Jeremiah
Through the Centuries

Wiley Blackwell Bible Commentaries

Series Editors: John Sawyer, Christopher Rowland, Judith Kovacs, David M. Gunn
Editorial Board: Ian Boxall, Andrew Mein, Lena-Sofia Tiemeyer

Further information about this innovative reception history series is available at
www.bbibcomm.info.

Forthcoming

Jeremiah
Through the Centuries

Mary Chilton Callaway

WILEY Blackwell

Registered Offices
John Wiley & Sons, Inc., 111 River Street, Hoboken, NJ 07030, USA
John Wiley & Sons Ltd, The Atrium, Southern Gate, Chichester, West Sussex, PO19 8SQ, UK

Editorial Office
The Atrium, Southern Gate, Chichester, West Sussex, PO19 8SQ, UK

For details of our global editorial offices, customer services, and more information about Wiley products visit us at www.wiley.com.

Wiley also publishes its books in a variety of electronic formats and by print-on-demand. Some content that appears in standard print versions of this book may not be available in other formats.

Library of Congress Cataloging-in-Publication Data
Names: Callaway, Mary, author.
Title: Jeremiah through the centuries / Mary Chilton Callaway.
Description: Hoboken, NJ, USA: Wiley-Blackwell, 2020. | Series: Wiley
   Blackwell Bible commentaries | Includes bibliographical references and
   index.
Identifiers: LCCN 2019049073 (print) | LCCN 2019049074 (ebook) | ISBN
   9780631231516 (hardback) | ISBN 9781118780756 (adobe pdf) | ISBN
   9781118780732 (epub)
Subjects: LCSH: Bible. Jeremiah–Commentaries.
Classification: LCC BS1525.53 .C35 2020 (print) | LCC BS1525.53 (ebook) |
   DDC 224/.207–dc23
LC record available at https://lccn.loc.gov/2019049073
LC ebook record available at https://lccn.loc.gov/2019049074

Cover Design: Wiley
Cover Image: Life of William Blake (1880), Volume 2, Job illustrations by Cygnis insignis is licensed under CC BY-SA

Set in 10/12.5pt Minion by SPi Global, Pondicherry, India

Printed and bound by CPI Group (UK) Ltd, Croydon, CR0 4YY

10 9 8 7 6 5 4 3 2 1

For Jamie
who always finds grace in the wilderness

Contents

Introduction

Commentary

The Blackwell Bible Commentaries series, the first to be devoted primarily to the reception history of the Bible, is based on the premise that how people have interpreted, and been influenced by, a sacred text like the Bible is often as interesting and historically important as what it originally meant. The series emphasizes the influence of the Bible on literature, art, music and film, its role in the evolution of religious beliefs and practices, and its impact on social and political developments. Drawing on work in a variety of disciplines, it is designed to provide a convenient and scholarly means of access to material until now hard to find, and a much-needed resource for all those interested in the infl uence of the Bible on Western culture.

Until quite recently this whole dimension was for the most part neglected by biblical scholars. The goal of a commentary was primarily, if not exclusively, to get behind the centuries of accumulated Christian and Jewish tradition to one single meaning, normally identified with the author's original intention. The most important and distinctive feature of the Blackwell Commentaries is that they will present readers with many diff erent interpretations of each text, in such a way as to heighten their awareness of what a text, especially a sacred text, can mean and what it can do, what it has meant and what it has done, in the many contexts in which it operates.

The Wiley Blackwell Bible Commentaries will consider patristic, rabbinic (where relevant), and medieval exegesis, as well as insights from various types of modern criticism, acquainting readers with a wide variety of interpretative techniques. As part of the history of interpretation, questions of source, date, authorship, and other historical-critical and archaeological issues will be discussed; but since these are covered extensively in existing commentaries, such references will be brief, serving to point readers in the direction of readily accessible literature where they can be followed up.

Original to this series is the consideration of the reception history of specific biblical books arranged in commentary format. The chapter-by-chapter arrangement ensures that the biblical text is always central to the discussion. Given the wide influence of the Bible and the richly varied appropriation of each biblical book, it is a difficult question which interpretations to include. While each volume will have its own distinctive point of view, the guiding prin-ciple for the series as a whole is that readers should be given a representative sampling of material from different ages, with emphasis on interpretations that have been especially influential or historically significant. Though commenta-tors will have their preferences among the different interpretations, the material will be presented in such a way that readers can make up their own minds on the value, morality, and validity of particular interpretations.

The series encourages readers to consider how the biblical text has been interpreted down the ages and seeks to open their eyes to diff erent uses of the Bible in contemporary culture. The aim is to write a series of scholarly com-mentaries that draw on all the insights of modern research to illustrate the rich interpretative potential of each biblical book.

John Sawyer
Christopher Rowland
Judith Kovacs
David M. Gunn

Acknowledgments

Well over a decade ago, John Sawyer entrusted me with the task of writing the Jeremiah volume for the Blackwell Bible Commentary series. His patient editorial support made it possible for me to search out the sources, sometimes translate them, and weave them into a reception history. Judith Kovacs had originally challenged me to write a proposal for the book, and with characteristic generosity offered critical and creative support throughout the writing, even though as New Testament editor of the series she did not have to read a word. Her friendship and insights have been a sustaining presence. David Gunn has given crucial help with multiple readings, corrections, and above all encouragement and advice about the pictures. Rebecca Harkin has ably steered me through the shoals.

Early in my graduate studies Professor James A. Sanders introduced me to the Hebrew text and the passionate persona of Jeremiah. Later, as my *Doktorvater* on another topic, he directed me to the deep theologies and holy sense of humor in Jewish exegetical traditions. His wise teaching planted the seeds for this book.

Two editors have patiently worked over every detail of the manuscript to correct my lapses. I am indebted to Cynthia Shattuck for her expert readerly eye and merciless editor's pencil, which made the book leaner and better. Caroline McPherson put the manuscript into final shape, dealing graciously with late changes and bibliographic challenges.

Graduate students Alex Hwang and Jennifer Jamer located troves of Patristic sources and put them into a usable form, sometimes hunting down the Greek original. Ankie Wiegerink and Jan van dear Staak generously translated an eighteenth-century Dutch text about Ebed Melek, which proved to be a challenge even for native Dutch speakers.

Fordham University has supported the project with two sabbatical leaves and a grant to help pay for permissions to publish images. Colleagues Harry Nasuti, J. Patrick Hornbeck, and Elizabeth Johnson have offered important insights and friendly goading in equal measure. Graphic designer Marc Tremitiere made many of the pictures in the book possible by expertly scanning my trove of antique prints into high-resolution images. Marta Martin Pérez and Ariadna Fernendez at the publishing company M. Moliero generously made available high-resolution images from the *Bible moralisée,* which are a linchpin in the reception history of Jeremiah.

The rich but sometimes arcane resources that provide the raw material for reception history are housed in libraries around the world. I am indebted to the patient and creative assistance given by librarians at the British Library, Bibliothèque nationale de France, Fordham University Library, Houghton Library of Harvard University, New York Public Library, Pierpont Morgan Library, and Union Theological Seminary Rare Books Collection.

I am grateful for the persistent challenge posed by members of the Writing/ Reading Jeremiah Group of the Society of Biblical Literature, and the opportunities they gave me to test and refine ideas about the reception of Jeremiah. In addition, Walter Brueggemann, Robert Carroll, Andrew Mein, Kathleen O'Connor, Carolyn Sharp, and Lou Stulman have generously offered support and asked sometimes discomfiting but always generative questions. Members of the Columbia University Hebrew Bible Seminar have offered constructive critiques in a formal setting together with helpful resources informally. The nine superb essays on the reception of Jeremiah in *The Book of Jeremiah: Composition, Reception, and Interpretation,* edited by Jack R. Lundbom, Craig A. Evans, and Bradford A. Anderson (Brill 2018) appeared after my manuscript was substantially complete, so I was regrettably not able to incorporate their insights. Likewise, Mark Leuchter's essay in *The Oxford Handbook to the Book of Jeremiah* was not available. I take these omissions as a good sign that reception history of Jeremiah has become significant in biblical studies.

Special thanks to Hannah Boone Callaway for help with translating and understanding important eighteenth-century French texts about Jérémie, and for insights into French political history and humor. Equally valuable were her expert readerly eye and persistent challenges to make the narrative compelling.

Finally, my beloved Jamie has made this book possible. His extravagant care, creative problem solving, insightful comments, and good-humored support are embedded in every page. He reminded me early and often that Jeremiah speaks to the present, whenever that is.

Jeremiah the Man

"He was the most compassionate of the prophets."
Gregory Nazianzus, *Oration* 17, 373 CE

"It was this good man's unhappiness to be a Physician to a dying State."
John Trapp, *A Commentary upon Jeremiah,* 1660

"Jeremiah is by no means wanting either in elegance or sublimity, although, generally speaking, inferior to Isaiah in both ... His thoughts indeed are somewhat less elevated ... but the reason of this may be, that he is mostly taken up with the gentler passions of grief and pity, for the expression of which he has a peculiar talent."
Robert Lowth, cited in B. Blaney, *Jeremiah, and Lamentations. A New Translation with notes ... 1784,* p. 8

"Every thing relating to Jeremiah shows him to have been a man of an equivocal character."

Thomas Paine, *Age of Reason* II, 1795

"Jeremiah has a kind of feminine tenderness and susceptibility; strength was to be educed out of a spirit which was inclined to be timid and shrinking."

F.D. Maurice, *Prophets and Kings of the Old Testament: A Series of Sermons*, 1853, p. 370

"He was set by God's hand as a solitary beacon on a lofty tower, in a dark night, in a stormy sea; lashed by waves and winds, but never shaken from his foundations.

Christopher Wordsworth, Bishop of Lincoln 1875, *The Books of Jeremiah, Lamentations, and Ezekiel in the Authorized Version*, p. x

"Jeremiah's ministry may be summed up in three words: good hope, labour, disappointment."

John Henry Newman, *Parochial and Plain Sermons, Vol.8* Sermon 9. 'Jeremiah, A Lesson for the Disappointed' p. 127

"Of the truth of his conviction he never had a moment's doubt; he knew that Jehovah was on his side, that on Him depended the eternal future. But, instead of the nation, the heart and the individual conviction were to him the subject of religion."

Wellhausen, *Prolegmena to the History of Israel*, Trans. John Sutherland Black, Allan Menzies p. 491

"There are always Jeremiahs who go about saying that we have never had such bad times."

Daily Express, 23 February 1928

"In the midst of danger he was brave. In the midst of trouble he was true. In the midst of confusion he was calm. In the midst of dark he was a flame."

Roy L. Smith, *Writing Scripture Under Dictators*, Nashville: Abingdon-Cokesbury, 1943, p. 60

"Jeremiah was a weak and timid man, but God's power worked in him."

George André, *The Prophet Jeremiah*, Sunbury, PA: Believers Bookshelf, 1988

"We hear him as he secretly talks with God."
Martin Luther King, Jr. 'The Significant Contributions of Jeremiah to
Religious Thought' (unpuslished seminary paper, 1948) in
The Papers of MLK, Jr. Vol. 7, p. 181

"He was accused of fantasizing, being stubborn, disturbing the peace and
being an enemy of the people, as have those in every age even up to the
present day who were seized and possessed by God."
Dietrich Bonhoeffer, sermon, 21 January 1934, DBWE 13, p. 347

"Jeremiah was truly the genius of torment and dissent; the Euripides, the
Pascal or the Dostoevsky of the Old Testament."
Thomas Römer, 'La conversion du prophète Jérémie à la thèologie
deutéronomiste,' 1997

"Polarity of emotion is a striking fact in the life of Jeremiah. We encounter
him in the pit of utter agony and at the height of extreme joy, carried
away by divine wrath and aching with supreme compassion."
Abraham Joshua Heschel, *The Prophets*

The Book

"The book of Jeremiah is all doom."
Talmud, Baba Batra 14

"In order that nothing be lacking in the sense even though much is lacking in the words, I have prepared the warp and the woof for you; you
yourself will weave the most beautiful garment."
Jerome, *In Hieremiam*, Prologue

"Frequently in the first part there is something in a later chapter which really
took place before that which is spoken of in an earlier chapter. So it seems as
though Jeremiah did not compose these books himself, but that the parts
were taken piecemeal from his utterances and written into a book. For this
reason one must not worry about the order or be hindered by the lack of it."
Martin Luther, Preface to the Prophet Jeremiah, 1532

"It is a necessary thing to the understanding of the prophets to know the
stories of the times wherein they prophesied."
Myles Coverdale, Marginal Note to Jer. 1:1, 1535

"We may all very profitably read the Prophet Jeremy, who is full of incitation to repentance and new obedience."

John Trapp, Commentary on Jeremiah, 1660

"The prophecies of Jeremiah, which are related historically, are also taken from various chronicles; for not only are they heaped together confusedly, without any account being taken of dates but also the same story is told in them differently in different passages."

Benedict Spinoza, A Theologico-Political Treatise, 1670

Were I … to write in such a disordered manner, no body would read what was written, and every body would suppose, that the writer was in a state of insanity. The only way to account for the disorder is, that the book is a medley of detached unauthenticated anecdotes, put together by some stupid book-maker, under the name of Jeremiah."

Thomas Paine, The Age of Reason, Part II 1795, Paris, pp. 48, 52

"The prophet's *individuality* is so impressed on his writings as to disarm suspicion of their authenticity."

Christopher Wordsworth, Bishop of Lincoln, 1875, The Books of Jeremiah, Lamentations, and Ezekiel in the Authorized Version, p. x.

"Though it was 'the *word of the Lord,*' these communications were 'words of *Jeremiah;*' his personality, temperament, experiences, style of thought, modes of expression, are all stamped upon these Divine messages. Inspiration does not obliterate, scarcely subordinates individuality."

Preacher's Complete Homiletic Commentary, Vol. 17: 8, Funk & Wagnalls, 1892

"As a lad I started to read the Scripture through according to the familiar schedule, three chapters each weekday and five on Sunday, by which we were assured that in a single year we could complete the reading of the Book. I got safely through Numbers and Leviticus, even Proverbs did not altogether quench my ardor, but I stuck in the middle of Jeremiah and never got out. I do not blame myself, for how can a boy read Jeremiah in its present form and understand it?"

Harry Emerson Fosdick, The Modern Use of the Bible, 1930, p. 21

"It is a hardy adventurer who decides to brave the book of Jeremiah."

Andrew Shead, www.matthiasmedia.com

"The book of Jeremiah does not contain stories about arks or whales or a talking donkey. The stories in this book can be a little difficult for children to understand."

Annabelle Lee, eHow Contributor to site for children's
activities for Jeremiah Bible Stories

Actualizations

"I myself was initiated under Moses the God-beloved into his greater mysteries, yet when I saw the prophet Jeremiah and knew him to be not only himself enlightened, but a worthy minister of the holy secrets, I was not slow to become his disciple."

Philo of Alexandria, *Cherubim* II.49

"Jeremiah's case is the case of all the Ministry, placed between two gulfs, two seas, two rocks, two fires: God's curse, and the world's hatred."

John Hull *Lectures upon the Lamentations of Jeremiah*, 1620, p. 6

"Although he were not ... free from all fault (for he had his out-bursts) yet he was ... a man of singular sanctimony and integrity, good of a little child, a young Saint, and an old Angel; an admirable Preacher ... a pattern to all Preachers of the Gospel."

John Trapp, *A Commentary or Exposition upon the Book
of the Prophet Jeremiah*, London, 1660, p. 219

"How comes it that such ancient faith has so wholly faded from among Christian mankind? Where shall we to-day look for a preacher, fearless, plain-spoken, earnest, sincere, like Jeremiah? If he were among us, would he fare much better than the prophet?"

Cunningham Geikie, *Hours with the Bible:
From Manasseh to Zedekiah*, 1887, p. 158

"Jeremiah has proved a sympathizing companion and comforter in seasons of individual suffering and national calamity from the first destruction of Jerusalem down to the siege of Paris in our own day."

In Preface by the General Editor to Carl Wilhelm Eduard
Nägelsbuch's *Book of Jeremiah*, 1871, p. i

"Children, being with God does not make one happy. We learn this from Jeremiah."

Dietrich Bonhoeffer, children's meditation, 1927, in *The Young Bonhoeffer*, p. 514

"Jeremiah was a bullfrog."

Hoyt Axton, 1971

"Among the prophets Jeremiah seems to me the most 'modern' of sensibilities, kin to the wager of Paschal, Kierkegaard's bleak isolation and abandonment, Hopkins' dark night, let us dare say, kin to Graham Green's: 'My salvation is: I do not believe my disbelief.'"

Dan Berrigan, *Jeremiah: The World, the Wound of God*, Minneapolis: Fortress, 1999, p.88

" Who reads Jeremiah for pleasure?"

M.D. Aeschliman, Review of *Jonathan Swift: A Hypocrite Reversed*, *National Review* October 24, 1986, p. 54

"'He's a right Jeremiah.' That means a depressing and pessimistic person who will be the wet blanket at every party."

Alan Pain, *I am Jeremiah* (*Don't Laugh*), East Sussex, Kingsway, 1990

"What's wrong with America is not a very complicated question. It can put in just a few words from the Prophet Jeremiah."

Darryl Walker, *America's Return: Solutions from the Prophet Jeremiah*, Tate Publishing, 2016

"Jeremiah puts us on edge with ourselves."

Renita J. Weems in *Global Bible Commentary*, ed. Daniel Patte, Nashville: Abingdon, 2004, p. 224

Introduction

Jeremiah's brooding figure inhabits modern culture as an ancient prophet who often seems surprisingly like us. His deep emotions of grief and rage expressed with unvarnished honesty even to God make him a spiritual model, and his strong sense of self over against his contemporaries resonates in a world that encourages individual expression. One of the most famous images of Jeremiah in modernity, Rembrandt's *Jeremiah Lamenting the Destruction of Jerusalem*, embodies this brooding figure. Rembrandt inverts the traditional iconography that highlighted the city with Jeremiah lamenting outside its walls by moving

Jeremiah Through the Centuries, First Edition. Mary Chilton Callaway.
© 2020 Mary Chilton Callaway. Published 2020 by John Wiley & Sons Ltd.

the burning city to the darkened margin and drawing the viewer to the illuminated face of an introspective old man (Figure 1). The absence of conventional
artistic markers for prophecy, such as a scroll, together with the inward gaze of
the prophet direct the viewer away from the destruction of Jerusalem into the
troubled soul of Jeremiah.

Our understanding of what it means to be a person, and the experience of a
subjective inner life as we understand it, was most likely not known to the
original Jeremiah. Rembrandt projects onto the ancient prophet an early
modern sense of the self, especially the idea of interiority that had been developing since the fifteenth century (Callaway 2004: 48–62). We intuitively read
Jeremiah in light of these concepts that are so natural as to be almost invisible
to us, but readers in the centuries before early modernity knew a different

FIGURE 1   Rembrandt van Rijn, *Jeremiah Lamenting the Destruction of Jerusalem.*
Rijksmuseum, Amsterdam.

prophet. In fact, what seems most familiar about Jeremiah is actually foreign to him and to centuries of his earlier readers. How did Jeremiah stray so far outside the pages of his book? The answer, and the story of Jeremiah's evolution from ancient prophet to icon of the spiritual self, is the work of reception history.

Theory and Practice of Reception History

To understand reception history and why it matters we turn briefly to its origins in the philosophical hermeneutics of Hans-Georg Gadamer. In considering what it means to understand a text, Gadamer challenged the fundamental premise of modernity that readers can intellectually transpose themselves into another age. The idea that we can leap over the abyss of history is flawed because the very habits of thought by which we understand the past are themselves the product of history and the content of that abyss. The thought experiment of placing oneself in a historical situation is limited because that self was formed by effects of the historical situation being investigated. Our consciousness and modes of thinking are not objective and universal, but "historically effected." Habits of thought and assumptions that have been inherited for centuries become invisible as their historical origins are eclipsed, and they seem part of the natural order. To understand a text from another era therefore requires becoming more aware of the ways in which our thinking have already been influenced by that era; in Gadamer's terms, we approach history as already its product. The "abyss of history" is therefore not an empty chasm but the fertile ground in which our own understanding is rooted, "filled with the continuity of custom and tradition, in the light of which everything handed down presents itself to us" (Gadamer 1989: 297). The distance between us and the past enables understanding when its thick texture discloses our basic assumptions about reality as products of history and culture. Gadamer's ideal of understanding happens when we actively engage the past neither as otherness foreign to the present, nor as essentially like us, but as illuminating our present understanding while simultaneously changing it.

Gadamer's insights are particularly important for a reception history commentary of Jeremiah because of the prophet's significance in the developing idea of the self in Western intellectual history and of interiority in Christian spiritual tradition. His *Wirkungsgeschichte*, or history of effects, explores the ways that readers have appropriated texts to address their own circumstances, and highlights the effects of these re-readings on cultures and in history. Over time, many interpretive traditions became an invisible penumbra surrounding the biblical text, sometimes overshadowing it so much that subsequent readers assume them as they read. These traditions also became virtual interlinear notes, invisibly but indelibly inscribed above the written words. Eve's "apple" in Genesis 3 is a clear example of this phenomenon, as are the "three kings" in Matthew 2. The historical and social consequences of these unwritten aspects of a text can be both destructive and beneficial; by bringing them into the light reception history tries to clarify some of these effects.

Reception history identifies uses of a text that have had lasting effects and explores their immediate political and cultural context to clarify contingencies that may have been catalysts. Less visible than these contingencies, but equally important, is the influence of inherited modes of thinking. The subtle influence of *mentalitè,* the worldview within which people read or heard the Bible, is often transmitted along with particular interpretations. Hence the pressure of history, understood as the demands of a particular crisis together with the more gradual processes that influenced the way people understood their world, shape the ways that Jeremiah has been read and dictate the marks that the prophet and his book have left. Reception history lingers in the space between a particular reading and the cultural context in which it was produced, asking what indelible marks these have left on the text. This reception history commentary presents the specific texts and traditions of Jeremiah that have most profoundly influenced readers down the centuries, highlighting their effects. The receptions can take the form of political tracts, fictional adaptations, liturgical practices, and artistic images, to name only a few. Reception history is in some ways similar to the contemporary challenge of understanding the "other." What at first appears inscrutable or offensive can become, with patient engagement and a hermeneutic of hospitality, at least comprehensible, often enlightening, and at times treasured.

Jeremiah in Three Guises

Reception history of Jeremiah includes three distinct aspects of the biblical text: words of the prophet, narratives about the prophet, and the figure of the prophet. In every era all three are in play, separately or by creative combination. Prophecies are the direct speech of the prophet pronouncing "the word of the Lord" found in collections of prophetic oracles such as chapters 2–10 and 30–31. The literary form of poetic parallelism used across the ancient Near East, together with graphic images and arresting forms of speech, led scholars to conclude that these words represent something close to the speech of the historical prophet. Ancient redactors separated these prophetic words from their original context even before the book of Jeremiah was complete and arranged them into groupings whose logic for the most part still eludes scholars. This loosening of historical moorings indicates that from the beginning, Jeremiah's words were shaped to address subsequent generations. Jewish and

Christian readers in every age have in one sense continued the work of the ancient redactors, assuming that the prophet's words were addressed to Judah but also contained other meanings, intended by God for later readers. These readers often found in Jeremiah's raw poetry a voice for their own political and personal circumstances.

Narratives comprise half the material between 1 and 36 and all of 37 to 45, making Jeremiah uniquely story-rich among prophetic books. Since the early twentieth century, scholars have distinguished several different types of narratives that reflect the earliest reception of Jeremiah.

The largest category constitutes brief stories that describe Jeremiah performing a symbolic action whose meanings are explained in extended speeches. These speeches offer multiple interpretations of the original event, suggesting that debate about causes and outcomes of the Exile was shaping the Jeremiah tradition. A second type of story, represented by chapters 26 and 36 among others, features artful narration and dialogue to portray strong resistance to the prophet. These stories also offer evidence of early reception shaping the Jeremiah tradition to explain the destruction of Jerusalem. Chapters 37–45, set in the last years of Jeremiah's life, offer another type of narrative, marked by some literary coherence and realistic details. Conflict over whether the true remnant of Israel is the exiles in Babylon, those who fled to Egypt, or those left in Judah is apparent in these stories. All of the narratives in Jeremiah support the scholarly consensus that the book is the final product of lengthy and contested claims to the prophet's legacy by post-exilic communities.

The *figure* of Jeremiah inhabits the biblical text, but ultimately eludes its boundaries. He is the slipping character that readers have created in the dynamic between the biblical text and their own cultural contexts. While prophecies and stories provide a solid textual foundation, the figure of Jeremiah is a synthesis of fragments and intimations, forged in the imaginations of readers and built up over the centuries. It represents a surplus of meaning that often seems at odds with the biblical text and, although more elusive, it is at the heart of Gadamer's *Wirkungsgeschichte,* history-of-effects, of the text. By the second century BCE, this figure had slipped the confines of the biblical text, assuming new guises and voices. In the Commentary he is often glimpsed when Jews and Christians, trying to be faithful in perilous circumstances, put on his mantle.

Jeremiah in Antiquity

Jeremiah as book and as persona is the product of two catastrophes. The destruction of Jerusalem by the Babylonian army in 586 BCE and of the Second Temple in 70 CE by the Roman army mark inflexion points in the reception history of the prophet. The formation of early Judaism after the first, and of rabbinic Judaism after the second, are contexts in which evolving Jeremiah traditions began to be fixed. Yet these events were also catalysts for new receptions of the prophet, particularly in ways that harnessed discourses of contemporary culture to respond to the trauma of defeat and the fear that God was absent.

Early Judaism

Evidence of developing, and contested, traditions within the book suggests that groups in Judah and Babylon in the sixth century both claimed Jeremiah's legacy. Exiles in Babylon arranged his prophetic words, added commentary to interpret them, and shaped narratives about his life, but "submerged voices" from the Judean community bear witness to alternate receptions of Jeremiah (Sharp 2003). William McKane's widely accepted description of the Jeremiah scroll as "a rolling corpus" aptly describes the early stages in its production as a process in which early texts triggered commentary leading to an expanded text (McKane 1986). Additions included narratives about Jeremiah in conflict with kings, priests, and people in Jerusalem that developed the prophetic persona as both threatening and sorrowful. These narratives about the people's rejection and persecution of Jeremiah paradoxically functioned as words of hope in the exile because they helped explain Judah's destruction as YHWH's plan rather than Nebuchadnezzar's victory. The narratives also brought life to the exiles by presenting Jeremiah as an embodiment of their trauma and the voice of their anger and despair. His rage against God reflected their own reality and his tears became theirs. That the "biblical" Jeremiah is a literary figure constructed from irretrievable historical fragments that were shaped for the needs of the community shows that "the word of the Lord" is always historically contextualized, contingent, and in need of translation. The slipping figure of Jeremiah is already evident in the book that bears his name.

The textual tradition offers further evidence that reception of the Jeremiah tradition was contested even during its formation. The Hebrew text is about one eighth longer than the Septuagint, primarily because of honorifics such as "the prophet" frequently added to Jeremiah's name, "oracle of the Lord" occurring almost 50 percent more times, and brief introductions such as Jer. 2:1–2 and 7:1–2. Several longer passages in the Masoretic Text (MT) appear to be expansions of the Septaguint (LXX) (see Commentary at 33:14 and 39:4). More significantly, the Septuagint places the "Oracles Against the Nations" at chapter 25:14 while the MT places them after chapter 45 and makes the prophecy of Babylon's fall the climactic word. Our earliest manuscripts are five scrolls from Qumran, of which three generally agree with MT, while two more fragmentary scrolls reflect the content of the Septuagint against the MT (see Commentary on Jer 10). Septuagint most likely translates a now lost Hebrew version that disappeared after the Hebrew text was normalized, probably by the early second century CE. In the richly productive era of Second Temple Judaism, therefore, two or three versions of Jeremiah coexisted comfortably. Our canonical Jeremiah is clearly the end product of centuries of reception by multiple communities in Babylon, Judah, and Egypt.

While some early Jewish communities were developing multiple texts of Jeremiah, others were already interpreting and expanding Jeremiah's prophecies and persona. Biblical and deutero-canonical books written between the fifth and second centuries progressively heighten Jeremiah's authority and elaborate his persona. 2 Chronicles 36:22 and Ezra 1:1 describe the decree of Cyrus as "in order that the word of the Lord through the mouth of Jeremiah be accomplished." In the second century BCE, Daniel reports puzzling over Jeremiah's words "in the scrolls" that the exile would last 70 years (Dan 9:1–2), which did not happen. The solution that Jeremiah meant 70 *weeks* of years (490 years) transformed the prophecy into the future to give hope in time of persecution. That the solution came only by revelation from the angel Gabriel shows a new reception of Jeremiah's words as encoded mystery whose deeper meaning cannot be perceived by human understanding (Newman 2017: 237). Finally, Jeremiah becomes a supernatural figure in the Hellenistic narrative of 2 Maccabees, which offers two distinct images. In the first, Judas Maccabeus encourages his soldiers before a crucial battle by recounting his vision of Jeremiah appearing to him as an aged man "of wonderful authority" and handing him a golden sword, "a gift from God" (2 Macc 15:6–16). The other image, linking Jeremiah with the lost Ark of the covenant, persists for centuries. As the temple burns, the prophet orders tent and ark to follow him to a cave on Sinai, where he hides them and seals the entrance "until God gathers his people together again and shows his mercy" (2 Macc 2:18).

Stories about Jeremiah's preservation of the Ark in 2 Macc take on new life in response to the Roman destruction in 70 CE. *Lives of the Prophets* describes Jeremiah having the Ark swallowed up in a rock, on which he inscribes with his finger the seal of the divine name while proclaiming that at the resurrection the Ark would emerge from the rock and appear on Mt. Sinai. 4 Baruch, called in Greek manuscripts "The Things Omitted from Jeremiah the Prophet," offers the most elaborated version of Jeremiah hiding the Ark and vessels of the Temple (see Commentary on Jer 22:29). The synagogue at Dura Europos, on the eastern edge of the Roman Empire, preserves an image of Jeremiah as custodian of the Ark. In what is probably the earliest extant illustration of Jeremiah, the fresco shows the prophet with the facial features, hairstyle, and toga distinctive to Roman art (Figure 2). The prominent scroll signifies Jeremiah as a biblical prophet, but also confers authority as a poet in Roman tradition. The veiled object at left is the Ark, hidden and guarded by Jeremiah until the

FIGURE 2   Jeremiah with scroll and Ark. Wall fresco in the synagogue at Dura Europos.

End-time. The placement of this portrait flanking the Torah shrine and adjacent to scenes from the Ark Narrative of I Sam 4–6 reinforces the association of Jeremiah with the lost Ark (Kessler 1987). This early Jeremiah offers hope for both earthly and eschatological restoration of Israel.

In addition to miraculously preserving the Ark, Jeremiah also preserves human life. In *Lives of the Prophets* his prayers expel crocodiles from Egyptian waters, and the dust of the place where this occurred was reported to have healing powers. This tradition of miraculous healer casts the prophet in the image of wonder-worker common to the ancient Mediterranean world, and extends into the Middle Ages. *Lives* also reports that Jeremiah was "thrown down by stones" in Egypt by his own people. This begins the tradition of Jeremiah's martyrdom that extends into the sixteenth century (see Commentary on Jer 44).

Two fragments of a scroll found in Cave 4 at Qumran add another dimension to the prophet's persona. Part of a lost Apocryphon of Jeremiah, they present Jeremiah as a new Moses warning Israel to obey the Law in their new land. The larger fragment describes him accompanying the exiles "to the river" (presumably the Euphrates), where he reminds them "concerning the words which God had commanded him… so that they should keep the covenant of the God of the fathers in the land of their captivity" (Diamant 2013: 16). This Jeremiah is "the prototypical Jewish leader in the new age of spiritual 'exile' in the Hellenistic world" (Davis 2014: 173) For the members of the community at Qumran, who had withdrawn to live in caves in the Judean wilderness because of corruption of the priesthood in Jerusalem, Jeremiah was authoritative because of his persona. This fragment, taken with the multiple textual forms in use at Qumran, shows two important aspects of the reception of Jeremiah. The text of what would become canonical Jeremiah was still pluriform in the late second century BCE, and the adaptable figure of Jeremiah as teacher and leader carried authority apart from his words.

Philo of Alexandria is the first to adapt Jeremiah to the discourse of neo-Platonic philosophy. Writing as a Jew in the culturally diverse intellectual world of Alexandria, Philo adopts Greek exegetical use of allegory for his own interpretation of the Scriptures. Literal meanings of words become a vessel for deeper meanings, as the body is for the soul. Philo's primary motive was to render the sacred texts of the Jews not as primitive and irrational but as fonts of true wisdom. Of Philo's three quotations from Jeremiah, two appear in the synagogue liturgy, in readings on one of the Sabbaths preceding the Ninth of Ab (see Commentary on Jer 2 and 3). Jeremiah is one of only five biblical authors named by Philo, perhaps because the prophet's costly insistence on the one true deity resonated with Philo's own experience as a Jew in Alexandria. Philo sees in Jeremiah a fellow lover of virtue and "right reason" who is drawn unwillingly into conflict with wicked and foolish adversaries (see Commentary Jer 15). In a cultural environment where the teacher–disciple relation defined identities, Philo the philosopher boldly declares himself a disciple of Jeremiah: "I myself was initiated under Moses the God-beloved into his greater mysteries, yet when I saw the prophet Jeremiah and knew him to be not only himself enlightened, but a worthy minister of the holy secrets, I was not slow to become his disciple" (*Cherubim* II.49). Philo's re-signifying of Jeremiah as sage and teacher seeded a rich tradition of reception for centuries.

Josephus shrewdly adopts Jeremiah's persona to curry favor with the Romans occupying Jerusalem in 66 CE. In *Jewish War* he describes at length his efforts to persuade his countrymen in Jerusalem to surrender to the Romans. Mocked and attacked, he reminds them that Jeremiah had similarly counselled Zedekiah to surrender to the Babylonians yet was not put to death. "But you… assail with abuse and missiles me who exhort you to save yourselves, exasperated at being reminded of your sins" (*Jewish War* V. 391–393). Josephus bends Jeremiah's story so he can vest himself with the prophet's authority and appear favorable to the Roman authorities (Cohen 1982). Eighteen years later, his re-telling of biblical and early Jewish history in *Jewish Antiquities* gives more attention to Jeremiah than any other prophetic book. Jeremiah's bizarre actions and graphic prophetic language are replaced with rational arguments that would appeal to Josephus's educated Greek readers. The narrative highlights Jeremiah's accurate prophecy that the Babylonians would take Jerusalem, which Josephus links with "the recent capture of our city." Josephus presents a Jeremiah whose experiences mirrored some of his own during the Roman invasion of Jerusalem and destruction of the Temple in 70 CE, to defend his own pro-Roman position with his Jewish readers.

The Developing Biblical Tradition

Reception of Jeremiah in antiquity not only generated expanding traditions about the prophet, but also affected the shape of the Bible. Early Jewish tradition attributed the book of Lamentations to Jeremiah, probably because of the biblical words that he "lamented a lament for Josiah" (2 Chron 35:25). A number of verbal parallels in the poetry of Jeremiah and Lamentations added weight to the idea that Jeremiah was author of both books. Lamentations in the Septuagint opens with a line not in the Hebrew: "When Israel was captured and Jerusalem made desolate, Jeremiah sat weeping and lamented this lament over Jerusalem." With this addition the developing persona of Jeremiah was written into the first translation of the Hebrew text. In the early fifth century CE, Jerome's Latin translation further expanded the image of Jeremiah as weeping prophet by adding to the Septuagint's prologue "with sorrowful spirit, sighing and moaning, he said… " Christians rearranged the Jewish order of Scripture, moving Lamentations from its traditional location with other Writings to place it immediately after Jeremiah. These changes to biblical text and canon during crucial stages of their development show that early reception of Jeremiah as the weeping prophet influenced the final shape of the Bible. In what may be the first visual representation of the weeping prophet, John of Damascus' ninth-century Greek collection of short biblical and patristic texts *Sacra Parallela* presents Jeremiah in a pose that will have lasting effects (Figure 3).

Early Christianity

In their descriptions of Jesus, early Christians merged the words of Jeremiah in the Scriptures with the persona of Jeremiah elaborated in Jewish tradition. Jesus as miracle-worker made some think that Jeremiah had

FIGURE 3   John of Damascus, *Sacra Parallela*. Bibliothèque Nationale de France. Grec 923, fol. 258v. Constantinople.

returned (Matt 16:13–14). All four Evangelists portray Jesus as Jeremiah in their narratives of the money-changers in the temple (see Commentary on Jer 7). Similarly, I Cor 11:25 and the Synoptic Gospels present Jesus as the one who fulfills Jeremiah's prophecy of the new covenant. Hebrews 8 explicitly identifies the early Christian community as heirs of Jeremiah's new covenant, and by the third century CE the church designated its authoritative texts as Old Covenant and New Covenant (see Commentary on Jer 31). Hebrews 11 invokes the prophet "stoned to death" among its models of faith for Christians to emulate. Luke 19:414–8 uniquely weaves four Jeremiah traditions into an image of Jesus as prophet. As Jesus enters Jerusalem he weeps over the city and prophesies its destruction, evoking Jeremiah (Jer 14:17). Then he purges the temple, quoting Jer 7:11. Luke ends the scene with the comment that the religious leaders and the leaders of the people sought to kill him. In these eight verses Luke presents Jesus as a prophet with Jeremiah's characteristic traits of weeping, prophesying the destruction of Jerusalem, defending the sanctity of the temple, and being in the crosshairs of the religious leaders' sights. Luke's description of Jerusalem as the city "who kills the prophets and stones the ones sent to her" evokes the apocryphal tradition that Jeremiah was stoned while exhorting his people. More Lucan parallels are presented in the Commentary on Jer 5:31; 9: 17–22; 15:9; 22:5; 38:15. Luke's Jesus as prophet in the tradition of Jeremiah provided a paradigm by which the Lucan community could understand the story of Jesus, as well as its own persecutions, authenticated by Scripture and tradition.

Patristic writers mining the Scriptures to support theological arguments generally did not find a resource in Jeremiah; even the 350 citations by Augustine tend to be part of his trademark rhetoric of biblical vocabulary. Three notable exceptions are Origen of Alexandria, Jerome, and Theodoret of Cyrus. In the Commentary they provide prime examples of the two dominant Christian approaches to Jeremiah in antiquity. Origen's *Homilies on Jeremiah* (c. 250 CE) offers one of the earliest and most influential readings. Pastoral and attentive to the Greek text of Jeremiah, Origen typically used allegorical and even mystical exegesis help shape the Christian identity of his congregation (Torjesen 1995: 18). His sermons follow a four-step pattern that begins with the Scriptural verse, elucidates its plain sense, develops its spiritual teaching, and finally appeals to the congregation by placing them in the world of the text (Torjesen 1995: 21). The homilies adapt Jeremiah to classical rhetorical techniques designed to elicit emotion and to persuade because Origen wants to instruct his listeners and move them to repentance. He frequently interprets Jeremiah's words with reference to "the Savior" and the Christian life, but also to his unorthodox neo-Platonic ideas, such as the pre-existence of souls. His presentation of Jeremiah in homilies shaped by the rules of classical rhetoric serves his goal of developing a Christian consciousness in his listeners. In the judgment of patristic scholar Charles Kannengiesser, S.J., "Origen remains the only interpreter in the early church who has read Jeremiah according to a theological and spiritual vision of the Christian life and a coherent idea of the faith" (Kannenngieser 1975: 318).

Jerome favored a more literal and historical approach than Origen, though he used allegorical interpretation to show Jeremiah as a prefiguring of Jesus and to address contemporary conflicts in the church. Jerome's training in the classical poets gave him eloquence, while his study with rabbis gave respect for the historical context of Jeremiah. His monumental *In Hieremiam Prophetam* reflects prodigious linguistic knowledge of Greek, Hebrew, Aramaic, and other languages as well as Christian and Jewish traditions. His commentary helped establish the authority of the Hebrew text over the church's use of the Septuagint. Yet even with his historical approach, like Josephus he clearly found in Jeremiah's story resonance with his own situation. In 385 CE, he was driven from Rome by opponents and established a monastery in Bethlehem, and when Rome was sacked by Vandals in 410 he began to take in refugees. When he started his commentary in 415 he was an old man; in 416 his monastery was burned, along with his vast library, by an attacking horde presumably sent by his enemies.

Jerome found in Jeremiah a man like himself, almost crushed by strife and contention. His commentary reflects sustained engagement with opponents whom he saw as dangerous to the church, notably Pelagius, whose optimistic theology rejected original sin and argued that human will could overcome evil. He also rejects the work of Origen, whom he had earlier described as second only to the Apostles as a teacher of the church but now describes as "the heretic" or "the one who goes astray with allegory." He often presents exegetical traditions from Origen in order to refute them; ironically, after the church destroyed Origen's writings, Jerome's commentary preserved some of his ideas. Jerome found in Jeremiah a prophet whose words addressed the pressing issues of the contemporary church. When he died in 420 CE he had completed 32 chapters of what he called in the preface "the warp and woof" from which his reader would weave the most beautiful garment. His commentary was transmitted and completed by Rabanus Maurus in the ninth century, from whom it was taken into the *Glossa Ordinaria,* which insured its influence into the sixteenth century. In addition to the commentary, Jerome's translation became the church's Jeremiah in the form of the Vulgate Bible. His prologue was always included with the biblical text; acting as sentinel it instructed readers to understand Jeremiah in the double context of ancient Judah and the Gospel. Jerome's own discomfort with Jeremiah's graphic images and violent language is apparent in his opening sentence that describes him as "more rustic in language" than other prophets. This judgment persists without attribution in commentaries through the nineteenth century.

In popular religion of late antiquity Jeremiah was revered as thaumaturge and martyr, with shrines at the major locations mentioned in the biblical text. The earliest traditions describe a gravesite in Taphanes "near Pharaoh's palace, because the Egyptians held him in high esteem" for getting rid of crocodiles. The same tradition relates that Alexander had Jeremiah's remains moved to Alexandria, where they encircled the city for protection from snakes (*Lives of the Prophets* 2). In the sixth century, three pilgrim accounts describe visits to the "pool" into which Jeremiah was thrown, naming different locations in Jerusalem (see Commentary on Jer 38). A Byzantine account mentions a church of Jeremiah in Anatoth.

Jeremiah's status as saint and martyr is signaled by his prime position on the northern wall of the sixth-century Basilica of Saint Apollinare in Ravenna, one of the earliest images of the prophet. Holding an open scroll, he faces Moses

FIGURE 4   Prophet Jeremiah. Basilica of San Vitale, Ravenna. De Agostini Picture
Library/Bridgeman Images.

receiving a closed scroll from God's hand; the two signify the old and new
covenants. The walls of Jerusalem remind viewers that his prophecies came
true, and become a standard part his iconography throughout the Middle Ages.
The golden crown highlights the tradition of his martyrdom and the nimbus
marks him as a saint (Figure 4). He overlooks a large lunette portraying the
hospitality of Abraham and the binding of Isaac, stories which have
Christological interpretations resonating with those of Jeremiah himself.

The Liturgical Jeremiah

Jeremiah's multiple identities as martyr, prefiguring of Christ, and prophetic
voice calling to repentance gave him a significant place in liturgies throughout
the church year. From the fourth through the tenth centuries, lectionaries in

different regions varied, but all included Jeremiah for the church's major feasts and fasts (Lurz 1992). The liturgical Jeremiah appears in two forms: as prophetic voice and as a persona representing Christ. The prophetic voice revealed the righteous branch on Christmas Eve (23:2–6), foretold the Lord appearing from afar on Christmas (33:10–22), and proclaimed the promise of a Davidic descendant on the throne of Israel at Epiphany (33:10–22). Jeremiah's contrast between idols and the true God made manifest in the Lord (10:6–16) was heard at the solemn blessing of the water on the eve of Epiphany, and catechumens at their baptism heard the narrative of divine mercy in Israel's history of disobedience (Jer 32:16–25). At the Easter Vigil, the new covenant was often heard (Jer 31:31–34) and in Easter week the command that Jeremiah not marry (Jer 16) made an invitation to amendment of life central to Easter worship. At Pentecost, worshippers heard Jeremiah's prophecy that God would gather the exiles from every country and give them one heart and one way (Jer 32:36–44). Throughout the year, Jeremiah was also heard marking days special to particular regions. In Constantinople, Christians heard readings from Jer 2–3 to commemorate the 740 CE earthquake that they attributed to divine anger at iconoclasts. In the monastery at Mosul, monks mourned the fall of Nineveh with Jeremiah's voices of lamentation (Lam 5) and warning to keep the Sabbath (Jer 17:21–27). Early reception of Jeremiah as a martyr gave him a designated feast day in the Christian calendar. Although it varied somewhat, the most common date was May 1, still observed in the Greek Orthodox church.

All lectionaries reflected the early reception of Jeremiah as typological figure of Christ by presenting his voice most intensively in Passiontide, the two weeks before Easter. Jeremiah 1–3 was read during Lent in almost all lectionaries, and Jeremiah's suffering (Jer 20) was a staple of Holy Week. On Maundy Thursday, the fulfillment of Jeremiah's prophecy of a new covenant was made explicit in the words of institution over the cup of wine (see Commentary on Jer 31:31), and on Good Friday Jer 11:18–20 described the crucifixion. In the Syriac church, Jeremiah in the cistern (Jer 38) was read from Good Friday through Easter, foreshadowing Jesus' descent into death and resurrection. In addition, at the predawn monastic service for the last three days of Holy Week, monks sang parts of the Lamentations of Jeremiah, thereby taking on the voice of the suffering prophet in their devotions. The association of Jeremiah with Holy Week grew over the centuries and had destructive effects for medieval Jews, when the voice of Jeremiah became the voice of Jesus in the Reproaches (Lam 1:12) sung on Good Friday, inciting Christians to violence against their Jewish neighbors. Early reception of Jeremiah as a martyr gave him a designated feast day in the Christian calendar. Although it varied somewhat, the most common date was May 1, still observed in the Greek Orthodox church.

Rabbinic Judaism

In the literary riches of rabbinic Judaism the figure of Jeremiah slips the confines of the text to become more pious but also more outrageous in his speech. Translation of Jeremiah into Aramaic for study and especially for reading aloud in the synagogue shaped a unique Jeremiah whose words combined biblical tropes with contemporary concerns. Targum Jonathan, which became an authoritative translation, provided the text for the *Haftarah,* the reading from the prophets to accompany the Torah reading. Three characteristics influenced its reception of Jeremiah. First, the translators heightened divine transcendence by reinterpreting anthropomorphic images, so that instead of "I" God says "my word" and Jeremiah's accusations of divine deception are softened by a word or two into deception by false prophets. Second, translators often added a few words to adapt a prophecy to the circumstances of the congregation, especially pressures from Gentile rulers. Finally, prophetic words were supplemented to make them conform to current theological beliefs, especially eschatological doctrines of resurrection and the age to come. For Jews in the synagogue, Jeremiah represented both ancient prophetic tradition and a contemporary voice that was equal parts warning and consolation.

Rabbinic midrash imaginatively interprets Scripture to fill in gaps and make connections with other scriptural texts and rabbinic traditions, often in the context of contemporary circumstances. This reception of Jeremiah from late antiquity into the eleventh century created a distinctly Jewish prophet whose fraught relation with the Holy One refracted contemporary experiences and attitudes. *Pesikta de Rab Kahanna* 13 is a midrashic homily for the first of three Sabbaths preceding the Ninth of Ab, when Jer 1:1–2:3 was the *Haftarah* reading. It uses an early set of rabbinic traditions elaborating Jeremiah's lineage imaginatively constructed from the union of Rahab and Joshua, whose eight descendants are all characters in the book of Jeremiah. *Pesikta* also links God's warning that Canaanites not driven out of the land will be "as thorns in your eyes, and pricks in your sides" (Num 33:55) with Jeremiah as troublemaker prophet. As a descendant of the Canaanite Rabab who was not driven out, Jeremiah would "thrust words into you as will be thorns in your eyes and pricks in your sides" (Braude and Kapstein 2002: 256). Rahab and Jeremiah bookend Israel's life in the promised land, marked by the consistency of divine judgment: "Rahab to Jeremiah is a metonymy for the Israelites in the land of Israel from conquest to destruction" (Jassen 2016: 18). For worshippers hearing the homily, Jeremiah was not only a thorn for Jerusalem, but also for evaluating their own lives.

Pesikta Rabbati, the collection of sermons for special Sabbaths and holy days that originated in Palestine between the fourth and seventh centuries, incorporates traditions from *Pesikta de Rab Kahanna* into a unique format. Piska 26 is the first in the sequence for the three Sabbaths of preparation for the solemn observance on the Ninth of Av, and the congregation would have just heard Jeremiah 1 as the *Haftarah*. This Piska is unusual because it does not proceed in the usual way by linking disparate Scripture texts, but tells Jeremiah's story elaborated with midrashic traditions of divine interventions. It is framed by Jeremiah's encounter with a mythic woman, first at birth when he accuses his "mother" of adultery, and after Jerusalem is destroyed when he comforts the mourning Mother Zion. From his cry of anguish at birth for the fate of his people, to the final scene on the smoking ruins of the city, this Jeremiah is driven by love for his people. His harsh words against God are occasioned by Jerusalem's suffering, not his own, though the hostility of the princes against him is colorfully embellished. Most notably the Piska elaborates the tradition of 4 Baruch to show Jeremiah's devotion to his people as so great that God had to use deception to get him out of Jerusalem so that it could be destroyed (see Commentary on Jer 20). Introduced as one of the "four supremely perfect creatures in Scripture whom God Himself had formed," yet left stateless and friendless, this midrashic Jeremiah addresses Jewish experiences of subjugation and loss of land in late antiquity. Its portrait of Jeremiah as both shrewd and pious influences reception of the prophet in all three Abrahamic religions.

Medieval Jeremiahs

The reception of Jeremiah from 1100–1400 includes complex debates and imaginative images whose influence persists into the present. The Commentary highlights the influence of Jeremiah in two aspects of medieval culture. The first is the complex relation between Jews and Christians. In these centuries, Jews and Christians encountered Jeremiah in such different media, weighted with centuries of different traditions, that one might wonder whether the Hebrew *Yermiyahu* of rabbinic midrash and the Latin *Hieronymus* of the church's traditions even refer to the same character. Yet close contact between Jews and Christians, particularly in northern France, meant that the two receptions of Jeremiah developed in a complex engagement of cooperation and hostility. A second aspect of Jeremiah's influence in medieval culture highlighted in the Commentary is the way the figure of the prophet slips between the typological figure of Christ and a developing theology of the humanity of Christ.

Jeremiah in Medieval Christianity

Christians knew Jeremiah through multiple media and in diverse settings. Monks and educated clergy studied Jerome's sixth-century Latin translation in the *Glossa Ordinaria,* which surrounded the biblical text with patristic commentary. For laypeople, paraphrased Bibles that presented a continuous narrative with illustrations became popular. Everyone from bishops to beggars knew the Jeremiah portrayed in the stained-glass windows that colored the interior of cathedrals and the stone sculptures that flanked their doors. Ordinary Christians knew Jeremiah as a character in the mystery plays often performed in churches and outdoors, especially in the holy seasons of Advent and Lent. Wealthy patrons knew a different Jeremiah in their beautifully illustrated Books of Hours and other devotional literature. As these sources appear often in the Commentary, an introduction to their important characteristics is offered here.

The *Glossa Ordinaria*

A major pedagogical change in the late eleventh century affected the way Jeremiah was read. Men training for administrative duties were educated through school texts of Latin poets annotated with marginal and interlinear notes on rhetoric and logic. Scholars teaching in the newly created cathedral schools wanted to use the Bible instead, but no Bible with appropriate notes existed. Out of this practical need, some scholars argue, the *Glossa Ordinaria* was created. The basic text had already been created by Rabanus Maurus in the tenth century, in the form of large volumes of biblical books supplemented with Jerome's commentary. This format was expanded with more patristic commentaries filling the margins and brief interlinear notes that trained the reader in various forms of textual analysis and logic. Often the brevity of the notes, especially on Jeremiah's images, made the reader do the intellectual work of making connections (see Commentary on Jer 4:7 and 19).

Preserving theological commentaries from late antiquity, in a format from the tenth century, with additions reflecting twelfth-century concerns, the *Glossa* on Jeremiah offers a diachronic compendium of almost a millennium of Christian reception of the prophet. Its influence persisted from the twelfth well into the seventeenth century. In the fifteenth century, it was one of the early printed books; in the sixteenth century, it was formative in Martin Luther's education; in the seventeenth century, it was part of John Donne's library and informed his sonnets. The *Glossa* is a rich trove to be used with an alert historical consciousness. Its frequent presentation of Old Testament texts as negative foil for Christianity create "a subversive reading" that erases Israel's identity (Signer 1997: 593). See for example the Commentary on Jeremiah 1:5, 3:15-18 and 11:19.

Narrative Bibles

The proximity of the cathedral of St. Pierre to the Jewish quarter in the northern French city of Troyes is a contingency of history that affected the way medieval Christians understood Scripture. When Peter Comestor was Dean of the Chapter

(1147–64), Rashi's grandson Rabbi Tam lived in the neighborhood and attracted students from all over France. Peter Comestor had grown up in Troyes and was acquainted with the school of Rashi. Although there is no proof of interaction with particular Jews, there is ample evidence that Comestor used Jewish traditions in his work. When not in Troyes he was at the collegiate abbey of St. Victor in Paris, a center of biblical studies where the *Hebraica veritas* was prized and the work of Rashi and his heirs was habitually consulted. In this mix of intellectual currents, Peter Comestor wrote his narrative paraphrase of the Bible, a work that would influence reception of Jeremiah until vernacular Bibles were introduced in the sixteenth century. Officially recognized by the Fourth Lateran Council in 1215, it was one of three books required for theological study in Paris, along with the *Glossa* and the Sentences of Peter Lombard. Its effects on the reception of Jeremiah took hold immediately, as the curriculum for theology students at the cathedral school of Notre Dame, while the Abbey of St. Victor used it as an introduction before beginning study of the Bible and the *Glossa*. By the time they arrived at Jerome's text of Jeremiah, these future preachers and teachers had a firmly set horizon of expectation about who Jeremiah was and what he signified.

Comestor's fusion of biblical and apocryphal traditions into a compelling story created a new Jeremiah. The story occupies 26 columns inserted into an abbreviated paraphrase of 2 Kings and Tobit; by contrast, Ezekiel is only six columns long. It begins midway through the account of Josiah's reign with the title "the holy prophet Jeremiah" and draws together disparate biblical, apocryphal, and secular traditions. In the tradition of Isidore of Seville's chronicle of world history, Comestor includes two *Incidentia* correlating Jeremiah's life with the reigns of the Roman kings Ancus Marcius (640–616 BCE) and Tarquinius Priscus (616–579 BCE). By weaving theological and historical elements into an engaging story, Comestor's mix of history, moral instruction, and hagiography created a Jeremiah whose influence would dominate reception of the prophet until the sixteenth century.

The *Historia*'s Jeremiah is both interpreter and giver of divine signs. In his own day he rightly interprets divine signs, but the people inevitably misread or dismiss his own prophetic signs. Comestor's purpose becomes most clear toward the end of the story, when he includes legends from the ancient *Lives of the Prophets*. Jeremiah twice gives signs to the reader, one Christological (the virgin and child) and the other eschatological (the Ark). Comestor's legendary Jeremiah related to contemporary readers by modeling a hermeneutic of interpreting signs. In twelfth-century Europe, interpretation of Scripture focused on the relation between signifier and signified, particularly what Augustine had called transferred signs (*signa translata*). In these higher-level signs, the idea signified by the prophet's sign becomes itself a new sign pointing to a higher spiritual sense. Comestor's wonder-working Jeremiah, who offered readers clues to divine signs, perfectly reflected medieval thinking.

This new Jeremiah began to circulate well beyond the university in 1289 when Guyart des Moulins translated Comestor's book from Latin into French and added moralizing commentary along with colorful pictures. The *Bible historiale* was so popular that Paris booksellers prepared different versions, from large lavishly illustrated volumes to small tracts, to accommodate the disparate incomes of their clientele. In Guyart's book, French readers encountered for the first time an engaging Jeremiah who spoke their language, whose story they could read for themselves. In one fourteenth-century contemporizing version, an illustration shows the prophet with the halo of a Christian saint, holding a book and teaching a group of seated men wearing medieval tunics and buskins.

Picture Bibles
Jeremiah as contemporary voice against corruption in secular culture and church hierarchy appeared with vigor in early thirteenth-century France. Artists began producing elaborate Bibles that inverted the usual proportion of text to image, thereby introducing a radically different way of reading the Bible. These picture Bibles could be illuminated manuscripts fit for a king or inexpensively printed pocket-size volumes with block prints. They continued to be produced and widely circulated in multiple formats for the next 400 years. Common to all was the juxtaposition of Old Testament scenes with their typological interpretation in a New Testament scene or a contemporary moralizing scene. Three different formats of these graphic Bibles offer a glimpse into the reception of Jeremiah in medieval devotional literature. The *Bible moralisée*, made for King Louis IX, later called St. Louis, in the decades after 1226, is one of the most significant: 27 folios, with 8 roundels on each, offer 216 small, elaborately detailed and exquisitely colored medallions illustrating the book of Jeremiah. He is an ancient prophet set in a medieval city where kings have golden crowns, soldiers wear coats of mail, and ancient Israelites wear the conical hat of medieval Jewry. The brief commentary combines quotations from the *Glossa Ordinaria* with contemporary warnings. This monumental work deserves attention for its pivotal place in the medieval reception of Jeremiah and for its role as progenitor of images reproduced in stained-glass windows and popular books into early modernity. Two excellent reproductions exist, but as there is no translation of the Latin texts accompanying the moralizing roundels, all translations in the Commentary are my own.

A brief look at the society in which it was produced helps explain the complex reception of Jeremiah in the *Bible moralisée*. By the early thirteenth century, northern France had become economically prosperous and intellectually vibrant. Trade with other parts of Europe was brisk, and the practice of money-lending at interest made capital available. Universities and cathedral schools were flourishing in Paris as well as other cities. Economic and demographic expansion brought prosperity and intellectual advances, which inevitably were attended by the dangers of greed, pride, and the lure of secular teaching (Lipton 1999: 138). The presentation of Jeremiah in the *Bible moralisée* reflects deep ambivalence in the church toward this economic and intellectual prosperity. Aristotle was censured even as theologians in the universities were embracing his philosophy. The use of dialectic imported a new discourse into theology, and the mediating role of human reason through logic was viewed as a threat to the authority of patristic teachings long established in the church. A related intellectual crisis was brewing in biblical exegesis. Jews were assumed to have a kind of inside knowledge of Scripture because they knew Hebrew, and increased interaction between Jews and Christians led to Christian scholars studying Hebrew. Patristic allegory enshrined in the *Glossa* therefore had to compete with a new emphasis on philology and the plain sense of Scripture.

The *Bible moralisée* confronted these threats with its many illustrations of Jeremiah prophetically confronting money-lenders and philosophers, as well as corrupt clergy (see Commentary on Jer 20:14–18). Jeremiah functions as signifier of distinctions in medieval society, especially saint and sinner, Jew and Christian. Throughout the work, the barefoot prophet is clothed in a brown monastic robe while others wear bright colors, pointed shoes, and sometimes the conical hats that signify Jews in medieval art. This artistic convention coaches the medieval reader from the outset to identify with Jeremiah as a Christian.

From the twelfth through the fifteenth centuries, a smaller picture Bible, later called *Biblia Pauperum*, circulated in northern Europe. In the fifteenth century, the new technology of the woodblock made wide distribution of this picture Bible possible. Versions in Dutch, German, and French, and an early edition using John Wycliffe's illegal English translation, suggest that laypeople used it for private devotion. This picture Bible invited medieval Christians to prayerful study of the ways that the stories of the Old Testament prefigured the life and Passion of Christ. Each page presents a scene from the Gospels flanked by images of two Old Testament stories. The scenes are framed by two prophets above and two below, each holding a banderole proclaiming a prophecy of the Gospel event featured in the central scene. In some versions all prophets except Jeremiah wear distinctive hats, generally the pointed caps common in images of medieval Jewry and used to designate Old Testament characters. Jeremiah is often bare-headed, perhaps as a visual sign of his identity as the mourning prophet. In a fifteenth-century printed version (Henry 1987), he appears ten times, making him the most frequently quoted prophet after Isaiah. Some of the ten associations are well-known from the *Glossa Ordinaria* (see Commentary on Jer 11: 9, 19; 25:10; 31:22), while others appear to be new associations between Jeremiah and the Gospels (see Commentary on Jer 12:7).

Medieval Jewish Sources

Medieval Jewish reading of Jeremiah integrates the *peshat,* the plain sense, with *drash,* which often displays the playful approach to Scripture characteristic of Judaism. Rabbi Solomon ben Isaac (1040–1105) was a master of bringing the two together in Bible commentary. Vintner by day and scholar by night, Rashi compiled a commentary on the Bible whose influence was immediate and long-lasting. While earlier works used biblical texts in the context of homilies, liturgical poems (*piyyutim*), or collections of midrashim, Rashi's focus was interpretation. In response to elaborate allegorical and mystical interpretations, Rashi's pithy comments keep the reader grounded in the world of the text by focusing on its historical and linguistic aspects. Still, there are allusions to the precarious situation of eleventh-century French Jews, as in the resonance Rashi gives to Jehoiakim burning Jeremiah's scroll (see Commentary on Jer 36).

Rashi remains the most widely read of the twelfth-century Jewish exegetes, but others have important contributions to the reception of Jeremiah as well. Jewish scholars in Muslim Spain had already been emphasizing the *peshat* over against midrashic interpretations by emphasizing grammar and philology. Bringing familiarity with Arabic, they were able to challenge fanciful etymologies with linguistic ones. When some of them emigrated to Provence in the early part of the twelfth century, they broadened the influence of these exegetical methods. David Qimḥi (1160–1235), known by the acronym Radak, combined his linguistic expertise with the midrashic focus on religious teaching of his native Provence, in the crucible of twelfth-century rationalism. Rashi and Radak are the primary voices in the Commentary representing the rich tradition of Jewish exegesis from the eleventh through the thirteenth centuries.

In Jewish liturgy since antiquity, Jeremiah has been most closely associated with Tisha B'Ab (the Ninth of Ab), the day of remembrance for the destruction of the Temple. In two of the three Sabbaths of Admonition leading up to this major fast day, readings from Jeremiah dominate the lectionary. On the first Sabbath, the *Haftarah* (reading from the prophets) reading is Jer 1:1–2:3; on the second the *Haftarah* continues with Jer 2:4–28 and 3:4. On Tisha B'Ab the mourning of the worshippers is echoed by God in Jer 8:13–9:23. Liturgical poems called *piyyutim* use Jeremiah on this day of mourning, which also remembers medieval and modern massacres of Jews (see Commentary on Jer 9). The liturgical Jeremiah offers hope as well as tears; on Rosh Hashanah the three shofar blasts are accompanied by three groups of biblical verses, culminating with Jer 31:20. Jeremiah's image of the Lord dandling Ephraim on a knee has been recited on Rosh Hashanah since the fifth century CE (Fishbane 2002: 275). On the second day of Rosh Hashanah the *Haftarah* is Jer 31:2–20 (see Commentary).

Jeremiah in Islamic Tradition

For Muslims, Jeremiah was a prophet and holy man who prepared the way for Muhammad. The Qur'an does not mention Jeremiah, but a story in Surah 2 gave rise to rich traditions about him. A traveler passed a ruined city and wondered how even God could give life to it. To illustrate divine instruction to doubters, God made the man sleep for a hundred years, then brought him back to life and asked how long he had slept. When the man said a day, God corrected him and proceeded to clothe the skeleton of his donkey with flesh and revive it as the man watched. This legend is likely derived from the early Jewish tradition of Abimelech's 66-year sleep at the fall of Jerusalem (see Commentary on Jer 39). The active presence of highly educated Jewish converts to Islam in the Arabian peninsula of the eleventh century explains this interreligious reception.

The Qur'an story is also linked with Jeremiah in the tenth-century *Lives of the Prophets* (*Qisas al-Anbiya*) by Persian author Ahmad Ibn Muhammad Thalabi. Such stories about biblical prophets mentioned in the Qur'an became an important literary genre in Arabic literature because Muhammad is called the "seal of the prophets" (Surah 33:40). Understanding the prophets who came before him therefore deepens readers' understanding of Muhammad. Thalbi's version opens by noting that teachers disagree over whether the prophet is Ezra or Jeremiah, but he narrates it with Jeremiah's name. When Jerusalem fell, Jeremiah fled to the wilderness. He later returned on his donkey, with a basket of figs, but when he saw the ruined city, he said "How shall God give this city life after death?" God removed Jeremiah's soul for a hundred years and his donkey died, with the figs beside him. After seventy years God brought the exiles back to rebuild Jerusalem. Thirty years later he revived Jeremiah, eyes first so he could watch God's work. A voice from heaven called to the bones of his donkey to gather together, then to be covered with flesh, and finally to come to life. The legend ends by suggesting that Jeremiah still lives: "And God preserved Jeremiah alive and he is the one who is found in the wilderness" (Brinner 2002: 577). In the Qur'an, the unnamed traveler teaches about unbelief; in the tenth-century elaboration Jeremiah has become a sign of divine life-giving power. In the fourteenth century, Rashid al-din, a Jewish convert to Islam, included the story in his *Universal History* (*Jami' al-Tavarikh*). An illustration from the earliest extant manuscript shows Jeremiah watching his donkey coming to life, with two baskets of fresh hundred-year old figs nearby (Figure 5). Drawn as an Asian sage in an Islamic work containing stories adapted from Jewish sources, this is a multi-cultural Jeremiah.

FIGURE 5   Ms Or 20 f. 13v The Prophet Armia, miniature from the "Jami' al-Tawarikh" of Rashid al-Din, c. 1307. University of Edinburgh Library/Bridgeman Images.

Early Modernity

The risk of reading early modern culture as a rough draft of our own thinking haunts this part of reception history. In Gadamer's terms, our modern consciousness has been "historically effected" by momentous developments in early modernity which are now so natural as to be nearly invisible. The Jeremiahs of early modernity therefore seem natural because our own habits of thought and assumptions about the Bible have already been shaped by intellectual developments in this era. For our modern historical consciousness to be aware of its own otherness from the past, it must foreground the horizon of the past as distinct from its own. Yet this same historical consciousness has already been formed by the continuing tradition, especially early modern humanist tradition. Three aspects of this tradition in particular bear on reception of Jeremiah. First, Jewish and Christian scholars in the Renaissance emphasized the individual human person shaped by a particular context as the vehicle of divine revelation. While Jerome had apologized that divine revelation was clothed in the inelegant garments of Jeremiah's crude (*rusticus*) speech, Isaac Abarbanel (1437–1508) relished this human factor. That the young Jeremiah was "forced to express that which God commanded him in the language to which he was accustomed" in his village explains not only his lack of eloquence but also the many grammatical problems and textual irregularities in the Hebrew, which Abarbanel attributes to the prophet's lack of education (Saebø 2008: II.209). Jeremiah fascinates Rabbi Abarbanel precisely because of his humanity, which in the form of his idiosyncratic speech shines forth in the divine revelation on the sacred page. A second critical factor is the technology of the printing press. Gutenberg had printed about 200 large Bibles by 1455, many of which went to monasteries and universities for study. A significant aspect of these Bibles, besides the clear print, is the absence of interpretation. Unlike the *Glossa Ordinaria*, Gutenberg's Jeremiah had no notes, and apart from Jerome's traditional Prologue no competing voices. Jeremiah spoke for himself. Further, the clean flow of uninterrupted text invited continuous reading of longer units, and interpretation in light of adjoining passages. Not long after Gutenberg's printed Vulgate, the first printed Bible in Hebrew appeared in Soncino, Italy, making Jeremiah in the original more available to European Jews and to Christian scholars. Inexpensive printed Bibles in vernacular languages became available across Europe and England, eagerly read by Christians and Jews and interpreted to bring courage and solace in difficult circumstances. Finally, humanist scholarship changed the understanding of what it means to read the Bible as history. Origen and his student Jerome had always treated history as the plain sense before moving to allegorical interpretation, but in fifteenth-century Europe the discovery of classical antiquity that led to the Renaissance brought a new sense of the distance, and difference, of the past from the present. This sense of historical distance, joined with the emphasis on the human person mentioned above, radically changed the reception of Jeremiah in ways that reverberate into the present. If in the past Jeremiah had been for Christians primarily a figure of Christ, in early modernity he becomes in addition an embodiment of their own struggles.

The Reformers take on Jeremiah's Persona

Two major figures of the Reformation represented in the Commentary, Martin Luther and John Calvin, made lasting changes in the figure of Jeremiah. Luther's translation appeared in 1534, 12 years after his New Testament. His lively rendering made Jeremia, as Luther called him, accessible and his choice of German words made him a prophet for the church in crisis. By using the technical ecclesial verb *predigen* (preach) to translate a variety of Hebrew verbs meaning simply to call out or to speak, Luther conjures up a prophet like the contemporary preachers troubling the German church. This is no accident. In 1528, already charged with treason and heresy, Luther writes, "Thus they soon cry that we who teach the Gospel are disturbers of the whole world. This was the experience of Christ, of Jeremia, and all others" (Luther 17: 176). The Preface to his translation of Jeremiah (1532) draws a parallel between the impending doom of Judah and Luther's apocalyptic sense of his own era: "We learn from Jeremia among others that, as usual, the nearer the punishment, the worse the people become; and that the more one preaches to them, the more they despise his preaching… So it goes everywhere even now. Now that the end of the world is approaching, the people rage and rave most horribly against God. They blaspheme and damn God's word, though they well know that it is God's word and the truth." While Luther was translating Jeremiah, Germany suffered several plagues and the Peasants' Revolt; Luther himself was often in hiding or on the run. His identification with the prophet is explicit in his Preface: "It is indeed a wicked and miserable time, even worse than that of Jeremia. But so it will be, and must be. The people begin to feel secure and sing, 'Peace; all is well.' They simply persecute everything that accords with the will of God and disregard all the threatening signs." His Preface clearly directs his readers to appropriate Jeremiah's words for the present crises, and see Luther as his heir.

Adding to the popularity of Luther's Bible were the lively woodcuts by Lucas Cranach, Luther's friend in Wittenburg. With their biblical characters depicted as sixteenth-century Germans, set in a reassuringly familiar European landscape, these illustrations reinforced Luther's hermeneutic that Christians read themselves into biblical stories. Jeremiah is repeatedly pictured in scenes of confrontation with angry mobs and officials. These images would draw readers' attention to the narratives of the prophet's opposition to the religious establishment, inviting them to draw parallels with Luther's preaching (see Jer 27-28 and 38).

Calvin likewise identified with Jeremiah as one who spoke God's truth and endured persecution from hostile parties on all sides. He had lived in exile from his native France for 30 years, but was also in conflict with Lutherans because of his theology. In 1557–58, he delivered a series of lectures on Jeremiah to the Theological School in Geneva. Two associates published them in the original Latin in 1559; by 1565 they were available in French, and in 1620 an English translation was published in London. Calvin's three-volume commentary is the longest and most detailed Reformation work on Jeremiah, and is still used today. The lectures address Jeremiah's Hebrew idioms and historical circumstances along with Calvin's theological reading. Each section ends with a prayer whose theme appropriates Jeremiah for the Christian life (see Commentary on Jer 1:5 and 20:2). Calvin sometimes describes Jeremiah's historical setting as if it were the sixteenth century: "The Book of the Law was unknown; so that every one indulged his fancy in inventing many impious forms of worship... fabricating for themselves many absurd things" (Calvin 1989: 1:27). He likens Josiah's discovery of the Book of the Law in Jeremiah's youth to the Reformers' bringing the Bible to Christians, and he introduces his exegetical lectures as part of this same renewal of the Book. Calvin repeatedly finds the political situation in Geneva mirrored in Jeremiah's Jerusalem. Polemics against Rome are woven into exegesis, and readers are encouraged to see in Jeremiah a model of Christian resistance and endurance under persecution. In his dedication Calvin writes, "If Jeremiah himself were now alive on earth, he would add, if I am not deceived, his recommendation; for he would acknowledge that his prophecies have been explained by me not less honestly than reverently; and further, that they have been usefully accommodated to present circumstances" (Calvin 1989: I:xxiii).

Jeremy Emboldens Faithful Outlaws in England

The humanist reception of Jeremiah influenced the English Bible from the beginning, and the effects persist into the present. The story begins late in the fourteenth century with Oxford scholar John Wycliffe, who thought that English Christians should be reading the Bible. The Archbishop of Canterbury and King Henry IV were not amused, and in 1401 vernacular Bibles were outlawed. Wycliffe and his associates produced several translations that circulated throughout England in the form of small manuscript books that could be easily hidden; their popularity is evident in some 200 copies still extant in spite of persistent attempts to destroy all traces of them. Wycliffe's second edition replaced Jerome's prologue with a contemporary introduction to explain why Jeremye, as the prophet is called in early English, matters. The prologue emphasizes God's desire for sinners to repent so that they might live, using the examples of Nineveh and Sodom as keys to reading Jeremye. Noting that the book of Jeremye often details the time of prophecy, Wycliffe has his readers ask, "What to me is the time of the story?" so that they can learn the spiritual significance of Judah's last days. Wycliffe's Jeremye adds to the traditional foreshadowing of Christ a contemporary preacher, whose warnings can save those who have ears to hear. Most provocatively, this Jeremye calls Christians into a direct relation with God, without help from the clergy.

Some 50 years after Wycliffe, another illicit translation into English presented the prophet as model for sixteenth-century Christians. While William Tyndale was in prison for publishing an English New Testament, his colleague George Joye published *Jeremye the Prophete* from exile in Antwerp. Joye's 1534 Preface is more important in the reception history of Jeremiah than his translation from Latin, though he did coin some Jeremianic words in English, such as backsliding and saving health. He is primarily interested in the *person* Jeremy as a model of inner conviction. His Preface establishes Jeremy as a companion for dangerous times when English Christians were risking their lives for the word of God, just as the prophet had done in his own day. Joye finds in Jeremye affirmation of his own illicit work of bringing the word of God to his people, and his own sense of betrayal by his countrymen: "Neither could the unkind dealing of his own folk of Anatoth, nor yet the false behavior of the rulers against him, once turn his mind from them. There could no king for all their threatening, prisoning and punishing make him to shrink or cease from his office that God called him unto" (Joye 1534). Joye hints at the similarity between the prophet and himself, as well as his imprisoned friend William Tyndale: "… his fortune (as be the fortunes of all true preachers before the world) was most miserable and hard, as one of those that preached the word of the Lord God both prudently and constantly unto his death. Which constancy, most commendable in any preacher, could not come but of a perfect and firm faith in God." Joye also presents Jeremye as a model English gentleman, worthy of imitation by English Christians. Writing about the prophet's response to being carried away to Egypt by his enemies, Joye writes, "For he exhorted them sweetly and lovingly, he rebuked sharply and earnestly and preached evermore faithfully and constantly. So that if we behold his faithfulness, he is fervent. If we consider his erudition and doctrine, he shineth. If we look upon his prudence, it is right savory and well seasoned. If we behold his godliness, he exceedeth. And as for his constancy, it is invincible and beareth away all the victory." Joye's Preface encouraged readers to see in the prophet a fellow traveler in dangerous times whose faith made him bold in the presence of enemies.

The next year Myles Coverdale published a complete English Bible in Antwerp, adding Joye's translation of Jeremy, as Coverdale spelled it, to the books that Tyndale had translated before he was executed. The woodcut of Jeremy encourages readers to apply the prophet's story to the present conflicts in England. Alone on a hill overlooking a city with a fortress resembling an English cathedral, Jeremy is dressed in contemporary breeches and boots, a persona in whom readers can see themselves (Figure 6). As Jeremy interprets God's signs to carry out his prophetic task, so the reader should perceive in the text what God is saying and do it. The illustration draws readers into the new act of reading and interpreting the Bible, suggesting that the word of God that came to Jeremy is equally available in Coverdale's translation.

The King James or Authorized Version of 1611 complicates reception of the prophet, whose name for the first time is spelled Jeremiah. Its extraordinary and continuing influence for over 400 years has put his words and story into the hands of English speakers across the world, yet its Elizabethan language gave him a distant voice locked in the past. Aiming for a translation that would seem

FIGURE 6 Headpiece to Jeremiah in the Coverdale Bible 1535. Reproduced by permission of the Syndics of Cambridge University Library.

familiar, the translators worked with the 1568 Bible used in churches. English, however, was evolving rapidly, and by 1611 the language of that Bible was beginning to sound archaic. While the Jeremy of the illicit sixteenth-century Bibles spoke directly to the reader in language like theirs, the Jeremiah of 1611 was distanced. Words already obsolete like cockatrices (8:17) and wroth (37:15) make him sound quaint. On the other hand, the translators included marginal notes revealing problems in the Hebrew text and alerting readers to alternate possibilities. By making this Bible transparently a *translation*, they constantly reminded readers that Jeremiah inhabited ancient Israel, however much he might sound like an English Christian.

Jeremiah in Early Modern Europe

In seventeenth-century Europe, Jeremiah embodied two dominant religious phenomena of political action and private devotion. Calvin's theological emphasis on the hidden depths of the human heart as the primary locus of encounter between God and Christian dominated

Protestantism. His language not only rejected Catholic sacramentalism, but also reflected contemporary fascination with the idea that the human person was above all an interior space in which the most significant religious encounters took place. Affective piety as a form of private devotion for lay Christians had of course been known in Catholicism at least since Thomas à Kempis' fifteenth-century prayer manual *Imitation of Christ,* and the *Devotio moderna* movement of lay Christians that it inspired. For the reception of Jeremiah, however, Jan van der Straet's engraving seems to mark a turning point (Figure 7). This Jeremiah as a contemporary Dutchman at prayer replaced traditional images of the prophet with a new understanding of him as a fellow Christian seeking inner communion with God. Rembrandt's *Jeremiah Lamenting the Destruction of Jerusalem,* painted 17 years after van der Straet's engraving, combined the medieval pose of Jeremiah lamenting with an introspective figure focused more on an interior reality than on the Jerusalem in flames nearby (see Figure 1). Like van der Straet, Rembrandt used a living model, thereby humanizing Jeremiah as though he were a contemporary of his Dutch viewers.

The same culture that held dear a perception of Jeremiah's rich interior life with God prized equally his confrontation of political powers. As embodiment of bold confrontation with kings, Jeremiah was enlisted in the debates about the relation between religious and political authority. Throughout medieval Europe, kings had ruled by divine right, and Christians were taught allegiance to their sovereign second only to God. Some seventeenth-century political philosophers upset this longstanding arrangement by arguing for a new

FIGURE 7 The Prophet Jeremias. Jan van der Straet, called Stradanus. *Icones Prophetarum Veteris Testamenti* Antwerp 1613. Private collection.

relation between the individual and civil authority, based on humanist ideals rather than traditional religion. Spinoza's reading of the Bible, and his use of Jeremiah, was part of his political argument that civil authority must rest on a compact of the governed that balances the natural rights of the individual with the welfare of the society. His argument rested in part on the model of covenant in the Bible, which showed that Israel had to agree willingly to be ruled by divine law (Exodus 24). Even God, the supreme Sovereign, ruled with the consent of the governed. Further, the human sovereign was himself under divine law, and if his command abrogated this law his subjects had no duty to obey (see Commentary on Jer 29). Spinoza's writing is but one example of widespread questioning in the seventeenth century that shook the foundations of traditional political theology. When this bedrock of society began to shift,

both royalists and critics of the divine right of kings saw in Jeremiah a powerful ally. Illustrations of Jeremiah in seventeenth-century Bibles document
the reception of Jeremiah as a political figure representing the ideals of
humanism.

For Europeans challenging the divine right of kings, this ancient prophet
who confronted his king was newly compelling. An important example
appears in the dramatic engraving in the popular picture Bible *Theatrum
Biblicum,* first produced by Dutch Protestant Claes Jansz Visscher in 1643
(Figure 8). The prophet stands before Zedekiah with a hand gesture clearly
evoking Socrates conversing with Aristotle in Raphael's 1510 fresco *The School
of Athens.* The two figures are engaged in passionate but rational dialogue, in a
setting whose every detail conveys sixteenth-century humanism. The perfectly
proportioned architecture, the open book and scientific device on the table,
even the soldiers in conversation visible through the open door, all frame
Jeremiah as a rational humanist, while his pointed hat marks him as a biblical
prophet. Refusing to accept the king's decision as God's desire, this Jeremiah is
a model of humanist ideals emboldening the viewer to confront divine power
with human reason.

FIGURE 8   Jeremiah before Zedekiah. *Theatrum Biblicum* 1643. Rare Books Division,
The New York Public Library, Astor, Lenox and Tilden Foundations.

Jeremiah in the Counter-Reformation

Protestant claims on Jeremiah as contemporary prophet of the Reformation met with a Catholic response revitalizing the church's traditional teaching that he was an ancient prefiguring of Christ. In 1568, a group of English Catholics at Oxford fled for safety to Flanders, where they established the College of Douay and began an English translation from the Church's official Latin Bible. The short preface to Jeremiah (1609) instructs readers to understand him according to ancient church tradition. He was "a special figure of Jesus Christ, in the persecutions he underwent for discharging his duty; in his charity for his persecutors; and in the violent death he suffered at their hands: it being an ancient tradition of the Hebrews, that he was stoned to death by the remnant of the Jews who had retired into Egypt." In presenting the martyrdom of Jeremiah as authoritative, the translators place him firmly under the aegis of the church and patristic tradition. This reception of Jeremiah primarily as a figure of Christ received scholarly support in the work of Michael Ghislerius, an accomplished scholar-priest in Rome. Ghislerius had discovered a manuscript of Origen's homilies on Jeremiah in the Vatican Library, translated them into Latin, and published the first printed edition of this long-lost resource. In 1623 he produced an extensive commentary to counter the directions in which Jeremiah was being taken by humanists. Written in Latin, it adhered to a medieval format of presenting a catena of patristic sources and a traditional arrangement of plain and spiritual senses. The title page repeatedly proclaims a Jeremiah formed by patristic traditions (Figure 9). A crucifix at the top is framed by the traditionally Christological words of Jeremiah 11:19 (see Commentary). In the center, two large figures present Jeremiah and Baruch as equals, each holding his book. This image references the Council of Trent's ruling, against the Protestants, that the books of the Apocrypha have the authority of Scripture. Baruch here is not only Jeremiah's scribe, but an inspired sacred author. Between these figures two cherubim hold an image which is at once the woman of Revelation 12:1–6 and the Virgin Mary. The text refers to Jeremiah 31:22 (see Commentary). The three scenes across the bottom from Jer 38, Lamentations 1, and the apocryphal stoning all have Christological interpretations in patristic tradition. The inclusion of Jeremiah's martyrdom on the cover of a 1623 book highlights Ghislerius' intention to draw Jeremiah back into a traditional Catholic Christological interpretation against the tide of humanist interpretation.

Jérémie in French Society

In seventeenth- and eighteenth-century France, Jérémie slipped easily between political opposition, religious sentiment, and literary parody. His voice emboldened protests in the crisis of 1648 when the ambitious and hated Cardinal

FIGURE 9   Title page of Michael Ghislerius, *In Ieremiam prophetam commentarii* (1623). By kind permission of the Andover-Harvard Theological Library, Harvard University.

Mazarin took control over the regency of nine year-old king Louis XIV. Mazarin had established a blockade of Paris to starve its people into submission, provoking protest in the form of hundreds of pamphlets denouncing him and his tax agents who were profiteering in a time of crisis. These Mazarinades, as the pamphlets were soon called, often channeled the voice of a historical character to conceal the author's identity from the authorities. In this desperate situation, Jérémie spoke across the centuries and Jerusalem became Paris in a Mazarinade titled *La Jerusalem françoise: ou les propheties de Jérémie sont naïvement expliquées suivant ce qui arrive à present* (The French Jerusalem, or the prophecies of Jeremiah interpreted for the present). The anonymous author shrewdly divides his pamphlet into three "days" to reflect the church's tradition of worship on the last three days of Holy Week, when readings from Jérémie dominate. To justify his contemporizing, the author reminds readers that although Jérémie's words were originally addressed to ancient Jerusalem, they were subsequently interpreted by the church to signify Christ's passion. "We are blind if we cannot see how these words we interpret about others also apply to us... I want to show you now that when God warned the Jews what was going to happen to them, he also wanted to warn us of what we may have to fear." With this trope he encourages his fellow citizens in the drama being played out on the streets of Paris: "You will surely see that the prophet's predictions are even now being accomplished, for I have not shrunk back from the significance of this great prophet." Jérémie's voice gives authority and political cover to the author's seditious charge that the primary cause of the current disasters is Cardinal Mazarin. The author finds a contemporary analogue to Nebuchadnezzar's violation of the Temple in Mazarin's treachery: "The enemy who has stretched out his hand on that which we hold most dear is Mazarin... It is Mazarin, I say, who treacherously and recklessly entered God's sanctuary when he made himself Cardinal, a title that he carries against the will of God, who had never approved of him because of his corrupt life." With the voice of Jérémie, the author undermines the Cardinal's authority and rallies beleaguered Parisians against him. He shows that Paris can be loyal to her God and king while rejecting Cardinal Mazarin, thereby weakening the longstanding bond between church and state. Like the original, Jérémie is faithful yet subversive, giving cover in a dangerous time for seditious political rhetoric against the religious establishment.

Jérémie's voice is also used to parody Cardinal Mazarin, along with French aristocracy, in Paul Scarron's long mock-heroic poem *Virgile travesty* (1653). While the anonymous Mazarinade of 1648 used the church's Jérémie of Holy Week to challenge Cardinal Mazarin, Scarron invoked the tradition of the weeping prophet in order to skewer him. In a burlesque of Virgil's *Aeneid*, Scarron speaks to political crisis through satire, as his rupture of Virgil's classical genre encodes the rupture in legitimate authority during the regency of Louis

XIV. His send-up of the epic hero is a thinly disguised unmasking of contemporary French aristocrats, mocking their self-esteem and undermining their assured place in society (Assaf 1990: 277–279). In this comic work, Jérémie appears four times, always to parody Virgil's description of an emotional scene. In Book I "Aeneas does a Jeremiah, and soaking his wan face he cries with exquisite perfection, even when nothing is wrong." Caricaturing Queen Amata's distress that Aeneas has ruined her daughter's wedding plans, Scarron jokes, "She made a Jeremiah, and wept until she was bleary-eyed." His colorful phrase *faire le Jérémie* (to make a Jeremiah), especially in the context of such ludicrous exaggerations, skewers the religious sentiment developing around the weeping Jérémie and undermines Cardinal Mazarin's authority.

The tears parodied by Scarron were treasured in the Baroque church, where engaging the emotions in personal piety led to new interest in Jérémie. His tears were often a model of religious sentiment for French Catholics, and became an established idiom in art and poetry. When the renowned Bishop Jacques Bousset delivered his funeral oration for the French widow of King Charles I in 1669, he invoked the prophet's tears. Reflecting on the horrors Queen Henrietta Maria had experienced at the hands of English Puritans who beheaded her husband and sent her into exile, Bousset exclaims, "Who can narrate her sorrows, or describe her weeping? Non, messieurs, even Jérémie himself, who has no peer in mourning disasters, did not suffer such sorrows" (Bousset 1892: 67).

Jérémie as French Rebel

As he had in England and Germany, Jérémie embodied the conflict in France over translation of the Bible into the vernacular. Ever since the royal edict of 1551 prohibiting vernacular Bibles, French Catholics in seventeenth-century France generally knew the prophet from a patchwork of second-hand sources. Like their medieval forebears, they knew him primarily from Holy Week liturgies as prefiguring the suffering Christ, and from sculptures that often flanked the doors of their cathedrals. Scholar and educator Nicholas Fontaine wanted students at the Jansenist school in Port-Royal to read the Scriptures, so he produced a story-book Bible in the vernacular to circumvent the law. *L'histoire de Vieux et du Nouveau Testament* (1670) presented the Bible as a continuous narrative divided into short chapters, each featuring a contemporizing illustration full of dramatic action, taken from Matthäus Merian's popular *Icones Biblicae* (1630), and closing with edifying words from an ancient patristic source. Fontaine explained that the pictures offered his young readers a way for the important lessons of sacred history "to go through their eyes into their souls."

His Jérémie is a bold rebel prophet. The short narrative presents "a man of admirable virtue" whom he intends as a model for his students, replacing the traditional prefiguring of a suffering Christ with a young man bravely confronting his enemies. Fontaine engages his young readers by presenting Jérémie as their contemporary, "who began to preach at the age of fifteen." Deftly creating the gripping story of a prophet "whose courageous independence soon drew men's hatred," Fontaine's Jérémie reflects the introspective temperament and moral courage prized in his Jansenist community at Port-Royal. His narrative is a barely disguised description of his own conflicts with the church: "He was not surprised by their evil plots and threats against him, or the tortures that they prepared for him. Far from becoming more timid in his prophecies, he became more fiery than ever." Omitting Jérémie's tears, Fontaine writes, "This holy man suffered the abuses of his enemies with heroic courage." A large illustration of the defiant prophet being lowered into a cistern (see Commentary on Jer 38) would appeal to Fontaine's young readers far more than traditional images of a weeping Jérémie. Fontaine maintains his contemporizing interpretation to the end, even in the patristic teaching that he subversively transforms into a battle cry: "This is what St. Cyprian means when he says, 'A man of God who has God in his heart, reverence for God before his eyes, and God's truth in his mouth may be killed, but he cannot be mastered'" (Fontaine 1670: 308). Fontaine wrote from the Bastille, where he had been imprisoned in 1664 on charges of treason because of his Jansenist theology, and his description of "the weak king who could not resist" the demands of his princes to imprison Jérémie is a thinly veiled critique of Louis XIV.

Jérémie Speaks Elegant French but Remains Stubbornly Hebrew

Fontaine's colleague at Port-Royal, Louis-Isaac le Maistre de Sacy, published a translation of Jeremiah into French in 1693, making the prophet's full story more widely known. As a Jansenist Sacy, like Fontaine, embraced humanism and the idea that lay Christians should study Scripture. He had been imprisoned in the Bastille (1666–68) for translating the New Testament into French, and during his two and a half years there he worked on translating the Old Testament. Although his translation of Jérémie into stylish French reflected the Jansenist insistence on encouraging Christians to read the Bible, it was in some ways traditionally Catholic. Each chapter includes a long explication, "Sens Litteral et Spirituel," that blends historical explanations with moralizing comments from patristic theologians. Sacy's widely read Jérémie reflected an uneasy amalgam of reason and empirical knowledge with medieval piety and supernatural prophecy.

Like Jérémie, Sacy was at first reviled by all parties. His book guided readers with the church's spiritual interpretations, yet church officials condemned it; he made a vernacular Bible available, but humanists scorned it for its stylized

French. Sacy had transformed the otherness of ancient Israel into *le classicisme,* "a very particular literary style reflecting the language and self-conscious values of the French court and aristocracy" (Schwarzbach 2008: 567). Sacy's French was the voice of Jérémie for almost 200 years, from 1670 until the middle of the nineteenth century. Yet even this elegant translation could not tame what Jerome had criticized as Jeremiah's "rustic" style. Hebrew poetry had elements as alien to cultured Frenchmen of the seventeenth century as to Jerome in the fifth century. An introduction to an 1837 edition of Sacy's translation suggests that even in French Jérémie was exotic: "Fragments of meaning, broken phrases, interrupted and *louche* expressions, using singular for plural and past for future, disorganization of speeches, little order in the narrative: these are problems common to the style of ancient authors. We perhaps do not like their writing because we are ignorant of the nature of their language" (*La Bible,* Paris, 1837: Vol. 3, 274 my translation).

Holy Terror: Jérémie in Popular Culture

While the educated read Jérémie in Sacy's literary French, the poor and the unlettered in the countryside knew a different prophet. In the early sixteenth century, enterprising printers in Troyes had begun producing small inexpensive books bound in blue sugar paper. Named *bibliothèque bleue* for their covers and usually sold by itinerant peddlers, these books were eagerly consumed until well into the nineteenth century. Along with almanacs and romances, short narratives that made the Bible accessible were popular. One example is *Histoires abregées de l'Ancien Testament* (1685), a moralizing story Bible for young people that abridged Fontaine's 1670 *L'histoire* mentioned above. While Fontaine's Jérémie was part of a humanist education encouraging students to think for themselves, in this widely circulated *bibliothèque bleue* the prophet remained safely within church tradition. The preface describes the purpose as "sowing in their young hearts the seeds of virtue, whose fruits will appear in time," because "the Holy books should be used to teach, to reprove, to correct, and to show the way to godliness and righteousness." To this end, the book "presents in a manner simple and appropriate for all kinds of minds the great wonders that God has done for his people," with the purpose of evoking both grateful wonder and "holy terror at seeing the judgments of God." In his six appearances the prophet models Christian virtues for young French Christians. He speaks only truth: "Jérémie chose to endure tormenting from the nobles who saw him as their enemy, rather than give the Jews the false words they wanted to hear." He shows forgiveness to his persecutors when his prophecies of doom came true: "He consoled them in this affliction [Exile], promising that God would deliver them at the appointed time." Making Jérémie an example of selfless loyalty motivates the fanciful re-writing of Jer 43:5–7: "Seeing that he could not dissuade the people from going to Egypt, he chose to accompany rather than abandon them." The final scene re-writes 2 Macc 15:12–16 to present a pious Jérémie. In the original, Judas Maccabeus encourages his men by recounting his dream in which the high priest Onias shows him a vision of Jeremiah handing him a golden sword for the battle. *Histoires* omits the sword, instead describing Jérémie as a model Catholic, "one who does not cease offering his prayers to God for all the people."

Jérémie turned a profit for peddlers of "blue books" by offering personal devotions and fishing tips. A book for praying the stations of the cross enlists Jérémie to motivate emotional response to Jesus' passion. In the thirteenth station, where the women of Jerusalem weep for Jesus (Luke 23:27), the author praises tears with a list of saints who wept, including "the holy prophet Jérémie." This prophet "used the silent eloquence of his eyes, which wept to appease God's anger and to move him to pity, and he urged Jerusalem to do the same" (Paviliers 1775: 50). Jérémie is here a model of Baroque piety designed to engage the emotions of readers.

One "blue book" in particular illustrates how the penumbra of extra-biblical traditions continued to develop, creating a prophet continually slipping from definition. A Jérémie who is part magician and part practical advisor appears in the popular *Le Secret des Secrets de Nature* (1679). The title page promises "extracts from *Petit Albert*," a popular hybrid of almanac and magic spells, published in 1668. The author confides "a good secret for catching many fish in rivers or ponds, which was given to me by Capitaine Jérémie, a genuine Egyptian" (p. 75). A recipe instructs readers to make a paste of cheese, flowers, wine, oil, and rose water, form it into little balls, and throw them into the water to attract fish. A variant of this piece of folk magic had been enjoyed by readers since Peter Comestor's twelfth-century *Historia Scholastica* that narrated the prophet's miraculous powers over the creatures in Egypt's waters, traditions that originated in the first-century CE *Lives of the Prophets*. Originally part of medieval theological education in Paris, Comestor's wonder-working Jérémie now surfaces in seventeenth-century popular culture long after humanist scholars in the universities had set him aside.

Jérémie Evokes Both Tears and Snickers in Eighteenth-century France

The figure of Jérémie was so deeply embedded in French culture that in the vitriolic debates of the eighteenth-century French Enlightenment, opposing sides could equally claim him as their own. On one side were the *philosophes*, who followed Descartes' principle that certainty comes only from sense perception and reason; on the other side were Catholics for whom the church's tradition, including Scripture, brought revealed truth. For the *philosophes,* religion was suspect, but Jérémie as a trope of emotion run wild was amusing. Voltaire, one of the most famous *philosophes,* knew just how to use him. In an infamous episode one evening early in 1760, Catholic aristocrat Jean-Jacques Lefranc, who had just been admitted to the prestigious French Academy, delivered a debut lecture that turned out to be his last. Lefranc had studied Hebrew in order to translate some of the Bible into metered, rhyming French, and his book *Poésies Sacrées* had made his reputation. His lecture on that fateful evening focused on castigating intellectuals who were discarding religious truths for Enlightenment rationalism. In the audience were many *philosophes* who had voted to admit him, and they were outraged by his arrogant manner and discourse. Voltaire quickly published a ditty that became famous and helped destroy the man's reputation. The meter of the French exactly imitated Lefranc's sacred poems:

> Savez-vous pourquoi Jérémie
> A tant pleuré pendant sa vie ?
> C'est qu'en prophète il prévoyait
> Qu'un jour Lefranc le traduirait.
> Do you know why Jeremiah
> Spent so much time crying?
> He could foresee his fate:
> Lafranc his words would translate. (Voltaire 1877:560).

Voltaire's scathing verse is evidence that the figure of Jérémie lamenting had become a useful cultural icon, even among rationalists who had little use for the Bible.

Catholics also enlisted Jérémie's tears, as laments for True Religion attacked by fashionable intellectuals, just as Judah's holy city had been invaded by impious Babylonians. A notable example is *Jérémie, Poëme en quatre chants,* the ambitious set of illustrated poems by Catholic priest and Sorbonne educated poet Desmarais. Published in 1771, at the height of Voltaire's career, the poems adopt Jérémie's voice in a thinly veiled attack on Voltaire and the *philosophes,* whom Desmarais calls the new adversaries. An expanded second edition in 1772 includes a long poem titled "L'Incrédulité," warning that the enemies of religion roamed the land like a hideous monster seeking to destroy faith, as Jérémie had sought to destroy him. The frontispiece signals that this Jérémie, though found in the Scriptures, has slipped into Paris to warn of disaster (Figure 10). The author describes the frontispiece as "an antique window covered by a curtain displaying the title. To signify the devastation of the holy place, a corner of the curtain is raised, revealing a Levite overthrown to the ground, bathed in his blood: he still

FIGURE 10 Frontispiece to Jérémie, *Poëme en Quatre Chants*, by M. Demarais. Paris 1771.

holds the censer, a sign of his high office" (Desmarais 1771: 11 my translation). All of these aspects of the Temple encode the eighteenth-century Catholic church in France: the Levite with censer is the priest at Mass, and the Ark is the Tabernacle which holds the Sacrament in every church. Desmarais' narrative poems about Jérémie will raise the curtain to reveal the prophet's sad story, and its warnings about the present.

In five vignettes, these poems interweave the story of Jérémie, the Passion of Christ, and the troubles of contemporary French Catholics. Demarais' Jérémie embodies the Baroque aesthetic of intense emotion extravagantly expressed. The over-wrought tone of the heroic couplets that this prophet speaks gives new meaning to the trope of the weeping prophet. He bemoans his fate, "Exposed to the mocking laughter of incensed people, rejected, misunderstood, confused, threatened, full of disgrace, intoxicated with bitterness." All of this in elegant, rhyming courtly French, which models Desmarais' view of "the necessity of accommodating the genius of Hebrew poetry to the taste of our time." Desmarais' Jérémie encodes the painful experiences of French Catholics smarting under the intellectual critiques of the *philosophes* and the undermining of their political power in the ruling Parlement. Three of the six illustrations particularly embody Desmarais' fusion of Jérémie, Christ, and the attack on True Religion into a single narrative (see Commentary on Jer 20, 38, and 44). Traditionally pious yet artistically *au courant,* the prophet's exquisitely sensitive sorrows are designed to evoke similar emotions in readers: "It is gratifying for a sensitive soul to be agitated with Jérémie, a writer so full of godly feelings," Desmarais writes. This reception of Jérémie fortified beleaguered Catholics against the crisis of Enlightenment mockery; in the longer term it helped fashion the prophet as embodiment of the modern virtues of religious sensibility and interiority.

Jeremy Weeps for England's Pleasant Land

The figure of Jeremiah became both Puritan and Royalist throughout the violence and treachery of the English Civil War (1642–51). When the Puritans' Parliament imprisoned King Charles, Royalists used the voice of the prophet as political cover to rally support, as in a 1648 anonymous pamphlet entitled *Jeremiah Revived: though in his Prison; or his Lamentations paralleled.* The author's subversive intentions are clear on the title page: "Being a mournful representation of the King and His Kingdom's wretched condition." Like Jeremiah, the pamphlet juxtaposes outrage and sorrow, indictment and pleading. Similarly, the young Royalist Jeremiah Rich showed his poetic abilities and political cunning in *Jeremiah's contemplations on Jeremiah's lamentations, or, England's miseries matched with Sion's elegies* (1648). The dedication invokes the tradition of England as Jerusalem to sound the alarm against the Puritans. Recalling that "these two Ladies, Israel and England, were the Darlings of God, the Daughters of Heaven, the Wonder of the Earth, and yet the Envy of the World" only highlights their disgrace. The poet protests the Puritan destruction of images in

England's parish churches, encoding his complaint as Jeremiah's lament over the Babylonian sack of the Temple in Jerusalem:

> And now the furious Foe hath stretched his hand
> On her rich Ornaments, and pleasant Land:
> And 'cause he thought this not enough to do,
> Thy Sanctuary is polluted too.

Rich's descriptions of the present disasters had roots in his habitual reading of Jeremiah in English, which evoked a non-linear juxtaposition of indictment, hope, guilt, and salvation. His *Jeremiah Revived* presents a complex reading of "England's miseries" inflected with the contradictions embedded in the biblical book of Jeremiah.

Shortly before Charles I was executed, John Quarles also used Jeremiah's voice for mourning as well as indictment. Quarles had taken up arms against the Parliamentarians while a student at Oxford, and he was exiled in Flanders when he wrote *Fons Lachrymarum: or A Fountain of Tears: from whence doth flow Englands Complaint* (first published 1648). In his preface, Quarles instructs his readers: "I here present to thy view a Fountain, from which doth flow, Complaints, Lamentations, and Meditations, three necessaries for these times. Never were Complaints more frequent than they are in this Age of obduracy and oppression; nor Lamentations more requisite, than in these Lachrymable Times; nor Meditations more commendable, than in these days of uncertainty." The graphics of the title page evoke Jeremiah in multiple ways (see Commentary on Jer 9:1).

Puritans actualized Jeremiah as fervently as their Royalist enemies. John Milton wrote *The Reason of Church-Government* (1642) in part to discredit the authority of bishops. In a preemptive rhetorical move that establishes his religious credentials, he styles himself a new Jeremiah, reluctant but driven to speak: "When God commands to take the trumpet and blow a dolorous or a jarring blast, it lies not in man's will what he shall say, or what he shall conceal. If he shall think to be silent, as Jeremiah did, because of the reproach and derision he met with daily, and all his familiar friends watched for his halting to be revenged on him, for speaking the truth, he would be forced to confess as he confessed, 'his word was in my heart as a burning fire.'" Like the prophet, Milton says he is reluctant to "embark in a troubled sea of noises and hoarse disputes," but is driven by divine promptings to speak "those sharp, but saving words which would be a terror, and a torment in him to keep back." Those sharp words are evident when he contrasts his own willingness to pay the cost for prophetic truth-telling with prelates who "strive to keep to themselves to their great pleasure and commodity those things which they ought to render up." Like Jerusalem's corrupt priests, England's bishops are leading the people to ruin, and Milton sees himself as a contemporary Jeremiah.

Milton's prophetic indictments in Jeremiah's voice refashioned the ancient prophet into a modern man obeying his conscience. As God spoke to Jeremiah, divine promptings speak in Milton's conscience, which he calls "God's Secretary," and to ignore them would rob him of all peace. In combining Jeremiah's burning fire with the vocabulary of conscience and self-reflection, Milton inscribes an early modern sense of the self into the prophet's words. This potent voice, constructed from Milton's synthesis of Jeremiah and his own experience, persists even when political circumstances change. As the prophet had emboldened him in the optimistic days of Puritan ascendancy, he also gave justification to Milton's alienation 18 years later, when the restoration of Charles II to the throne spelled Puritan defeat (see Commentary on Jer 22 and 44).

Jeremiah in Early Humanist Struggles with the Bible

In the debates about revelation and human knowledge that set Scripture against the insistence on empirical evidence, Jeremiah appeared equally often as a figure of piety and of human reason. Spinoza wrote his *Theologico-Political Treatise* (1670) partly to demonstrate that governments ruled not by divine will but human consent, in order to insure peace and freedom. In the spirit of Humanism, he challenged the divine authorship of the Bible by exploring the very earthly nature of its composition. "The method of interpreting Scripture is no different from the method of interpreting Nature," he writes in chapter 7, and Jeremiah offered a compelling example. Promising because of its clear historical setting, the book's chaotic chronology ultimately undermines its divine authority for Spinoza. The prophecies, "taken from various chronicles" are "heaped together confusedly, without any account being taken of dates but also the same story is told differently in different passages." Jerome had resolved the problem by saying that Jeremiah was writing prophecy, not narrative, but in the context of early modern humanism, the chronological disarray of Jeremiah offered evidence of the Bible's human origins.

The received tradition of Jeremiah as the weeping prophet offered evidence for Spinoza's insistence that ideas originating from God are always mediated through and bear the marks of individual human personalities. In chapter two of *Theologico-Political Treatise* he writes: "I discount the fantastic view that the prophets had human bodies but nonhuman minds, so that their sensations and consciousness were of an entirely different order from our own" (Spinoza 1951: 30). He describes prophetic thought using Descartes' signature formula for human reason, "clear and distinct ideas," to emphasize its human quality. In an epistemological claim that came to have far-reaching consequences, Spinoza argues that revelations to prophets were shaped by their unique temperaments, knowledge, and beliefs. "If the prophet was of a cheerful disposition, then victories, peace and other joyful events were revealed to him; for it is on things of this kind that the imagination of such people dwells. If he was of a gloomy disposition, then wars, massacres, and all kinds of calamities were revealed to him." By suggesting that Jeremiah prophesied destruction *because of* his naturally dour temperament, Spinoza uses the traditional image of the mourning prophet to make a new claim about the role of human personality in divine revelation. The revolutionary nature of his argument in the developing notions of the individual self that characterize modernity is clear in hindsight.

In England Jeremiah spoke to rationalist challenges against Scripture's claims to truth. John Smith was one of the Cambridge Platonists who wanted to reconcile the Bible with humanism, and his "On Prophecy" (1660) reads prophetic literature with the empirical mindset of a seventeenth-century scientist. The question of whether some of Jeremiah's bizarre actions were "real, or only imaginary, and performed upon the stage of fancy" was crucial for Smith. The relation between knowledge derived from sense perception and the knowledge of an ethically formed will – reason and faith – is a central question of the era. For Smith, whose library included works of Descartes, prophecy is as central to moral knowledge as sense perception is to scientific knowledge. In the beginning of his discourse on prophecy, Smith evokes Jeremiah to make his claim that the God who made us able to converse rationally with one another would not make us deaf to the divine voice that breaks rock. Jeremiah's experiences of the divine word as physical sensation like fire or a hammer nicely fit Smith's Cartesian criterion of a clear and distinct sensation. The stumbling-blocks to reason are the bizarre actions and descriptions that strain credulity (see Commentary on Jer 23:9). Smith explains that the bizarre actions that Jeremiah narrates in the first person are apparitions made to the imagination and acted out symbolically, while third-person narratives are "a real history concerning himself" (Smith 1660: 222, 225). In a language tinged with Cartesian vocabulary he instructs doubters how to read Jeremiah: "The mode of Jeremiah's language insinuates a literal sense by speaking altogether in the third person... and so must be of some real thing and that which to sense and observation had its reality" (Smith 1660: 225). For faithful readers filtering Scripture through the fine mesh of empiricism, Smith's work on Jeremiah offered a reasonable solution to their problems.

The eighteenth century brought new problems of reconciling the Book of Scripture with the Book of Nature. Matthew Tindal's *Christianity as Old as the Creation* (1730) argued that since human reason can discover God's will for human ethical action, the Bible is a superfluous product of irrational cultures.

Problems in Jeremiah add to reasons for people to set the Old Testament aside as a guide to moral teaching (see Commentary on Jer 27:1, 7:22–23, and 20:7). These texts portray the kind of authority from which Tindal and other Enlightenment thinkers wanted to free humanity. Tindal's work had wide circulation and generated a robust response. One was Daniel Waterland's "Six Offensive Passages in Jeremiah Explained," part of his large work *Scripture Vindicated* (1734). Waterland does not dispute the rationalist way in which Tindal framed his critique of Scripture, but responds in detail to show Tindal as an inept reader. He chides Tindal for not recognizing figurative language that "added new force and dignity to the Prophet's message, made it the more awful and solemn in the delivery, and gave it the advantage of a deeper and more durable impression" (Waterland 1734: 89). Not content with refuting Tindal's charge of the irrationality of Scripture, he argues that Jeremiah actually conforms to eighteenth-century literary norms. Waterland repeatedly responds to Tindal with philological and literary arguments to show that Jeremiah is in fact rational. In accepting Tindal's premise that the Bible could be read and judged like any book, Waterland showed how deeply Enlightenment principles had taken root in the church. In a culture where Scripture was being judged by standards of rationalism, biblical scholars wanted to bring ancient Israel to life by making its culture and geography real and therefore believable.

Benjamin Blaney united Enlightenment scholarship with devotion in his influential academic commentary. The discovery that parallelism was the structuring framework of Hebrew poetry was still new, and Blaney's Jeremiah was the first to speak English in this distinctive form. The typography of his translation made Jeremiah read more like ancient Hebrew poetry, but his archaic Tutor English kept him safely in the church. Jeremiah's "expressions in the bitterness of his soul" were an aesthetic as well as a religious problem, but Blaney tamed them with his judgment that they "demand our pity rather than censure." Blaney's Jeremiah "was in truth a man of unblemished piety and conscientious integrity; a warm lover of his country, whose miseries he pathetically deplores." This Enlightenment Jeremiah was intended to unite rational and spiritual powers so that they would not be at war in the heart of the believing Christian as they were in the culture.

Reception of Jeremiah was permanently marked by the effects of Jean-Jacques Rousseau's theories of education. His writings detailing the balance between protecting and perfecting children were reflected in the work of British educator Mrs. Sarah Trimmer. A founder of the institution of Sunday school and of charity schools, Mrs. Trimmer thought religious instruction crucial to maintaining an orderly society. She offered her young readers an ancient Judean Jeremiah with lessons pertinent to eighteenth-century England. Her two-volume *A Help to the Unlearned in the Study of the Holy Scriptures, being an attempt to explain the Bible in a familiar way* (1782–85) intends "to produce a *rational faith*, and a right practice, founded immediately upon the word of God." Mrs. Trimmer's Jeremiah reflects Rousseau's revolutionary idea that children are innocent and impressionable, requiring protection as well as education. In Scripture "numberless passages… abound with incidents and doctrines much beyond the comprehension of young persons" (Trimmer 1785:7–8), so her book includes "only those parts which appear to me proper to be read by young persons" (Trimmer 1785: 10). Readers see no hint of resistance, anger, or strong language; rather Mrs. Trimmer's Jeremiah is like a prescient adult among naughty children whose foolishness is made apparent to her readers. Her influential work, reprinted into the mid-nineteenth century, closes with "… Let the fate of the Jewish nation warn you before it is too late, for *though he is dead he still speaks to us*" (Trimmer 1785: 436).

Nineteenth and Twentieth Centuries

The Paradox of Jeremiah in the Nineteenth Century

The figure of Jeremiah in the nineteenth century embodies a paradox of history. Archeological explorations of the Holy Land promised evidence of the historical Jeremiah, and European explorers coming into contact with Bedouin herdsmen in Palestine assumed that they were seeing "the world of the Bible." Knowledge of the historical cultures of the ancient Near East became part of Christian education, and publishers of family Bibles included illustrations of *realia* encouraging readers to imagine Jeremiah living in ancient Judah. At the same time, scholars presented Jeremiah as a sensitive, introspective individual who resembled his readers. The prophet's words for them demonstrated that the history of Israel was a story of religious consciousness evolving from primitive belief to inner spiritual experience. The idea of evolution dominated England and Germany, with geologists demonstrating physical changes in the earth over millennia and Darwin showing that species developed over time by adapting to their environments. Reception of Jeremiah reflected these intellectual currents. Julius Wellhausen's history of Israel used the model of evolution to argue that while the eighth-century prophets had a more developed religious sense than their predecessors, it was in Jeremiah that the most highly evolved true religion appeared. "Instead of the nation, the heart and the individual conviction were to him the subject of religion," Wellhausen wrote, distinguishing Jeremiah from Amos and Hosea (Wellhausen 1885: 491).

Wellhausen's Jeremiah was created from an alchemy of scientific studies in evolution combined with German Romanticism and Lutheran theology, where sensibility and a receptive heart marked the highest stage of religious evolution. Two of Wellhausen's contemporaries permanently changed the reception of Jeremiah. Heinrich Ewald's influential commentary had already described Jeremiah as "the evening star of the sinking days of prophecy." Ewald designated six texts as "spontaneous outpourings of the heart" (*herzensergiessungen freien*) and "personal lamentations" (*Selbstklagen*), which he described as Jeremiah's deep despondency and bitter indignation at his constant persecution (Ewald 1868: 71, 179). For Ewald, these words of "angry and bitter rebellion about being so completely misunderstood and relentlessly persecuted" were at best "pardonable" (Ewald 1868: 71). Decades after Ewald had identified these six prayers, Berhnard Duhm designated them "Confessions," a term that has subsequently defined the reception of Jeremiah. Duhm's *Jeremia* (1901) highlights them as a window into the prophet's inner life and a prototype of Protestant prayer (see Commentary on Jer 15:10 and 20:14–18). Duhm also interpreted the narratives of persecution in a distinctly Protestant way to make Jeremiah a model for his readers: "He is the first true religious martyr, though unlike many early Christian martyrs seeking future reward he was not a fanatic, so his bravery is greater and more commendable (Duhm 1901: 14). Duhm constructs a Jeremiah who is not like Catholics seeking salvation through works, but a proto-Protestant throwing himself on the mercy of God and praying in his own personal idiom. If medieval readers saw in Jeremiah a figure of Christ, readers have seen in him since the late nineteenth century Duhm's spiritual hero in whom genuine feeling was a measure of inner conviction guiding right behavior.

Duhm's modern Jeremiah took root beyond the West. An American missionary to India in the 1920s used him to show that the Christian Scriptures were compatible with Indian culture. Troubled by a movement advocating that the Indian Christian Church should reject the "materialism" of the Old Testament in favor of the spirituality of Hinduism, the Rev. E.W. Felt published a short work with the Christian Literature Society for India. In *Jeremiah, Prophet and Hero* Felt acknowledged that the prophetic books emphasize "human activities in the world" rather than the "the relation of the individual human soul to the Divine Spirit," but argued that the prophetic focus on justice "corrects and supplements the predominant emphasis in Hinduism on a purely individual salvation and a static order" (Felt 1923: 2). Felt aimed to "make Jeremiah real and living" by "placing his life and teaching over against the environment of Hinduism." Merging European biblical scholarship with the vocabulary of Hinduism in India, Felt wrote that Jeremiah was rare among the prophets because "he boldly proclaimed the vanity of any change of conduct not based in spiritual rebirth" (Felt 1923: 78), and that Jeremiah's laments "were but the outbursts of a heroic soul, struggling to attain unity of purpose and peace in conflict with his lower self" (Felt 1923: 84).

Jeremiah for Children

Educators in the nineteenth and twentieth centuries fashioned a surprising array of Jeremiahs to help shape the character of young people according to the norms of their time. Some threatened, some offered stories of danger and adventure, and others were presented as role models for young Christians. These versions of Jeremiah learned in childhood lingered in the imaginations of adult readers, and remain an influential part of reception history.

Protestant children in nineteenth-century America found in Jeremiah a stern teacher. The American Sunday-School Union in Philadelphia published *The Life and Prophecies of Jeremiah* (1836) as part of an innovative curriculum designed for broad distribution. Each chapter of this small book weaves together Jeremiah's story in the context of biblical history and earnest moralizing. The treachery of Jeremiah's enemies offers a lesson: "How often the young feel angry with those who give them faithful advice! How apt they are to abuse or ridicule them! Yet such advisers are their best friends... Let such take warning by the fate of the men of Anathoth, who threatened to kill Jeremiah for his fidelity" (26). Its final pages on the sacking of Jerusalem place Jeremiah at the heart of the paradox of suffering in Protestant theology: "All this desolation and sadness are the wages of sin." On the other hand, Jeremiah's hard life is portrayed as undeserved and borne with sturdy faith, as he "believed in the Lord, and persevered for forty years in declaring his word" (78). This Protestant Jeremiah "bore all his sufferings in patience and faith" and "was not saved by his righteousness, but by the mercy of God through faith" (79–80). Finally, lest child readers dismiss Jeremiah as ancient history, the author warns, "His voice still speaks to us from the Bible, and every sinner should listen to it as seriously as if he were one of the rebellious Jews to whom he spoke when on earth. For the same God is our God..." (80).

Young Americans reading Frances Manwaring Caulkins' influential 1841 *The Children of the Bible: As Examples and as Warnings* experienced Jeremiah as moral exemplar. A New England historian and prolific author of Bible studies, her work also reflects the theology of her Puritan ancestors. The epigraph for her chapter on Jeremiah reads, "Piety persecuted in this life – the reward hereafter" and presents Jeremiah as a tragic figure, "a sight for angels to admire" who teaches children a sobering lesson:

> Not always in this vale of tears
>   Hath virtue its reward;
> The prophet lived a life of fears,
>   In grief he numbered all his years,
> His heart was sorrow's chord.

Though a Protestant, Caulkins couldn't resist the tradition of "ancient writers" that Jeremiah "was stoned to death by the Jews" in "a martyr's bloody death." The last stanza teaches her young readers to understand Jeremiah as model for a life that does not count the cost of holiness:

> Thus Jeremiah wept and bled,
> As through this world he passed:
> Thus are the saints through trials led;
> With foes they meet, on thorns they tread,
> But win a crown at last.

The single illustration shows a patient Christ-like Jeremiah in the stocks (see Commentary on Jer 20). Caulkins' young readers found in Jeremiah a model of religious sentiment and patient suffering.

The end of the nineteenth century brought German "scientific" exegetical approaches to the Bible, which had a profound effect even on instructing children about Jeremiah. In 1904, Methodist Episcopal minister Jesse Lyman Hurlbut criticized children's Bible story books like Caulkins' for teachings and moral reflections not contained in the biblical text. Hurlbut's own *Story of the Bible for Young and Old* sought "to avoid all doctrinal bias" and promised that "the results of recent knowledge in Bible lands and Bible history are used as far as is suitable in a book for children." History has its limits, however: "The publishers have not allowed scenes of blood or such as would be repulsive to people of taste. There is a realism in some modern views of Oriental manners and customs, which may be accurate, but is not pleasing and does not promote reverence" (Hurlbut 1904: 12). Text and pictures teach Hurlbut's young readers that this prophet belonged to a distant and exotic past, yet like Hurlbut himself was above all a preacher trying to change people's behavior. Equally influential was Charles Foster's *Bible Pictures and What They Teach Us* (1886), intended to be "simple enough for little children to understand, and at the same time instructive and interesting to those of riper years." Foster's preface unwittingly echoes Nicholas Fontaine's words about religious instruction 300 years earlier: "Pictures are the delight of children, who sometimes receive impressions from them that are never afterward wholly effaced." Foster hopes that his stories about "how good is rewarded and evil punished" will train youthful minds "to look up to God as noticing and recompensing our every action (Foster 1886: preface). The picture of Jeremiah lowered into a cistern on a rope transforms Jer 38 into an exciting adventure (Figure 11).

A significant change occurs in the mid-twentieth century, when young readers are encouraged to emulate Jeremiah's steely courage. As a young pastor preaching to German children, Dietrich Bonhoeffer warned, "Children, being with God does not make one happy. We learn this from Jeremiah" (Bonhoeffer

Jeremiah is being lowered down into the dungeon. These wicked men have tied a rope around him and they are letting him down by it. Yet Jeremiah is a good man. He is a prophet. God has sent him to tell these men of the punishment that will come on them if they do not

mind him. But they are angry with Jeremiah. They want to kill him. They have asked the king if they may not put him into this deep pit. The king has given them leave. So they are lowering him down. There is mire at the bottom, and Jeremiah will sink into the mire. But God will remember him and send men to take him out again.

FIGURE 11   A children's Jeremiah from Charles Foster, *Bible Pictures and What They Teach Us* (1893). Private collection.

2002: 514). American children in 1942 saw a young, defiant Jeremiah pictured as a character in DC Comics "*Picture Stories from the Bible*." Written by M.C. Gaines in collaboration with Protestant, Catholic, and Jewish leaders, it appeared when the comic-book format was only a decade old. In six full-color

FIGURE 12   Jeremiah resists the government. D.C. Comics, *Picture Stories from the Bible*. Private collection.

pages of action and conflict, Jeremiah has the appearance of an ancient Israelite but the character of a young American (Figure 12). He admonishes people about social injustice, outwits kings, shows bravery in prison, defies tyranny, and remains loyal to his people when offered safety by the enemy. Jeremiah's Geneva cap and his defiant retort, "Imprison me, but you cannot kill these ideas!" evoke Martin Luther. Young readers find no trace of tears or doubt in this sturdy fellow who is a hero to emulate. Gains' comic book has remained in print more than half a century.

Jeremiah offers a far different lesson for readers of Arthur S. Maxwell's ten-volume *The Bible Story* (1955), which includes ten brightly colored illustrations showing Jeremiah in Orientalizing as well as contemporary settings (Figure 13). Accompanying a picture of Jeremiah as a young reader pondering God's call is Maxwell's encouragement: "Perhaps someday God will call you into His service. If so, remember His promises to Jeremiah...And don't be scared of people" (Maxwell 1955: 179). Maxwell's Jeremiah embodies the virtues of obedience and strong character found in his many other books

FIGURE 13   Jeremiah pictured as the young reader of Arthur S. Maxwell's, *The Bible Story* 1955.

for children and models the benefits of faith: "This rather bashful young man," introverted and afraid of crowds, was transformed: "God would take away all his fear, all his feelings of weakness, and make his sagging backbone like an iron pillar" (Maxwell 1955: 178–179). Likewise, the Jehovah's Witness *My Book of Bible Stories* (1978, 2004) offers Jeremiah as model for shy young men embarking on their mission. The chapter titled "A Man Who Is Not Afraid" begins, "See the people making fun of this young man" and highlights Jeremiah's determination in the face of ridicule and rejection (Figure 14). The first study question asks young readers heading out to face a hostile world, "As Jeremiah's example demonstrates, what qualifies a person for Jehovah's service?"

Jeremiah as model of bearing up under teasing and bullying is the lesson in a 1949 Bible story book, where the torment of the stocks includes the prophet having his feet tickled with a feather, along with public ridicule. The "othering" of Jeremiah's enemies by Orientalizing dress may warn young readers against being bullies like them, but it also subtly communicates the idea that the bad guys look different (Figure 15).

A Jeremiah wrestling with his identity appears in books for teenagers. Virginia Millikin's 1954 *Jeremiah, Prophet of Disaster: A Novel Biography of the Prophet Jeremiah* adapts the biblical text to the accessible format of a chapter book about a character not too different from the readers. Jeremiah is a teenager

FIGURE 14   Jeremiah models resisting ridicule. *My Book of Bible Stories,* Watchtower
Bible and Tract Society, 1978. Private collection.

struggling with his growing awareness that "he had been marked by Yahweh as
a prophet," which will mean losing friends and alienating family. Human
dreams and intuitions replace divine speeches, and Judah's history is the back-
drop for the story of Jeremiah's inner development. Millikin engages young
readers with the lively, pretty Tabitha as a soul-mate with whom Jeremiah is in
love but gently tells he cannot marry. Toward the end he confides to Baruch
that "each human heart will be a place of worship," that "it was bigoted of me to
think that his messages could come only to me and other prophets," and that
being the chosen people means "clearing the way for other nations to come to
him." Milliken's Jeremiah foreshadows Christianity, teaches her young readers
the theological universalism of liberal Protestantism, and models self-sacrifice
by relinquishing his girlfriend.

FIGURE 15   Jeremiah bullied. Children's story Bible from the early twentieth century.
Private collection.

Norman Habel's *Are You Joking, Jeremiah?* (1967, 1970) engages teens by
giving them acting parts in a dramatic reading about a rebellious, feisty prophet.
Using slang and tropes from teenage popular culture, the script presents a dialogue between "Jerry" demanding surrender to the enemy or complaining to
God, and the "Kids." Habel blurs the lines between ancient Israel and contemporary church, making Jeremiah a subversive prophet challenging complacent
Christians, and the Kids being themselves by talking back. At one point the
Kids respond to Jeremiah's call for surrender to Babylon, "What would they
say? What would our phony people say/If we interrupted any pastor/By
screaming from the choir loft?… If we were asked to choose for God/In a final

nuclear war?" (Habel 1970: 61). Habel's popular play offered a Jeremiah who spoke the language of American teenagers and challenged the religious certainties of their parents.

The graphic novel offered a format for making Jeremiah speak to contemporary adolescents. Using the stylized format of Japanese manga, the Manga Bible (2007) tells his story with simple, angular black-and-white drawings and minimal text. Jeremiah is introduced in the context of Zedekiah's dilemma during the Babylonian occupation of Jerusalem in Jer. 37: "… somewhere buried in the belly of this political stalemate was the prophet Jeremiah." He appears as an imprisoned teenager, asking himself how he got into this mess, and answering, "Oh, I remember; I told the truth." After being hoisted out of the cistern in a basket, he addresses an exotically wicked looking Zedekiah: "I'm getting bored of repeating myself over and over again. Judah is being judged for her idolatry and injustice" (Manga 2007: 126). This teen Jeremiah for the twenty-first century models faithfulness as political action, courageously confronting corrupt authority whatever the consequences.

Jeremiah in War Time

Amidst the horrors of two world wars, the figure of Jeremiah appeared in new and urgent forms. Stefan Zweig's 1917 play *Jeremiah: A Drama in Nine Scenes* is a mix of biblical tropes and contemporary political comment that drew early praise from Thomas Mann and later censoring by the Nazis. The story of Jerusalem's destruction becomes in the play the story of Austria-Hungary's destruction in the war. Zweig's Jeremiah is, like himself, driven to despair by his self-consciousness as God's prophet doomed to watch his people destroy themselves. Yet the last scene, titled "The Eternal Way," presents Jeremiah encouraging the exiles on the road. "God's are the ways on which ye shall walk. Made wise through suffering, Wanderers, chosen of God, on, through the world!" (Zwieg 1922: 330). A Babylonian soldier watching them channels Zweig's own fierce challenge to nationalism: "Who can conquer the invisible? Men we can slay, but the god who lives in them we cannot slay. A nation can be controlled by force; its spirit, never" (Zwieg 1922: 336). Zweig's writings were outlawed in Nazi Germany, but printed in the Netherlands in 1939, where this politically dangerous Jeremiah spoke again.

The ancient figure of the lamenting Jeremiah appeared in a new form after *Kristallnacht,* "the night of broken glass." The deadly attacks on Jewish neighborhoods in Germany and Austria in November 1938 galvanized Jews and Christians, and American artist Louis Rosenthal designed a medal to raise money to bring Jews out of Germany. The traditional image of a mourning Jeremiah is contemporized to a mourning Jew holding an open

FIGURE 16 Louis Rosenthal charity medal, 1938. Private collection.

text reading 1938 (Figure 16). Angel wings behind him signify those who lost their lives in the pogrom. On the reverse, three hands hold an eternal flame, with the inscription, "in the union of faiths we are fortified to serve mankind."

Reinhold Niebuhr, called "an American Jeremiah," repeatedly invoked the prophet to warn Americans about the intentions of Hitler and the dangers of listening to false prophets of peace (see Jer 20 and 27–28). Methodist educator Dr. Roy L. Smith wrote a study guide on Jeremiah and other seventh-century prophets titled "Writing Scripture Under Dictators." He contemporizes Jeremiah as one of the "godly men who were compelled to do their work under the suspicious eyes of dictators holding the power of life and death" and "harried by means of a gestapo that was both pagan and callous" (Smith 1943: 3). British scholar L.E. Elliott-Binns published *Jeremiah: Prophet for A Time of War* in 1941 with the Student Christian Movement Press. Elliott-Binns draws parallels between Jeremiah's time and his own, in the reality of many nations drawn into war, and especially "the impression that civilization is poised on the brink of the abyss" (Elliot-Binns 1941: 44). He also poignantly compares Jeremiah's descriptions of women and children destroyed in war (6.11; 11.21; 15.9) with the European reality that "every man, woman and child is in the front line" (Binns 1941: 46). He uses Jeremiah's confrontations with the powerful to call his British readers to "earnest study and mental effort," warning that "the fruits of ignorance, deliberately cultivated, are to be seen in Germany to-day" (Binns 1941: 173–174).

American poet Virginia Dunbar registers the horror of Pearl Harbor and impending war in her 1942 poem "Word to Jeremiah" (Commentary Jer 4). In the same year, Leonard Bernstein composed his "Jeremiah Symphony," which wove Hebrew chants with contemporary tonalities to make Jeremiah's voice startlingly contemporary. The three movements – Prophecy, Profanation, and Lamentation – represent Jeremiah's futile attempts to change the people, "the destruction and chaos brought on by the pagan corruption within the priesthood and the people" (as Bernstein notes in the score), and lamentations for the destroyed Jerusalem.

In 1944, Theologian Paul Tillich invoked Jeremiah to counter Nazi propaganda that branded doubters as defeatists: "My German friends! Don't be misled by the word *defeatism!* Take on the responsibility of being branded as defeatists for the sake of the truth… Jeremiah was such a prophet. He took upon himself the difficult work of foretelling the destruction of Jerusalem. He was hated and unpopular with the Jews, just as he would be today with the Nazis" (Tillich 1998: 159). Dietrich Bonhoeffer often drew strength from Jeremiah during his activities in the Confessing Church against the Nazi party (Jer 38 and 45). Artist Marc Chagall transformed the centuries-old artistic tradition of Jeremiah lamenting in his 1933 "Solitude," painted the year that Hitler was elected Chancellor of Germany (Figure 17). The mourning figure has the traditional pose of Jeremiah, but his prayer shawl and cradled Torah scroll signify Judaism. The burning city in the background is both Jerusalem and the Jewish towns destroyed in Russia. The juxtaposition of this multi-layered figure with two of Chagall's signature images, a white heifer symbolizing sacrifice and a violin signifying the Eastern European shtetl, suggest that this new Jeremiah mourns for European Jews past and present.

In the aftermath of the war, Jeremiah sometimes challenged Christians to acknowledge their Semitic roots. For some Jews, centuries of presenting Jeremiah as a prefiguring of Christ had stripped the Hebrew prophet of his true identity. Irving Layton, a Canadian Jewish poet who served in the army during World War II, identified with the large statue of a lamenting Jeremiah whom he describes as trapped inside the Catholic cathedral in Montreal. This Jeremiah epitomizes "Christian appropriation and reinterpretation of Jewish symbols"

FIGURE 17   Marc Chagall, *Solitude*, 1933. Tel Aviv Museum of Art. © Artists Rights Society.

(Sherman 2010: 154) yet remains for the poet a fellow Jew. Layton's 1956 poem "On Seeing the Statuettes of Ezekiel and Jeremiah in the Church of Notre Dame" describes a Jeremiah Christianized, "with Palestinian hills quite lost in this immense and ugly edifice." The poem begins by addressing the two prophets as fellow Jews: "They have given you French names and made you captive, my rugged troublesome compatriots" and ends with these lines:

> Yet cheer up Ezekiel and you Jeremiah
>   who were once cast into a pit;
> I shall not leave you here incensed, uneasy
>   among alien Catholic saints
> but shall bring you from time to time
>   my hot Hebrew heart
> as passionate as your own, and stand
> with you here a while in aching confraternity.
>   (Layton 1989: 52)

The American Jeremiad

One of most persistent marks of Jeremiah on American culture is the rhetorical genre that has come to be called the American jeremiad. The term jeremiad is attributed to English writer and abolitionist Hannah More, who wrote in 1790, "It has been long the fashion to make the most lamentable *Jeremiades* on the badness of the times" (Roberts 1845: I.110). The form had been widespread in England more than 100 years before More named it. During the English Civil War, from 1642 to 1660, Puritan divines as well as their opponents frequently preached sermons whose structure and rhetoric drew on Jeremiah. The occasion was often a crisis threatening the welfare of the whole people, and the preacher's task was to bring the community to repentance. In sermons indicting Royalists and Papists for their ills, Puritan preachers would also exhort their congregations to acknowledge their own sin and seek forgiveness. These sins would be contrasted with the original calling of the people, described as the Covenant by which God had lovingly bound them to himself. Divine displeasure brought the grievous present condition, which would grow worse without public repentance and amendment of life. This demand came with assurance of divine faithfulness and mercy. Hence the sermons were a dizzying mix of doom and hope, pride in a shared founding story and shame in failing to live up to it. English preachers often addressed large congregations during liturgies that were not in the church calendar but ad hoc responses to disastrous events. The context was both civic and ecclesial, drawing the entire nation into a day of penitence. These Fast Day sermons were often published, ensuring that their influence would persist well beyond the crisis that they addressed.

The Puritans who established the Massachusetts Bay Colony brought with them the religious sensibility that created the jeremiad as well as its rhetorical form. Like their English counterparts, these colonial sermons were often preached on public occasions proclaimed by civil magistrates and featured a catalogue of recent calamities linked with widespread sinful behavior in the community as well as a demand for amendment of life. Two distinctive adaptations, however, have brought significant consequences in American history. First, the colonists' jeremiads substituted their own covenant with God for the biblical covenant. John Winthrop's sermon "A Model of Christian Charity," written and preached aboard the ship Arabella in 1630, had described the colonists as a new Jerusalem in covenant with their God and each other: "For we must consider that we shall be as a city upon a hill. The eyes of all people are upon us. So that if we shall deal falsely with our God in this work we have undertaken, and so cause him to withdraw his present help from us, we shall be made a story and a by-word through the world." Winthrop echoes Jeremiah in vocabulary as well as form, characterizing sin as dealing falsely (Jer 6:13; 8:10) and its consequence becoming a by-word (Jer 24:9), but dealing falsely meant to fail in the project of establishing God's rule in America. Second and third generation Puritans realized that they had not yet fulfilled their high calling of being God's elect in a new promised land and their jeremiads lamented the gap between original vision and contemporary reality. The "Great Design" had been compromised by mundane realities of economics and politics, interaction with other colonies, and the distraction that worldly success was bringing to the original errand in the wilderness. Present ills were interpreted as divine punishment for the colonists' betrayal of the promises of a once glorious past; these jeremiads created a pervasive sense of failure intended to lead to amendment of life and reaffirmation of identity. One historian writes, "In an effort to overcome this incongruity of obvious prosperity amid felt declension, they not only defined consciousness of failure as punishment for failure; they also decided that to fail in a designation sublime was after all to fail with a difference... In lamenting their sad decline, New Englanders subtly thanked their God and notified the world that they were yet were not as other men, that they, despite all, were a chosen people dedicated to perfection" (Minter 1947: 50). The jeremiad ironically became a genre of celebration that memorialized the colonists' original vision and led to American exceptionalism.

The second American adaptation of the jeremiad is a reinterpretation of the call to repentance. Early on this prophetic demand became tinged with American optimism. The theological idea that God accepts the prayers of the penitent and helps the sinner reform remained, but increasingly became subordinated to the sense that when America had lost her way, she could find it again by grit and determination. As the jeremiad entered political discourse the call to repentance was transformed into a call to civic action. The goal was still a return to the idealized past in which the sacred mission of the nation had been given, but the original call for penitence was replaced by an American can-do optimism. The jeremiad evolved from the problem of dealing falsely with our God to not being true to ourselves. This transformation was to have a lasting effect on the formation of American character.

During the debates about slavery and throughout the Civil War, speakers of both the Union and the Confederacy used the jeremiad to link the current crisis with abandonment of a glorious past and its values. American historians point out sustained use of jeremiads in the political rhetoric of the temperance movement, nativism, and teaching evolution, but the narrative arc of the jeremiad also characterized the speeches and sermons of Martin Luther King, Jr. Reinhold Niebuhr consciously modernized the jeremiad in his persistent arguments that sin characterizes even the best humans and their actions, which he often coupled with harsh critiques of America's social sins of greed and pride (Davis 1986). Yet like the jeremiad, Niebuhr's insistence on the power of sin was coupled with a belief that Americans were called to persist in overcoming its immediate manifestations in society. If Niebuhr made the jeremiad a rhetorical fixture of social critique in liberal thought, in the 1970s the Christian Right defined America's sins differently, and made their own jeremiad a fixture of public discourse. One historian characterizes the sustained power of Jeremiah's legacy, "As a story, the jeremiad contains both great hope and deep sorrow, hope at the nations' promise or previous achievements, and sorrow at its current moral or spiritual state… both the hope and the sorrow are integral to the jeremiad's power, as they are to the prophetic tradition on which American Jeremiahs model themselves" (Murphy 2009: 119).

Jeremiah's Voice in American Culture

In 1955, Allen Ginsberg published "Howl," his transformative poem graphically expressing prophetic anguish at his apocalyptic vision of civilization on the edge of destruction. Ginsberg was seeking a way to express his "prophetic illuminative seizure" in a way that would draw readers into the experience of prophetic consciousness (Portugés 1984: 162). Jeremiah's use of a rhetorical catalogue, as complaints against God, sins of Judah, and visions of devastation, captivated Ginsberg because it encouraged in the reader free association without linear or logical thinking. In his poem, Ginsberg inflects Jeremiah's rhetorical form, which he called litany, with the emerging Jazz improvisations of Lester Young and Charlie Parker that used a repeated cadence to introduce a series of different riffs (Portugés 1984: 171). The opening section is a catalogue of "the best minds of my generation destroyed by madness," inspired by Jeremiah's cadences as well as his graphic images of sexual activity and catastrophic violence. Ginsberg described his vocation as poet-prophet, and much of his poetry refracts Jeremiah's longing for Judah's conversion together with his alienation and suffering, the price paid for seeking a transcendent reality in a society devoted to "Moloch," as described in "Howl" Part II. The title "Howl" alludes to the phrase "I howl for Moab" in Jeremiah's mock-dirge for the destruction of Moab (Jer 48:31).

   A more intimate Jeremiah appears in a century of writings from Evangelical authors who encourage readers to find in the prophet a tutor and exemplar for their personal life. Early twentieth-century reception of Jeremiah as a spiritual giant teaching Christians how to pray is merged with the self-help movement in these books. A sampling of titles illustrates this use of the prophet. *Morning and Evening Walks with the Prophet Jeremiah*; *Run with the Horses: The Quest for Life at Its Best*; *Lessons on Living from Jeremiah*; *Jeremiah, the Prophet Who Wouldn't Quit: How to Keep Going When You Feel Like Giving Up*; and *Pray Through Your Dungeon: Reflections from the Book of Jeremiah*. In these books the prophet is fashioned as spiritual friend guiding readers to overcome personal obstacles in their lives. The titles join American utilitarian principles and optimism with Jeremiah's "spiritual biography" to create a prophet rarely found in earlier reception history.

Jeremiah confronts the hope and despair that the life and assassination of Martin Luther King Jr brought to America in the writing of Chicago-born African-American scholar and novelist Leon Forrest. Forrest's first acclaimed novel *There Is A Tree More Ancient Than Eden* featured the Rev. Pompey c.j. Browne, a "wild, 6'7 Negro minister." In an evocative piece written in 1979 and later added to the re-issue of the novel in 1988, Forrest channels the voice of Jeremiah through Browne's sermon preached at the Cross-Roads Rooster Tavern on the twelfth anniversary of Martin Luther King's death. The dream-like allusive sermon titled "Oh Jeremiah of the Dreamers" interweaves allusions to Jeremiah and King's life: "Montgomery 1955: 'Oh outlaw Martin … what didn't he set out to see? The new covenant of the desegregated Heart?' Birmingham, 1963 (after the bombing of the 16th Street Baptist Church). 'Vaulted Martin wept … Oh that I might weep a fountain of tears over their beloved ashes … Almighty God have you placed this iron yoke about my neck "to learn me" of the weight of wingless justice?'… April 4, 1968: Oh Jeremiah of the dreamers… ordained in the womb before He formed you – and Lord we hardly knew you. Of the merchandizing of King's legacy: "And upon every high hill and every green tree: the dangling worship of flesh and branded form – our unbridled scent for transforming … Is there no balm in Gilead?"' (Forrest 1979: 73). In the analysis of one scholar of Forrest's work, the sermon reflects the bitter disappointment brought by the resurgence of racism in the 1980s. Yet the sermon was added to the 1988 re-issue of Forrest's novel in a final section titled "Transformation." In this context the use of Jeremiah to interpret King teaches the central character of the novel that "his individual grief is connected to a larger historical reality of suffering and death. This realization of the place of individual suffering in a larger pattern opens up the possibility of transformation and transcendence" (Cawelti 1997: 39).

Leonard Nathan's 1996 poem "Jeremiah Lamenting the Destruction of Jerusalem," eloquently portrays one Jeremiah slipping into another.

> One by one, Rembrandt
> is losing his paintings to forgers
> and it doesn't much matter
> and it doesn't much matter
> that the man who posed
> for the prophet wasn't a prophet
> or that the names keep changing –
> Jerusalem yesterday,

> Sarajevo today,
> Jerusalem perhaps
> Again tomorrow, or Troy
> or Los Angeles, layer
> after layer down to bedrock where tears
> leave no fossils.
>   Only
> the reason for grief remains
> constant, the thing outside
> the frame of the painting, the thing
> that Jeremiah stares down at
> in a place the Lord has placed him,
> a dark place "as they
> that be dead of old," or is he
> looking inward?

What Leonard Nathan did with words, Doug Johnson did in his 1991 reception of Rembrandt's Jeremiah, titled "Lamentation for the Ages" (Figure 18). These two receptions can appropriately launch the reader into the Commentary.

Practical Notes for Using the Commentary

The Commentary explores texts from every chapter of Jeremiah that have left significant marks on Western culture. I have presented each text in a chrono-logical narrative to highlight the nature of reception history as both conversation and debate taking place across centuries. Each reception reflects a particular historical context, but often engages previous readings as well. In this narrative form, I try to highlight the reception of Jeremiah not as a cabinet of historical curiosities but as a process in which readers repeatedly are shaped by the prophet and his earlier readers even as they leave their own mark on him. Each new Jeremiah is a bricolage of past Jeremiahs, reconfiguring pieces of the tradi-tion into a contemporary shape.

There is minimal judgment on the many polemical and vitriolic battles into which Jeremiah has been drawn, notably between Catholics and Protestants, and especially against Jews. However, because it is useful to consider the her-meneutical principles and the presuppositions about Scripture that shaped such receptions of Jeremiah, the Commentary will engage the tension between constitutive and prophetic hermeneutics in religious communities. In the *constitutive* hermeneutic readers assume the identity of the prophet, reading words of judgment against their own enemies and words of comfort to support

FIGURE 18   "Lamentation for the Ages." Doug Johnson.

themselves in their present trials. With the *prophetic* hermeneutic, however, readers assume that the prophet stands over against them to challenge, judge, and effect change. As Gadamer demonstrated, hermeneutical assumptions influence readers most potently when they are habitual and invisible, seemingly part of the natural order. Encoded in the discourses of culture, they become embedded in traditional interpretations of texts and often in the texts themselves, with far reaching consequences. In times of political turbulence, opposing sides both enlisted Jeremiah in their cause. Reception history brings to light their implicit hermeneutics as well as the normative interpretations and historical effects that they generated.

The readers represented in the Commentary, like the readers of this volume, encounter the prophet in three contexts: the text of the Bible, the surplus of meaning left by previous readers, and the circumstances of their own lives. The Commentary highlights particular ways that one or more of these contexts shaped particular receptions of Jeremiah. Sources are presented in their own voice as much as possible, preserving archaic diction, though not spelling. As a reminder of our distance, I have often used the form of the prophet's name appropriate to the sources being presented. The effort required from the reader is offset by the benefit of hearing the source as representative of a different *mentalité*. Resisting the impulse to replace unfamiliar discourse with our own helps maintain the tension inherent in reception history. Gadamer showed that we initially understand the past at a point where it merges with our own horizon of expectation; it expands our horizon only when we recognize its otherness. To that end, I have tried to engage readers in material that is initially alien and disrupts settled assumptions about familiar texts. The goal is to help readers discover new Jeremiahs and new reasons for cherishing the original.

Word of the Lord or Words of Jeremiah? (Jer 1:1)

Readers from the beginning wrestled with the complex relation between divine speech and its human record. Septuagint begins "The word of God that came to Jeremiah…" but the Hebrew reads "The words of Jeremiah son of Hilkiah… which was the word of the Lord to him." Dead Sea scrolls of Jeremiah offer evidence that multiple versions co-existed, some supporting what became the Masoretic text and others the Septuagint. The Septuagint,

Jeremiah Through the Centuries, First Edition. Mary Chilton Callaway.

though later than our Hebrew text, translates an earlier Hebrew version no longer extant. Why does this matter? For redactors of Jeremiah in the exile the uncontrolled nature of prophecy was a problem, hence seven references to a scroll (25:13; 30:1; 36:2, 28, 32; 45:1; 51:63) highlight the authority of the written text as privileged repository of the divine words. Historians suggest that exilic redactors codified their version of the Jeremiah tradition to emphasize an authoritative scroll, as in Jer 1:1, partly to counter voices of the remnant in Judah who heard or read the prophet differently (Sharp 2011: 35–46). Reception history displays persistent engagement with the complex relation between divine word and human writing. Jerome reassures readers that both the Hebrew and Greek of Jer 1:1 identify Jeremiah's words as the word of the Lord, which by the fifth century had already taken on the technical sense of "Scripture" (Jerome 1960).

Jeremiah persists as human site of the divine word and contested text in medieval interactions between Jews and Christians. The *Bible moralisée* illustrates Jer 1:1 with the prophet in the traditional pose of lament, holding an open book, surrounded by four Jews with hands raised in gestures of opposition (Figure 19). The historical prophet rejected by his people here becomes the book whose Christological interpretations are rejected by medieval Jews. At least 26 more roundels throughout *Bible moralisée* show Jeremiah with an open book in images designed to contrast the church's teaching over against that of Jews, philosophers, heretics, or even other Christians. The accompanying interpretive roundel shows Jerome at his desk translating Jeremiah into Latin and the bishop authorizing his translation as the church's scriptures. The two roundels together address contemporary disputes about biblical interpretation. In thirteenth-century France, Christian scholars who knew Hebrew, especially at the Abby of St. Victor in Paris, sometimes challenged the church's traditional allegories. The beginning of Jeremiah addresses these debates by visually identifying the book on Jeremiah's lap, which signifies his original Hebrew words, with Jerome's Vulgate, shown firmly under the ecclesial authority of a saint and a bishop.

The effects of Jeremiah as book and person are apparent in Figure 20, a copper-plate engraving that appeared in Cornelius Martinus Spanghoe's 1784 Dutch picture Bible entitled *Very Correct Discourse of the History of the Old Testament*. The codex, pen, and distinctive face contemporize Jeremiah for eighteenth-century readers as a consumer of the divine word, mirroring their own experience with the Bible.

Nineteenth-century readers were reassured that their individuality mattered to God. Jeremiah's "personality, temperament, experiences, style of thought, modes of expression, are all stamped upon these Divine messages. Inspiration does not obliterate, scarcely subordinates individuality" (Jellie 1892: 17:8).

Figure 19   Jeremiah as author of his book. © *M. Moleiro. The Bible of St. Louis, vol.2,* f.130r.

Twice the text urges reading Jeremiah 1:1 as evidence that God uses "the true self," an idea that would surely have puzzled Jeremiah's redactors.

Jeremiah Before Birth (1:4–5)

Reception begins in Sirach 49:5–9, a poetic narration of Israel's history from the beginning to the author's own time around 180 BCE. Prominent in Sirach's praise of Jeremiah is "sanctified a prophet in the womb." Paul permanently influences reception by combining Jeremiah with Isa 49:1 to claim that God set him apart in his mother's womb and *called* him (Gal1:15). Paul's change marks Protestant theology from the sixteenth century forward (see below).

FIGURE 20   Jeremiah 1:1. Cornelius Martinus Spanghoe, 1784. Private collection.

In the third century CE, Jeremiah's conception becomes part of Christian speculation about the nature of the soul. Origen argued that Jeremiah offers evidence for the neo-Platonic teaching that souls are pre-existent. Reading the verbs "formed" and "knew" as two chronologically distinct divine actions, Origen argued from Gen 2:15 (God formed Adam from the earth) that "formed" indicates physical creation subsequent to knowing. When God knew him, Jeremiah already existed as a soul but not a body. Origen's use of Jeremiah to support pre-existence of souls met with fierce resistance. Jerome comments: "Not that he existed before conception, as the heretic [Origen] believes, but rather that the Lord, for whom deeds not yet done have already happened, knew his future" (Jerome 1960: 4). For Jerome the allegorical sense of Jer 1:5 is apparent in John 10:38: "Before he came forth from his mother, he was sanctified in the womb and known to the father; indeed, he was always in the father and the father was always in him" (Jerome 1960: 5). Jerome's Christological reading of Jer 1:5 contributed to the early identification of Jeremiah with Jesus, which persisted through the Middle Ages.

The verse also figured in passionate arguments against Arius and his many followers who held that Christ was not co-eternal with the Father, but came into existence at birth. In his list of the genuine books of Scripture, Gregory Nazianzus describes Jeremiah as "the one called before birth" (Gregory Nazianzus 1890: 7), while no other prophet in his catalogue is given more than a name. Ambrose more than once invokes Jer 1:5 to argue against Arian teaching, citing Jacob and Jeremiah as examples of those existing and indeed appointed before birth. Ambrose uses Jeremiah to explain the unusual phrase in John 1:18 on the pre-existence of Jesus in the bosom of the Father: "The Father's womb is the spiritual womb of an inner sanctuary, from which the Son has proceeded just as from a generative womb... The Father speaks of that womb through the prophet Jeremiah (1:5). Therefore, the prophet showed that there was a twofold nature in Christ, the divine and the fleshly" (Wenthe 2009: 4–5). The description of Jesus in the Nicene Creed as "eternally begotten of the Father" reflects the victory of this idea.

In the eleventh century, Rashi challenges Christian use of Jeremiah's origins with rabbinic hermeneutics. Reading with the Targum "I established you" and "I appointed you," Rashi finds in Jeremiah fulfillment of the mysterious promise to Moses, "I will establish a prophet like you" (Deut 18:18). That both texts use establish, and that Moses and Jeremiah both reproved Israel and prophesied for 40 years, signals that the texts interpret each other. Rashi's countering of Christian allegory with classic Jewish exegetical principles gave French rabbis support in their debates with Christian scholars.

The thirteenth-century *Bible moralisée* pictures Jeremiah's birth as Christian allegory (Figure 21). A nativity scene of reclining mother and watchful father clearly evokes images of Jesus' birth, but the midwife holds up a fully formed miniature prophet who receives a book from God's hand. The visual allusion to Luke's nativity story offers a hermeneutic to readers, encouraging them to see Jesus in Jeremiah from the very beginning of the book. The visual trope linking God, the prophet, and the book also reminds readers of the divine origins of the text in their hands. The accompanying roundel reinforces Jesus as a figure of Jeremiah by showing him, like Jeremiah, holding an open book. The text instructs that Jer 1:5 foretells Christ, "who called all the nations through the apostles" as Jeremiah was prophet to the nations.

FIGURE 21   The birth of Jeremiah and its allegory. © M. Moliero Editor. *Bible of St. Louis*, vol. 2, f. 130r.

The artist used the patristic tradition preserved in the *Glossa Ordinaria*, which glosses Jer 1:5 by writing "Father" over "the Lord" and "the Son through whom all things [were made]" over "his hand." God's commission to Jeremiah is explained as "the Father to the Son" and explained by Ps 2:8 ("Ask and I will give you the nations as your inheritance"). This elaborate tradition linking the origins of Jeremiah and Jesus continues in the storied thirteenth-century stained glass of Sainte-Chapelle in Paris. Of seven windows devoted to Jeremiah, one shows the prophet kneeling to receive an ornate book from God, whose right hand is raised in a priestly blessing. Another image, now in the Victoria and Albert Museum in London, shows a swaddled newborn being handed to his reclining mother. The rest of this image is no longer extant, but art historians conclude that the lancet portrays the thirteenth-century French tradition of Jeremiah's birth prefiguring Jesus. That King Louis IX was patron of both the

Bible moralisée and Sainte-Chapelle suggests that this shared artistic tradition is a thirteenth-century innovation in the reception of Jeremiah.

Reading the divine "I chose you" as instructive of Christian vocation becomes the norm in the sixteenth century, but it has one precedent. In the eleventh century, Peter Damian used Jeremiah constructively to teach his monks that God chooses people at different times of life, some in youth, others in old age (Damian 1998: 4:321).

One of the most far-reaching effects of Jeremiah's "call" is the way Calvin draws it into his discourse of predestination and vocation. He paraphrases, "Before I formed you in the womb, I destined you for this work, that you might undertake the burden of a teacher among the people." For Calvin, Jeremiah's experience is not unique, but universal: "Sanctification is the same as the knowledge of God...not mere prescience, but that predestination, by which God chooses every single individual according to his own will, and at the same time appoints and sanctifies him" (Calvin 1989: 1:37). Calvin's reformist sensibilities redefine the priestly term sanctified with a theology of individual call for every Christian, though "call" also acquired a technical sense of professional ministry. The annotation of the Geneva Bible uses Jeremiah 1:5 to buttress the authority of Protestant clergy by replacing the hands of a bishop with God's call: "The scripture uses this manner of speech to declare that God has appointed his ministers to their offices before they were born, as in Isa. 49:1, Gal. 1:15." The language of the call was explicitly written into the biblical text in the first legal English translation of the Bible, when Miles Coverdale introduced his 1537 translation of Jer 1 with the words, "He declareth first hys callinge." Even the King James Version (1611), printed at the king's direction without marginal glosses, includes as a heading for Jer 1 "The time, and the calling of Jeremiah," and most Bibles in English still use the term "call" in their headers for Jer 1. In the Scottish Presbyterian *First Book of Discipline* (1560) God's call to the individual is authenticated by the ecclesial call to a particular community: "In a church reformed... none ought to presume either to preach, either yet to minister the Sacraments, till that orderly they be called to the same." This process of selecting a minister remains a hallmark of Protestantism, where an offer of employment is "a call." cvc but the language of call is rooted in the reception of Jer 1:5 in the sixteenth century.

The most widely circulated illustration of Jer 1 in the seventeenth century reinforces the received tradition of Jeremiah as Christian minister. In 1630, the Swiss-German engraver Matthäus Merian published *Iconum Biblicarum,* his collection of some 250 Bible illustrations accompanied by descriptive quatrains in multiple languages. His picture contemporizes the traditional iconography of the prophet outside Jerusalem by placing him above a European seaport, gazing directly at the reader, mouth open in speech as if addressing the viewer

Ieremias Prophiteert over Ierufalem

FIGURE 22   Jeremiæ the Prophet. Matthäus Merian, *Iconum Biblicarum* 1630. Private collection.

(Figure 22). The anthropomorphic God of medieval art is here replaced with the Calvinist preference for rays from a heavenly divine name. A 1650 printing includes an English quatrain describing Jeremiah as a Puritan preacher:

> Jerusalem in sin abounded so,
> Made it her bus'ness, and her God her foe,
> That Jeremy was call'd, was call'd and sent
> To show what plagues must come, or she repent (Visscher n.d.: 86).

Merian's picture of Jeremiah as preacher was widely reproduced for 200 years in Bible picture books in England and Germany, and on Delft tiles around the hearth in Dutch kitchens.

Nineteenth-century interest in the historical Jeremiah merged with German Romanticism to produce a Jeremiah who was both ancient and contemporary. The illustration in F.B. Meyer's 1894 book for young readers, *Jeremiah: Priest and Prophet,* has none of the supernatural elements of earlier art, but presents the reader with a boy pondering an inner religious experience (Figure 23). In marked contrast with traditional representations, this "call" occurs inside a

THE CALL OF JEREMIAH.

Figure 23   A nineteenth-century imagining of Jeremiah receiving God's call. F.B. Meyer. 1894. Private collection.

house. The architecture of the windows was known to British explorers of the Levant, and the three scrolls provide a veneer of Orientalism that evokes antiquity, but this Jeremiah is remarkably similar to Meyer's young readers. His hand on the scroll suggests that its words have just brought revelation, signaled by his intent gaze toward the heavens. Like Meyer's readers, this Jeremiah experiences the divine summons as personal conviction after studying the Scriptures. That the prophetic experience is a model for nineteenth-century Christians is evident in Meyer's exposition: "In every age of the Church young eyes have eagerly scanned this paragraph; and have dared to cherish the hope that since youth did not disqualify Jeremiah, so it would not render them unfit for the special service of God. The only thing to be sure of is that God has really called you… There is first the consciousness of a strong inward impulse… which often surges up pure and strong in the soul." The divine voice to Jeremiah here becomes interior conviction confirmed by emotional experience and unique in each young life. Even in adversity one can be comforted "by the thought that you are being fitted for some high purpose that has not yet been made known" (Meyer 1894: 12–13, 20).

Meyer's use of Jer 1 as a template for individual spiritual experience was the norm by mid-twentieth century. In 1941, an influential British scholar read Jer 1:5 as metaphorical language for divine preparation, as Calvin had, but substituted the language of psychology for Calvin's vocabulary of predestination. Commenting on the verse in his popular *Jeremiah: A Prophet for A Time of War*, L.E. Elliott-Binns writes, "Such a preparation is always provided by God for His instruments, however long the actual call may be delayed and whatever its outward circumstances. There are those to whom His voice comes as they wander in some lonely garden at the cool of the day; there are others who hear it beneath the blaze of a midday sun upon the open highway. But whenever the time and wherever the place, the true servant of God is ready to welcome the divine message, to recover which his mind and conscience have long been preparing him" (Elliott-Binns 1941: 78). The idea that God worked slowly and persistently in hidden ways until the divine will erupted in a flash of recognition into Jeremiah's consciousness remakes Jeremiah from an inscrutable prophet of antiquity into a familiar modern fellow.

Developments in historical-critical exegesis in the first part of the twentieth century bolstered the link between Jer 1 and the call of a Christian minister with evidence from the new discipline of form criticism. In 1956, E. Kutsch of Tübingen used form criticism to explain similarities between the narratives of Moses (Ex 3), Gideon (Ju 6), and Jeremiah 1. Kutsch concluded that Jeremiah's objection was not biographical but literary, an essential component of the traditional Israelite form used to narrate the *Berufung* (call) of a prophet. His unspoken debt to Calvin's use of "call" illustrates the way that reception of a biblical text over time merges with the text itself. In 1965, "call" as a literary form entered the English-speaking world in Norman Habel's influential study. Habel's contribution to the reception of Jeremiah is twofold. He established the term "call narrative" and he resisted Kutsch's claim that Jer 1:5 is a literary retroversion rather than an historical account, arguing that it was "public proclamation" of "an inner compulsion from God" intended to establish authority (Habel 1965: 306). This combination of German form criticism with contemporary psychological language reflecting the experience of his readers contributed to making Habel's reading normative. Today, most contemporary annotated Bibles use the term "the call of Jeremiah," showing that the reception history of Jer 1:5 has been virtually inscribed into the biblical text of Jeremiah.

A Prophet to the Nations (1:5)

Jeremiah's puzzling job description as "prophet to the nations" often led readers to understand Jeremiah as prophet of weal to themselves (Israel) but of woe to others (the nations). Under pressure of persecution, Jews in antiquity interpreted Jeremiah as bringing judgment against the Gentile nations. Targum Jonathan uses Jer 25:15 to interpret 1:5 in this way: "I designated you a prophet who should make the nations drink a cup of cursing" (Hayward 1987: 46). The fourth-century rabbinic *Sifre* to Deuteronomy, however, argues that Jeremiah is a prophet to his own people who behave like the nations (Hammer 1987: 202). Rashi follows this tradition, using the plain sense of a similar phrase in Jer 25:15 to show that the nations being judged include Israel. Early Christian readers used a different hermeneutic, typically understanding the nations in a positive way as themselves, Gentiles brought into the church. Similarly, the *Glossa Ordinaria* quotes Origen and Jerome to explain that the words refer to Jesus, "who was especially a prophet to the Gentiles and through the apostles called all nations." In the early fourteenth century, Nicholas of Lyra explained in his preface to Jeremiah that the divine purpose in the prophet was the good of the church universal, which is gathered from all the nations. By the turn of the twentieth century, most scholars explained the words as the work of sixth-century redactors addressing exiled Judeans, giving hope that God would destroy the nations who were their enemies.

Resisting God (1:6)

Jeremiah's resistance made him a model for many readers. Jerome read humility: "He prays for deliverance from a task that he cannot do because of his age. Moses expresses the same modesty, saying his voice was slight and thin; but while that adult is reproached, this boy, adorned with modesty and reserve, is excused." Two influential Byzantine church fathers used the verse for the dual purpose of defending their own reluctance and establishing criteria for a true Christian leader. Shortly after Gregory Nazianzus was ordained in 361 by his father the bishop, he fled to a monastery in the desert. On returning several months later to assume his ministry, he countered accusations of prideful disobedience in an Easter sermon: "For it is a good thing even to hold back from

God for a little while, as did Moses, and Jeremiah" (Schaff 1894: 203). Later, he invoked Jeremiah against the practice of local aristocrats, often barely Christian, who eagerly sought the episcopate to increase their power and prestige: "Jeremiah was afraid of his youth, and did not venture to prophesy until he had received from God a promise and power beyond his years" (Schaff and Wace 1894: 227). Jeremiah's reluctance, understood as humility, here becomes a model for true episcopal leadership. Similarly, Chrysostom uses Jeremiah to indict ambitious churchmen who would adopt the self-affirming rhetoric of the culture: "See how righteous men are free from self-regard, and how their writings under-rate themselves. Who would not blush to write this? But they were not striving for fame and ambition" (Migne 1844–55: 20:750). Two centuries later, Gregory the Great, influenced by the former Gregory's writings and compelled by his own circumstances in Rome, again invokes the model of Jeremiah. When the pope called him out of his beloved monastery to serve as papal ambassador to the emperor in Constantinople, he was reluctant but obedient. His sixth-century Pastoral Rule, which lays out the qualities of a good bishop, compares Jeremiah's reluctance with Isaiah's eagerness. "Notice how they spoke with a different voice, but [their words] did not emanate from a different source of love." Isaiah yearns to serve through the active life of preaching, "while Jeremiah, who zealously clings to the love of the Creator through the contemplative life, opposes being sent to preach. Therefore, what one laudably sought, the other, just as laudably, avoided" (Demacopoulos 2007: 39). This distinction between active and contemplative modes reflects Gregory's understanding of varieties of Christian vocation, and illustrates another way that Jer 1:6 contributed to developing Christian spirituality.

Jewish and Muslim traditions likewise read Jeremiah's reluctance as virtue. Targum softens his objection by adding "Hear my prayer" and changing "speak" to "prophesy." To this humility Rashi adds a note of realism, paraphrasing Jeremiah, "I am not worthy to reprove them. Moses reproved them shortly before his death, when he was already esteemed in their eyes… I come to reprove them at the beginning of my mission." In the eleventh-century Islamic *Lives of the Prophets,* Jeremiah's resistance is interpreted as the Muslim virtue of holy submission: "'I am weak if You do not give me strength; powerless if you do not help me.' God responded, 'I shall inspire you'" (Thalabi 2002: 558).

The sympathetic readings of Jerome and Gregory the Great dominated medieval exegesis through their reproduction in the *Glossa Ordinaria,* but in the sixteenth century, Calvin expressed palpable discomfort with Jeremiah's "refusing what God enjoined." He begins by describing Jeremiah as politically astute, refusing so that "he might clear himself from every suspicion of rashness, for we know how much ambition prevails among men… most men too readily assume the office of teaching, and many boldly intrude into it." Calvin continues, "If anyone asks, whether Jeremiah acted rightly in refusing what God enjoined? The answer is that God pardoned his servant" because of his modesty. Calvin advises his readers, "As we ought to undertake nothing without considering what our strength is, so when God enjoins anything, we ought immediately to obey his word as it were with closed eyes." Jeremiah is therefore a model of the two-step response: consider what the shoulders can bear before volunteering, but go when God calls.

The Geneva Bible's marginal note attributes Jeremiah's reluctance to spiritual maturity, because foreseeing great destruction he "was moved with a certain compassion on the one hand to pity them that would thus perish, and on the other hand by the infirmity of man's nature, knowing how hard a thing it was to enterprise [attempt] such a charge." Jeremiah here is a model for Protestant preachers, especially those in exile. This reading of Jeremiah as model of Christian leadership persists in John Trapp's influential commentary. Perhaps tempered by the loss of the Parliamentarians in the English Civil War, he reads in Jeremiah's resistance only humility: "True worth is ever modest; and the more fit any man is for whatsoever vocation, the less he thinketh himself: for-wardness argueth insufficiency" (Trapp 1660: 221).

Some great men saw themselves in Jeremiah and used him to buttress their own narratives. Unable to control conflict in the colony he had established in Hispaniola, Columbus was arrested in 1500 and brought back to Spain in chains by the royal governor. The next year he wrote his *Book of Prophecies,* in which he presented biblical texts that he argued supported his claim that he had been chosen by God to evangelize the Indians and take Christianity to the ends of the earth. Citing Jer 1:5–7, he presents himself as "a man to fulfill God's purpose." Identifying with the twin themes of divine call and human rejection in Jeremiah gave Columbus courage to endure (Columbus 1997: 4). Luther also saw himself in Jeremiah. Tormented by the sense that his preaching was not effective, he identified with the prophet who railed against the impossible task that God had imposed. Lecturing on Isa 45:9, he cites Jer 1:6: "So I was often tempted [to question God] in my calling to the point that I had regrets. If I had been aware of these things first, I should not have undertaken to proclaim the Gospel. But let God see it through." In the year this was published, Luther told the congregation in Wittenberg that he "would rather preach to mad dogs, for my preaching shows no effect among you, and it only makes me weary" (*LW* 17:128–129).

By the late nineteenth century, readers saw in Jeremiah's response a sensitive conscience afflicted by ambivalence. August Strindberg evokes it in his 1872 historical drama *Master Olof,* about a young sixteenth-century monk tormented by the conflict between corrupt church structures in

Sweden and the new teachings of Martin Luther. In the opening minutes of the play, Olof's friend Lars challenges him to bring Luther's teachings to Sweden, overriding Olof's objection that he is too young by reminding him of Jeremiah:

> Lars. Do not say you are too young.
> Olof. No, for there are plenty of others who say it.
> Lars (takes out a roll of paper, which he opens; for a while he stands looking at Olof; then he begins to read) "Then the word of the Lord came unto Jeremiah: 'Before I formed thee in the belly I knew thee...'
> Olof (leaping to his feet). Did the Lord say that?
> Lars. "Thou therefore gird up thy loins and arise, and speak unto them all that I command thee."
> Olof. ... I feel myself choking when I think of these poor people who yearn for salvation. They are crying for water – for living water – but there is no one who can give it to them.
> Lars. Tear down the crumbling old house first, you can do that. Then the Lord Himself will build them a new one... You were born to give offence, Olof; you were born to smite. The Lord will heal.
> Olof. I can feel the pull of the current; I am still clinging to the sluice-gate, but if I let go, I shall be swept away...What storms you have raised in my soul... Help me, O Lord! I go (Strindberg 2006: 3–4).

To portray the Swedish hero, Strindberg merges Jeremiah with the conscience of Luther and the religious sensibilities of nineteenth-century Swedes. Students in Sweden still study the play for its dramatic presentation of the origins of Sweden's independence from Denmark and Rome, while Master Olof himself is revered as a founding father.

A twentieth-century psychoanalytic study describes Jeremiah's resistance as a significant psychological experience common to biblical prophets and having lasting influence in Western history. The author, a practicing psychiatrist, writes about prophetic calls, "This utter subjugation to the will of God results in a peculiar combination of meekness and grandeur... This ambivalent attitude appears clearly in the consecration of Jeremiah." Drawing on Freud's Oedipal theory of ego development in the male, in which the dominating father is incorporated into the personality as the superego, the author describes a prophetic call as the reversal of this process in adulthood. "The retrojection of the superego... to some anthropomorphic heavenly figure... is what is subjectively experienced as God... The feeling for God is derived from the feeling for the father. Upon this emotional basis is founded the relationship between the prophet and his God." Reliving the child's ambivalence toward the father's power, the prophet naturally is "steeped in ambivalence, if not outright rebellion" (Arlow 1951: 374–397).

Filling Jeremiah's Mouth

The startling idea of God's hand touching Jeremiah's mouth discomfited Jewish and Christian exegetes. Targum replaces "hand" with "the words of his prophecy" which God arranged in Jeremiah's mouth. Jerome offers two comments to counter charges that God's hand forced Jeremiah. The first discloses God's gracious accommodation of Jeremiah's humanity: "In the literal sense his hand was sent forth appropriately, in order that seeing the form of human limbs Jeremiah would not recoil from the touch of the hand." This explanation persisted into the sixteenth century in an interlinear note in the *Glossa Ordinaria*. Another comment explains, "Jeremiah's mouth was touched, and the word of the Lord bestowed on him, so that he would receive confidence to preach." Illuminated medieval Bibles often portrayed Jerome's pastoral interpretation of a gracious deity enabling the prophet. One of the most frequently illustrated scenes in Jeremiah, it is often enclosed in a historiated initial V that begins the first word of the book, *Verba*. Dozens of examples from the twelfth through sixteenth centuries appear in Vulgate Bibles across Europe. One striking illumination from a fifteenth-century British Bible shows Jeremiah with the pointed beard of a Jew, an artistic convention designating a prophet, yet he kneels with folded hands like a Christian receiving the bread of the Eucharist (Figure 24). Viewers would see the similarity of God's action to priests placing the bread into a Christian's mouth.

A notable exception to the illuminations of a willing partnership between God and prophet is the twelfth-century Winchester Bible's initial illustration, which is unique for its lively portrayal of emotion (Figure 25). The young prophet's body bends away from God, visibly expressing his protest. Yet the diagonal of his resisting body crosses the one created by God's gaze on his troubled eyes and hand touching his mouth. The locked eyes of prophet and deity at the visual center of the picture create a personal dimension that draws the viewer into the scene. Further, by picturing God in liturgical vestments, with a hand in the formal pose used for priestly blessing as if to protect the prophet's mouth even as it is being filled with scorching words, the artist contemporizes Jeremiah's story for medieval viewers. This unusually human Jeremiah could sustain medieval Christians confronting questions about their own vocation and fears about their capabilities.

The idea that God put his words into the prophet's mouth was crucial for the Protestant argument that authority to minister came not from the institutional church, but directly from God. Calvin read this verse of Jeremiah as a warrant: "This passage ought to be carefully observed; for Jeremiah briefly describes how a true call may be ascertained... when he brings forth nothing of his own...who teach not according to their own fancies, but faithfully deliver what God has committed to them."

FIGURE 24   God places the word in a receptive Jeremiah's mouth. British Library
Royal MS 1 E IX ("The Bible of Richard II") folio 193r.

The Job Description (1:10)

Since the early twentieth century, scholars have argued that the original formula had only four verbs because the pairing of uproot/demolish with build/
plant reflects the literary convention of chiasm used often in biblical poetry.
Further, the Hebrew words present verbal assonance, a hallmark of prophetic
speech. Ancient listeners would hear linntosh /lintotz and livnot /lintoah.
The phrase recurs in part or whole throughout Jeremiah, functioning as a
leitmotif by which exilic redactors unified Jeremiah traditions and adapted
them for their new circumstances (Jer 29:5; 32:15). In later centuries, church
and synagogue both tended to read their enemies as the object of Jeremiah's

FIGURE 25 Winchester Bible, f148. ©The Dean & Chapter of Winchester, 2019.
Reproduced by kind permission of the Dean & Chapter of Winchester.

"demolish" and themselves as the referent of "build." Targum Jonathan inserts
the words "over the house of Israel" before the positive verbs, which it translates as "to build and to establish." Rashi refers approvingly to the Targum,
but supplements build and plant with the warning "if they heed." This contemporizing persists into the eighteenth century, when John Wesley suggests
that "either the former words [uproot and tear down] relate to the enemies of
God, and the latter to his friends; or rather to both conditionally: if they
repent he will build them up… if they do not, he will root them up."

Origen enlists the verse in his fight against Gnostic teaching that dismissed the Old Testament because "the God of the Law is crude" and not related to the Gospel. He writes that the order of Jeremiah's verbs reflects the wisdom and compassion of the divine teacher: "In Scripture we always note that those acts which are 'unpleasant-seeming,' as I will name them, are listed first, then those acts which seem gladdening are mentioned second." Origen further spiritualizes the text with his interpretation that evil must be uprooted and the building of evil demolished in the soul before God can plant and build (Origen 1998: 20–22). Gregory of Nyssa brings Origen's idea to eastern Christianity in his Homily on Ecclesiastes 3:3, "a time to demolish and a time to build." The order of the verbs teaches that "we must first tear down the buildings of evil in us and then find a moment and a clear space for the construction of the temple of God which is built in our souls, whose fabric is virtue" (Gregory of Nyssa 1993: 107). Jerome interprets Jeremiah's task as his own struggle against Pelagius and other heretics in the fifth-century church: "Plantings not from God and buildings constructed on sand are perverse teachings that must be uprooted and demolished so that the church's truth can be planted and built" (Jerome 1960: 6–7).

Puritans also used Jeremiah 1:10 to authorize and further their own mission. A note on this verse in the Geneva Bible instructs readers, "He shows what is the authority of God's true ministers, who by his word have power to tear down whatever lifts itself up against God: and to plant and assure the humble and such as give themselves to the obedience of God's word, and these are the keys which Christ has left to loose and bind." The image of the keys, long used in Catholic tradition to refer to the Pope, become here a polemical warrant for the authority of the Bible instead. In the verbs of Jeremiah's commissioning Puritans found support for their own task of challenging religious authorities.

An example of twenty-first century reception comes from British pastor David Perry in Figure 26. His web-based visual theology project (visualtheology. blogspot.com) contemporizes Jeremiah's verbs as mandates to act for social justice.

God's Pun (1:11–12)

Jerome understood that the meaning of Jeremiah's vision was expressed in a pun on the Hebrew words "almond" (*shaked*) and "watching" (*shoked*), so he preserved the play on words in his Latin rendering, *virga vigilanta*, "a watching branch." The first English Bibles translate his Latin; John Wycliffe (1395) offers "a yerde wakynge" and Coverdale (1535) "a wakynge rodde," but in 1560 the

FIGURE 26 Contemporary reception of Jeremiah's commission. *Visual Theology.*
By permission of The Rev. David Perry, England.

Geneva Bible translates the Hebrew phrase, "rod of an almond tree." In Jewish
tradition Maimonides uses the verse to illustrate his exegetical principle that
words in prophetic parables can be interpreted according to their etymology
(as Jerome had done). This use of Jeremiah's plain sense challenged the increasingly allegorical exegesis of medieval Christianity.

Images associated with rod and almond generated allegories that persist into
modernity. They begin with Origen, who associates the "priestly mystery" of
Aaron's blossoming rod that produces almonds (Num 17:8) with the blossoming almond branch of Jeremiah, one of the priests of Anathoth (Origen 2009:
42). The almond's three parts, bitter hull, protective shell, and edible seed, teach
us how to read Scripture to be nourished by the fruit of God's word. The bitter
hull is the literal sense, the shell is the moral teaching necessary in this life,
and hidden within these coverings is the seed, the sweet wisdom of God that
nourishes the saints. Origen's tripartite scheme of interpretation, "the threefold
mystery that runs through all the Scriptures" lays the groundwork for the later
four-fold sense of Scripture. The multiple meanings Origen finds in Jeremiah's
almond branch are preserved in the margins of *Glossa Ordinaria*, read from the
twelfth until well into the sixteenth century.

Jerome uses Origen's method to link Jeremiah's almond branch with the rod
of Ps 23:4, which he interprets as comforting because it corrects: "Just as the nut

tree has the most bitter bark and is encased in a very hard shell, so that when the harsh and hard parts have been pulled off the fruit is found to be very sweet; so every rebuke and effort of self-control seem bitter in the present, but the sweetest fruit will appear" (Jerome 1960: 12). Jerome's ascetic attempts to tame his own passions, including several years in a desert monastery, may also shape his interpretation. Its influence persists into seventeenth-century England, where it is paraphrased in John Trapp's widely read commentary with a Puritan touch: "So is a good man made better by afflictions."

The almond branch is not described as flowering, but Christian tradition makes it so. Twice in the Bible a dead *virga* (branch) is said to come spontaneously to life: in Aaron's staff (Num 17:8) and Jesse's stump (Isa 11:1). Jerome reads Jer 1:11 in light of these images to show that the almond branch signifies Christ's resurrection. *Glossa* makes Jerome's moral and Christological interpretations standard throughout the Middle Ages.

In modernity, supernatural visions were replaced with the ideal of encountering revelation in the ordinary, so Jeremiah's almond branch encouraged readers to be alert for such experiences in their own lives. In his influential biography of Jeremiah, George A. Birmingham, Canon of St. Patrick's Cathedral in Dublin, explains that Jeremiah's vision differed from others in the Bible: "It was of things entirely common-place… which all men like him… had seen repeatedly, which had no meaning for them, or for Jeremiah himself, until God interpreted them… He had seen it many times before… Hardly could this be called a vision, any more than the sight of the first snowdrop is to us…It is not a supernatural vision; it is spiritual interpretation of the common-place" (Birmingham 1956: 45–46). In a similar psychological vein, *Expositor's Dictionary of Texts* makes Jeremiah's experience familiar for the preachers it addresses. Jeremiah is "a thoughtful and tender-hearted man who must have brooded over the sins and follies of his people," worrying about who will speak for God, until "there gathers within him half unconsciously the feeling that his is the voice that must be lifted up… in one sublime moment, the whole wonderful meaning of his career… is flashed upon him" (Robertson et al. 1910: 650).

Jeremiah's vision evokes the Enlightenment ideal of revelation as a partnership between divine will and human reason in a 1782 painting of Jeremiah by American artist Benjamin West. Commissioned by George III to decorate the royal chapel at Windsor Castle, West planed an ambitious scheme of paintings narrating the history of progressive revelation in the Bible. The chapel was to be called the Chapel of Revealed Religion to highlight its Enlightenment theology. Part of the altarpiece included a triptych of Moses giving the Law, flanked by Isaiah having his lips purged and Jeremiah seeing the almond branch. A young Jeremiah faces the viewer, resisting an angel who holds up a beautifully

FIGURE 27   Benjamin West, The Call of Jeremiah, 1782. Musée des Beaux-Arts de Bordeaux.

flowering almond branch (Figure 27). The branch appears as a symbol of revelation, as it separates angel and prophet while also drawing the two into the same plane. West replaces the traditional God-the-father figure with a delicately rendered angel, an artistic trope for revelation in eighteenth- and nineteenth-century art. West's paintings were never installed, as the increasingly irascible king began to suspect his colonial loyalty, but his Jeremiah endures to offer a window onto eighteenth-century idealizing of revelation.

What's Cooking? (1:13–16)

Ambiguity in the Hebrew of verse 13 and problems in the transmission of the text have given readers latitude to play with the image of the cooking pot. The Hebrew reads "a pot blown upon," while the Septuagint reads "a pot burning underneath." Beginning with Origen, Christians saw a surplus of meaning in Jerome's fiery cauldron. Its origins in the north make it a code for the devil, who sets up his throne in the north (Isa 14:13). Reading almond rod and cauldron together, Origen writes that Jeremiah "saw that life was in the almond rod and death was in the boiling cauldron. For life and death are set before our face, and Christ, in the mystery of the almond is indeed life, but the devil, in the figure of the boiling cauldron, is death. Therefore if you sin, you will place your portion with the boiling cauldron; but if you act justly, your portion will become in the rod of almond with the great high priest" (Origen 2009: 42).

Some readers drew meaning from the pot's boiling contents, others from the fire under it. In tenth-century France, Rashi focused on the pot's bubbling contents. His language evokes a kitchen hearth where the pot is about to boil over; he uses the familiar French *boillant* (written in Hebrew letters) to explain the puzzling Hebrew. For "its face," Rashi continues the culinary image with *ses ondes,* its "foam," perhaps describing the scum that accumulates on the surface of boiling stock. Rashi wants his French readers to visualize Jeremiah's alarming image in the context of their own kitchens and also to understand the historical reference to Babylon.

In Christian medieval art, the pot boils and flames, signifying Jeremiah's fiery task. Many medieval Bibles begin the book of Jeremiah with a historiated initial V because in Latin *verba* (words) is the first word. The decorated initial is enlarged and filled with a scene offering readers an image to guide their interpretation. In some French Bibles from the thirteenth and early fourteenth centuries, a rounded V frames a scene of the young prophet facing God, who gazes intently from the opposite corner. Between them a cauldron spews flames from top and sides, a literalized picture of Jerome's burning pot. This illustration offers visual exegesis to lead readers beyond the plain sense to contemplate Jeremiah as mediator of the fire of God's word (5:14; 20:9) and wrath (4:14) in their own lives. These contemplations would be deepened by Gregory's influential allegorical exegesis, which interpreted the pot as the human heart inflamed by the devil's suggestions. Following Origen, Gregory links Jeremiah's pot burning from the north with Lucifer's boast that he will set up his throne in the divine assembly "in the far north" (Isa 14:12–13). In this allegorical exegesis Lucifer's would-be throne is the human heart. Gregory's move from biblical geography to monastic spirituality influenced readers for centuries. In a sign of the shifts taking place in biblical interpretation in the fifteenth century, later editions of the *Glossa* incorporate Nicholas of Lyra's comments at the bottom of the page. A fierce defender of the Hebrew, Nicholas rejects Gregory's allegory by noting that the Vulgate's pot of burning fire is unlikely, while the Hebrew's boiling pot makes sense. Nevertheless, Gregory's allegory surfaces in John Trapp's Puritan commentary: "Man's mind is the pot."

During the Reformation, Jeremiah's boiling cauldron appeared in many woodcuts which were essentially political cartoons. Idioms like "stirring the brew" for inciting social change and "smelling the roast" for suspecting trouble appeared frequently in pamphlets, and woodblock illustrations used the pot to comment on events (Matheson 2001: 11). One 1530 woodcut plays with traditional iconography, showing the flaming pot not in the sky, but on the ground, over a raging fire. Out of its mouth looms a protesting head, mouth open in speech; surrounding it stand an approving host of bishops and rulers. Behind them Jeremiah, seated in a desolate landscape, points out the scene to God, who peers down from the sky in traditional fashion (Figure 28). The head evoked the shocking events in Nuremberg, when in 1527 Wolfgang Vogel, an Anabaptist, was summarily tried and beheaded. He had written a pamphlet calling on "king, princes and lords" of his city of Bopfingen to repent for removing his successor from the pulpit; the uneasy judges sent it on to the Nuremberg council for advice. With the Peasants' Revolt a very recent memory, the council acted peremptorily to snuff out any hint of insurrection against authority. The cartoon's inversion of the traditional image of Jeremiah's vision, and the figure of God with the crown, scepter, and orb of European monarchs, suggests radical political commentary. Jeremiah's vision was sufficiently embedded in the popular imagination to make the political cartoon dangerous.

By the turn of the eighteenth century, the boiling pot was emblematic of the trouble that Jeremiah would stir up and the suffering he would endure as a result of his prophetic words. Figure 29 shows an engraving from a popular Dutch picture highlighting the pot in its dramatic image of an anthropomorphized God commissioning a submissive young Jeremiah. The scene in the immediate background reinterprets the story of the yoke in Jer 28 by showing the high priest, looking like a bishop, seizing Jeremiah. In the distance, Jeremiah is dropped into the cistern. To the right, Jeremiah is portrayed with the two baskets of figs (Jer 24), another allusion to the boiling pot of conflict the prophet's words stirred up.

An intriguing possibility for nineteenth-century reception of Jer 1:13 is Freud's description of the id, the "lower third" of the human psyche that represents instinctual impulses and desires. In his 1933 lectures, Freud describes it as "a chaos, a cauldron full of boiling agitations" ("Vergleichen, nennen ein chaos, einen Kessel voll brodeinder Erregungen"). The Bible in Freud's boyhood home, which he read starting at the age of seven, was Ludwig Philippson's *Die Israelitische Bibel,* which juxtaposed Hebrew and German texts accompanied

FIGURE 28   Political cartoon from *Flugblätter der Reformation und des Bauernkriges*. Widener Library, Harvard University.

by extensive annotations. Philippson's notes focused on explaining the realia of ancient Israel in the mode of the Enlightenment Wissenschaft des Judentums movement that had begun a few decades earlier. Customs, objects, places, and peoples were described in terms of the contemporary Middle East, and accompanying drawings added to the sense of the Bible as product of a real if exotic culture. It also made the Bible intellectually respectable for educated Jews who understood themselves as part of European culture. Philippson's lengthy note at Jer 1:13 begins, "The second allegory uses a boiling cauldron (*einen Kessel*) directed from the north at sinful Jerusalem and the cities of Judah to signify a king coming from the north. A cauldron full of boiling water in later Arabic poetic speech is also an expression for a destructive king" (Philippson 1839: 2:6:935, my translation). The note elaborates the cauldron's boiling contents three more times. The influence of Philippson's annotations and illustrations on Freud is well documented, and Jeremiah's boiling cauldron mediated through these annotations may have helped shape Freud's language of the id as a boiling cauldron.

Jerem. *La vision d'une chaudiere bouillante, etc* ɔ:I.72.
I.9-13. Gezicht van eenen ziedenden pot enz.

FIGURE 29   The boiling pot. Engraving by Matthias Scheits for *Tableaux de vieux et nouveau testament*. Amsterdam 1710. Private collection.

Thomas Aquinas takes the beginning of Jeremiah's prophecies as the place to introduce the traditional corpus of all Jeremiah's words: "Here begins the prophecy of Jeremiah himself, now placed into the job of prophet. It is divided into three parts: in the first (Jeremiah) he prophecies captivity, in the second (Lamentations) he laments, in the third (Baruch) he leads the captives to penance. The book of Jeremiah is divided into the prophecies against Judah and the prophecies against the nations; prophecies before the fall of Jerusalem and prophecies after it" (Aquinas 2013, my translation). Thomas' divisions into ever smaller units of meaning focus on the textuality of Jeremiah rather than the

Jeremiah Through the Centuries, First Edition. Mary Chilton Callaway.
© 2020 Mary Chilton Callaway. Published 2020 by John Wiley & Sons Ltd.

theology. This focus is evident also in the attention he gives to the literal sense, including what each rhetorical form tells readers about the author's intention. Thomas' repeated taxonomies of the text reflects the influence of Aristotle, but their popularity in French universities also responded to Jewish critiques of Christian exegesis as privileging the allegorical sense over the plain meaning.

God's Lawsuit (2:1–13)

Jeremiah's vivid images of Judah as bride of the Lord stand in a long chain of reception. For sixth-century Judah, they contemporized. Hosea's earlier story of Israel as God's adulterous wife; they are subsequently developed more luridly in Ezekiel 16 and 23. In modernity, scholars identify the images as part of a traditional genre of prophetic speech portraying divine judgment as a courtroom drama. In a lawsuit for breach of covenant the Lord is both plaintiff and judge; Judah is the defendant and all creation is witness. Jeremiah's mix of sexual and forensic images in this chapter had consequences for centuries.

Jerome interprets verse 6 as an allegory of the Christian pilgrimage toward God, glossing the poetic phrases as steps in the spiritual ascent from world of woe to heavenly home. Being led out of Egypt is the ascent in this world, while trekking through inhospitable and unmarked land describes the difficulty of the journey and hostility of a world where no virtuous person ought to settle. A land of thirst signifies that we are not meant to be content here but long to go higher, and the shadow of death teaches that whenever we stop to rest, the devil has spread out his snares. The land where no one lives points ahead to the heavenly home, the only place where perfection is attained. Jerome uses Jeremiah to combat the popular Gnostic teaching that spiritual perfection can be achieved in this life. In *Glossa Ordinaria,* Jerome's phrases appear as interlinear notes over the text of Jer 2:6, instructing Christians for centuries in his spiritual allegory of Judah's history.

In medieval churches, Christians heard Jeremiah's prophetic indictment of his people turned against contemporary Jews. The Good Friday liturgy paired Jeremiah's words with Jerusalem's reproach of passers-by in Lam 1:12, with devastating effects. The *Improperia* (Reproaches) sung during veneration of the cross begin with Jer 2:5–7 spoken by a sorrowful Christ reproaching his people – "the Jews." The re-imagining of Jeremiah's words on the lips of Jesus in the Good Friday liturgy transformed these verses into a Christian polemic against Jews. Singing the Reproaches began around the eleventh century, and Christians in medieval towns used them as justification for pogroms. This liturgical use of Jeremiah fueled the idea of Jews as "Christ-killers" well into the twentieth century.

The established practice of reading Jeremiah during Holy Week included the monastic office of Matins on Palm Sunday, when Jer 2:12–17 was read with verses 18–22 and 29–32 as three lessons separated by responses from the Psalms. After the third lesson the monks heard part of a sermon from Pope Leo which described the Jews as being inflamed with "unrighteous hatred." Jeremiah's call to the heavens (verse 12) as witness in God's lawsuit against Judah became on the lips of monks an appeal to the heavens to shudder at the sight of the rejected messiah.

In *Pilgrims Progress*, John Bunyan, using the Geneva Bible, merges Jeremiah's image of the land of the shadow of death (verse 6) with the valley identically described in Psalm 23:4. Quoting Jeremiah, Bunyan interprets this valley as "a land that no man (but a Christian) passeth through." On the only route to the Celestial City, it is a narrow valley road bordered by a pit and a quagmire and inhabited by "hobgoblins, satyrs, and dragons." Bunyan dramatizes the terror by including fiends who "whisperingly suggested many grievous blasphemies to him, which he verily thought had proceeded from his own mind" (Bunyan 1859: 50–51). In Bunyan's Puritan imagination, Jeremiah's valley signifies temptation to sin, and the Psalmist's voice sustains him through the dangers.

The marginal note in *Brown's Self-Interpreting Bible* displays the historical realism that particularly interested inquiring readers in the nineteenth century. The puzzling "land of the shadow of death" was either a place where the only shadows were cast by "the monuments of the dead," or where "every shadowy retreat was the lurking place of some murderous robber, or ravenous beast" (Brown 1859). Readers could imagine with a shudder the ancient Hebrews trekking through dark graveyards and on roads patrolled by highway robbers, the very places they themselves would avoid.

The mention of distant travels in verses 10–11, particularly the word "coastlands," attracted Christopher Columbus, for whom the verse was a mandate to convert the native peoples of the islands he wanted to explore and a prophecy about himself (likewise Jer 3:17 and 16:19).

Leaky Cisterns or Living Water? (2:12–13)

Jeremiah's memorable images of leaky cisterns and living water found new interpretations in every era. For Hellenistic Jews living under the Seleucids, Jeremiah's fountain of living water becomes a warning in Baruch 3:12 where it is a fountain of true wisdom in danger of being forsaken for the allure and false wisdom of Hellenistic culture. Philo similarly urges Jews not to be like those who "dig in madness for themselves but not for God," whose cisterns (souls) need to be constantly filled with worldly instruction. "All the receptacles of the ill-conditioned soul are crushed and leaking, unable to hold in and keep the inflow of what might do them good." He warns that the rational soul is sustained not by human wisdom but by "the ever-flowing spring of living" and "the deep sources of knowledge from which the draughts of reason are drawn," which means contemplation of the divine (*On Flight* 197).

Traditional Jewish and Christian interpreters were keen to identify Jeremiah's two evils. The Epistle of Barnabas reads the living waters as a figure of baptism, actualizing Jeremiah's words against contemporary Jews "who will not receive the baptism that brings the remission of sins, but will build for themselves" (11:1–2). Jeremiah's broken cisterns become in the Epistle's citation a "cistern of death," a polemical designation for the Law. Justin's second-century *Dialogue with Trypho* expands this polemic, contrasting "those who are willing to drink the water of life" with "you who do not believe us who draw your attention to what has been written" (chapter 114). Jerome instead uses allegory to warn his educated Christian readers against contemporary theologies, especially Pelagius' teachings of self-perfection, warning that the land where God's fountain of living waters flows also offers many cisterns full of waters from turbulent and muddy sources. Rashi similarly reads the verse as a warning against false teaching. He explains that if Israel had simply exchanged her deity for another, that would be one evil, but forsaking God for idols is a second. As a vintner, Rashi knew about irrigation and he points out that a cracked cistern introduces muddy water that makes the walls cave in. In the fourteenth century, Nicholas of Lyra contemporizes Jeremiah differently, instructing monastic readers that Jeremiah's two evils are avoiding prayer and the study of Scripture.

An early English translation of Jeremiah evokes the broken cisterns in the conflict between Rome and England. In 1534, George Joye of Cambridge University published his translation of Jeremy the Prophete as an individual book, with a 13-page preface to guide readers; 4 pages are devoted to verse 13. The living waters are theologically explained in the Christological language of John 4:10–15, but the broken cisterns are explained with Protestant polemics: "Jeremy" speaks against "these damnable delvers the bishops of Rome and their fashion [type], delving and digging up their muddy and miry stinking dykes all for to feed their own carnal affects, to maintain their glistening glory and to increase their filthy lucre and establish their falsely usurped power..." Joye ends with an implicit lesson in reading Scripture: "But as for their pestilent pits, they may hold none of those lively refreshing waters which Christ offered unto the Samaritan woman, and daily offereth them unto us to call us from these popish puddles, unto himself the very perpetual springe of everlasting life" (Joye 1534). Joye uses Jeremiah's image to instruct new readers of the Bible in English, guiding them to interpret the Old Testament in terms of the New and of their own lived experience, in equal measure.

Jeremiah's cisterns likewise figure significantly in the closing paragraph of *The Translators to the Reader,* the unusual defense of the project of the King James Bible. Exhorting readers holding this new translation in their hands to read it faithfully, and warning against receiving such a treasure lightly, they write, "Ye are brought unto fountains of living water which ye digged not; do not cast earth into them with the Philistines, neither prefer broken pits before them with the wicked Jews." In the margin is written "Gen 26,16 and Jerem, 2,13." The translators join Jeremiah's fountains with Isaac's wells, which the Philistines had filled in, to provide biblical metaphors for the full range of their enemies. The Philistines are Catholics, who cast earth into the living water of the Bible by using Jerome's Latin and mixing biblical text with church teaching. The "wicked Jews" are more complicated, since English churchmen identified with biblical Israel as a people chosen by God for a special destiny in the world. King James I was so deeply invested in this idea of England as the new Israel that he saw himself, and was described by others, as the English Solomon. If England represented the true Israel, then contemporary Jews presented a low-level but persistent threat to English self-understanding simply by their visible presence as heirs of Abraham. Their preference for Jeremiah's "broken pits" was, for readers of the King James translation, a reference to their fidelity to Jewish law, seen by Christians as useless and broken.

By the late eighteenth century, Jeremiah's cisterns represented an inner drama of the heart, evident in Charles Wesley's hymn based on Jer 2:3:

> Ah! Lord, with late regret I own,
> I have the double evil done,
> Forsook the Spring of life and peace,
> And toil'd for earthly happiness…
> Now for my double sin I grieve,
> Again the broken cisterns leave…
> Fountain of true felicity,
> Eternal God, spring up in me,
> And fill'd with life, and love, and power,
> My heart shall never wander more
> (Wesley 2012: 3)

Here Jeremiah's indictment of Judah is transformed into the language of personal salvation and his fountain of living water has become the "Spring of life and peace" that warms the heart.

A Puzzling Verb Becomes a Word of Salvation (2:20)

A problem in the Hebrew of verse 20 generated contradictory spiritual lessons. The Hebrew verb that looks like "you have broken" is in fact an archaic form identical to "I have broken." Not knowing this archaic form, translators of the Targum turned the indictment of Judah into a word of salvation: "I have broken the yoke of the nations from your neck." A tenth-century Masoretic note instructs readers to substitute "I will not transgress" for the verb in the text which looks very similar but means, "I will not serve" [idols]. Jewish readers therefore understood Judah to be penitent rather than defiant. Septuagint and Jerome, on the other hand, present God accusing a rebellious Judah: "You broke my yoke… you said, I will not serve." Medieval Christian readers of the *Glossa* read the words "of marriage," written above "yoke" and "husband" above "I will not serve." With these brief interlinear notes, *Glossa* turns Jeremiah's indictment of Judah into a contemporary warning about uncontrolled women, and *Bible moralisée* illustrates it with two bare-legged medieval girls wielding hammer and saw against chains on their ankles.

Sixteenth and seventeenth-century English translators likewise did not know about the archaic second-person feminine Hebrew form, and the Geneva Bible reads, "I have broken thy yoke and burst thy bonds, and thou said, I will no more transgress, but like an harlot thou runnest about…" Protestants found in the verse a lapse from grace to sin. For Methodist Charles Wesley Israel's story encoded the evangelical experience, and his hymn based on Jer 2:20 evoked the fervor known to many:

> Yes, Thou didst my soul release,
> (This fills up my guilt and pain,)
> From the bands of wickedness,
> From my old oppressor's chain!
> Never more will I transgress,
> Such was then my solemn vow:
> Farther still from God I roved,
> Sunk in vile idolatry.
> Now command my sin to cease,
> Break, and now renew my heart
> (Wesley 2012: 5)

Wesley's verse transforms Jeremiah's indictment of Israel into the drama of personal sin and redemption at the center of the new movement of English Methodism. The plea to "break my heart" poignantly adapts a version of Jeremiah's words to this experience.

Prophetic Pornography (2:20–25)

Jeremiah's indictments in 2:20–25 use some of the most graphic sexual imagery in the Bible. Hosea had used the metaphor of adultery for Israel's breach of covenant with YHWH a century earlier (Hosea 2:1–13; 4:7–14), and Jeremiah elaborates with peculiar vocabulary and unseemly metaphors, describing Judah variously as an adulteress, prostitute, and animal of insatiable lust. Judah's behavior "on every high hill and under every green tree" is described in verse 20 with the graphic wordplay *tsoa zona. zona* is the common term for prostitute, but *tsoa* is a rare Hebrew verb that occurs in only two other places, where it describes tipping a wine vat for pouring (Jer 48:12) and the bent-over posture of prisoners (Isa 51:14). Jerome cleverly translates with *prosterno,* "to throw oneself to the ground," used by Cicero to denote prostitution. Jeremiah's "high hills and leafy trees" signified for Jerome the worldly literature of classical Rome and the artful rhetoric of orators like Cicero. As an educated Roman, Jerome had been dismayed by the simple and even crude literary style of the Scriptures, which he found at first a stumbling-block to his faith. In his experience, Jeremiah's words reflect the seductive intellectual culture of Rome: "Anyone who is first educated in Christian and sacred writings but later desires worldly literature (high hills) and pleasing speech (leafy trees) throws himself before demons who promise erudition and deep knowledge but corrupt the souls of believers and make them spread their feet to all who pass by." Jerome's warning is contemporized in the twelfth century to indict philosophy, especially the retrieval of Aristotle that led to scholasticism being taught at the University of Paris. The illustration of Jer 2:20 in *Bible moralisée* shows a monk being instructed by a philosopher while another monk turns away in horror.

Jewish tradition plays with both plain and spiritual senses. The Targum, perhaps in light of its liturgical use, avoids Jeremiah's sexual image, paraphrasing, "You worship idols." David Kimḥi follows this allegorical sense: "You wander as a harlot. Just as a harlot goes from place to place seeking lovers, living first with one and then with another, so did you worship first one idol and then another one" (Rosenberg 1995: 1:16). Rashi privileges the plain sense, and since Jeremiah's peculiar verb reminded him of a rabbinic Hebrew word meaning bed, he understands it as "recline," explaining that "this is an expression of a bed and a sheet" (Rosenberg 1995: 1:15–16). Rashi's enduring influence is apparent in the contemporary translation of the Jewish Publication Society, "You recline as a whore."

English translations reflect the same uncertainty about Jeremiah's verb as the ancient versions, some portraying a female in frenzied activity, others suggesting languid seduction. Wyclif's English is indebted to Jerome, translating "under each branchy tree thou were thrown down as a strumpet." Coverdale translates it "like an harlot thou runnest about," and John Trapp's 1660 commentary vividly evokes the Puritan trope of Catholics as whores who "runnest a-madding and a-gadding after Idols." Calvin explains Jeremiah's "high hills" as Judah's foolish belief that God is localized in order to ridicule the Catholic practice of keeping a consecrated host on display in churches as an object of devotion: "And at this day the case is the same with the Papists; for the devotion, or rather the diabolical madness, by which they are carried away, is of a similar kind" (Calvin 1989: 1:110).

While patristic, medieval, and early modern commentators sought the religious meaning of Jeremiah's sexual images, historical-critical exegetes tried to illuminate the sociological context and literal connotation of the images. The classic Hebrew-English lexicon (BDB) defines Jeremiah's rare verb simply with the words, "in sensu obscoeno." Mid-twentieth century excavations in Syria yielding Canaanite religious texts and statues led scholars to imagine licentious coupling at shrines to Baal; for example, John Bright writes in the Anchor Bible commentary, "Reference is to the fertility cult, whose rites included sacred prostitution and the ritual self-dedication of young women to the god of fertility" (Bright 1964: 15). Although without clear evidence and now generally discredited, this reception of Jer 2 remains embedded in many commentaries. More recent scholarship interprets the rare verb *tzoa* ("tip over") in light of ancient sexual practices of having intercourse bending over in a standing position. Ancient near eastern art offers some evidence for this interpretation (Carroll 1986; Holladay 1986; Lundbom 1999). Most modern translations avoid Jeremiah's image altogether. The Scofield Reference Bible, with its emphasis on personal trust in God, simply directs its readers to fidelity: "He accuses them of choosing other, and impotent, gods." Like the ancient Targum, the Good News Bible replaces metaphor with explanation: "The Sovereign Lord says, 'Israel, long ago you rejected my authority; you refused to obey me and worship me. On every high hill and under every green tree you worshiped fertility gods.'"

Jeremiah's metaphor of infidelity changes in verses 23–25 to an image of Judah as an animal in heat. Discomfort with these verses begins with the ancient versions, which differ significantly from the Masoretic text and from each other. Jerome misunderstands "in her month" as when she is menstruating; Septuagint translates "in her humiliation." Targum changes Jeremiah's metaphor of the camel in heat easily found by the males she seeks to a more edifying statement teaching that whoever seeks Torah will find it. In medieval Jewish tradition, "in her month they will find her" is interpreted as the end of pregnancy, when a woman would be easily overtaken and captured. Kimhi interprets it metaphorically as the Ninth of Ab, the day of mourning for Jerusalem, when people's sins, which run free all year, finally overtake them. In the *Glossa,*

Nicholas of Lyra elucidates "in her month" as reference to Jewish law forbidding sexual intercourse while the wife is menstruating. "This is because," he supposes, "she was thought to be overly licentious (*luxuriosa*). With this image the ardor of idolatry in Israel is described." Calvin does not hesitate to name the "impetuous lust" and insolence of the female dromedary. If his readers wonder whether such behavior is possible, he invites them to consider "the Papists" with their statues and superstitions.

Jeremiah in the Synagogue (2:4–28)

Verses 4–28 have been part of Jewish worship since at least the first century BCE (Cohen 2007: 487–489). They provide the *Haftarah,* the reading from the prophets paired with the Torah portion read in the synagogue, to accompany Num 33–36, which describes how the land is to be divided among the 12 tribes. These verses of Jeremiah have been read for over 2000 years on the second of three Sabbaths of Admonition leading up to the solemn Ninth of Av, the remembrance of the destruction of the temple, and of subsequent Jewish sufferings. In this liturgical context Jeremiah's indictments offer an explanation of the Exile as divine correction and exhortation to holy living in the present. While Christians tended to read Jeremiah's warnings triumphantly against Jews, Jews read the same words in a liturgical season of penance bringing both judgment and hope.

A Rare Allusion to God the Father (3:4,19)

Only a handful of verses in the Hebrew Bible refer to God as father: Jer 3:4,19; Isa 63:16; and Isa 64:7 are the earliest traces of rare traditions in which Israelites called the Lord "father." Jer 3:19 draws on the ancient poetry of Deut 32:4–9, using its trope of God as father who created Israel and gave them the best heritage, only to be betrayed. In Jewish liturgical tradition, Jeremiah's re-signification of these ancient verses is part of the liturgy of repentance. Like Jer 2:4–28,

Jeremiah Through the Centuries, First Edition. Mary Chilton Callaway.

it concludes the *Haftarah* on the second of the three Sabbaths of Admonition before the Ninth of Ab.

In medieval Christian art, Jeremiah is sometimes pictured opposite Peter because of this verse; the fourteenth-century *Taymouth Book of Hours* offers a beautiful example (British Library MS Yates Thompson 13). On one side of a two-page spread of Psalm 95, a bearded Jeremiah holds a banderole evoking Jer 3:*19 patrem vocabis me dicit* (He says, you will call me father). On the facing page, the apostle Peter appears holding a banderole inscribed with the first sentence of the Nicene Creed, with the key words *patrem omnipotem* – "Almighty Father" – enlarged. Medieval readers would understand Jeremiah here as one who prefigured Peter and his spiritual heir, the Pope. This typological use of Jer 3:19 appears more ominously in an image from the elaborate *Petites heures de Jean de Berry* (BnF, Mandragore Catalogue, MS. Latin 18014). The prophet, wearing the pointed cap of medieval Jewry, stands gesturing with his right hand to a model of a cathedral, and with his left to a haloed St. Peter. The banderole in his left hand reads, *patrem invocabitis qui terram fecit et conditit caelos* ("You will call me father who made earth and established the heavens"), conflating Jer 3:19 and 10:12. The page offers a clear illustration of the contemporary ideology of church triumphant over synagogue, using the traditional practice of enlisting the Jews' own prophet as witness against them. Further underscoring this polemic is the image of Paul's conversion in the upper left corner of the page, directly diagonal from Jeremiah, implicitly asking why Jews can't convert as Paul did. Jeremiah appears in order to indict Jews who do not acknowledge the fulfillment of these words. The visual layout of the page bears witness to the way medieval Christians used Jeremiah to address their own uneasiness at the continuing faithfulness of Jews to God's covenant with them, a faithfulness that challenged Christian self-understanding as God's true people.

The Septuagint's translation initiated a new interpretation that shifted the focus from father to daughter: "Did you not call me house and father and prince of your virginity (*parthenia*)?" This verse captured the imagination of Philo, who heard it in the synagogue every year in the *Haftarah* reading. In his neo-Platonic metaphysics, virginity symbolized the ideal state of the soul in communion with God as well as the communion between God and virtue. In *Cherubim* II.49 Philo writes, "I myself was initiated under Moses the God-beloved into his greater mysteries, yet when I saw the prophet Jeremiah and knew him to be not only himself enlightened, but a worthy minister of the holy secrets, I was not slow to become his disciple. Out of his manifold inspiration he gave forth an oracle spoken in the person of God to Virtue the all-peaceful: 'Did you not call upon Me as your house, your father and the husband of your virginity?'" (Philo 1929). Philo here extols the person of Jeremiah as spiritual teacher, a Judean prophet in the garb of a Hellenistic mystagogue, and calls

Jeremiah by name rather than his usual formula "one of the prophets," highlighting the personal significance of his engagement with the prophet as sage. Jeremiah is for him a teacher of Hellenistic metaphysics, presented in words known to every Jew from the liturgy of the most solemn season. Here is evidence that toward the end of the first century BCE, exegetical mining of the texts was paralleled by blossoming traditions about the persona of Jeremiah.

Holy Forgetting (3:15–18)

These verses present layers of scribal editing that continually defer fulfillment of the prophecy to an ever more distant future, from the exiles' return to Judah, to an eschatological vision. At the center (verse 16) is the Ark of the Covenant, which was lost when Nebuchadnezzar's troops burned the temple. In this extraordinary verse, which paradoxically envisions the loss of Judah's most holy object as a sign of hope, the overloaded syntax of the second sentence captured readers' attention. Are all four verbs simply variations of "they will not remember," or do they signal different traditional uses of the Ark? Rather than variations of "they will not remember," in Jewish tradition the four verbs blossomed into different occasions of hope. Targum Jonathan paraphrases: "They will no longer tremble or fight with it in their midst." In thirteenth-century France, David Kimhi, whose father had been expelled from his native Spain, reads Jeremiah's "nor shall it be done anymore" as "you will not need to take the Ark out to battle because the nations will not envy you, and there will be no more wars." Rashi reads another kind of hope: "Your whole assembly will be holy, and I will dwell there as in the Ark."

The image of the "forgotten ark" has a long afterlife in Christian tradition. It begins with Jerome's unusual addition of an alternate translation in his rendering of verse 16: "the ark of the pact – or testament," as he also does for Jer 31.31. His use of *testamentum* would signal for his readers the book designated by the church as *Vetus Testamentum* (Old Testament), a connection he encourages by commenting that the Ark held the Law of Moses. Jerome's interpretation of the "forgotten ark" taught that Christians were not "enslaved to obsolete sacrifices but pursue spiritual worship." For medieval Christians, Jerome's comment became Jeremiah's witness to the Mass. A note over the word "ark" in *Glossa* directs readers to Jerome's comment in the margin, where Jerome's *cultum* (worship) has been changed to *cibus* (bread). For medieval Christians, Jeremiah's words become evidence that the Mass supersedes all Jewish practice. Puritans in the sixteenth century likewise interpreted Jeremiah's prophecy as the beginning of their own worship and biblical interpretation. A note in the Geneva Bible instructs its Protestant readers, "This is to be understood of the coming of Christ: for then they will not seek the Lord by ceremonies, and all figures will cease." The traditional anti-Jewish interpretation here becomes instead an anti-Catholic critique of liturgical practices and allegorical biblical interpretation. Matthew Poole's 1683 commentary continues this Protestant polemic in its explanation of the unusual piling up of phrases in verse 16: "God foreseeing... the pleas that the corrupt wit and invention of man would find out for the retaining of these rites, and by consequence their lothness to forego them, he useth such a heap and variety of expressions... that he may leave no room for doubting."

Jeremiah's prophecy of a restored Jerusalem replacing the Ark as God's throne generated rich images. Jerome's zeal for intellectual precision and a disciplined spiritual life, apparent in his ongoing feuds with Origen's disciples as well as cosmopolitan Romans, appears in his interpretation of God's throne in the present as "everyone who believes with a perfect mind." In the eschatological future, the throne will be the church, "Jerusalem" to which all nations will come. Jerome's double interpretation of the throne is inscribed into Jer 3:17 in the *Glossa*, where "church" (*ecclesia*) is written above Jerusalem. Jerome's gnomic words about believing with a perfect mind have been rendered "all believers made perfect," written over the word "throne." Jeremiah's vision of Jerusalem drawing together the nations becomes for medieval Christians a vision of the church as God's throne. Nicholas of Lyra usually prefers the historical sense, but here offers an allegory of the throne as the heavenly "church triumphant," where Jesus is enthroned at God's right hand, as well as the earthly "church militant" where Jesus appears seated with his disciples, present for medieval Christians in the "throne" of the Mass.

3:24–25

These verses of Judah's repentance were prayed in 1544 by English Christians using the little book *Certain prayers, and godly meditations of holy men and women: taken out of the Bible*. Small books of biblical prayers were popular in sixteenth-century England, where they scored a political point by making parts of the forbidden English Bible a source of personal prayer. Jer 17:14–18 and 31:18–19 are also included as prayers, making Jeremiah seem like a fellow Englishman at prayer.

A Subversive Translation (4:1–2)

In Chaucer's *Canterbury Tales,* the Pardoner invokes "holy Jeremye" on swearing falsely: "Thou shalt swear truthfully thine oaths and not lie/ But swear in judgment and in righteousness." Making his own translation from the Vulgate, Chaucer slyly made a bit of Jeremiah widely available even as Wyclif was being prosecuted for circulating the Bible in English. Chaucer's use of the vernacular "lie" glosses Jeremiah's words and makes him contemporary, increasing readers' appetite for an English Bible.

Jeremiah Through the Centuries, First Edition. Mary Chilton Callaway.
© 2020 Mary Chilton Callaway. Published 2020 by John Wiley & Sons Ltd.

The Circumcised Heart (4:4)

Jeremiah's metaphor of the circumcised heart reflects Deuteronomy, where it is both command (Deut 10:16, "Circumcise the foreskins of your hearts") and promise (Deut 30:6, "The Lord your God will circumcise your heart..."). Paul's appropriation of "circumcision of the heart" in Rom 2:25–29 to argue that Gentiles could be part of the covenant with Abraham re-signifies Jeremiah's metaphor as a legal definition of what counts as circumcision. The Epistle of Barnabas in the second century CE turns Paul's use of Jeremiah into anti-Jewish invective. Arguing that God had never intended circumcision in the flesh and that Jews had been misled by an evil angel, the author links Jer 4:4 with images of hard hearts and stiff necks in Deut 10:16 to indict "the Jews" (*Ep Barn* 9:5). Jeremiah's prophetic words aimed inside his own community are reinterpreted in this second-century Christian writing as invective directed at Jews outside. This polemical reception of Jeremiah via Paul persists in Christian writers in the West (Justin Martyr) and the East (Theodoret).

   Anti-Jewish traditions attached to Jeremiah's circumcision of the heart take on new virulence in the art of the early Renaissance. Fra Angelico's fresco in the basilica of San Marco shows Mary and an aged Joseph holding the naked baby Jesus over a small altar, about to be circumcised by a high priest. Three artistic details emphasize the metaphorical distance between Jesus and the Jews. The holy family all have a golden nimbus, while the high priest wears a pointed hat evoking the distinctive cap of medieval Jews. The vulnerability of the naked baby is heightened by the large figure of the priest looming over his genitals with two sharp stones. The priest's apron and the basin on the table ominously portend blood about to be shed. A scroll floating above the scene with the words of Jer 4:4 is paired with one below with the words of Luke 2:21. As the obedient parents faithfully fulfill the Law, Jeremiah's words signal for the medieval viewer that this is the end of Jewish law and the coming of the new law of Christ. This scene with its prominent display of Jer 4:4 is the subject of many fifteenth- and sixteenth-century altarpieces. Noteworthy is Luca Signorelli's rendering of the scene, which includes an image of Jeremiah holding a banderole with his words about circumcising the heart. The altarpiece was installed around 1491, when synagogues in Ravenna were destroyed during the expulsion of the Jews. For viewers accustomed to multiple levels of meaning in biblical stories, this rendering of the circumcision of the infant Jesus ominously prefigured the blood to be shed at the crucifixion. This reading of Jeremiah contributed to those occasions when Christians claimed the right to shed Jewish blood.

   Martin Luther's *On the Jews and their Lies* (1543) adopts the satirical voice of an imaginary interlocutor to turn Jeremiah's words against Jews in Luther's world: "Jeremiah, you wretched heretic, you seducer and false prophet, how dare you tell that holy, circumcised people of God to circumcise themselves to the Lord? Do you mean to imply that they were hitherto circumcised physically to the devil, as if God did not esteem their holy, physical circumcision? And are you furthermore threatening them with God's wrath, as an eternal fire, if they do not circumcise their hearts?… I advise you not to enter their synagogue; all devils might dismember and devour you there." Such anti-Jewish use of the verse persisted into seventeenth-century England. In his popular commentary (1683), Matthew Poole paraphrases Jeremiah, "Take away that Brawniness [callousness] and Obstinacy that… is upon your hearts." He encourages his readers to identify the Jews as the target of Jeremiah's prophecy by adding as cross-references Rom 2:29 and Acts 7:51, in which Stephen uses "stiff-necked people" together with "uncircumcised in heart" in his speech to the Jewish council.

Circumcision of the heart as a moral trope persisted in Jewish teaching. Targum interprets, "Return to the worship of the Lord, and remove the evil of your heart." Nineteenth-century eastern European Jewish scholar Malbim, who resisted efforts at modernizing Judaism yet wrote his Bible commentary to speak to contemporary Jews, adapts Jeremiah's metaphor to classical pietist thinking. Actualizing Jeremiah for a people losing the divine voice in the din of modernity, Malbim writes that Jeremiah speaks to them. Warning against adaptations to contemporary culture that weaken Jewish law, he describes their hearts as enveloped by a covering that makes them insensitive to inspirations leading to goodness. Jeremiah calls them to remove this foreskin so their hearts will become sensitive and responsive to God's commandments (Rosenberg 1995: 1:35). Arguing that Jeremiah's language has influenced developing ideas of the self, Timothy Polk writes, "What is at stake… is the 'self,' the self of Jeremiah, the many selves of Judah and Jerusalem, and ultimately the selves of the book's readers" (Polk 1984: 37).

Reading Metaphor (4:7)

Glossa Ordinaria includes an interlinear note above lion reading, "Savage Nebuchadnezzar, who circles like a lion, seeking whom he might devour." This language triggers recollection of 1 Peter 5:8, which compares the devil to a prowling lion. A brief note on the lion's lair continues the image: "That is, from evil, or hell (inferno)." Jeremiah's words become part of the *Glossa*'s project of training medieval readers to see multiple meanings juxtaposed in a scriptural image. The prophecy of desolate land and unoccupied cities in ruins is decoded in an interlinear note reading, "The church ravaged by heretics." This gloss distills Jerome's longer comment to focus readers' attention on the danger of heretical teachings by philosophers. The lapidary nature of these interlinear glosses left readers to do the work of making connections and gave them practice with allegorical interpretation.

Does God Deceive? (4:9–10)

The suggestion in 4:10 that God might purposely deceive his people caused consternation for centuries. Jerome explains that Jeremiah is merely confused by contradictory visions of destruction and salvation. Rashi softens the sense by supplying the vernacular French *tenter* (tempt), suggesting that the false prophets' promise of peace "tempted" people. The Geneva Bible reassures readers that God did not deceive humanity, but sent false prophets to punish the people's "rebellious stubbornness." In the seventeenth century, Matthew Poole reassures readers that the first word, "Ah," attests that Jeremiah's words are "breathed out in the great sorrow and sighing of Soul." He also offers the option of reading the words as a question: "How can it possibly be, that thou shoudst suffer thy people to be thus deluded by their false Prophets, thou being a God that canst not lie, Titus 1:2?" In his Enlightenment defense of the Bible, *Scripture Vindicated* (1732), Daniel Waterland rejects the Puritan explanation that the prophet was "overwhelmed with Grief and Anxiety, and so uttered such Things as he would not have done upon cool and serious Reflection." Waterland assumes instead that God merely allowed people to be deceived by false prophets. He notes that in verse 18 Jeremiah "takes Care to remove all Pretense of charging God, by throwing Blame upon the People themselves." By appealing to verse 18 to explain verse 10, Waterland engages the Enlightenment principle of attending to larger context in biblical interpretation to undermine the Deist critique that the Bible is full of superstition. The effect of the verse in modernity is clear in John Skinner's psychological explanation: "That which is characteristic of Jeremiah is the dialogue of two voices within himself, one known to be divine, and the other consciously his own. As Hegel said of himself, he was not one of the combatants, but rather both of the combatants, and also the combat itself" (Skinner 1922: 48–49).

Body and Soul (4:19–22)

Readings of these graphic verses reflect changing ideas about the body and human emotion. Jerome reads verse 19 as God's sorrow, as when Jesus mourns for Lazarus and weeps over Jerusalem. He contemporizes his interpretation with the addition, "God says this also when he discerns noises and dissension of sedition in the church." Elsewhere, Jerome invokes Jeremiah's innards as evidence for the practice of metaphorically ingesting Scripture. Commenting on Ezekiel eating the scroll, he writes, "When by assiduous meditation we shall have stored the book of the Lord in the treasury of our memory, we fill our belly in a spiritual sense, and our bowels are filled, that we may have with the Apostle the bowels of mercy (Col 3:12), and that belly is filled concerning which Jeremias said: 'My bowels...'" (Carruthers 2008: 209). Nicholas of Lyra in the fourteenth century reflects increasing interest in the connection between corporeal and spiritual experience: "Here fittingly the prophet's grief is assumed into his body. Violent emotion overflows from a joyful or suffering mind to the body." In early modernity, this somatized grief is a mark of authenticity in a preacher. The Geneva Bible actualizes Jeremiah's anguish as the struggle of true ministers, who are "lively touched with the calamities of the Church, so that all the parts of their body feel the grief of their heart." Jeremiah's cry "I cannot keep silent" touched Luther, as the words describe his own tormented experience. Linking this cry with the prophet's futile attempt to withhold the word in 20:9, Luther imagines himself as Jeremiah: "He could not keep silent because his conscience (*Gewissen*) was driving him" (*LW* 17:344). Luther's application of "conscience" to Jeremiah was part of his redefinition of a traditional word that had meant awareness of sin but came to signify fidelity to one's personal conviction.

By the eighteenth century, Jeremiah's innards were subject to scientific scrutiny. In his influential 1784 commentary aiming to make the Bible intellectually respectable, Oxford scholar Benjamin Blayney explains, "Walls of the heart undoubtedly meant the pericardium, a membrane which sits loose about the heart." He offers a physical description of grief working its way from the bowels to the pericardium and finally to the heart itself, "where becoming too big to be contained, it breaks forth in outward expression." Twentieth-century commentary shifts to psychological experience, and in the wake of World War I English commentator Leslie Elliott-Binns writes, "This section is of great interest as being the first of several similar revelations of Jeremiah's own feelings... his tender soul is now torn by realizing the fate which is coming upon his native land" (Elliott-Binns 1941). In his still influential *Prophecy and Religion,* John Skinner sees in Jeremiah the beginning of "personal religion." These verses "are not the direct word of the Lord to Jeremiah, but the effect of that word on a sensitive human heart, which gives forth its own peculiar tones like the Aeolian harp when its strings are swept by the wind... the poems have their end in themselves, in the artistic utterance of personal emotion; and only in secondary application do they become a medium of enlightenment or instruction or warning to others" (Skinner 1922: 35–52).

Apocalypse Now (4:23–28)

In this terrifying vision, Jeremiah reverses the order of events in Gen 1 to portray God systematically deconstructing creation, and the use of the rare term *tohu-wa-bohu,* an onomatopoetic term for chaos in Gen 1:2, suggests a link between the two texts. Reversal of creation imagery in ancient Near Eastern magical incantations invoked a curse, which Jeremiah adapts to prophetic warning. By replacing the climactic blessing of the seventh day with divine rage, he calls down judgment on Judah (Fishbane 1971: 161–162). Jerome applies this vision to the church, which has offended God by persecution and heresy. To forestall criticism by sophisticated readers, he uses the Greek term *hyperbole,* explaining the absence of light as human blindness because of terror, and mountains moving to signify that they offer no refuge. Jewish tradition, however, plays with the literal sense: one medieval rabbi clarifies the puzzling image of moving hills by explaining that the unique verb is derived from the root "to be light." The hills' great weight keeps them grounded, but the Lord made them light, and they skittered around (Rosenberg 1995: 42). Jeremiah's vision resonated with medieval emphasis on the Day of Judgment; perhaps as a precaution to readers, *Glossa* has *hyperbolicos* prominently above verse 24. To further insure against literalism it notes twice that "the face of God" in verse 26 means simply the divine presence. Still, readers are warned that the divine wrath is "aroused by the vice of the people, the cause of all the disasters." A different lesson comes from Thomas Aquinas' commentary, whose scholastic approach encourages linking verses together. He argues that because Jeremiah's cry of anguish in verse 19 comes before his vision of punishment, God has compassion even in judgment.

In the twentieth century, Jeremiah's bleak vision offered language for another kind of devastation. After the bombing of Pearl Harbor in 1941 and America's entry into the war, poet Virginia Dunbar contemporized Jeremiah's bleak vision (Dunbar 1942: 171):

Word to Jeremiah

Struck to stone is the beautiful flock.
The nightingales are turned to rock.
 Struck to stone are the virgins fair
With golden arms and gleaming hair.
  And on the hills of wilderness –
  No human foot, nor hand, nor voice.
  No blood runs along the bone
That has this day been struck to stone.
  O, Jeremiah, rest in peace
While we fulfill your prophecies.

Contradiction as Problem and Opportunity (4:27)

The contradiction between the two parts of this verse engaged readers since the third century. Will God completely destroy or not? Taking the problem as an opportunity, Origen creatively reads the Greek translation of Jeremiah's words to mean, "I will not destroy you until the consummation" – that is, the coming of the kingdom of God (Origen 1998: 69). A key piece of Origen's theology was that divine judgment is never complete until the Last Day, when the kingdom comes. Even the devil, given enough time, might be saved. This radical view of God's grace, supported by a creative reading of Jer 4:27 and 5:18, was one reason that Origen was condemned as a heretic. In Jerome's view, Origen's exegesis contradicts the doctrine of original sin and advocates the Pelagian teaching that with God's help people are capable of overcoming sin. Jerome counters Origen in part by his own explanation of Jer 4:27 at work in history: "God's anger is blended with mercy; the earth will be made desolate but not finished off, so that some remain who know his mercy." His words are reproduced in *Glossa* twice, here and at Je. 5:10, alerting readers that any apparent contradiction is not in Jeremiah, but in the inscrutable nature of God's mercy.

In early modernity, Calvin tried to hold this textual contradiction together with the historical reality of the Exile and "the richer truth" of divine softening so the faithful would not despair. A marginal note in the Geneva Bible similarly invites readers to see themselves in the verse, a "residue to be his church, and to praise him in the earth." In the early twentieth century, the contradiction in the verse helped drive the new exegetical method of redaction criticism; in his 1901 commentary, Bernhard Duhm argues that the words of hope were added by a scribe in Babylon in order to update Jeremiah's prophecies for the exiles. This verse, together with 5:10 and 5:18, helped establish the scholarly consensus that scribes in Babylon edited Jeremiah's words and shaped the scroll.

Dressing Down a Gussied-Up Female (4:29–31)

Jeremiah adopts traditional prophetic images of the people as a loose woman (Hos 2; Isa 1:21–23; 3:16–17) to denounce Jerusalem's unfaithfulness. Ezekiel 16 and 23 elaborate Jeremiah's metaphors with graphic descriptions and violent stories. In the first century CE, the author of Revelation appropriates Jeremiah's image of the woman dressed in scarlet and adorned with gold to describe the enemy "Babylon," updating her by adding the purple of the Roman Empire to her clothing (Rev 17:1–6). Jerome actualizes Jeremiah's biting words in his own satirical jab at married Christians. In the bitter debate among fourth-century Christians in Rome about whether Eastern practices of celibacy and ascetic marriages were necessary for spiritual perfection, Jerome had been ostracized for his strong position that serious Christians should remain single, or if married limit sexual activity and if widowed not re-marry. Some 21 years later, writing his commentary on Jeremiah, he found the prophet's image apt for his venom: "This should be understood in a spiritual sense against those who have squandered marital devotion and the chastity of true faith." Interpreting the feminine adornments as positive but ultimately useless, he writes, "'Though you clothe yourself in scarlet' – that is, you have taken on faith in the blood of Christ – 'though you adorn yourself with golden ornaments' – you have a habit of judgment and spiritual understanding – 'though you paint your eyes with liner' – you have an eagerness for mysteries and for knowing the hidden things of God – 'you gussy yourself up in vain'. You prepared these for your lovers, but your narrow bed does not have enough room, nor does God accept, the ornaments with which you have enticed your lovers until now." Christians who complicate their faith with marriage and sex are portrayed as Jeremiah's floozy.

Puritans read Jeremiah's words as indictment of decoration in any form. The Geneva Bible's note "Neither thy ceremonies nor rich gifts shall deliver thee" interpret Jeremiah's metaphorical whore as the Catholic Church. Matthew Poole's commentary offers a practical warning to his Puritan readers: "It is observed that they that paint much make their skins withered."

Nothing Bad Will Happen to Us (5:12)

The Hebrew idiom in the mouths of Jeremiah's opponents reads literally "he is not," shorthand for "he is not the cause of events." In the Hellenistic culture, informed by Greek philosophy, the phrase caused consternation because it was read as a denial of God's existence. By adding one word the Septuagint softens it to, "These things will not happen." Targum, however, which often promotes a theology of divine control of history, expands Jeremiah's caricature of false prophets to "Good things do not come to us from him." Jerome translates it

Jeremiah Through the Centuries, First Edition. Mary Chilton Callaway.
© 2020 Mary Chilton Callaway. Published 2020 by John Wiley & Sons Ltd.

similarly – "He is not the one" – and ends his comment warning, "The church should attend to this when it overlooks and denies God's foresight." His comment suggests that Jerome knew the Targum tradition and found it useful for Christian instruction against popular Epicurean philosophy (Hayward 1985: 104). This teaching that events are random rather than rewards or punishments was popular in the Roman Empire, and anathema to Jews and Christians. *Glossa* preserves a simplified version of Jerome's comment, showing that Jeremiah's text continued to influence debate about divine action in human life.

Divine Fire Consuming Human Wood (5:14)

For patristic writers, Jeremiah's image of the prophetic word as consuming fire offered a solution to several perplexing New Testament passages. Jerome deftly combines Jeremiah with the alarming picture of God as a devouring fire in Hebrews 12:29 and Paul's warning to the Corinthians against false use of the Gospel. The divine fire is purifying, Jerome warns in a polemic against Gnostics and other unorthodox teachings "to consume any hay, wood or straw we might build on the foundation of Christ." Cyril of Alexandria paradoxically turns Jeremiah's image into comforting words to explain Jesus' troubling claim, "I came to cast fire on the earth" (Luke 12:49). Interpreting the devouring fire of the divine word as the gospel, he argues that it kindles people to a holy life full of the Spirit that burns within them. Jeremiah here prefigures Jesus firing up disciples with word and spirit" (Wenthe 2009: 54). In the seventeenth century, John Trapp's ominous reading echoes Jerome's warning: "Oh fear this fire! Vengeance is in readiness for the disobedient; every whit as ready in God's hand as in the minister's mouth."

Eyes Have They But See Not (5:21)

Readers in late antiquity were curious about the pathways between physical sensations, the intellect, and spiritual understanding, so Jeremiah's words had resonance. Jerome combines the prophetic indictment of Judah's failure to see with contemporary Roman moral discourse to make Jeremiah seem like a philosopher, interpreting: "We ought to know what is right using our natural senses." Theodoret of Cyrus likewise condemns those who "did not use their bodily senses as they should" and "though endowed with reason, preferred irrationality." Reflecting the growing importance of monastic life in the fifth century, John Cassian refashions Jeremiah's words to indict intellectuals who claim perfect knowledge of Scripture but are "entangled in vices." They have eyes and ears (intellect) but cannot "penetrate to the very heart of Scripture and the mysteries of spiritual meanings" (Schaff 1894: 443). Jeremiah bears witness to the monastic rule that knowledge belongs to those who live a holy life and who read with the eyes of the heart (Reventlow 2009: 74).

In the early twentieth century, Jeremiah's words became a selling-point for eyeglasses (Figure 30). A 1924 advertisement by the American Optical Company invokes the verse to warn readers of the *Saturday Evening Post*. "Its meaning was, of course, a spiritual one; yet may we not apply these words to a condition which exists today? What could better describe the unconscious victims of our own Age of Eyestrain – with fine-print books, glaring artificial

FIGURE 30   "Was Jeremiah speaking to you?" Advertisement from *the Saturday Evening Post* 1924.

lights and flickering motion pictures. Who are they, these people 'that have eyes and see not'? Millions! At least one in five Americans don't see well." Here is evidence that Jeremiah was broadly recognized and authoritative in the popular culture of early twentieth-century America.

An Appalling and Horrible Thing (5:30–31)

Jeremiah's acerbic description of the collusion between religious leaders and people is a fixture of English and American rhetoric. English Puritan preacher Thomas Brooks uses it in the first of his "Seven Characteristics of False Teachers," whom he calls "man-pleasers" (Brooks 1671: 333). Calvin satirizes "the common people" who follow priests, propped up by false prophets defensively saying, "What can we do but to follow our bishops?" During the English Civil War, Jeremiah's prophecy was a useful subterfuge for illegal criticism of the Parliament. Likening the desperate condition of England to ancient Judah, an anonymous poet adopts Jeremiah's voice to denounce the Parliament in the 1648 pamphlet titled "Jeremiah Revived: though in his Prison… Being a mournful representation of the King and his Kingdom's wretched condition." The author writes that the people seek living bread and sound doctrine to refresh the soul, "but are seduced & deceived, for thy Prophets prophesy lies and thine adversaries the Sectaries love to have it so: these have destroyed God's true Religion, cast his public Worship and Service out of their assemblies, rejected his sacred Ordinances, laid violent hands upon his loyal Servant their royal Sovereign the King… beat, imprisoned, and robbed their fellow-subjects." Jeremiah's false prophets become code for members of Parliament, and Judah's gullible people are their Protestant supporters.

"A Wonderful and Horrible Thing is Committed in the Land" is the title of a political tract by Isaac Hillyard first published in New York in 1814 and widely reprinted. Hillyard uses the King James Version's (KJV) seventeenth-century translation "wonderful," which signified causing amazement. In the raging debate over whether the US should continue in the war against Britain, New England clerics preached vigorously against the War of 1812 because shipping interests were at stake. Hillyard, who supported the war, used Jeremiah's words about false prophets proclaiming what people want to hear in order to undermine these preachers: "I know of no other place in Scripture where crimes are prefaced with 'horrible,' and by that I conclude this is one of the highest crimes" (Hillyard 1816: n.p.).

Jeremiah's prophetic image of three different wild animals destroying the inhabitants of Jerusalem (verse 5) is interpreted in Jewish tradition as the four empires that conquered Judah in antiquity. The lion is Babylon, the wolf is Media, the leopard is Greece, and the fourth is Edom, code for the Roman Empire. The midrash offers hope in its claim that Israel's enemies did not defeat her by their own power, but as agents of the divine plan to bring her back from idolatry (Bialik and Ravnitzky 1992: 378).

Jeremiah 6

Two Roads Diverged (6:16)

Jeremiah's metaphor of standing at an intersection to choose a road is embedded in Western imagination. The Parson in Chaucer's *Canterbury Tales* evokes it in his prologue when he prays,

> Jhesu, for his grace, send me wit
> To show you the way, in this journey,

Jeremiah Through the Centuries, First Edition. Mary Chilton Callaway.
© 2020 Mary Chilton Callaway. Published 2020 by John Wiley & Sons Ltd.

> Of that same perfect glorious pilgrimage
> That is called Jerusalem celestial.

His words use the medieval tradition of literal and spiritual meanings to make Jeremiah's "good way" the road on which the pilgrims travel to Canterbury as well as their lifelong journey toward heaven. Jeremiah's "find rest for your souls" becomes for Chaucer's readers "Jerusalem celestial." Two centuries later, the marginal note to 'the ancient paths' in the Geneva Bible limits the path its readers should choose to one: "In which the patriarchs and prophets walked, directed by the word of God: signifying that there is no true way, but that which God prescribes." Although drawing on the Catholic tradition of Nicholas of Lyra, whose gloss had identified Jeremiah's ancient paths as "Abraham, Isaac and Jacob, and other holy fathers," the Geneva Bible's note directs its Puritan readers to look not at the church's tradition but into the word of God – the very Bible in their hands – for Jeremiah's paths. Since the mid-twentieth century, readers have contemporized the paths in the poetic idiom of Robert Frost, "Two roads diverged in a yellow wood." This modern reception of Jeremiah shifts the focus away from the object, the good way of the ancient paths, to the subject's dilemma of choice.

Buying Salvation (6:20)

Jeremiah's indictment of religious leaders who profit from injustice culminates in the rejection of expensive incense and meat sacrifices. Jerome began a long tradition of adopting the words to condemn Christians getting rich by extortion and violence and planning to buy redemption through an offering to the church. *Glossa* reproduces Jerome's indictment in the context of medieval Christianity, and *Bible moralisée* illustrates it with a picture of monks rejecting a bin-full of money from two wealthy donors. Nicholas of Lyra boldly expands Jeremiah's words to indict contemporary priests whose eucharistic offerings, "made acceptable by their faith and vows," are nevertheless rejected by God because they are unfaithful and disobedient to their vows. His words in fifteenth-century printed editions of the *Glossa* had a wide circulation and contributed to the discontent with clerical corruption before the Reformation.

Jeremiah as Fortress and/or Refiner (6:27)

Reception history of this verse offers a historical cross-section of evolving approaches to an unstable text. The image of Jeremiah as metal-worker testing for impurities opens with a noun unique in the Bible (*baḥon*), though the related verb *bahon,* appears at the end of the verse ("and assay their ways"). The first word closely resembles an unrelated rare word for fortress (*bahan,* Isa. 32:14). Early in the text's history, a well-meaning but confused scribe may have glossed Jeremiah's neologism for "assayer" with the common word for "fortress," thereby encouraging readers to understand the verse in light of God's designation of the prophet as a fortress in 1:18. Ancient versions preserve images of assayer and of tower. Septuagint and Vulgate maintain the image of testing, but Targum combines the images: "I have made you as one tested, like a fortified city." Rashi reads "I have made you the strong one and you shall test their way" noting that *bahon* is an expression of strength used by Isaiah. In the thirteenth century, David Kimhi highlights the allusion to Jeremiah as "fortress" in 1:18 and suggests a deliberate wordplay *bahon/bahan* to show that God has made Jeremiah strong for the job of testing his people (Rosenberg 1995: 63). Kimhi's reading uses a literary approach to Scripture that flowered in medieval European Judaism. In response to Christian allegorical readings that found Christ potentially everywhere in the Hebrew scriptures, some rabbinic schools developed sophisticated approaches to the *peshat,* the contextual sense. Kimhi's approach of imagining a human author playing with language to describe the relation between God and Jeremiah anticipates modern biblical scholarship.

English translations, beginning with the 1568 Bishops Bible, combined these two images even when the result was somewhat unclear. The Geneva Bible reads, "I have set thee for a defense and fortress among my people, that thou mayest know and try their ways." A marginal note adapts Jeremiah's task of measuring Judah's compliance with Torah to Puritan theology's interest in distinguishing the redeemed from the damned: "to try out the godly from the wicked as a founder doth the pure metal from the dross." Calvin uncharacteristically supports the Vulgate against the Hebrew Bible, perhaps because the image of the prophet as watchtower and fortress resonates with his own difficult experiences. He explains that God's servants need knowledge gained from watching and "undaunted courage" from being fortified. The KJV "tower and fortress" persisted until 1946, when the Revised Standard Version (RSV) translated it as "I have made you a tester and a refiner," though a footnote offers "fortress" as an alternative reading.

A Den of Thieves (7:1–15)

This chapter and its parallel in chapter 26 bear witness to the complex development of traditions that resulted in the book of Jeremiah. Chapter 7 describes Jeremiah indicting his fellow Judeans for their illusions that the presence of the temple will keep them safe even as they violate the Covenant, while chapter 26 narrates the hostile reaction to this speech. Prophetic attack on sacrifice without obedience had been an established tradition since the eighth century, but speaking against

Jeremiah Through the Centuries, First Edition. Mary Chilton Callaway.
© 2020 Mary Chilton Callaway. Published 2020 by John Wiley & Sons Ltd.

the protective powers of the Temple was a political act. Jeremiah's condemnation of hypocrisy in the fraught political context of sixth-century Jerusalem was a resource for later readers who took courageous stands against powerful religious interests. In their narrative of Jesus driving out the money changers, Matthew, Mark, and Luke present Jesus as acting with the authority of Jeremiah. In all three accounts, Jesus justifies his violent actions by quoting Jer 7:11: "Has this house, which is called by my name, become a den of robbers in your eyes?"

In the fourteenth century, Nicholas of Lyra, whose additions to the *Glossa Ordinaria* later influenced Martin Luther, contemporizes Jeremiah's words with a gloss describing "Christians who build chapels with plundered wealth, or give alms for the work of the church, believing themselves saved by these without amending their faults." With this comment, Nicholas enlists Jeremiah to attack the corrupt use of indulgences in the late medieval church. Dante puts Jeremiah's image into the mouth of St. Benedict to condemn the degradation of Benedictine monasteries: "What once were abbey walls are dens of thieves" (*Paradiso* 22:27). In seventeenth-century philosophical discourse, Jeremiah's words supported a humanist argument for separate authorities of government and religion. Spinoza's *Theologico-Political Treatise* used reason to argue that the two are based on different forms of authority, and thought and speech about religious matters are therefore not legitimately controlled by government. A significant part of his argument is that the revelation of Scripture, whose object is obedience, is distinct from ordinary knowledge. He argues that the Bible therefore is holy and uncorrupted "insofar as it teaches what is necessary for obedience and salvation," otherwise it is merely an object of superstition (Spinoza 1951: 167). Spinoza presents Jeremiah as a philosopher teaching that Solomon's Temple is the Temple of God only when visited by those who defend justice as God requires; otherwise it is just a den of evil-doers. His reception of Jer 7 made it a permanent part of the humanist argument distinguishing divine from human authority.

Jeremiah's requirement for entrance to the Temple in verse 3 takes an unsavory turn in late nineteenth-century American immigration debates. A political cartoon by the popular Frank Beard shows Uncle Sam barring the way to a caricatured Eastern European Jew, laden with bags labeled disease, poverty, and Sabbath desecration. The tag line from Jer 7:3 demanding amendment of ways implicitly equates the Temple with America and the immigrant as one of Jeremiah's law-breaking hypocrites (Beard 1899: n.p.).

A Troubling Contradiction (7:21–24)

The contradiction between Jeremiah's claim that the Lord did not command sacrifices and the multiple instructions for sacrifice in the Torah was a source of discomfort for some and delight for others. Rashi read the plain sense of "the day that I brought them out of Egypt," invoking the obedience required at Sinai in Ex 19:5, while Christians used it to justify their limited adherence to Torah. Jerome made an elaborate distinction between the first tablets of the ten commandments and the elaborate laws of sacrifice given after the incident of the golden calf. The first he called "the true religion of God's commandments" while the second he described as a concession to the people's weakness for eating meat. Jerome's final comment claims that inability to keep the law made "the grace of the Gospel necessary." Jerome's Christianizing explanations of Jeremiah's words are preserved in the *Glossa,* where they became more virulent in the context of anti-Judaism in medieval France. Above "burnt-offerings" (*holocaustomata*) in 7:21 readers see a simplification of Jerome's comment that sacrifices were just an excuse to eat rich meat turned into an innuendo about Jewish greed.

Calvin likewise contemporizes Jeremiah, adding to medieval attacks on Jews his own derision of "pompous exhibitions of ceremonies" in the Catholic church: "For when the Papists perform their trumperies, when the monks and the sacrificing priests fill the churches with their noises, when they practice their childish mummeries, and when they delight themselves with music and incense, they think that God is satisfied, however full of obscenities and filthiness their whole life may be: they are hardened in that false confidence by which the Jews were inebriated."

Jeremiah's taunt to "add your burnt offerings to your sacrifices and eat the flesh… for when I brought your ancestors out of Egypt, I did not command them concerning burnt offerings or sacrifices" contradicts Leviticus 1 and 3, which commands that the meat be consumed in the fire of sacrifice. This contradiction fueled anti-religious writings in the Enlightenment. In his provocative book *Christianity as Old as the Creation: or, the gospel, a republication of the religion of nature,* Deist Matthew Tindal argued that the ethical teaching offered in Christianity is also available in nature and through reason. Religion merely adds superstition, and Jer 7:21 is one of his examples of the superiority of reason to Scripture. In his widely circulated response, *Scripture Vindicated,* Daniel Waterland dismisses Tindal's "short censure upon this text… leaving the Reader to imagine that Scripture contradicts itself" with the claim that "such as attend to the Sense of Scripture more than to the Sound of Words, will easily perceive how the Case stands." With this rejection of Tindal's literal reading, Waterland then appeals to the Enlightenment principle of individual motive: "moral Performances without the Obedience of the Heart, are nothing; and positive Performances without the like Obedience, are nothing: But the sincere obeying of God's Voice in Both, is true religion, and true Morality" (Waterland 1732: 3:67–72). Jeremiah 7:21 thus left its mark on the Enlightenment problem of reconciling reason and religion.

Jeremiah 8

Reading Jeremiah as Science (8:7)

Jeremiah's image of stork and turtle-dove knowing their times drew the interest of seventeenth-century churchmen eager to reconcile the Bible with Enlightenment empiricism. In 1695, Puritan preacher and scientist Charles Morton wrote an influential tract using Jeremiah's words to propose an answer to the age-old question of what happened to birds who disappeared in fall and returned in spring. In *An Enquiry into the Physical and Literal Sense of Jer. 8:7,*

Jeremiah Through the Centuries, First Edition. Mary Chilton Callaway.
© 2020 Mary Chilton Callaway. Published 2020 by John Wiley & Sons Ltd.

Morton drew on his reading of Copernicus's demonstration that the moon is proximate to the earth and his knowledge that gravity and air resistance are not present outside the earth's atmosphere. Noting that storks ascend together in one flock, he proposed that birds fly for two months to reach the moon, or perhaps some closer "aetherial islands," reside there and then fly back to earth (Morton 1744). After a series of arguments based on observation, Morton enlists Jeremiah for corroborating evidence. Translating the Vulgate *tempus iteneris* as the time of their *journey* rather than their coming, Morton argues that Jeremiah describes a significant trip for the birds, and that "in the heavens" signifies a place distinct from the earth. Morton uses Jeremiah to demonstrate the early Enlightenment principle that the book of God and the book of nature are entirely compatible, a lesson he taught in his post as vice president of the newly established Harvard University. Morton's friend Cotton Mather read his work with interest, and gave it widespread dissemination by incorporating its argument into his own commentary on Jeremiah in his *Biblia Americana,* the first Bible commentary published in America.

Jeremiah's birds became part of a defense against the threat of Darwin in John Kitto's popular *Pictorial Sunday Book.* An English Evangelical scholar of the early nineteenth century, Kitto aimed to engage young people in Scripture with a book showcasing the realia of the biblical world. Jer 8:7 offered an opportunity for two full pages of scientific drawings of biblical birds, which Kitto's young readers could pore over instead of the usual texts on offer for Sunday afternoon. Most notable is his reference to *Bridgewater Treatises,* a multivolume work written by astronomers, geologists, naturalists, and doctors to demonstrate "the Power, Wisdom, and Goodness of God, as manifested in the Creation." First appearing in 1833, the *Treatises* were reprinted in revised editions into the 1880s and functioned as a bulwark for Christians looking to natural theology to counter the threats that new discoveries in evolution and geology posed to their faith. For his young readers, Kitto quoted *Bridgewater Treatises* at length on the migration of birds, concluding that it offers "abundant reasons for thankfulness to the Almighty Father of the Universe, for the care he has taken of this whole family, and of his creature man in particular... by the beauty, motions, and music of the animals that are his summer or winter visitors... thus the swallow gladdens the sight both of the Briton and African... What can more strongly mark design and the intention of an all-powerful, all-wise, and beneficent Being?" (Kitto 1845: 119). Kitto enlisted Jeremiah's birds to equip the faithful against the new threats that science posed to religion. His *Pictorial Bible* was reprinted in 1866, seven years after the publication of *On the Origin of Species,* in which Darwin used bird migration in his argument for evolution. In the early twentieth century, Jeremiah's birds were also popular in books of picture puzzles "designed especially for the boys and girls to stimulate a greater interest in the Holy Bible." Here, the influence of Audubon's realistic drawings is apparent on nineteenth-century artist Frank Beard, who makes Jeremiah a source of useful ornithological knowledge in *Picture Puzzles, or How to Read the Bible by Symbols* (Figure 31) (Beard 1903: 22).

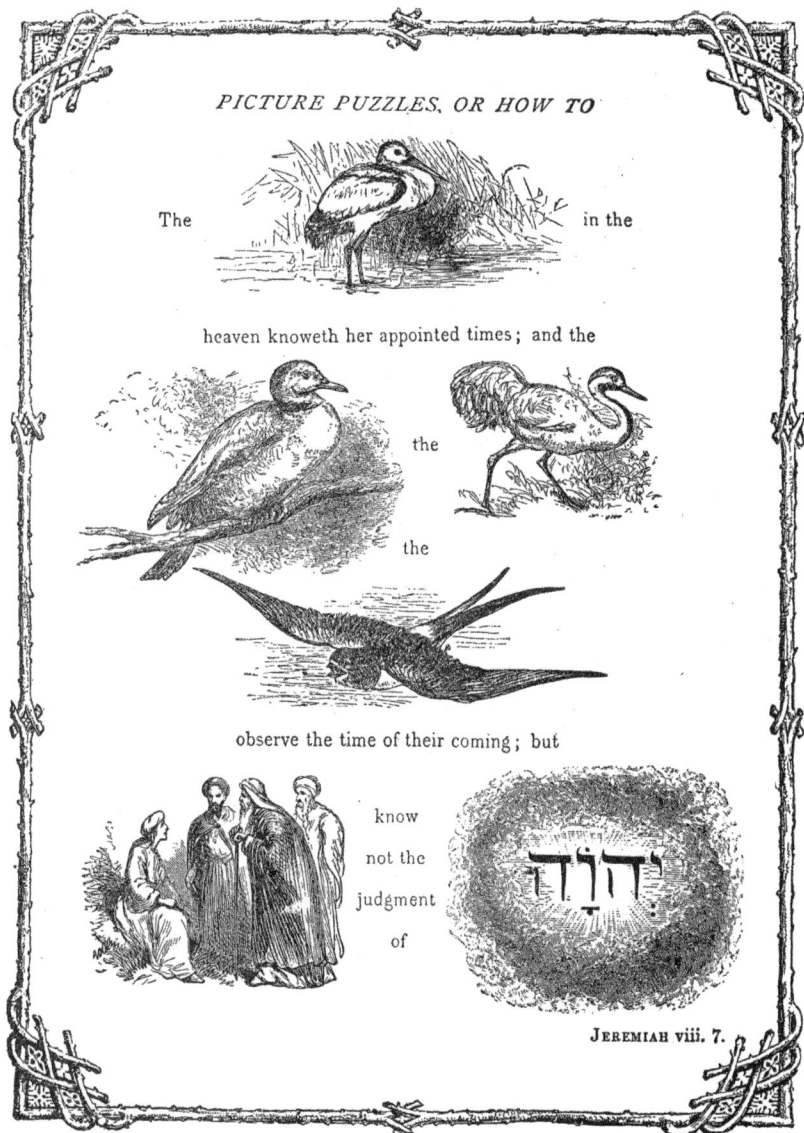

FIGURE 31   Jeremiah's birds. Frank Beard, *Picture Puzzles, or How to Read the Bible by Symbols* (Beard 1903: 22). Private collection.

The Balm of Gilead (8:22)

Jeremiah's metaphor had a long afterlife. Jerome appealed to the balm in Jer 46:11 (of Egypt) and 51:8 (of Babylon) to describe both plain and figurative meanings: "resin [*resina*] of Gilead stands for both repentance and medicine." Targum contemporizes the balm as words of Scripture, and encourages the synagogue congregation not to err as Judah had but to use the balm. Rashi elaborates Targum's tradition with his interpretation of the balm as "righteous men from whom to learn so that they should improve their ways." In the European pogroms of the twelfth and thirteenth centuries, the balm of Gilead becomes the life-giving miracle for which suffering Jews long. David Kimḥi glosses Jeremiah, "Is there no righteous person whose merit moves God to forgive God's people and deliver them?" (Rosenberg 1995: 81).

In early modernity, the balm of Gilead treated a different wound. The first English Bibles translated the rare Hebrew word with *resyn* (Wycliffe 1395) and *triacle* (Coverdale 1535). Balm was introduced by the Geneva Bible (1587), accompanied by a polemical note: "Meaning that no man's help or means could save them… Or else deriding the vain confidence of the people, who looked for help at their Priests, who should have been the Physicians of their souls, and dwelt at Gilead, Hosea 6:8." This note enlists Jeremiah in the Puritan critique of the Catholic church, particularly the clergy, as false balm. The addition of Hos 6:8, which describes Gilead as a city of evildoers, makes clear the political intention of the note.

This reading of the wound as an objective state of the soul for which the balm of grace was the only salve soon became complicated by changing perceptions of the body. Sixteenth-century Europe and England experienced a retrieval of Galen's second-century Greek treatise on the physiology of the four humors that described four basic bodily fluids as sources of four different temperaments, and equated an imbalance of these fluids with all manner of ills both physical and emotional. Interest in Galen's analysis of the body's interior was heightened by the sense of "inwardness" and perception of the human interior as the locus of interaction with God that had been developing since the fifteenth century. In early seventeenth-century English Christianity, therefore, Jeremiah's ancient balm became an important trope in the discourses of preaching, eagerly applied by churchmen of all persuasions. One of the earliest was Thomas Adams, a priest whose service ranged from country church to the Chief Justice of the king's bench. In 1614, he preached "The Sinners' passing-bell, or Physicke from Heaven," in which he determined to "prescribe to these sick times some spiritual physicke." He wanted "to beget in us a sense of the sins we have done, of the miseries whereby we are undone and to rebuke our forgetfulness of God's long-since ordained remedy, the true intrinsic Balme of his Gospel" (Adams 1614: 165–166).

Early seventeenth-century paradoxical fascination with the human interior as both appallingly physical and also the divine dwelling-place is clear in his comments that "inward diseases are as frequent as outward; those by disquiet of mind as those by disquiet of body… Were our bodies but half so diseased as our souls are, a strange and unheard of mortality would ensue… The flesh is made a gentleman, the mind a beggar." He condemns those whose worldly ambition lead them to harden themselves "to prefer Machivelli to Moses, Ishmael's scoffs to Jeremie's tears" (288). Adams also warns his congregation against purveyors of false cures by enumerating the standard enemies of English Christians. "Mahomet would challenge this Balm to grow in his garden, and bids us search for it in his *Choran*. The apostate Jews affirm it to grow in their synagogue, and point us to the Talmud. The Pope plucks us by the sleeve and tells us that he only hath the Balme and shows us his Mass-book" (Adams 1614: 293). Finally, Adams teaches his congregation that Jeremiah's balm is ready to hand to be applied uniquely by each Christian. "Your diseases are as different in your consciences as in your carcasses. This balm is ready, soon had, and cheaply: let not this make you distain it." Adams adopts the developing discourse of the human interior to describe Jeremiah's balm as the Gospel, but tailored to heal the specific sins and sorrows of each individual.

Joseph Hall, bishop of Norwich, reading Jeremiah's balm of Gilead on the more Catholic side of English Protestantism, equated it with the sacraments of the church. His 1646 treatise, *The Balm of Gilead: or, Comforts for the Distressed; both moral and divine,* like Adams used the language of spiritual solace for the individual: "To all the distressed members of Jesus Christ, wheresoever, whose souls are wounded with the present sense of their sins, or of their afflictions, or with the fears of death and judgment, the author humbly recommends this sovereign Balm which God hath been pleased to put into his hands for their benefit, earnestly exhorting them to apply it carefully to their several sores… through God's mercy, they shall find thereby a sensible ease and comfort to their souls" (Hall 1863: 1). This balm of Gilead was the sacrament given by God to bishops and priests to offer Christians whose wounded souls needed healing.

A similar use of Jeremiah's image appears in Robert Herrick's "White-Hall, before the King."

> My God, I'm wounded by my sin,
> And sore without, and sick within:
> I come to Thee, in hope to find
> Salve for my body, and my mind.
> In Gilead though no Balm be found,
> To ease this smart, or cure this wound;
> Yet, Lord, I know there is with Thee

All saving health, and help for me.
Then reach Thou forth that hand of Thine,
That powers in oil, as well as wine.
And let it work, for I'll endure
The utmost smart, so Thou wilt cure.

(Herrick 1823)

Set as an antiphonal prayer to be sung by choir and congregation, Herrick interprets Jeremiah in terms of Anglican theology. The balm is found not in Gilead but "in oil, as well as wine," symbolizing the sacraments of anointing and Eucharist. Hall and Herrick, with their appeal to the experience of individual introspection, were a turning point in the reception of Jeremiah 8:22.

Balm came to seventeenth-century America in an Election Day sermon preached by Thomas Walley in a small Cape Cod town (Figure 32). He describes the sickness as "a Burning Fever amongst us, a Fire of Contention in Towns, in Churches; Fuel is laid upon this fire daily. What Town, or what Church is there that is free from this Disease?" Gilead's balm is "healing Ordinances, the Preaching of the Gospel, the Seals of the Covenant of Grace, Magistrates that would heal the Sicknesses of Sion, and Ministers that mourn for the hurt of the daughter of Sion. Surely this day New-England is sick… the Country is full of healthful bodies, but sick Souls." Walley appeals to "Gilead's Physicians," civil and religious authorities, to effect healing, and to his congregation "to encourage and strengthen the Hearts and Hands of those that God hath in a special manner made Physicians" (Walley 1670: 8, 20). In spite of its description of civil and religious ruin, the sermon overwrites Jeremiah's despair with its American optimism that the balm of Gilead is within reach.

Preacher James Strong understood the balm less politically in his 1676 sermon, "Balm in Gilead, or, A Spur to Repentance," which ends, "Oh how easy were our cure in our deepest straits, could we apply that Sovereign Remedy to our Sin-Sick Souls, which that great Physician hath provided!" (Strong 1676: 37). Strong's sermon perhaps provided the seed for John Newton's hymn, "The Good Physician," whose first stanza includes the lines, "There is but one Physician/Can cure a sin-sick soul" (Newton 2011: 50). Newton's hymn became forever linked with Jeremiah's balm in 1853 when American evangelist Washington Glass renamed the hymn "The Sinner's Cure" and added a chorus: "There is a balm in Gilead/To make the wounded whole/There's power enough in heaven/To cure a sin-sick soul" (Glass 1853: 68–70). His American optimism and Evangelical fervor permanently changed the original sense of Jeremiah's despairing question, "Is there no balm?" to an evangelical assurance that divine balm was always available to those who earnestly sought it.

The image of balm also took on new meaning among African American slaves. In the tradition of slave songs as coded messages, whereby a religious image communicated hope and even means of escape, the balm of Gilead

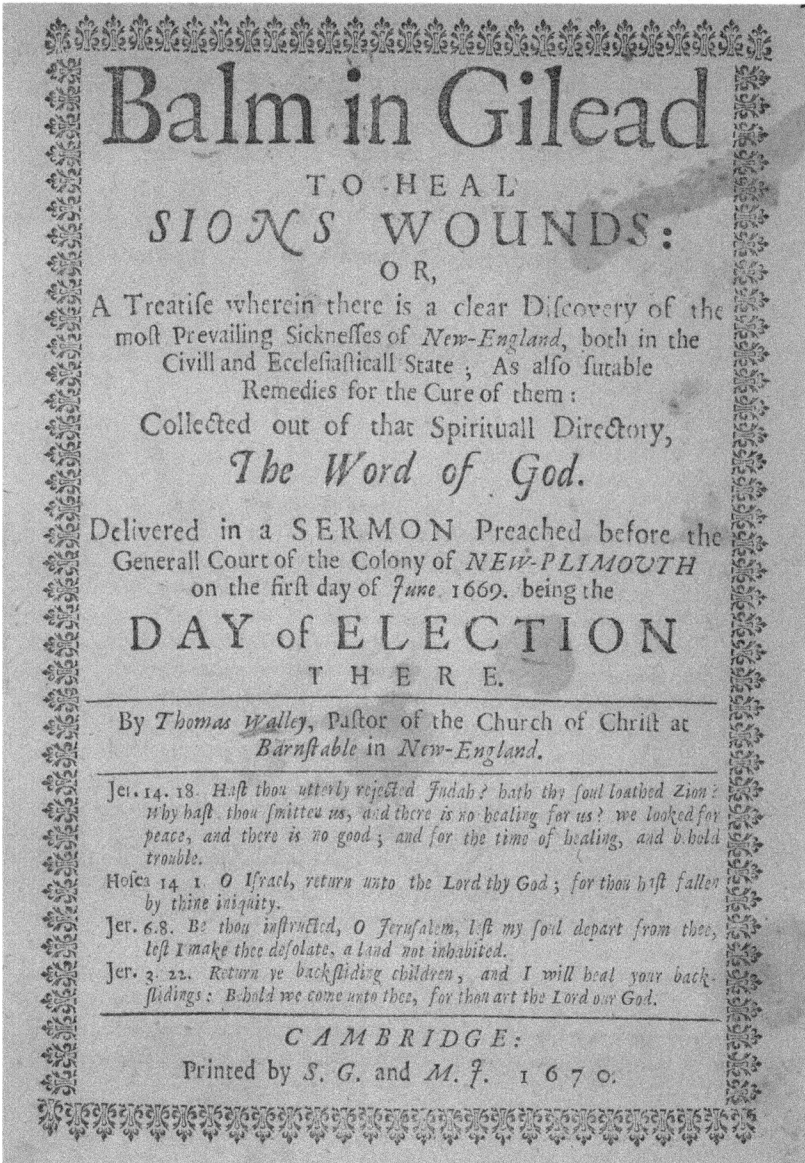

FIGURE 32 Election Day Sermon "The Balm of Gilead" preached in Cape Cod in 1670. Collection of the Massachusetts Historical Society.

sometimes signaled the possibility of freedom. In a 1967 sermon, "The Meaning of Hope," Martin Luther King Jr. wrote, "Centuries ago Jeremiah, the great prophet, raised a very profound question... He noticed the good people so often suffering and the evil people so often prospering. Centuries later our slave forefathers came along, and they too were confronted with the problems of life… They looked back across the centuries, and they took Jeremiah's question mark and straightened it into an exclamation point. And they could sing 'there is a balm in Gilead!" (Baldwin 1992: 64–65).

Straightening Jeremiah's question mark into an exclamation point began with the English Puritans and was later transformed in America. A different reception comes from Edgar Allen Poe, who invokes Jeremiah's balm as an elusive easing of the torment of a lost love. Near the end of his poem "The Raven" Poe addresses the unwelcome bird as "prophet" and asks, "Tell me truly, I implore: Is there – is there balm in Gilead? – tell me – tell me, I implore!" The raven's response of "Nevermore" echoes the despair of Jeremiah's original words in a Victorian key.

A Fountain of Tears (9,1,18)

Across the centuries, Jeremiah's tears remain one of his most distinctive traits, and the history of their reception reveals creative use in times of trauma as well as changing images of God. In four occurrences (Jer 9:1,18; 13:17; 14:17), God's tears for Judah are also the prophet's, in part giving rise to the ancient tradition that Jeremiah was also the author of Lamentations. In the second century CE, Jeremiah's fountain of tears became a new source of consolation. In the Jewish

Jeremiah Through the Centuries, First Edition. Mary Chilton Callaway.
© 2020 Mary Chilton Callaway. Published 2020 by John Wiley & Sons Ltd.

apocalyptic writing 2 Baruch, Jeremiah's scribe is introduced with the authority of the prophet's words, "I, Baruch, went to the holy place and sat on the ruins and wept and said: O that my eyes were springs, etc." The ruins on which he sits are the second Temple, but the telescoping of time that makes the destructions of 586 BCE and 70 CE a single event highlights the early Jewish belief that biblical history provides the pattern for contemporary events. Jeremiah's ancient image gave solace to Jews after the Roman army had reduced the temple to ashes. Jewish tradition still evokes Jeremiah's tears in the lectionary readings for the solemn liturgy on the Ninth of Ab, which remembers the two destructions of Jerusalem, as well as medieval persecutions and the Shoah. The Torah reading from Deut 4:25–40 is paired with Jer 8:13–9:23, making the ancient prophet's tears a contemporary expression of somber reflection on Jewish history.

Through the centuries, Jeremiah's tears have represented the pain of many who in their own time saw corruption of what they considered true religion. Chrysostom evokes them when he refers to his sorrow over the "grievous wound" of Christians putting wealth over care for the poor and even their own souls. His use of Jer 9:1 is an invitation to Christians to weep, and to change their economic priorities (Wenthe 2009: 81). Jeremiah's tears are evoked by Peter Damian not over money, but sex. During the church reforms of the eleventh century, this relentless reformer wrote to Pope Leo IX asking him to address the problem of pederasty and sodomy among the clergy. The lengthy letter *Liber Gomorrhianus,* written in 1049, includes "a tearful lamentation for the soul steeped in the mire of impurity." He compares this soul of the corrupted priest or monk to the violated sanctuary of the temple (Lam 1:4) because it has become "addicted to the filth of impurity." Asking "how shall I weep for you, unhappy soul?" he answers by adopting the persona of Jeremiah: "With the prophet, 'let my eyes run down with tears...' Truly the daughter of my people has suffered a grievous injury, because a soul that had been the daughter of the Holy Church has been cruelly wounded by the enemy of the human race with the shaft of impurity" (Damian 1990: 33).

Jeremiah's voice inspired twelfth-century poet Eleazar ben Judah ben Kalonymus from Worms to write this *kinah,* a lament for the martyrs of the 1096 Crusade:

> O that my head were water, and my eyes a fountain of trickling tears, that I might weep all the days and nights of my life for my slain children and babes, and the old men of my congregation,
> ... and indeed cry aloud: 'Woe! Ah! Alas! And weep greatly, even more copiously.
> My eye shall weep bitterly, and I will go to the weeper's field, and I will make those who are distraught and bitter of heart weep with me for the fair maidens and

tender children who were enwrapped in their school books, and were dragged to the slaughter... they were trampled and cast down like the dirt of the streets...
... my eye shall weep bitterly.

(Laytner 1977: 142)

Kalonymus' lament was incorporated as a *piyyut* into the Maḥzor, the prayer book used on the Ninth of Ab.

In the early twentieth century, when the dream of a Jewish homeland in Palestine was becoming a political reality, poet A.M. Klein used Jeremiah's tears as an outdated relic of Judaism's traumatic past.

> You cherished them as ancient gems, those tears
> Of Jeremiah; through that night for you
> These only shone; these jewels of the Jew,...
> But now forget them! Spurn them! The dawn nears!
> The Dawn arises, tinted white and blue.

(Klein 1990)

Saul Rabino's 1935 lithograph (Figure 33) merges Jeremiah as ancient prophet and timeless Jew mourning for his people. Rabino had emigrated from his native Russia in the previous decade, and watched with alarm as anti-Semitism rose in Europe after 1929. He created this image of Jeremiah in the year Germany passed the Nuremberg Laws that revoked citizenship from Jewish citizens. Rabino included the text of Jer 9:1 in English and Hebrew as part of the lithograph.

The fountain of tears became marks of sincerity in early modern writing. The Geneva Bible warns that Jeremiah's "great compassion toward his people" because of the destruction hanging over them speaks directly to contemporary readers, "a special note to discern the true Pastors from the hirelings" – "True ministers are lively touched with the calamites of the Church so that all the parts of their body feel the grief of their heart." These hirelings are Catholic and Church of England clergy, who in contrast to true shepherds (Puritans) do not care about the destruction of their people. This new understanding of Jeremiah's tears as signs of authenticity will become widespread by the nineteenth century. Meanwhile, in the seventeenth century, the tears again play a political role, this time against the Puritans in the English Civil War. In 1649, John Quarles published *Fons Lachrymarum: or a Fountain of Tears: from whence doth flow England's Complaint*. The volume includes a paraphrase of Lamentations, using Jeremiah's voice to bemoan England's troubles when a Parliament controlled by Puritans turned against Charles I and banished the Royalists. Like Jeremiah, the personified England alternates between private grief and public indictment:

OH THAT ONE WOULD MAKE MY HEAD WATER, AND MY EYES A FOUN-
TAIN OF TEARS, THAT I MIGHT WEEP DAY AND NIGHT FOR THE
SLAIN OF THE DAUGHTERS OF MY PEOPLE.' (JEREMIAH)
מי יתן ראשי מים. ועיני מקור דמעה. ואבכה יומם ולילה את
חללי בת עמי. (ירמיהו)

FIGURE 33   Saul Rabino, "Jeremiah." 1935 lithograph. Private collection.

> O that my eyes were Oceans, that I may
> Drown all my sorrows in one stormy day
> Oh grief to speak it: Are there not a sort
> Of willful people that can make a sport
> At others ruins, whose pretended zeal
> Hath bred much mischief in this Common-weal?
> Are there not those that would pretend to be
> Reformers, yet deform a Monarchy?
>   (Quarles 1649: 16)

The trope of Jeremiah's fountain of tears gives cover for Quarles' dangerous political tract (Figure 34).

Young Royalist Jeremiah Rich likewise showed political cunning in *Jeremiah's contemplations on Jeremiah's lamentations, or, Englands miseries matcht with Sions elegies* (1648). As he reflects on the bitterness of the English church's sorrow, and the parallels between "these two Ladies, Israel and England, the Darlings of God, the Daughters of Heaven" he "could not choose but sometimes

FIGURE 34   Title page of *Fons Lachrymarum* with illustration of King Charles. The Huntington Library.

bathe my Subject with my Tears, and following the precedent of the sad Prophet, wish that mine eyes were Rivers of Waters" (Rich 1648: 1–2). Puritans like John Trapp also invoked Jeremiah's tears. He comments on 9:1, "A wonderful wish of this weeping Prophet, and to be taken up by God's faithful Ministers, considering the woeful condition of their perishing people, posting to perdition… Such waters will be turned into wine, at the wedding-day of the Lamb; for which purpose also they are kept safe in God's Bottle, Psalm 56."

In the nineteenth century, Jeremiah's tears become the authenticating mark of a caring heart. In *Beacon Lights of History*, a fourteen-volume history of the world from "the old pagan civilizations" to America, New England minister John Lord includes an entire chapter on Jeremiah, "a sad and isolated man." It begins with a Victorian tribute to the prophet's exquisitely tuned emotions: "Jeremiah was not bold and stern, like Elijah, but retiring, plaintive, mournful, tender. As he surveyed the downward descent of Judah, which nothing apparently could arrest, he exclaimed: 'Oh that my head were waters…' Is it possible for language to express a deeper despondency, or a more tender grief? Pathos and unselfishness are blended with his despair. It is not for himself that he is overwhelmed with gloom, but for the sins of the people" (Lord 1883: 2:362). Jeremiah's tears contribute to the Victorian ideal of sentiment as the manifestation of a finely tuned soul. In the mid-twentieth century, biblical scholars demonstrated that the trope of weeping and the language of Jer. 8:18 – 9:1 is heir to ancient Near Eastern poetry of lamentation; the tears are not necessarily autobiographical, but represent traditional language of mourning. In spite of this scholarly recognition of the ancient precursors of Jeremiah's tears, early modern and nineteenth-century receptions became virtually inscribed into the text by readers' assumptions and by editorial notes. With their implications of emotional sensibility and interiority, they make Jeremiah into a contemporary of his readers.

Late twentieth-century readers used the passage to support a theology of divine pathos and the image of God suffering, although this idea had been rejected in antiquity. The Hellenistic Jewish translators of the Septuagint had dismissed the anthropomorphic image of a weeping deity that made the Lord seem like one of the Greco-Roman gods, and rendered verse 18 to describe the people weeping because of the snake bites described in the previous verse. Targum similarly rejected the anthropomorphism by adding "says the prophet" to verse 18 to ensure that readers did not imagine God weeping. The sole ancient witness to the tears as divine appears to be Jerome, who boldly instructs readers of Jer 9:1, "This can be understood equally about the character of God and of the prophet." In 1962, Abraham Joshua Heschel introduced the English-speaking world to the idea that Jeremiah, among other prophets, shared in and embodied God's suffering, which he called divine pathos. Rejecting the philosophical ideal of God as unmoved mover, Heschel argued that biblical texts frequently portray the Lord suffering with and because of the covenanted people. Contemporary scholars have used Heschel's work to give new meaning to Jeremiah's tears. One writes, "The tears of God are part of the imaginative literary enterprise that ruptures theological language. The book's lead character breaks from his role as dominating, proud male, cruel architect of war, and for a brief poetic interlude embodies and participates in the pain of the people… Divine tears suggest a deity who vacates sovereignty and historical transcendence, at least temporarily, and relates in vulnerability to the other, the daughter of my people" (O'Connor 1999: 401).

Internalizing the Prophet's Cry (9:2)

John Henry Newman gives Jeremiah a nineteenth-century voice in his poetic elaboration of verse 2. His poem Jeremiah, written December 22 1832, "off the coast of the island of Galita," is torn by despair like Jeremiah's mixed with guilt that a Christian should express such feelings. Newman had just been forced out of his position at Oriel College, Oxford after ten years of service, because the provost thought the pastoral care he gave his students was not part of an academic tutor's responsibilities. Embarking on an extended trip in the southern Mediterranean with a close Oxford friend, he wrote a number of short poems combining biblical and personal themes. Jer 9:2 is included as a superscription to this poem.

> 'Woe's me!' the peaceful prophet cried,
> 'Spare me this troubled life;
> To stem man's wrath, to school his pride,
> To head the sacred strife!
> 'O place me in some silent vale,
> Where groves and flowers abound;
> Nor eyes that grudge, nor tongues that rail,
> Vex the truth-haunted ground!
> If his meek spirit err'd, opprest
> That God denied repose,
> What sin is ours, to whom Heaven's rest
> Is pledged, to heal earth's woes?'
> (Newman 1891: 309)

For Newman, the legacy of Jeremiah is the cry of a sensitive spirit thrown into controversy and rejection. His nineteenth-century sensibility found in the prophet a kindred spirit and validation for a complaint against God.

Death Climbs in the Windows (9:21)

Jeremiah's unsettling description of death climbing through the windows gives new life to ancient Near Eastern religious traditions. In the Baal epic, architects of Baal's new palace do not want to cut windows for fear that Mot (death) will enter them. In Old Babylonian texts, the Babylonian demon Lamashtu is described entering through windows to infect the young (Lundbom 1999). Jeremiah's ominous image of death stealthily entering his unwitting victims' windows captured the imagination of Christian theologians, who made it an allegory of temptation entering a person. Gregory Nazianzus writes that the prophet warns against "the occasions which the Evil One gets against us from sources within ourselves: bringing upon us the death that comes through the windows, as Holy Scripture says, that is, through the senses" (Gregory 1890: Oration 27). For Jerome, "This can also be understood spiritually, because death

from sin enters through all the senses to destroy the soul." St. Caesarius of Arles revises Jeremiah in a sermon for clergy he is training: "Death is come into your souls through your windows." He explains, "Whenever there is something beautiful to see, sweet to taste, flattering to hear, pleasant to smell, or soft to touch, if we are careless about it we allow the purity of our soul to be corrupted by the evil desires which overtake it. Then is fulfilled in us what the Prophet says: 'Death is entered through your windows.' Indeed, through our five senses, as through doors, either death or life enters our soul" (Caesarius 1956: 207, 327).

This patristic reception of Jeremiah's image takes on new life in seventeenth-century England when John Trapp warns his Puritan readers, "The Ancients give us warning here to see to our senses (those windows of wickedness) that sin get not into the soul thereby, and death by sin." A visceral image appears in a popular seventeenth-century "Dance of Death" titled *Icones Mortis Sexaginta Imaginibus* (Figure 35). The engraving shows a figure on a ladder stealthily entering a house resembling a human face, with two casement windows representing the eyes. The sinister figure surreptitiously enters the stone tower through one eye/window, while someone within unwittingly opens the other. This image adds to the traditional spiritualizing interpretation of Jeremiah a distinctive seventeenth-century ambivalence about the human interior as both exquisitely spiritual and appallingly corporeal (Schoenfeldt 1999: 24). Here patristic warnings are translated into contemporary idiom to make Jeremiah's witness especially personal and unnerving. The engraving also captures the warning against false security in the Geneva Bible's marginal note: "Signifying that there is no means to deliver the wicked from God's judgements: but when they think to be most sure, & most far off, then they are soonest taken."

Superstition and Science (10:2–5)

In late antiquity, Jewish scholars used Jeremiah to refute fears of celestial omens that were common in Gentile cultures where Jews lived. One of the earliest, *Mekhilta de Rabbi Ishmael,* invokes Jer 10:2 to allay fears of lunar and solar eclipses, and later *Tosefta Sukkah* 2:6 teaches that when Israel is occupied with Torah they need not worry about omens. The Babylonian Talmud also uses Jeremiah to buttress Jews against the dominant culture's belief in astrology.

Jeremiah Through the Centuries, First Edition. Mary Chilton Callaway.
© 2020 Mary Chilton Callaway. Published 2020 by John Wiley & Sons Ltd.

"How on the basis of Scripture do we know that Israel is not subject to the stars?" The answer is in Jer 10:2, with the explanation that the gentiles are dismayed, but the Israelites are not (Neusner 2006: 10, 41, 283).

Jeremiah's indictment of idolatry is also used against superstitious fears of natural phenomena in seventeenth-century England. In 1605, a practical compendium, *The Doctrine of the Bible: or, Rules of Discipline,* answers the question, "Is it not lawful to fear the conjunction of Stars and Planets?" with "No, because the Lord in these words [Jer. 10:2] hath forbidden it." In the extended debates about whether the work of Copernicus and Kepler undermined Christian faith, English cleric John Swan was a persistent voice arguing that thinking Christians had an alternative to the false choice between an atheism that rejected the Bible and superstitious beliefs that ignored the new science of astronomy. When predictions of a solar eclipse in 1652 were causing "a great noise among the common people," Swan preached a sermon on Jer 10:2, "Signa Coeli: The Signs of Heaven" to model a proper Christian attitude to such phenomena. Arguing that superstition about natural astronomical occurrences was a form of idolatry, based on pagan fears that the gods have evil designs on humanity (Jer 10:5), he mocked those "old doting women" who feared the moon (Swan 1653: 8). Swan uses Jeremiah to show that the faithful should not fear the eclipse, a natural phenomenon, but remain "quiet in mind" in the knowledge of God's goodness. Jer 10:2 served as buttress for the seventeenth-century challenge of accommodating the Bible to scientific discoveries, offering comforting evidence that the Book of Nature and the Book of God agree. Swan's sermon had influence beyond the immediate crisis of the eclipse, as it was published and bound with his *Calamus Mensurans: the Measuring Reed, or The Standard of Time* (1653), in which he correlated biblical events with secular history to show that the Bible is rational. Swan was not alone in using Jeremiah to dispel superstitious fears about the impending solar eclipse; William Ainsworth's *The Marrow of the Bible,* which summarized the biblical books in poems of rhyming couplets, devotes one couplet to each chapter of Jeremiah. All of Jeremiah 10 is represented by the signs of the heavens in Jer 10:2. "Fear not heavens signs, can idols with God vie? 'Gainst foolish Pastors God aloud doth cry" (Ainsworth 1652: 120). Ainsworth invokes Jeremiah to liken pagan nations fearing signs in the sky to superstitious English clergy preaching fear about an impending solar eclipse.

Verses used to encourage Christians to accept aspects of contemporary culture in the seventeenth century can have quite a different meaning in the twenty-first. Jeremiah's description in verse 3 of "the heathen" cutting a tree out of the forest, setting it up, and decorating it is for some a clear indictment of Christmas trees; some zealous readers see in Jeremiah's words a clear prohibition of this practice as idolatrous. One minister of the Worldwide Church of God compares Christmas trees to similar heathen practices in the time of Jeremiah. "If the prophet were alive today, he wonders, what would he say about all the Christmas trees now decorating our Christian homes and Christian churches? Would he sound a similar alarm...? He probably would."

Who Will Not Fear You? (10:7)

These words of praise become part of a curse in the medieval *piyyut* (liturgical poem) recited during morning prayers on Yom Kippur. Fifteen short poems elaborating Jeremiah's words ask God to take vengeance against those who have persecuted Jews. The violent verbs exhorting God to punish persecutors (swallow, lop off, crush, shoot, make bleed) bear witness to the suffering of medieval Jews in Christian lands. The following verses describe idols of silver and gold with clothing of blue and purple, which may have evoked for medieval Jews the Christian statues outside cathedrals that they had to walk by daily (Yuval 2006: 119–121).

Wise Fools (10:12–16)

Jeremiah's contrast between divine wisdom and the stupidity of idols and their makers proved useful to theologians defending their writings against secular critique. Origen devotes an entire homily to the paradox of foolish wisdom in verses 12–14 to show Jeremiah prefiguring Christian theology: "Establishing the world by wisdom" in verse 12 signifies Paul's reference to Christ as the wisdom of God (I Cor 1:24). As a philosopher, Origen is captivated by Jeremiah's paradox that "every human has become foolish from knowledge," and explains Jeremiah with Paul's assertion that the best human wisdom is worthless compared to divine foolishness (1 Cor 1:25). Yet if the Word is the wisdom of God, who emptied himself in this life (Phil 2:7), then wisdom is an empty vessel, and divine wisdom is foolishness! Origen thus understands Jeremiah's words to mean the opposite of their plain sense precisely because he wants to invoke a paradox: by joining themselves to the Word, who is both the wisdom and the foolishness of God, Christians become foolish, which is to say wise. The homily ends with a kind of doxology, "And my Savior and Lord has assumed all of the opposites so that by the opposites he might dissolve the opposites, and we might be made strong from the weakness of Jesus and we might know wisdom from the foolishness of God, and after we have been introduced in these things, we might be able to mount up to wisdom, to the strength of God, Christ Jesus" (Origen 1998: 84). In the struggle of early Christian theologians to align the Gospel with Greek philosophy, Origen slyly elides logic and poetry. His homily uses Jeremiah to merge Plato's idea of true being that dwells above the heavens yet is accessible to the soul (Phaedrus 247) with the Christian teaching that divine wisdom is, paradoxically, accessible in the Word made flesh.

Origen's use of Paul to explain Jeremiah's rejection of human wisdom is repeated in Jerome's commentary and preserved into the fifteenth century in the *Glossa*. Nicholas of Lyra adds an apparently pious comment that "human knowledge is not able to reach such things." While this may have appeared to be a warning to readers on the eve of the Renaissance, Nicholas actually uses Jeremiah to invite scientific investigation by suggesting that "human knowledge" properly belongs to such earthly matters. Erasmus likewise subversively adopted Jeremiah's words because the contrast between human wisdom and the Gospel suited his own humanist polemic against the persistent influence of scholastic theology. *In Praise of Folly* (1504) uses satire in which a personified Folly praises herself, perhaps ironically imitating Wisdom in Sirach 24, to unmask the church's dominant theology as based on discredited scholastic philosophy rather than the true wisdom of the Bible. Erasmus quotes Jer 10:14, "Every man is brutish in his knowledge" and 9:23, "Let not the wise man glory in his wisdom," asking "And why, good Jeremiah, would you not have a man glory in his wisdom? Because, he'll say, he has none at all." Erasmus enlists Jeremiah for his argument that the apparent folly of the Gospel surpasses the wisdom of human learning, especially theology. Erasmus endorsed *Devotio moderna*, the late medieval lay movement that emphasized private prayer, spiritual reading, and a life based on imitation of Christ, and his reception of Jeremiah subtly supported its preference for daily practices over learned theology.

Hans Holbein the Younger, who illustrated *In Praise of Folly* with woodcuts, included a tongue-in-cheek portrait of Erasmus as Jeremiah. Holbein's caricature may be related to Erasmus' ironic words in the paragraph preceding his use of Jeremiah: "I could wish also that I might change my countenance, or that I had on the square cap and the cassock, for fear some or other should impeach me of theft as if I had privily rifled our masters' desks in that I have got so much divinity." Holbein's woodcut did in fact change Erasmus' countenance to that of an old man with a beard, the iconographic image of Jeremiah, yet wearing the square Geneva cap of a sixteenth-century cleric (Figure 36). While Holbein's joke plays on the received tradition of Jeremiah as dour curmudgeon to poke fun at his friend Erasmus, it also highlights Jeremiah as critic of the contemporary church.

FIGURE 36 Caricature of Erasmus as Jeremiah. Hans Holbein 1509. Print Collection, The New York Public Library.

Humans Are Not Masters of Themselves (10:23–24)

Verse 23 reinterprets the ancient wisdom tradition of Proverbs. Although Proverbs 19:21 and 20:24 contrast human frailty with divine omnipotence, Jeremiah's proverb used human frailty as an appeal for divine mercy. The Dead Sea Scrolls offer an early use of Jeremiah in pious prayer. Members of the Qumran community followed a rule that included a prayer acknowledging human efforts are but dust without God's help, quoting Jer 10:23 with this explanation: "Their justification belongs to God, and from his hand comes perfection of way" (Dupont-Sommer 1962: 102).

Chrysostom was troubled by the popular reception of Jeremiah's words as an excuse for moral failures: "This saying is bandied about everywhere – in households, in market places, in town, in cities, on land and sea and islands. Wherever you go, you will hear many quoting this: Scripture says, 'Peoples' ways are not their own.'" Incensed at seeing the verse invoked as a cover for moral carelessness or indifference, Chrysostom preached an entire homily on it, which became famous for articulating his "norms, definitions, and unalterable doctrines" for interpreting Scripture. Likening Scripture to a highway that is in some parts smooth and level but in others steep and rough, he reminds his congregation of the need for "an alert and attentive spirit" when navigating a steep road bordered by precipices. Jeremiah's words pose a hazard if they "slacken the hands of the zealous, extinguish enthusiasm, and deepen the apathy of the faint-hearted." Chrysostom's remedy to losing one's way on the road of Scripture was to pay attention to the context of a verse and even more to the consequences of one's interpretation. Chastising those who "mangle the limbs" of Scripture, he draws attention to Jeremiah's next verse as evidence that we do have free-will to choose our road, but only with God's help can we reach our destination (Chrysostom 2003: 8).

Medieval Jewish interpreters beginning with Rashi noted that the Hebrew reads "*the* man's way," therefore referring to a specific man. That man was Nebuchadnezzar, who did not invade Jerusalem by his own will, but because God directed his will in order to punish King Zedekiah. By extension, the verse suggests that tyrants who persecute Jews in any era have no real power of their own; as Rashi writes, "If it were not for your command, the enemy would have no power to destroy your Temple." During the first crusade this actualization of Jeremiah's words might bring a measure of comfort by suggesting that God remained in control and would ultimately destroy evil doers.

The most persistent influence of the verse is an affirmation of divine design in human life. Describing spiritual formation, John Cassian observes that the ordering of an aspirant's life does not result from his own efforts, but comes graciously from God: "The way of man is not his…" (Cassian 1994: 326). Calvin saw scriptural support for the theology of predestination of the elect. Jeremiah teaches us that "men greatly deceive themselves, when they think that fortune or the issue of events is in their own hands: for though they may consult most wisely, yet things will turn out unsuccessfully, unless God blesses their counsels… The Holy Spirit has by this one passage checked the boldness of those who claim for themselves more than they ought." Jeremiah's words, together with Prov 16:9, are pithily paraphrased in Thomas à Kempis' popular *Imitation of Christ*, "Man proposes, but God disposes." Shakespeare seemed to have had a similar reception of Jeremiah's proverb in mind when he wrote Hamlet's words, "There is a divinity that shapes our ends, rough-hew them how we will."

For George Herbert the verse was a model of genuine spiritual feeling. Writing to a country parson about preaching in 1633, Herbert suggests "turning often, and making many apostrophes to God," because "some such irradiations scatteringly in the sermon, carry great holiness in them. The prophets are admirable in this… And Jeremy, after he had complained of the desolation of Israel, turns to God suddenly, O Lord! I know that the way of man is not in himself, &c." (Herbert 1842: 18).

Correct Me, O Lord (10:24)

Targum relates the verse to the afflictions of the Jewish community: "The Lord has brought sufferings upon them, but with clement judgement: let not your anger be strong against them, lest they be few" (Hayward 1987: 80). Augustine's famous prayer, "Give me chastity and continency – but not yet!" echoes Jeremiah's bold intimacy in prayer. Calvin uses the verse to argue that God's punishment of the elect must be distinguished from his wrath executed against the reprobate. Although the outward appearance may be the same, punishment is evidence of paternal love that intends to correct in love, attending to what sinners can bear rather than what they deserve. This is an important text in the controversy over the meaning of suffering among the elect of the church.

Pour Out Thy Wrath (10:25)

These words, found also in Psalm 79:6–7, play a dramatic role in the Passover Seder. They are recited after the blessing at the end of the meal, when the door is flung open to the outside. This gesture probably began in the late twelfth or thirteenth century, when Christians accused Jews of using the blood of Christian children in their Seders. In the culture of mob violence during Holy Week, opening the door could be a gesture to prove that Jews had no secret rituals; the prophetic curse was aimed at those who incited pogroms with their slanderous lies (Gaster 1949: 65–66; Yuval 2000: 123–124). Some contemporary Haggadas change the prayer to "Pour out your love on the nations who know you, and on the kingdoms who call your name, for the good which they do for the seed of Jacob, and they shield your people Israel from their enemies."

Let Us Put Wood in his Bread (11:19)

The scheming words of Jeremiah's enemies in verse 19 presented both a problem and an opportunity for centuries. At issue are three Hebrew words that inscrutably say, "Let us ruin the wood with its bread." The Septuagint's literal rendering, "Let us throw wood into his bread" made this verse a prize for developing christologies of the early church. The verse begins with images of the prophet as an innocent lamb led to the slaughter by his enemies, and its resonance with Isa

Jeremiah Through the Centuries, First Edition. Mary Chilton Callaway.
© 2020 Mary Chilton Callaway. Published 2020 by John Wiley & Sons Ltd.

53:7 prompted Christians as early as the second century to read Jeremiah's words as prediction of the passion. Tertullian uses the verse in his ironic treatment of Marcion's claim that the body on the cross was not Jesus' true body: "It would contribute very well to the support of Marcion's theory of a phantom body, that bread should have been crucified! But why call his body bread, and not rather some other edible thing, say a melon, which Marcion must have in lieu of a heart! He did not understand how ancient was this figure of the body of Christ, who said himself by Jeremiah, 'let us cast the tree upon his bread', which means, of course, the cross upon his body" (*Against Marcion* 4.40; see also 3:19). Early Christian apologists also used Jer 11:19 as evidence that the crucifixion was not a sign of failure, but fulfillment of the divine plan revealed to the ancient prophets.

Origen implicitly criticizes this simple typology, noting that applying the enemies' scheming words to the crucifixion "is a matter requiring careful thought." He begins with a new christological interpretation: the bread is Jesus' teaching, by which we are nourished; the wood is the cross, by which the Jews wanted to bring scandal to Jesus' teaching. Origen then draws on Exodus to proclaim "a paradox": the wood has in fact made the bread better. Just as Moses put wood into bitter water to make it sweet for the Israelites (Ex 15:25), so the wood of the passion entering the Word made its bread sweeter to the world. Through the wood of the cross the bread "received power" and thus the word of Jesus' teaching is spread throughout the whole inhabited world. Origen concludes that the wood as symbol of the passion makes the bitter water of the Law sweet: "For I say that the Law not understood is bitter water, but whenever the wood of Jesus comes in and the teaching of my Savior finds a home, it is made sweet; and the Law of Moses read and understood becomes most pleasant" (Origen 1976: Homily 10.2, my translation). By applying Hellenistic allegorical ways of reading to the Old Testament, Origen altered its status in the church from vexing problem to treasury of images. In sum, the problematic verse 11 becomes an opportunity for Origen, as it explains Jesus' passion, predicts the spread of his teachings to the Gentiles, and reveals a hermeneutic for understanding the Old Testament.

Jerome explains simply, "This is clearly the cross on the body of the savior; for he himself said, 'I am the bread that comes down from heaven.'" Even the Antiochene exegete Theodoret, who usually favored the plain sense, adopted the christological reading. After showing that the lamb led to the slaughter describes Jeremiah, Theodoret abandons the plain sense when he comes to "wood in his bread": "This is not completely applicable to the prophet: how could wood be put on his bread? By contrast, the verse bears very closely on Christ the Lord: he called his own body bread (John 6:51). This bread they nailed to the wood, thinking to snuff out his memory." Only Ephrem the Syrian advocated the plain sense, "Let us throw poison in his bread" (Kannengiesser 1974: 893).

The christological interpretation of verse 19 was essentially inscribed into the Vulgate and persisted throughout the Middle Ages in the interlinear notations of the *Glossa Ordinaria*. The word cross floats over the word wood, and "the body of the savior who is bread" appears above bread. This reception of Jeremiah as signifier of the Mass is visibly displayed on the central portal of the north transept at Chartres Cathedral, where ten biblical figures are arrayed in facing pairs and Jeremiah is paired with Samuel. Samuel holds a knife and a lamb, in preparation for sacrifice; Jeremiah presents a large round disc engraved with a cross. Like a priest, he covers one hand with a drape of his robe so that it does not touch the host while he raises the other hand in benediction. In this set of sculptures greeting worshippers at Chartres, Jeremiah figures the sacrifice of the Mass encoded in Jer 11:19.

The link between this verse and the cross is visually reinforced in the fourteenth-century *Biblia Pauperum,* where the scene of Jesus carrying the cross includes Jeremiah looking down sadly with the words of 11:19 on a banderole beneath him. The verse also figured prominently in three liturgies of Holy Week. Reading Jer 11:18–20 on the Tuesday of Holy Week reinforced the typology of Jeremiah as Christ, but also of the prophet's enemies as Jews. On Wednesday, monks at Lauds heard Jer 11:19, followed by a hymn about the crucifixion. Singing Jer 11:19 in the Responses during Tenebrae on Maundy Thursday echoed the liturgy's dual focus on the bread and the cross. Such readings inflamed passions that led to Holy Week pogroms throughout Europe. Rashi counters the Christian reading with his comment emphasizing the plain sense of the verse: "Let us put poison into his food."

Two explosive issues were at stake in the reception of Jer 11:19 in the sixteenth century. The first was the contested meaning of the sanctified bread and wine. Of the received interpretation described above, Calvin comments, "The ancients perverted this passage in the most childish manner when they applied it to the body of Christ. The Papists too, at this day, boast wonderfully of this allegory, though they make the most absurd use of it; for they seek to prove by it that bread is converted, or, as they say, transubstantiated into the body of Christ... We see how extremely absurd this is; and it must appear ridiculous even to children." The second issue was the fierce debate about legitimate ways of interpreting Scripture. For the Reformers, the Catholic tendency to ignore the plain sense of Scripture in favor of allegories was writ large in Jer 11:19. Calvin insists the meaning is clear if taken in context: "Let us give him wood instead of bread; and this, by its hardness will hurt his teeth, ulcerate his throat, and cannot be digested so as to become nourishment." Significantly, Calvin grants that Jeremiah was a type of Christ, but rejects "the similitude of his body." His hermeneutic was still medieval enough to use some typology, but his Protestant sensibilities rejected the traditional Catholic interpretation.

The medieval reception of Jer 11:19 was explicitly rejected in Protestant translations. Luther's 1534 translation describes destroying the tree with its sap, the Coverdale Bible reads "We will destroy his meat with wood," and the Geneva Bible's rendering, which became standard, is "Let us destroy the tree with the fruit thereof." The marginal note explains that this means destroying both the prophet and his teaching. Matthew Poole's *Annotations* admits no alternatives to the Protestant reading: "The sense is plain, Let us not only put an end to his prophesying, but to his being also." The ancient Catholic tradition persisted in the Douay translation, "Let us cast wood on his bread," with the marginal note, "By consent of all Churches (saith St. Ierome) this is spoken of Christ." Today no English Bible translates the Hebrew of Jer 11:19 literally, but follows the King James Version's interpretive paraphrase, "Let us destroy the tree with its fruit."

Reception shifted decisively in the nineteenth century, when Heinrich Ewald designated Jer 11:18–12:6 the first of Jeremiah's six personal lamentations (*Selbstklagen*) (Ewald 1868: 179) (see Introduction p. xx).

A Lawsuit Against God (12:1–4)

The long reception history of the Job-like protest in verse 1 illustrates a Jeremiah slipping between censure and praise. For centuries the protest was an embarrassment and an offense to the faithful. In the fifth century, John Cassian reassured his monks that Jeremiah "never professes to doubt about the justice of God" (Cassian 1994: 373). Rashi, always mindful that biblical characters provide moral examples, suggested that the prophet's complaint is

Jeremiah Through the Centuries, First Edition. Mary Chilton Callaway.
© 2020 Mary Chilton Callaway. Published 2020 by John Wiley & Sons Ltd.

in fact pious: "I wish to argue with you so that you will let me know your way."
The potential danger of the verse increased in a Renaissance culture cele-
brating human capabilities. Calvin insists that an affirmation of divine justice
in 11:21–23 immediately precedes Jeremiah's accusation: "This order ought
to be carefully observed; for when we give way in the least to our passions we
are immediately carried away, and we cannot restrain ourselves within proper
limits and continue in a right course. As soon then as those thoughts, which
may draw us away and lessen the reverence due to him, creep in, we ought to
fortify our minds and to set up mounds, lest the devil should draw us on far-
ther than we wish to go. It is not only for the sake of others he speaks thus, but
also to restrain in time his own feelings." For Calvin, the present disorder in
the world can lead to dangerous questioning of God's just rule and sinful
inclinations. Jeremiah therefore teaches us to frame worldly observation and
dangerous emotions with praise of the creator and to restrain our impious
emotions.

By the seventeenth century, Jeremiah's prayer resonated with contemporary religious sensibility that held self-abnegation and spiritual confidence in
tension. When Parliament removed the leadership of the established church,
the Bishop of Salisbury adopted Jeremiah's protesting voice in his *Private
forms of prayer, fitted for the late sad-times.* The subtitle set the stage: "An
humble and submissive expostulation with God, when the Orthodox and
loyal Clergy were so mercilessly silenced, by that bloody Usurper, who by
Proclamation forbid them either to preach or pray publicly in Churches; or
privately in Families, not suffering them so much as to teach School." The
prayer for January 30, the day on which Charles I was executed in 1649,
begins, "O That thou wouldst hear me, O God, that thou wouldst hear me
once more, who am but Dust and Ashes, while I presume, yet with all humble
Reverence, to expostulate with thee the great and Glorious God, in behalf of
this persecuted and afflicted Church!" (Duppa 1660: 55). The bishop merges
Jeremiah's challenge to divine justice with Abraham's questioning in Gen
18:27 to give biblical support to his protest to God when the king, the titular
head of the church, was beheaded.

Puritans prayed Jeremiah's complaint as fervently as their opponents.
A scene in *Pilgrim's Progress* describes Pilgrim's dream of Christiana and her
boys approaching the gate to the Celestial City, threatened by a barking
"filthy cur." When the master finally comes down, Mercy falls to the ground
crying out, "Righteous art thou," reciting all of Jer 12:1 before adding her
complaint, "Wherefore dost thou keep so cruel a Dog in thy Yard, at the sight
of which such Women and Children as we, are ready to fly from thy Gate for
fear?" (Bunyan 1861: 155). Isaac Watts similarly justified his prayer of complaint with Jeremiah's words. Toward the end of his life he wrote a treatise

questioning the doctrine of the Trinity, prefaced by a "solemn address to the Deity" that is both an assertion of his belief and a justification of his questioning. It begins, "Righteous art thou, O Lord, when I plead with thee concerning thy judgments. Permit me, O my God and Father, to plead with thee concerning the revelations of thy nature and thy grace, which are made in thy Gospel: And let me do it with all that humble reverence, and that holy awe of thy majesty, which becomes a creature in the presence of God." Watts' friends persuaded him to burn the treatise lest it irreparably harm his reputation and the popularity of the hundreds of hymns he had composed. Only one copy survived.

Jeremiah's prayer takes on the voice of a destitute man in nineteenth-century England:

> Dark is my place and chill the night,
> No fire have I, nor candlelight;
> Come down, make good to me Thy word,
> O humble and right piteous Lord…
> Righteous art Thou – and I am poor,
> And know not good, but long endure;
> I charge it not on Thee, blest Lord,
> Enough for all Thy fields afford;
> But some have much and other none,
> The weak are robb'd, the mean undone…
> O Lord, how long? O Lord, how long?
> (*Sacred Songs.* 1880: 181)

Like the novels of Dickens, the poem protests abusive labor practices in nineteenth-century London. Jeremiah gives voice to the indictment of the pious wealthy who pray for the poor while exploiting them to get rich.

Another approach to finding treasure in discomfiting words comes from John Henry Newman. In a sermon preached at his Oxford parish titled "Jeremiah: A Lesson for the Disappointed," Newman eloquently holds up the prophet's many trials as a means to the spiritual prize of resignation. Jeremiah's "perplexity at the disorder of the world, and the success of the wicked" was part of his repeated disappointments that led finally to his "chastened spirit and weaned heart" (Newman 1891: 132–134). Newman identified with Jeremiah from his own bitter experiences with university and church, and he found in Jeremiah's complaint evidence that the crushing blows of failure prepare the hearts of God's servants to receive divine love.

A half century later, English Jesuit Gerard Manley Hopkins gives Jeremiah a modern voice in his famous sonnet of 1889, whose title is the first words of Jeremiah's complaint:

"Thou art indeed just, Lord, if I contend
With thee; but, sir, so what I plead is just."
"Why do sinners' ways prosper? And why must
Disappointment all I endeavor end?"

The figure of Jeremiah is also reflected later in the poem's contrast between nature's fecundity in springtime and the poet as time's eunuch. By the memorable last line, Jeremiah's complaint becomes in Hopkins' anguished prayer the plea of one thirsting for God's presence within: "Mine, O thou lord of life, send my roots rain." The reception of Jeremiah's challenge to God evolved down the centuries from discomfort to grateful recognition as ideas of interiority and then of self-expression took root.

Shameful Revenues (12:13)

English abolitionist William Wilberforce passionately invoked this verse as "a glowing coal" in a 1789 speech to the House of Commons. Arguing against slavery, he "cannot help remembering those terrible words that look you in the face out of the book of the prophet Jeremiah like a glowing coal, 'They shall be ashamed of your revenues...'" For Wilberforce, Jeremiah's words burned in the present, indicting the shameful profits of slave traders who trafficked in human lives. About 90 years later, Judge Robert Pitman invoked Wilberforce's use of Jeremiah to argue against "taxation of the liquor traffic" as a morally bankrupt means of battling intemperance (Pitman 1878: 396).

Jeremiah's Loincloth (13:1–11)

The startling images of Jeremiah's two 400-mile round trips to enemy Babylon, as well as God's "loins," disturbed readers. Did the prophet really make the long trek to the Euphrates twice to hide and later to retrieve a loincloth? Twelfth-century Jewish philosopher Maimonides, influenced by Aristotle and driven by his own scientific mind to make the Bible compatible with human reason, wrote, "This was allegorically shown in a vision; Jeremiah did not go from

Jeremiah Through the Centuries, First Edition. Mary Chilton Callaway.
© 2020 Mary Chilton Callaway. Published 2020 by John Wiley & Sons Ltd.

Palestine to Babylon, and did not see the Euphrates" (Maimonides 1904: 2:46). In the sixteenth century, Protestant reformers also struggled with their commitment to the plain sense of Scripture when some texts were simply an affront to reason. Calvin dismisses those who believe that Jeremiah went to Babylon with a disdainful, "What can be imagined more absurd?" Merging the medieval solution with contemporary anti-Jewish polemic, he writes:"It is then what Rhetoricians call a scene presented to the view; though the place is not changed, yet the thing is set before the eyes by a lively description. Thus the Prophet, as the Jews were deaf, exhibited to their view what they would not hear." Calvin's solution is widely disseminated in the margin of the Geneva Bible: "Prophecies uttered in fables have more force to persuade, than only words." Nevertheless, when the Enlightenment brought attacks on the Bible as an affront to human reason, Jer 13 was a prime offender. In *Christianity as Old as the Creation* Matthew Tindal argues that it was one of the commands to prophets which, "if taken according to the Letter, seem unworthy of God, as making them act like mad Men, or Idiots" (Tindal 1730: 1:229). In a spirited defense of Scripture against Tindal and the Deists, English theologian Daniel Waterland devoted ten pages in *Scripture Vindicated* to the problem of Jeremiah's trip, defending the literal sense with ingenious arguments that included a sophisticated linguistic suggestion that the Hebrew does not say "Euphrates," but rather the name of a town near Jeremiah's home. Still, he allows that the episode can reasonably be understood as prophetic vision or parable, and need not trouble thoughtful Christians.

Although images of Judah as a loincloth around God's hips and of God undressing discomfited many, Origen relished them. Linking Jeremiah's loincloth with the vision of what appear to be the hips of the enthroned deity in Eze 1:26–28, Origen uses neo-Platonic thought to interpret Ezekiel's fire below God's hips and amber above. The hips are the seat of generation, represented by fire and belonging to the earthly realm; the realm above the hips, represented in Ezekiel by pure amber, is the destination of the soul's ascent, the higher body of God. Origen uses his dualistic ideas of mystical ascent from the corporeal (fire) to the spiritual (amber) to explain the significance of loins: it is our task "to pass from our present condition in what is below to one in which we become a body of God above." Origen's interpretation was rejected by Jerome, but it influenced medieval mysticism.

Origen did offer an allegorical interpretation of the loincloth around God's hips that persisted throughout medieval Christianity. He wrote that after God had discarded the rotted loincloth, he wove a new one for himself "from the pagan nations." This is the church, which must remain "worthy of the hips of God." Origen's allegorical exegesis of God's loincloth was of interest because it addressed the nettlesome problem of Jewish fidelity to their covenant with God that so troubled medieval Christians. *Glossa* paraphrases Origen: "The unworthy Jews stood apart from God, and were thrown off by him; he did not remain unclothed, but wove for himself out of the gentiles the garment of the church." This anti-Jewish reading is highlighted in *Bible moralisée*, which pairs roundels of biblical scenes with allegorizing interpretations. The illustration accompanying Origen's words shows Jesus handing the new loincloth to a crowned female figure representing the church, his back to the downcast female figure of the synagogue.

Peter Damian also found opportunity in the *Glossa's* new loincloth. Rejecting a literal interpretation of Jer 13, he develops a spiritual allegory to combat resistance to the church's new requirement of clerical celibacy. If the church is the garment of Christ and worn by all its members, he argues, the loincloth, closest to the body, represents the clergy, who are brought more intimately into the service of God. The damp area of the rocks where Jeremiah hides the loincloth is "the portion of the clerical order that is living under the shadow of passionate desire and in a flood of lust." Like the decaying loincloth, "clerics become wholly rotten as in their drunkenness they fill their fat bellies with wine, and drown themselves in a flood of filthy lust and befouling passion. And so, they are good for nothing, for the more portly they become, the worse is their decay, as their souls waste away in horrid squalor" (Damien 2005: 156). The clergy's intimacy with God requires them to be unsullied, like Jeremiah's new loincloth.

In art from the eleventh century through the middle ages the loincloth was an image of the last judgment. The iconography is consistent: the prophet stands in or near flowing water, reaching into a crevice to place or remove a rolled-up piece of cloth. The first known representation of the scene is in the *Roda Bible* (1020) from Catalonia. Jeremiah stands at river's edge holding a rolled cloth near a rock. His gaze directs the viewer to a graphic and violent scene of Jerusalem attacked, signifying the loincloth as the ruined people. A similar iconography appears in scenes of the last judgment on the west front of the cathedrals of Notre-Dame and Amiens. The connection is obscure, but one art historian finds a clue in the medieval tradition of the four rivers of Paradise symbolizing the four cardinal virtues. The Euphrates is justice, and in the coded language of medieval art, the scene of Jeremiah with the loincloth at the Euphrates represents divine justice, displayed in the past through salvation history and anticipated in the Last Judgment. In this context, the loincloth represents all Christians, warned in the *Glossa* to cling to the Lord lest they be cast off into destruction. The link with judgment is also evoked in the stained glass of Ste.-Chapelle, which pairs the loincloth scene with images of drunken men from Jer 13:12–14, as Jeremiah's warning to the inhabitants of Jerusalem becomes a warning to medieval French Christians.

Bernhard Duhm's 1901 historical-critical commentary objects to the text's non-realistic tone, saying, "Only one who thinks of the prophet as a marionette could accept such a narrative device." He likens it to the "outlandish and naïve fiction of midrash" of I Kings 13, which has "no ingenuity, no feeling of real life, neither depth of inner life, nor truly instructive ideas, but is written for a simple audience." Duhm's anachronistic comparison with midrash and his discomfort with the loincloth image offers insight into his reception of Jeremiah. His evaluation that "For understanding Jeremiah himself, it has no value at all" reflects late nineteenth-century interest in and construction of Jeremiah's inner life and spiritual struggles. This German Protestant reception distances Jeremiah from anything Jewish.

By the late 1960s, in America, the exotic loincloth had become an asset. In the liturgical drama for teenagers *Are You Joking, Jeremiah?* by Lutheran pastor and biblical scholar Norman Habel it becomes a dirty undershirt. A hip Jeremiah says, "I wear a dirty undershirt!… Remember that I'm called to be the Word of God alive. I live his waiting wrath, I show his doom by all my ugly antics" (Habel 1967: 57). Jeremiah's image of underwear, far from an embarrassment, becomes a means by which Jeremiah engages teenagers with the Bible

Jeremiah's Tears (13:17)

In the political struggles between Royalists and Puritans in seventeenth-century England each party adopted the image of the weeping Jeremiah when persecuted by the other. An anonymous engraving shows the ancient prophet praying with a Bible in a contemporary English prison (Figure 37). Jeremiah's tears express the despair, at different times, of Puritans and Royalists who see the ruined figure of their church and state (see also commentary on 9:1).

Unsettling Images (13: 22–27)

Jeremiah's imagery in verses 22 and 27 surprisingly adopts words originally used by Nahum against the enemy city Nineveh to indict Jerusalem. Their sexual imagery puzzled and embarrassed translators for centuries. In the eleventh century, Peter Damian read the words literally, combining the image of the violated female with that of death stealthily coming in the windows (9:20–22) to condemn women living as mistresses of priests. The Geneva Bible took the opposite approach, directing readers away from sexual thoughts to other sins by offering a metaphor in its marginal note: "Thy cloak of hypocrisy shall be pulled off, and thy shame seen." In 1792, Brown's *Self-Interpreting Bible*

FIGURE 37 Jeremiah weeps in the English Civil War. Harley MS 5987 61 (engraving) / British Library © British Library Board. All Rights Reserved/Bridgeman Images.

used Jeremiah to condemn slavery: "An allusion to the barbarous custom of carrying away captives naked – a cruelty still practiced (alas! still practiced by some states called Christian!) against the miserable inhabitants of Africa. When, Lord, shall these fetters of Japheth fall from the arms of Ham?"

In the late twentieth century, the American Bible Society's Good News Bible (1992) seemed to direct Jeremiah's indictment of Judah at contemporary women with its translation: "If you ask why all this has happened to you – why your clothes have been torn off and you have been raped – it is because your sin is so terrible." The widely used New International Version (1973, 2011) renders verse 22, "And if you ask yourself, "Why has this happened to me?" – it is because of your many sins that your skirts have been torn off and your body mistreated." Evangelical preacher Eugene Peterson's contemporary version, *The Message* (2002), removes Jeremiah's sexual imagery: "Do I hear you saying, 'What's going on here? Why me?' The answer's simple: You're guilty, hugely guilty. Your guilt has your life endangered, your guilt has you writhing in pain." Feminist scholars have drawn attention to the harm that biblical images of Israel as a promiscuous and violated female have done, and in the *Africa Study Bible* (2017) Renita Weems addresses the dangers of images that can normalize sexual violence and make it appear permissible and even divinely sanctioned.

The Inn and the Manger (14:7–9)

The people's prayer that God rescue them from the drought devastating Judah includes the plea, "Why should you become like a stranger in the land, or like a traveler turning aside for lodging?" An early reception of Jeremiah's image appears in Luke's infancy narrative. The people's plea that God not be like a stranger but be in the midst of them is echoed in Luke's midrashic detail of the fully booked inn in Bethlehem (Luke 2:7). The newborn Jesus is not found "like

Jeremiah Through the Centuries, First Edition. Mary Chilton Callaway.
© 2020 Mary Chilton Callaway. Published 2020 by John Wiley & Sons Ltd.

a traveler turning aside for lodging," but in a manger. (Luke combines Jeremiah's image with Isa 1:3, where the manger symbolizes Israel's failure to know her God.) This midrashic use of Jeremiah highlights the baby as a sign of God's new relationship with humanity, not as traveler but native among them. Some three and a half centuries after Luke, Jerome also read Jeremiah's words as a figure of the incarnation, but to emphasize that Christ would lodge on the Earth briefly, as one passing through. This use of Jer 14:8 persisted throughout medieval Christianity. *Glossa* interprets Jeremiah's "stranger" (*colonus*) with an interlinear note quoting John 1:10 ("He came to his own, but they did not receive him"). Above Jeremiah's traveler (*viator*) a note directs readers to Psalm 19:5, which they would recognize as the antiphon for the Magnificat on the fourth Sunday of Advent. Medieval Christians clearly knew Jeremiah's image as a foreshadowing of Jesus' nativity as well as a source of anti-Jewish polemic. A late fifteenth-century French illuminated manuscript of Augustine's *City of God* that describes the Scriptures' foreshadowing of Christ (7.32) vividly displays the link between Jeremiah and the manger. Floating in the sky above a traditional Lucan manger scene is Jeremiah, holding a banderole clearly displaying Jer 14:8 in Latin.

Saints Alive (15:1)

The image of Moses and Samuel interceding before God fueled the fierce Reformation debate about whether Christians should pray through dead saints. The Geneva Bible translates, "Though Moses and Samuel stood before me," and highlights the hypothetical in its marginal note: "Meaning, that if there were any man living moved with so great zeal toward the people as were these two, yet he would not grant their request." The Douay Rheims (1610) counters by presenting

Jeremiah Through the Centuries, First Edition. Mary Chilton Callaway.
© 2020 Mary Chilton Callaway. Published 2020 by John Wiley & Sons Ltd.

the intercessions as a plausible event: "If Moses and Samuel shall stand before me," and interprets in its introduction, "Though Moses and Samuel should pray for this people…" A marginal note warns readers, "The Geneva Bible is corruptly translated contrary to the Hebrew and Greek." At issue is whether to understand the Hebrew imperfect as conditional (Geneva) or future (Douay). Calvin argued at length that while Christians ought to pray for each other, and the prayers of the saints for others are effective, this refers to living members of the church. "Extremely ridiculous are the Papists, who apply this passage to dead saints." Their reading of Jeremiah is "as good as the braying of an ass."

Woe is Me, My Mother (15:10)

Jeremiah's anguished cry became for centuries a mark of identity. Philo adopts it as the boast of one living faithfully in a hostile environment where a man of virtue is an unwelcome outsider: "'O my mother, how great didst thou bear me!' Great, not in power of body, but in strength to hate evil." His mother is Wisdom. Philo continues by inverting Jeremiah's despairing phrase, the Septuagint's "My strength has failed amid those who curse me," to the triumphant "nor did my strength fail from their curses." He enlists Jeremiah in contesting the dominant culture of polytheism and hedonism, and in his own spiritual battle. As son of his mother Wisdom, Philo's Jeremiah combats "the neighbors of his soul," fears, passions, and vices. Jeremiah, "possessed by divine inspiration" as Philo introduces him, models the life of wisdom and virtue as "a man of combat." (*Confusion of Tongues*: 13:49, 12:44). Philo's unusual appropriation of Jeremiah's mother as Wisdom influences Christian theology for centuries, beginning with Origen, who cites it with approval to address the theological controversy over Jesus' nature. Reading Jeremiah as a figure of Christ, Origen asks whether it is insulting to attribute the words, "Woe is me" to him. Citing Jesus weeping over Jerusalem (Luke 19:41), he concludes, "The Savior says, 'Woe is me, mother,' not to the extent he is God, but to the extent he is man" (Origen 1998: 140). Origen seized the opportunity to affirm the humanity of Christ alongside his divinity some 80 years before the Council of Nicaea would establish it as the church's teaching, turning Jeremiah's problematic words into a theological asset, and his reading persisted for centuries. Medieval readers of the *Glossa* saw *sapentia* (wisdom) written over "my mother" and were instructed in an adjacent note, "Not that we divide the persons, as the wicked do, but that he is both son of God and human."

In early modernity, Jeremiah's complaint posed a dilemma for Christians. Luther draws strength from the prophet who "had the same experience" as his own. Being a man of strife and contention characterizes those who fight against a corrupt church whose head "lay in the mire like a sow that snores when people gently scratch it behind the ears" (*LW* 23:291). The Geneva Bible annotation likewise urges readers to identify with Jeremiah, who "showeth what is the condition of God's ministers: to wit, to have all the world against them, though they give none occasion." For Protestants in exile in Geneva or lying low in England, this contemporizing made Jeremiah a fellow minister, and their own persecution a badge of authenticity. Calvin writes, "All faithful teachers are here reminded, that if they perform their office strenuously and wisely, they will surely be loaded with many calumnies, and be called tumultuous, or morose, or disturbers of the peace." John Milton, protesting against his burden of writing against the bishops of the church in 1642, writes, "This is that which the sad Prophet Jeremiah laments, 'Woe is me my mother...' And although divine inspiration must certainly have been sweet to those ancient prophets, yet the irksomeness of that truth which they brought was so unpleasant to them, that everywhere they call it a burden" (Milton 2007: 85). Yet Jeremiah's outburst also discomfited readers. Calvin calls it "evidence of an intemperate feeling," while Puritan scholar Matthew Poole instructs readers of his popular commentary that "The prophet in this verse cannot be excused from a great measure of passion and human infirmity" and warns them not to imitate Jeremiah.

Robert Burns gives Jeremiah a Scottish brogue to express the alienation of the poor in eighteenth-century rural Scotland:

> Paraphrase of Jeremiah, 15th Chap., 10th verse.
> Ah, woe is me, my mother dear!
> A man of strife ye've born me:
> For sair contention I maun bear;
> They hate, revile, and scorn me.
> I ne'er could lend on bill or band,
> That five per cent. might blest me;
> And borrowing, on the tither hand,
> The deil a ane wad trust me.
> Yet I, a coin-denied wight,
> By Fortune quite discarded;
> Ye see how I am, day and night,
> By lad and lass blackguarded!

Changing Fashions in Prayer (15:15)

Jeremiah's cry for vengeance discomfited Jewish and Christian readers for centuries. Targum Jonathan adds the poignant words used in Jewish prayers in time of trouble, "Let my memory come before you." It then softens Jeremiah's call for

God to bring retribution on his persecutors to "Let me afflict my enemy and pay back my pursuers." Jerome translates the Hebrew that clearly means "avenge me" with "deliver me" and the *Glossa* offers an interlinear explanation, "Blessed is the conscience that suffers dishonor for the Lord." Only in the sixteenth century did Christians read what the Hebrew said. The Geneva Bible accurately translates, "Avenge me," adding a cautionary note, "He does not speak this out of a desire for revenge, but wishing that God would deliver his Church from them who he knew to be hardened and incorrigible." Calvin writes that though "the prophet seems here to have been more angry than he ought, for revenge is a passion unbecoming the children of God," in fact he is justified. Distinguishing between private and public feelings, passions of the flesh, and zeal of the spirit, Calvin judges Jeremiah a model of "right zeal" because he excluded private feeling and "subjected himself to the guidance of the Holy Spirit." Here is a reading of Jeremiah designed to help Christians recognize and manage their unacceptable feelings.

At the turn of the twentieth century, after centuries of censure, Jeremiah's prayer became a spiritual treasure. When German scholar Heinrich Ewald described the words as part of his second "outpouring of the heart," they began to change from embarrassment to genuine feeling honestly expressed. Though somewhat disapproving, Ewald judged the words pardonable given Jeremiah's persecution (Ewald 1878: 69). A few decades later, Bernhard Duhm adopted Ewald's description, but introduced the term Confession and pronounced the words commendable for their integrity and spiritual power (see Introduction). Within about 20 years, John Skinner's *Prophecy and Religion* made Duhm's evaluation the norm in the English-speaking world. He vividly describes Jeremiah's struggle, as though he were an Englishman, between "fidelity to his prophetic commission and the natural feelings and impulses of his heart" (Skinner 1922: 210). Skinner describes Jeremiah as the one in whom "the perennial fountain of true piety – the religious receptivity of the individual" was unsealed, and as the beginning of "individual religion." Gerhard von Rad later concludes that Jeremiah's intimacy with God, his maturity of self-expression, and freedom in admitting his own failure manifests "the human spirit at its noblest" (von Rad 1965: 174). This reception of Jeremiah as model of interiority, individualism, and honest prayer appears in the annotations of many study Bibles. Reception of Jeremiah in the twentieth century, with its sympathetic psychological insight and treasuring of the individual, had replaced the moral censure of centuries.

Is Jeremiah Blasphemous? (15:18)

Jeremiah's charge that God is unreliable troubled readers for centuries. Septuagint reads, "It [my wound] has become like false water, without faithfulness." Using this Greek, Origen posits three meanings for Jeremiah's wound: his bodily suffering, Jesus' crucifixion, and "all of the just in whom he receives a severe wound." Reading "false waters" as a wound that "does not remain but passes away," Origen thereby turns verse 19 from a complaint into an assurance that suffering is temporary. Jerome adopts this interpretation, without attribution, as a useful model for Christian endurance of the wound of persecution: "In this I am consoled: it will be like water, false and passing by. Just as water flows and disappears, so every attack made by our enemies disappears because of your aid." Jerome's interpretation has an elegiac quality, describing his own situation near the end of his life when he was alone, bitter from the rejection he had endured, and displaced from his beloved monastery by a fire. He is "full of reproach and awaiting the sentence of my judge, which will show when the end comes that all sorrow and bitterness have disappeared like flowing water." Jerome's reassuring explanation of Jeremiah's discomfiting accusation persisted until the sixteenth century in the margin of the *Glossa,* where a note above "deceitful waters" instructs, "In this is consolation, for just as water flows away, so enemies' attacks will perish with your aid." The *Glossa* also softens Jeremiah's words with Jerome's suggestion, probably learned from rabbinic sources, that the speaker is a personification of the ruined Jerusalem, bitterly remembering the false words of prophets who promised her prosperity.

While medieval Christians were reassured that Jeremiah's shocking words did not mean what they seemed to say, medieval Jews reading Hebrew scripture knew otherwise. Rashi emphasized the plain sense, describing the deceitful waters from Jeremiah's perspective: "like one cut off from safety, because you have handed me over to suffer." He drew attention to Jeremiah's harsh words by glossing the Hebrew "deceptive" with the French *faillir* (failing), ensuring that his readers would understand. Rashi's comments would have made the prophetic cry resonate with the experience of his readers during the First Crusade.

When the first English translations of Jeremiah from Hebrew appeared, Christians were startled by Jeremiah's accusation against God. The 1568 Bishops Bible translates, "Wilt thou be as one that is false?" and the Geneva Bible reads "Wilt thou be me as a liar?" with a marginal note warning, "It appears that in the saints of God is imperfection of faith." A cross-reference to Jer 20:7 highlights the danger of Jeremiah's "impatiency" and "weakness." In his popular commentary, Matthew Henry also presents Jeremiah as a warning against expressing negative feelings: "It is the folly and infirmity of some good people, that they lose touch of the pleasantness of their religion by the fretfulness and uneasiness of their natural temper, which they humor and indulge, instead of mortifying it." Matthew Poole more sympathetically explains, "Jeremiah, though a great prophet of the Lord, was (as Elijah) a man subject to like passions with other men... It is a hard thing not to see, and yet believe." In the Enlightenment, Matthew Tindal's *Christianity as Old as the Creation* dismissed Jeremiah's accusation as nonsense: "Did not the Scripture suppose

Reason was able to teach Men of the meanest capacity that God could not be deceived himself, or deceive us, the prophet Jeremiah would not have said [this]" (Tindal 1730: 1:230).

In the twentieth century, words that had discomfited readers for centuries became a credential of prophetic authenticity. Writing about the test of true prophecy, Reinhold Niebuhr notes, "It is instructive that the same Jeremiah who spoke so uncompromisingly against the false prophets tried to return his prophetic commission to God. He was not certain that he was worthy of it, and he doubted his courage to maintain the integrity of the word of God against the resistance of a whole generation which demanded security from religion and rejected the prophet who could offer no security on this side of repentance… Thus the Church can disturb the security of sinners only if it is not itself too secure in its belief that it has the word of God. The prophet himself stands under the judgment which he preaches. If he does not know that, he is a false prophet" (Niebuhr 1965: 17). In the 1950s, J.P. Hyatt presents Jeremiah as exemplar of good mental health: "Jeremiah had the wisdom and ability to give utterance to his doubts and fears, even to shake his fist at God. From one point of view this may seem sacrilegious. Modern psychology would say, however, that it was a very salutary and wholesome thing for Jeremiah to do, as it was likewise for Job. Had Jeremiah kept his conflicts wholly within himself and not given expression to them, they might have caused him to break down" (Hyatt 1958: 69).

A Divine Reprimand Reconsidered (15:19)

The play on "return" captivated Origen, who read it as a promise to individuals. It is a "mystery" that refers to his theology of *apokatastasis,* the restoration of all souls to their original home with God (Origen 1998: 155–156). This included the possible rehabilitation of Satan, an idea that enraged Origen's contemporaries and contributed to their condemnation of him as a heretic. Jewish tradition preserved in Targum Jonathan contemporized God's response for the synagogue congregation: "If you turn the wicked to righteousness, you will establish my pleasure." Jerome, eager to refute Origen's reading and cognizant of Jewish tradition, interprets, "If you bring people back from sin I will bring you back to joy, and you will stand before my face like the angels." Invoking an eschatological image of angels around God's throne from Rev 8:2, Jerome replaces Origen's Gnostic restoration of souls with an orthodox image of the obedient servant rewarded with the beatific vision of God's face. The *Glossa* writes Jerome's interpretation over verse 19, encouraging medieval Christians to bring sinners into the church. Early modern Protestants resonated their own perilous situation with readings of Jeremiah as a preacher tempted to despair; the Geneva Bible explains in the margin, "If you forget these carnal considerations and faithfully execute your charge." Puritan Matthew Poole likewise warns readers that verse 19 is "rebuking his diffidence and distrust in God."

Prophetic Celibacy (16:1–4)

The command to celibacy posed problems and opportunities that fueled debates about sexuality. Jerome begins with the plain sense, invoking Paul's advice to Corinthian Christians not to marry, "for the time is short" (1 Cor 7:28–31). This is to spare the prophet "being tortured by the sufferings of a wife and children" when the Babylonians invaded. Yet Jerome cannot resist offering God's command to Jeremiah as evidence for his unpopular position that

Jeremiah Through the Centuries, First Edition. Mary Chilton Callaway.
© 2020 Mary Chilton Callaway. Published 2020 by John Wiley & Sons Ltd.

virginity is spiritually superior to marriage, and that widows should not re-
marry. He was engaged in a bitter fight against Jovinian, a Roman Christian
who argued that baptism, not ascetic practices, brought spiritual transformation. In this fierce debate about Christian life in the cosmopolitan culture of late
fourth-century Rome, Jeremiah's celibacy offered a trump card that Jerome was
eager to play. He perhaps overplays it in his argument that Jeremiah was sanctified in the womb "because he was predestined to the blessing of virginity" and
goes even further: when Nebuchadnezzar destroyed the temple, "he gave no
charge concerning the Holy of Holies, but did give him charge concerning
Jeremiah. For that is the true temple of God, and that is the Holy of Holies,
which is consecrated to the Lord by pure virginity" (*Against Jovinianus* I, 33).
Jerome's use of Jeremiah's celibacy took on new life in the medieval church, as
Christians studying Jeremiah in the *Glossa* read Jerome's words along with a
comment explaining that Jeremiah "was a virgin and chaste, and without children, so that he would be free to prophesy." Jeremiah here is enlisted to support
the emerging practice of celibacy for clergy in early medieval Europe.

For Rabbi David Kimḥi in early thirteenth-century France, the command
presented serious difficulty: "Was not Jeremiah worthy that his children be
saved in his merit? Young children die only because of the sins of the parents,
and Jeremiah had no sins for which his children should die." He concluded that
the key to understanding the command is "in this place." It means Anathoth,
because 11:21–23 proclaims that the city would have no remnant; hence, if
Jeremiah fathered children there, they would perish. Kimhi's interpretation
highlights the Jewish exegetical principle of interpreting a problematic text by
means of another using the same word or phrase. "Sons and daughters" appears
in 16:1 and 11:22 in similar contexts of destruction; therefore, one verse interprets the other.

The possibility that Scripture might support the practice of celibacy challenged early modern Protestants. Calvin argued that Jeremiah's celibacy was
intended only as "a living representation, in order to produce an effect on the
Jews," insisting that it does not commend celibacy in general, "as some foolish
men have imagined from what is here said." Rather, the divine word applied
only in the impending destruction of Jerusalem, not to the church. The first
English translation of Jeremiah authorized for Catholics, however, highlights
the prophet's celibacy with the note, "Jeremie not only lived single in the times
of tribulation, but also remained a virgin all his life." John Trapp's popular commentary rejects this implicit endorsement of celibacy: "It is very likely that this
befell the Prophet in a vision. Or if otherwise, it was but for a sign, and in regard
of the great calamity impendent, that he is here forbidden marriage, otherwise
lawful enough, and, in some cases, necessary. The contrary doctrine (such as
was that of the Tatian heretics, and Popish canonists) is a doctrine of devils,

1 Tim 4:1." Trapp aligns the errors of second-century ascetic theologian Tatian, who championed sexual abstinence, with papal decrees of priestly celibacy, setting both against the New Testament. In this seventeenth-century anti-Catholic rhetoric, God's command that Jeremiah remain celibate becomes an argument in support of marriage.

In modernity, Jeremiah's celibacy signals his full commitment to being God's prophet. In her young adult novel, twentieth-century author Virginia Millikin imagines the effects of the command on Jeremiah, as she narrates his relationship with the lively young Tabitha, prone to worship the Queen of Heaven along with YHWH. The command to celibacy is described as an inner intuition and commitment to the work of prophecy rather than a divine voice. Milliken presents a modern drama between Jeremiah and Tabitha from his call to the destruction of Jerusalem: "My dove," he murmured brokenly, "for your sake I wish you loved another. But I would want to murder him. Listen, child, Yahweh has called me to a mission that will last all my years. I cannot take a wife. You must understand that. It is killing me to say this but I must" (Milliken 1954: 37–38). The rest of the book weaves an imaginary tale of their love and friendship, even when she is deported to Babylon, throughout Jeremiah's lifetime. Milliken contemporizes the command to celibacy as evidence of Jeremiah's commitment to his vocation as prophet.

Hunters and Fishers (16:16–18)

Jeremiah's destructive fishers and hunters become life-bringers in early Christian tradition. Matt 4:18 uses the same Greek word for fishers that the Septuagint uses for Jer 16:16, which led to centuries of Christian allegory. Origen interpreted the fish as those who are caught and saved by Jesus' fishers, the apostles and their present-day heirs, who "hold from God a gift of word, woven as a net and bound together from the sacred Scriptures as a casting net" (Origen 1998: 166). They enable the fish to "come up from the sea and flee its harsh waves," die to sin, and receive another life. For Origen the life of the fish in the depths figures the soul before enlightenment; the transformed soul in the mountains is in a higher place. Jerome rejected Origen's neo-Platonic reincarnation of the soul but adopted his allegory to an orthodox Christian eschatology. His hunters are "churchmen or angels" who "at the end of time will hunt out whomever is holy from the mountains of lofty teaching, the hills of good works and the clefts of rocks." His image received new life in the Middle Ages. In the *Glossa*, Matt 4:18 appears above "fishers," and Jerome's "churchmen or angels" appears over "hunters." For medieval readers fearful of the last judgment, Jeremiah's image of fishers reminded them of their teachers in life and the divine hunters who would recognize their good words at the end.

The prophet's words affected the 2008 US presidential election when preacher John Hagee wrote in 2006 that Jeremiah's words described the Holocaust: "The hunter is one who pursues his target with force and fear. No one could see the horror of the Holocaust coming, but the force and fear of Hitler's Nazis drove the Jewish people back to the only home that God ever intended for the Jews to have – Israel" (Hagee 2006: 132–133). When Hagee elaborated his idea that God allowed the Holocaust in order to drive the Jews back to the land of Israel in sermons and media appearances, always quoting Jer 16:16, John McCain repudiated him and distanced himself from Hagee's support of his bid for the presidency. In response Hagee responded, "Well dear heart, be offended. I didn't write it, Jeremiah wrote it" (Gunner and Smith 2014: 119).

Jeremiah 17

Misplaced Trust (17:5)

Augustine cites this phrase 23 times, more often than any other verse in Jeremiah. In the context of the late Roman Empire, where self-sufficiency and achievement were prized above all, Augustine uses the verse often to support a radical challenge to contemporary culture. In *City of God* 15.18, he uses it to show that human effort cannot win salvation: "Consequently no

Jeremiah Through the Centuries, First Edition. Mary Chilton Callaway.
© 2020 Mary Chilton Callaway. Published 2020 by John Wiley & Sons Ltd.

one ought to trust in himself that he shall become a citizen of that other city... in the immortality of perpetual blessedness."

Is the Human Heart Deep, or Depraved? (17:9–10)

To appreciate the richness of this verse's reception we begin with the linguistic kaleidoscope that the seven words present. Is the human heart devious, as the Hebrew says, or deep (*bathus*) as the Septuagint reads? Similarity of the Hebrew words for devious (*'akob*) and deep (*'amoq*) in appearance as well as sound makes scribal error likely at some early point in the text's history. If so, the inattentive scribe has only enriched the verse, leading readers from the beginning to wrestle with what it says about human nature. Septuagint's "the heart is deep" echoes the Psalmist's complaint that people are untrustworthy because their outward actions belie the schemes hidden in their thoughts (Ps 64:7). On the other hand, the Hebrew *'akob* (devious) plays on Israel's poetic name Jacob (*yakob*), as Jeremiah in fact does in his pun in 9:4, using *'akob yakob* to describe the way even relatives deceive each other. Whatever the original text of Jer 17:9, from the third century BCE readers pondered the heart as both hidden and deceitful.

A second ambiguity comes from the possible confusion of the Hebrew word for human being (*enosh*) and the word for sick or desperate (*anush*). The consonants are the same, but different vowels yield different words. While the Hebrew seems to say, "The heart is devious and sick; who can know it?" the Septuagint reads, "The heart is deep and it is the man; who can know him?" This Greek version figured prominently in Christian polemics against two perceived enemies. In the first centuries of Christianity, it challenged the popular idea of Docetism, a Gnostic teaching that Jesus lived on earth in the guise of a man, but was actually pure spirit. This idea appealed to sophisticated Roman citizens embarrassed by the thought of God becoming human. In the late second century, Ireneus attacked Docetism by applying Jeremiah's question "He is man; who will know him?" to Jesus, and to the suffering servant of Isa 53:8 ("who will know his origin?"). Ireneus answers polemically that those to whom the Father has revealed him will know him.

The *Glossa* uses Jerome's Latin – the heart is perverse (*pravus*) and unknowable (*inscrutabile*) – but adds that the Hebrew is ambiguous and comments instead on Septuagint's "He is man, but who shall know him?" This allows polemic against another perceived enemy of the church. Using Patristic tradition that interpreted Jeremiah's "man" through the "man" of Isa 53:8, *Glossa* instructs its medieval readers, "This is said against the Jews, who say that Jesus was a man according to the flesh, but cannot understand his nativity."

Jewish faithfulness to their covenant was a persistently vexing problem for Christians, in part because it challenged their own self-understanding as the true heirs of Israel. Here the Septuagint is preferred over the church's official text, allowing Jer 17:9 to be enlisted in anti-Jewish polemic.

Jeremiah's words had lasting effects in debates about human nature. A medieval French sermon by Peter Blois (1135–1212) understands Jeremiah's image of the heart in terms of a closed book that will one day be opened for judgment: "The book of conscience is now closed, for 'deep and unknowable is the human heart, and who can know it?'... In other words, that book will be opened because what is now hidden in our hearts will be revealed; then everyone will appear naked, each carrying a fascicle of their works" (Sermo LXV, *Patrologia Latina* 207:754; cf Jaeger 2000: 50–51). Blois uses the Septuagint's "deep" to illustrate his image of each person's heart as a text closed until the Last Day, when it will be read.

Jeremiah's words became contentious in the Reformation debate about the practice of praying to saints. The Douay Rheims Bible (1610) annotates the verse with an unusually long comment. Thomas Aquinas had used Jeremiah's rhetorical question, "Who can understand humans?" to answer the medieval question of whether angels knew human thoughts. Thomas's response that angels do not know human thoughts because this knowledge belongs to God alone caused trouble later. When Protestants in the sixteenth century criticized the practice of praying to saints as not biblical, Thomas' words seemed to support their case. How can saints know the thoughts of our hearts if that knowledge belongs only to God? The marginal note in the Douay Rheims Bible reassured Catholic readers, "It is proper to God only by his own power to search the heart of man and to know his secret thoughts which men, nor Angels cannot naturally know; but holy Angels & glorified Saints do know the thoughts of men by light of glory when mortal men pray unto them." Catholic readers should therefore learn from Jeremiah to reject Protestant arguments and pray to the saints in confidence that their glorified nature allowed them to read human hearts and answer prayers.

Jeremiah's proverb reflected the common ancient belief that people are not always as they seem because thoughts and intentions are hidden from view. In early modernity, however, readers intuitively changed the sense to conform with their experience of interiority and their own unexplored depths. The devious and deceitful heart that for Jeremiah posed a danger to others became in the Western imagination a danger to itself. The Geneva Bible's marginal note warns, "Because the wicked always have some excuse to defend their doings he shows that their own lewd imaginations deceive them and bring them to these hardships." John Wesley explained that the heart is "deceitful in its apprehensions of things, in the hopes and promises which it nourishes, in the assurances that it gives us." Jeremiah lamented the way that the hidden purposes of others led to treacherous deceit, but Wesley added the warning that it is also "deceitful with reference to ourselves" so that "a man cannot know his own heart" (Wesley 1765).

Luther famously used Jeremiah's claim that God alone knows the heart to argue for autonomy of "the thoughts and inclinations of the soul" from political rule. In 1522, the Duke of Bavaria outlawed reading or discussing Luther's books, including his German New Testament. Luther's sermon, "Temporal Authority: To what extent it should be obeyed," uses Jeremiah to argue that the state had jurisdiction over one's body and property, but not over what one believed: "How can a mere man see, know, judge, condemn, and change hearts? That is reserved for God alone" (quotes Jer 19:9–10). Therefore, it is futile and impossible to command or compel anyone by force to believe this or that" (*LW* 45:107). Luther's use of Jeremiah to protect the inner person is part of the developing early modern idea of the self. The idea that the thoughts and feelings of the heart are privileged and beyond the reach of external authorities marks a decisive break with the *mentalité* that made the Inquisition possible.

In nineteenth-century German Romanticism, Luther's "secret heart" becomes a sensitive soul tormented by self-doubt, and Bernhard Duhm's explanation is still influential. Reading verse 9 as Jeremiah's *cri de coeur* and verse 10 as God's reassuring response, Duhm interprets, "Surely no one was more destined for this observation and disclosure than Jeremiah, who was powerfully influenced by emotions and moods yet had such an unvarnished, genuine soul that he could not conceal his errors from himself or the world. Perhaps these thoughts break out as echo of that inner storm to which 15:10ff bears witness. This thinking is yet another step to the discovery of the *servum arbitrium* (Luther's term for 'unfree will'), for which the time of full understanding of course had not yet come: the 'law in my members' (Rom 7:23) would first be discovered only after one had measured himself by another Law in vain... For devout people this is a comfort, first because Yahweh is witness to good intentions when the evil that one does not want breaks through; moreover it means that Yahweh gives succor to the good and will defend them before dark evil forces" (my translation). Here, Duhm has taken several decisive turns in the reception of Jeremiah. He invents a personality and inner struggle of the "historical Jeremiah" that resonate with his German readers; his description of an "unvarnished, genuine soul" that was "powerfully influenced by emotions" makes Jeremiah a model of religious Romanticism and German Protestant spirituality. In addition, by overwriting Jeremiah with Luther's reading of Paul, he makes the prophet a spokesman for the internal struggles of the good Christian, whose "good intentions" God sees. The lasting influence of Duhm's palimpsest of Paul and Luther onto Jeremiah is apparent in the notes of many academic study Bibles, which direct the reader to Rom 7:18–19. The modern reception is apparent in T.S. Eliot's 1934 poem "Choruses from 'The Rock,'" Jeremiah into his ironic prayer: "O Lord, deliver me from the man of excellent intention and impure heart: for the heart is deceitful above all things, and desperately wicked" (Eliot 1952: 105).

The Partridge (17:11)

The curious proverb about the partridge generated a rich variety of images. One of the earliest may be Luke 12:20, where Jesus' parable of the rich man storing up his goods shares some of the vocabulary of the Septuagint Jer 17:11, and ends with the man, like the partridge, being called "fool" (*aphron*) at the moment of his death. Complicating the image is the uncertain meaning of the Hebrew *dagar*, used only here and in Isa 34:15, to describe a mother bird tending to her eggs. Whether she is incubating or gathering them is not certain, but both Septuagint and Targum translate the verb as "to collect," thereby establishing the sense of the proverb and its reception (Sawyer 1978: 325). Further complicating the image, ancient translators read "partridge" (*kore*) in light of their own understandings of ornithology; for some the bird steals eggs and hatches them, while for others the bird steals the nest of another for laying her own eggs. Septuagint's double translation of the Hebrew *kore* as both partridge and, equally possible, "calling out" had lasting effects in Western Christianity. In a second- or third-century writing from Alexandria cataloguing allegorical interpretations of animals (*Physilogus*), the partridge signifies the devil: "The partridge sits on the eggs of another bird and makes them her own brood; when they have grown, each one flies to its own parents and leaves the partridge alone and bewildered. Thus Satan seizes [calls out] from the family those who are infants according to the spirit; but when they come of age they begin to recognize their own heavenly parents, Christ, the Church, the holy prophets and apostles, and they abandon Satan to himself, bewildered and disillusioned" (Bastiaensen 1990: 196). In a homily on Jer 17:11, Origen similarly develops the partridge "calling out" to gather what was not hers into an allegory of the devil calling out through Gnostic heretics, notably Marcion, to gather the faithful and lead them to destruction (Origen 1998: 181).

A different image appears in early third-century Rome, in Hippolytus' *De Antichristo*. Citing Jeremiah's "parable" and "simile," Hippolytus explains that the partridge is a vainglorious creature whose imitative call lures from the nest young birds who are not his own, but when their true father returns they forsake the deceiver. Just so the Antichrist, wishing to gain possession of those not his own, allures with false promises of deliverance but in the end is unable to save himself. The rich Patristic reception of Jeremiah's partridge persists through the Middle Ages. The *Glossa* inscribes over the verse, "LXX: The partridge calls out; it gathers what it did not produce" and "Diabolus," directing medieval readers to interpret Jeremiah's partridge as a warning about the devil's tricks. It continues the image of Satan with its note over the next words of Jeremiah's proverb ("he gets riches") that ominously reads, "Saying to you 'I will give all this to you if you fall down and worship me.'" Jeremiah's partridge here reminds readers of Jesus' temptation in the wilderness, to warn them against their own tempters. Finally, the *Glossa* instructs readers to heed the warning of Jeremiah's proverb, inscribing the alarming interpretation "at his judgment" over the biblical words "at his end."

Using the *Glossa*, Peter Damian writes in the eleventh century as abbot of his monastery to another abbot who harbors one of Peter's monks. Peter uses Jeremiah's image of the partridge sitting on eggs she did not lay to apply to "a person who belongs to the group that steals from the membership of others" and "breaks trust and takes away another's student," imitating "the example of the Antichrist" to shame his fellow abbot into returning the errant monk (Damian 1989: 291–292). The partridge becomes a symbol of deceit in medieval art; in one sixteenth-century Book of Hours, the opening page of the seven Penitential Psalms is illustrated with a border showing Isaiah and Jeremiah in the corners and an intricately detailed partridge in the center. Jeremiah's partridge beckons meditative readers, who would have to be wealthy to hold such a lavish book, to beware the dangers of wealth unjustly gained.

Rashi explains *kore* not as a partridge, but transliterates French *coucou* into Hebrew letters for his early medieval French readers, who knew that the cuckoo laid her eggs in the nest of another bird. He explains that the mother bird chirps to her chicks, "but those whom the cuckoo called will not follow when they grow up, for they are not of its kind. So is the one who gathers riches but not by right." Rashi thus adapts Jeremiah's partridge to the European cuckoo to highlight a moral teaching about unjust gain.

The Surprise of Divine Freedom (18:1–12)

Readers have molded Jeremiah's image of potter and clay into surprisingly different shapes. Three problems emerged from the beginning. First, what happened? The Hebrew suggests that the clay-becoming-vessel was ruined in the potter's hands, but the Septuagint says that the vessel fell from the potter's hands; clay is not mentioned. Unlike the efforts of historical-critical exegesis to determine one original meaning, reception history reveals a readerly insistence

Jeremiah Through the Centuries, First Edition. Mary Chilton Callaway.
© 2020 Mary Chilton Callaway. Published 2020 by John Wiley & Sons Ltd.

on multiplying meanings. Origen notes in his homily that while some draw meaning from Scripture as from a spring and others draw more deeply as from a well, all are equally nourished. Beginning with the more accessible water from the spring, Origen reads the vessel falling from the potter's hands as warning Christians in danger of falling from the hands of their maker while they are still being molded. This appropriation of Jeremiah's image for Christian life had already appeared in a second-century Greek homily (*2 Clement* 3:14), but Origen balances judgment with hope: when our bodies fall back to their original clay, the potter can refashion the clay into a more beautiful vessel at the resurrection (Origen 1998: 193–194).

Marginal notes in early English Bibles also focus readers on the clay of their own lives. A Geneva Bible note on verse 12, "As men that had no remorse, but were altogether bent to rebellion and to their own self will," contemporizes Jeremiah to condemn pride and self-will, in Puritan theology the most dangerous of sins. In contrast, Roman Catholics reading an English Bible for the first time were instructed to see hope. The marginal note of the Douay Rheims translation explains, "A potter can make a new vessel of the same clay being misformed in casting, so it be yet fresh, & moist, but God can also reform man being hardened in heart, as if he made a new pot of an old one, broken into pieces or deformed." The Catholic annotation uses Jeremiah to encourage perseverance by highlighting the divine power to transform the heart.

Origen describes his second interpretation, "water from the deep well," as the mystery of the two nations. Israel rebelliously fell from the potter's hands and the church is the new vessel fashioned from the clay. Though Origen warns that the church too can fall away or be ruined, his reading of the church as the divine potter's replacement vessel cast a long shadow. It is dramatically illustrated in *Bible moralisée*, which pairs the prophet watching a potter with Paul's conversion. The connection was perhaps triggered by the Vulgate's use of *conversus* in verse 4, and Paul's use of the potter image in Romans 9:19–24. The illustration presents a narrative of Saul first falling headlong from a horse bucking in terror, then with blinded eyes and outstretched arms being guided by Ananias. The Latin text explains that the clay vessel signifies Paul, whom God reshaped from a persecutor of the faithful into a vessel of election (Figure 38).

Origen's mystery of the two nations surfaced in early editions of the King James Bible. English readers found no marginal notes, as the king had ordered, but a brief summary at the chapter heading guided their understanding to an ominous contemporizing of Patristic theology: "Under the type of breaking a potter's vessel, is foreshowed the desolation of the Jews for their sins."

Water from Origen's "deepest well," the most difficult meaning of a biblical text, is the problem of divine nature. God's pronouncement that "I will change my mind" in response to Judah's behavior implies that God does not know the

FIGURE 38   Jeremiah's potter as an allegory for the conversion of Saul. © *M. Moleiro.
The Bible of St. Louis, vol.2,* f.130r.

future. Worse, the Septuagint uses the verb which Origen knew as the basis
for Stoic and Christian language of repentance (*metanoia*), turning away
from wrong-doing, which is impossible for God. These theological problems
of Jer 18 arose when readers struggled to accommodate the Scriptures to
Greek philosophy. The issue is not theoretical; Marcion's challenge that
Israel's deity is neither omniscient nor good threatened the unity of the early
church. Origen addresses this grave implication of Jer 18 by appealing to his
readers' knowledge of rhetoric. The language is figurative, not literal; like an
adult teaching a child, Scripture adapts the divine mystery to human ways of
thinking. God "pretends that he does not see your future so that he may preserve your self-determination." Just as God's wrath is not human, but a figure
of speech designed to motivate us to be better, so God's apparent ignorance of
the future is a figure of speech whose purpose is to encourage us with the

sense that we have freedom to affect our own destiny. Origen's concern with human freedom does not reflect Jeremiah's focus, which showcases divine power. Instead, the logical opposition between divine omniscience and human freedom that Origen poses reflects Greek philosophical debates current in his day, especially among Gnostic Christians, who adopted the Stoic teaching that the outcome of each life was predetermined. In Origen's words cited above, "self-determination" translates a contemporary Greek word meaning literally "by-one's-own-power." This technical term allowed Origen to use Jeremiah's potter in a theologically sophisticated argument that maintained both divine omniscience and human freedom, an interpretation that persists into the present (Origen 1998:193–196).

In early modernity, Jeremiah's suggestion that the divine mind might change posed a challenge by attributing the human weaknesses of mutability and contingency to God. Affirming patristic readings while also embracing Renaissance optimism, Erasmus writes, "We must not forget that here the Holy Scripture is speaking after the manner of men, as in other places also it does quite often, since there is no mutability in God" (Rupp 1969: 58). In the seventeenth century, however, Jeremiah's image undermined religious authority. In his influential *Theologico-Political Treatise* (1670) arguing that political and religious authority derived from different sources and should therefore have distinct jurisdictions, Spinoza found Jeremiah's image of God changing his mind useful for his argument. Noting in Chapter II of the *Treatise* that 1 Sam 15:29 asserts God's mind does not change, Spinoza explains the contradiction by appealing to differences in the nature and circumstances of the human authors of the Bible. He concludes "that God adapted revelations to the understanding and opinions of the prophets, and that in matters of theory without bearing on charity or morality the prophets could be, and in fact were, ignorant, and held conflicting opinions. It therefore follows that we must by no means go to the prophets for knowledge, either of natural or of spiritual phenomena" (Spinoza 1951: 40).

While Spinoza used Jeremiah to limit the Bible's sphere of influence, Thomas Paine used him to dismiss it altogether. In Jer 18 he found another example of the absurdities in the Bible, and more support for his rejection of all religion except a principle of Deism. In *Age of Reason*, Paine writes, "Everything relating to Jeremiah shows him to have been a man of an equivocal character; in his metaphor of the potter and the clay, he guards his prognostications in such a crafty manner as always to leave himself a door to escape by, in case the event should be contrary to what he had predicted." Paine contrasts verses 7–8 with 9–10 to argue that Jeremiah is simply hedging his bets: "According to this plan of prophesying, a prophet could never be wrong, however mistaken the Almighty might be. This sort of absurd subterfuge, and this manner of speaking of the Almighty, as one would speak of a man, is consistent with nothing but the stupidity of the Bible" (Paine 1796: 2:10).

Jeremiah's metaphor for God's judgment of nations becomes, in the early twentieth century, a prayer of personal piety. In 1902, American evangelist Adelaide Pollard composed a hymn titled, "Have Thine Own Way, Lord" in response to a major disappointment in her life. The first stanza shifts the focus of Jeremiah's image from divine power to individual religious experience: "Have Thine own way, Lord! Have Thine own way! Thou art the Potter; I am the clay. Mold me and make me after Thy will, While I am waiting, Yielded and still" (Barrows and Hustad 1968). Set to music by George Stebbins in the same year, it immediately appeared in three hymnals and persists as a popular hymn in Evangelical churches.

Jeremiah Smashes a Jug

The narrative of Jeremiah smashing a jug is based on a signature characteristic of Jeremiah's prophecies, the wordplay. The Hebrew for jug is *bakbuk,* an onomatopoetic word imitating the gurgling sound of pouring liquid. The divine threat in verse 7 uses the related verb *bakbak*: "I will pour out (*bakoti*) Judah's best counsel," signaling God's intent to destroy it. Commentators ancient and modern draw attention to the power of prophetic actions. Jerome notes here

Jeremiah Through the Centuries, First Edition. Mary Chilton Callaway.
© 2020 Mary Chilton Callaway. Published 2020 by John Wiley & Sons Ltd.

and elsewhere that Scripture "wants to teach people not only through the ears but also the eyes, because what is seen is remembered better than what is heard." This privileging of sight over hearing reflects Jerome's classical education and his own preference. Reflecting seventeenth-century sensibilities, John Trapp echoes Jerome by saying Jeremiah smashed the jug "that the eyes of the bystanders and beholders may affect their hearts." Modern scholars argue that such actions were not understood primarily as teaching aids, but rather prophetic performances of the divine word which set the prophecy in motion.

Christians applied Jeremiah's prophecies to their own enemies. Jerome saw his theological opponents, "heretics," as defiling God's word, and the innocent blood spilled (verse 4) metaphorically as Christians led astray by their teachings. Calvin used verse 4 in an anti-Catholic polemic that pits tradition against Scripture, deriding "Papists" for "the abominations" which they say "have been taught by our ancestors." John Trapp used verse 13 to contemporize Jeremiah's condemnation of rooftop offerings to other deities in a polemic against "chambers of imagery and their private chapels for idolatrous uses, as Papists also have." Trapp ends, however, with an exhortation that readers take Jeremiah's warnings to heart: "We may all very profitably read the Prophet Jeremy who is full of incitation to repentance and new obedience."

FIGURE 39   Jeremiah smashes the jug. *Brown's Self-Interpreting Family Bible*. Private collection.

The long reception history of the smashed jug as prophetic indictment against one's enemies is apparent in this nineteenth-century engraving in many editions of John Brown's

Self-Interpreting Family Bible (Figure 39) The orientalizing dress of the men of Jerusalem and the "realistic" Judean geography reflect popular use of scholarship that sought to recover the original setting of Bible stories. For families pondering the story, Jeremiah is distinguished from his audience of Jews by his undivided beard and uncovered head. Signaling his role as proto-Christian, he points upward to the heavenly Father, and down to the smashed flask as harbinger of doom for the "Jews" he addresses.

Ancient Jewish tradition explored the three-fold expression of divine intent in verse 5. Given the principle that no word of Torah is superfluous, the rabbis sought three different referents for Jeremiah's phrase "commanded not, nor spoke, nor thought." One rabbinic tradition uses these three phrases to explain three discomfiting stories. The first (I did not command it) responds to Jephthah's rash vow resulting in the sacrifice of his daughter; the second (I did not speak of it) is Mesha sacrificing his son to the god Chemosh; the third (I did not imagine it) explains Abraham's potential sacrifice of Isaac. Jeremiah teaches that God never thought Abraham would actually kill Isaac (Neusner 2006: 25, 294).

Jeremiah in the Stocks (20:1–6)

Jeremiah's rough treatment by the priest Pashur is described in only two verses, but Pashur represents in every age the religious tyrant who fears the truth and uses physical intimidation to suppress it. For Jerome, who described him as one who "corruptly abused the office of high priest by terrorizing with torture instead of teaching and correcting by word," Pashur represents all in the church who abuse power, especially over those who challenge their thinking. Stinging

Jeremiah Through the Centuries, First Edition. Mary Chilton Callaway.
© 2020 Mary Chilton Callaway. Published 2020 by John Wiley & Sons Ltd.

from the disgrace of being exiled from Rome by church authorities, then having his reputation for orthodoxy undermined by his former friend Rufinus, and finally having a suspicious fire at his monastery, Jerome felt the presence of Pashur in his life.

Jerome's use of Pashur to indict bishops gained new life in early thirteenth-century France in the *Bible Moralisée*. The roundel illustrating Jer 20 shows Pashur wearing the *pileum cornutum*, the pointed cap identifying Jews in medieval art. His right hand strikes Jeremiah's face, evoking Ananias ordering Paul to be struck on the mouth for defending himself against the Sanhedrin in Jerusalem (Acts 23:1–2). Two young men pull Jeremiah toward the dark door of a medieval dungeon in a scene that continues to evoke the narrative of Paul's arrest. Pashur is pictured as a medieval Jew to support the widespread Christian polemic that Jews misread and rejected their own prophets. The companion roundel contemporizes Pashur as a bishop who directs a man to beat a monk being forced into a prison like Jeremiah's in the roundel above. A Latin text slightly modifies Jerome's words to indict contemporary bishops: "This signifies many bishops who perversely abuse their office; they do not rule in order to persuade, but use torture to terrify from within." The seated figure of Pashur wearing vestments and mitre directing the proceedings against the monk provides a powerful critique of corruption in the medieval church. The contemporized Jeremiah figure may represent the Cathars, a mendicant order that started in the twelfth century to model poverty and to criticize corruption in the church, especially among bishops and clergy.

In the bitter politics of the English Civil War, the figure of Pashur fueled Protestant rhetoric. A marginal note in a sixteenth-century Bible advises readers, "It is no new thing (ye may see) for Bishops to persecute the Prophets of the Lord for their preaching of the truth and constancy." The Geneva Bible contemporizes with a heading that invites readers to find parallels between the prophet and English Puritans arrested under Queen Mary I: "Jeremiah is smitten and cast into prison for preaching of the word of God." The marginal note at verse 2 heightens the polemic against the Catholic church by describing Pashur as "this priest as a chief instrument of Satan." One hundred years later, Pashur has clearly been established as a fixture of English religious history. John Trapp's commentary uses the exaggerations of *Foxe's Book of Martyrs* to cast Pashur as Edmund Bonner, Bishop of London, who also imprisoned and sometimes executed enemies during the reign of "Bloody Mary." For Trapp's seventeenth-century readers, Pashur represented a perennial threat to religious freedom.

For French Catholics in eighteenth-century Paris, Pashur embodied the hostile *philosophes,* including Voltaire, whose critiques undermined the church's authority. In 1771, priest-poet Desmarais published "Jérémie, Poëme en quatre chants," which subtly turned Jeremiah's story into a contemporary manifesto.

One of the vignettes graphically embodies Desmarais' fusion of Christ, Jérémie, and the attack on True Religion into a single narrative. "The high priest strikes Jérémie" (Figure 40) portrays the stooped prophet in a scene clearly evoking the trial of Jesus, yet the setting is distinctly eighteenth-century Paris, signaled by the Bastille and a French woman nursing her baby. Desmaris describes "this sad scene" to evoke his beleaguered readers' emotions about ancient and contemporary attacks on their faith and to fortify them against Enlightenment mockery.

Reception history of Jeremiah's physical suffering reflects the uncertainty of the text. Jer 20:2 describes the punishment with a rare Hebrew technical term based on the verb meaning to overturn, though whether this refers to the prisoner or the instrument is unclear. Septuagint uses a rare term meaning a portcullis or other wooden structure that comes down. The ancient versions read so differently that Jerome threw up his hands in defeat, saying he used *nervum* "in the ordinary sense, which type of torture we read about also in Acts when the apostles Paul and Silas were imprisoned with their feet "bound together in wood" (Acts 16:24). The *Glossa* follows Jerome, instructing medieval readers with an interlinear note above *nervum* simply defining it simply as "a kind of torture." The thirteenth-century image from *Bible moralisée* shows a medieval dungeon, while an 1850 illustration from a New England children's book follows the early English translation of "stocks." Here the mild and Christ-like prophet holds a scroll, suggesting to the picture's young viewers that he suffered for God's truth (Figure 41). The wooden stocks contemporize ancient Judah into devices for punishment in colonial New England.

Divine Deception (20:7)

Jeremiah's accusation of divine seduction and deceit generated a richly paradoxical legacy of disapproval and awe that highlights reading strategies of the faithful when confronted with a disturbing text. Origen puts the problem starkly – either Jeremiah is lying or God is a deceiver – and confesses, "I am at a loss how I can accommodate the word" (Origen 1998: 217). The problem was not abstract for him because Marcion and other Gnostics were teaching that Israel's deity was just such an untrustworthy character and that the Scriptures consequently had no authority for Christians. With so much at stake, Origen does not suppress Jeremiah's accusation but seizes its opportunities. Insisting that the Bible describes God in dark and allusive speech, by which attributes like anger, regret, and deception are "of another kind" than their human counterparts and only analogies, Origen nevertheless insists that God actually does

Pag. 34 .

P. le Clerc inv

C. Macret Sculp

FIGURE 40   Jérémie in Paris. "Le Grande-Prêtre Frappe Jérémie." M. Desmarais 1771, Paris. Private Collection.

JEREMIAH IN THE STOCKS.

FIGURE 41   *The Children of the Bible: As Examples and Warnings.* Frances M. Caulkins, 1850.

engage in deception. Unlike its human counterpart, God's deception benefits the deceived. Origen draws analogies to a physician who slows healing of a wound for better results, or a father who conceals his affection in order to discipline his son. Key to Origen's argument is his shrewd observation that Jeremiah could only utter his complaint "when he had stopped being deceived, after he knew the benefit from the deception," because his words suggest that Jeremiah came to appreciate what God had done with him (Origen 1998: 226). Jeremiah's deception also teaches about Scripture, because the way God lures people according to their needs mirrors the way Scripture accommodates readers of different abilities. This divine pedagogy is a model of the experienced human teacher who sometimes speaks with multiple meanings in order to inspire all students. In Origen's brilliant homily, Jeremiah's troubling accusation becomes a rich trove of theological teaching about the nature of God, epistemological evidence for multiple levels of meaning in Scripture, and practical advice for teachers.

Early Jewish readers were equally perturbed by the suggestion that God might be deceptive. Targum shields the congregation in the synagogue service by translating Jeremiah's words as "You have confused me." Most Jewish traditions locate Jeremiah's complaint in the narrative of his life, and an early tradition known to Origen explains that the deception refers to Jer 1:10, when the prophet is set over nations and kingdoms. Not imagining that the job included indicting his own people, Jeremiah accepted the commission; on learning that Judah was included among the nations under judgment, he protested God's deceit. In a later development of this midrashic tradition, God realizes that he cannot destroy the city as long as the prophet, with the strong pillar of his deeds and the stony wall of his prayers, is within its walls. He therefore sends Jeremiah to Anathoth to take possession of his cousin's field (Jer 32). No sooner has the prophet left than an angel descends, sets his feet against the city walls, and breaches them. As the Babylonians surge in, four angels with torches set fire to the Temple. Meanwhile, on the road back to Jerusalem, Jeremiah sees smoke rising from the temple. Thinking that the people have repented and are making offerings, he rejoices, until he sees the heap of burned rubble and cries out, "You have seduced me, and I was seduced" (Braude 1968: 26.6). The midrash appears in a homily for one of the sabbaths just before the Ninth of Ab, a liturgical day of mourning for Jerusalem, and subsequently for the destruction of Jewish communities in European pogroms. Jeremiah's anguish poignantly resonates with the experience of Jews even as it affirms the power of the holy man. Even God had to resort to deception to outwit Jeremiah's loyalty to his people.

The eleventh-century Islamic *Lives of the Prophets* adapts this rabbinic tradition to Muslim teaching by removing the scandals of divine deception and Jeremiah's harsh accusation (see Introduction page xx). When Jeremiah weeps on hearing God's warning in 1:14, God promises not to destroy any of the children of Israel "until the command for that is by you." Folk wisdom is evident in the figure of God, who does not deceive Jeremiah, which would be unthinkable, but models virtuous triumph through cleverness. An angel disguised as a man with a legal problem appears to Jeremiah. He has been kind to his kinsmen, he explains, but they have disdainfully mistreated him. What should he do? Twice Jeremiah sends him back to intercede for them and to give them time to change. As Nebuchadnezzar's army begins to assemble around Jerusalem, the disguised angel appears a third time to Jeremiah, who now sits on the city wall rejoicing in God's promise to him. The man's kinsmen have become worse, the disguised angel tells Jeremiah, now doing something offensive to God. Incensed, Jeremiah replies with a prayer that God destroy them. No sooner were the words out of his mouth than "God sent a thunderbolt from heaven upon Jerusalem" (Al-Tha'labi 2002: 561). To Jeremiah's weeping and protestations of deception, God replies that it happened only because of "your legal opinion and your prayer." This distinctively Muslim Jeremiah is loyal to his people, dispenses wise legal advice, and is submissive to the divine will.

Discomfort with divine deception is apparent in medieval Christian sources. The *Glossa* reassures readers with Jerome's adaptation of the Jewish tradition that Jeremiah mistakenly thought God's commission to prophesy "to the nations" meant against Judah's enemies, not against his own people. Explanation of the people's ridicule in verse 8 continues the theme of misunderstanding, imputing to Jeremiah the imagined words, "Because everyone thought I was making it up." The *Glossa* also tries to tame the nuance of deception in *seduxisti* of verse 7 with an interlinear note offering *obtinuisti & polluisti*, "you possessed and profaned me." The attempt to make Jeremiah more pious continues in the *Glossa*'s inclusion of Theodoret's explanation: "The prophet was tormented not because of his own injury, but because the divine word was mocked." Finally, the effects of humanism are evident in Nicholas of Lyra's fourteenth-century addition to the *Glossa*. Dismissing the possibility that God, who is truth, could seduce or lead anyone into error, Nicholas suggests interpreting Jeremiah's protest in the context of imminent physical suffering. A considered decision to endure suffering, even if marred by doubts and fears, is commendable; indeed, it describes Jesus in his prayer that the Father let this cup pass from him. Jeremiah is therefore like Christ in his humanity, fearing suffering yet submitting to God's will. Nicholas ends with the interpretation of Jeremiah's bitter accusation as, "Nevertheless, not my will but yours." Nicholas' sympathetic comment displays interest in Jeremiah's human experience; in this respect it anticipates the new ways this text will affect readers.

Sixteenth-century reformers were keen to direct readers to a positive reading of Jeremiah's alarming words. Calvin's chief concern is the specter of doubting one's call. So serious is this possibility that he reads Jeremiah's words as ironic mimicking of the people's rejection of Jeremiah's warnings that Jerusalem would be destroyed. Far from feeling deceived, the prophet "possessed in his heart a firm conviction of the truth he delivered… Jeremiah speaks not here as a private individual, but as he knew that his calling was approved by God, he hesitated not to connect God with himself, so that the reproach might belong to both." Calvin's interests are clear when he suggests that "from this passage a useful doctrine may be gathered. All who go forth to teach ought to be so sure of their calling, as not to hesitate to appeal to God's tribunal whenever any dispute happens… As to their calling and doctrine there ought to be that certainty which Jeremiah exhibits to us here by his own example." Calvin thus turns a troublesome verse into an exhortation for care in discerning a call and consistent faithfulness in living it out. The Geneva Bible's gloss similarly sees Jeremiah as a fellow beleaguered saint, encouraging its Puritan readers to identify with him and to hear in his cry a warning against despair: "Herein appeareth the impatience which oftentimes overcommeth the servants of God, when they see not their labors to profit, & also feel their own weakness, read Chap. 15.18."

John Donne is the lone seventeenth-century voice to embrace Jeremiah's discomfiting erotic image of intimacy with God. In "Holy Sonnet 14" (1633),

Donne combines Augustine's paradox that serving God is perfect freedom with Jeremiah's voice. The sonnet begins, "Batter my heart, three-person'd God" and ends, "for I, except you enthrall me, never shall be free, Nor ever chaste, except you ravish me." As a poet of both erotic and religious longing, Donne was the first to adopt Jeremiah's violent language as prayer.

Seventeenth- and eighteenth-century readers looking to the Bible for practical guidelines found both danger and comfort in Jeremiah's accusation. Matthew Henry reminds his Puritan readers opposing the established church, "Lively preachers are the scorn of careless unbelieving hearers." He warns against indulging one's feelings, because as Jeremiah "was tempted to quarrel with God" and "to quit his work" his words are a warning "lest we should be at any time weary and faint in our minds under our lesser trials... It is the folly and infirmity of some good people that they lose much of the pleasantness of their religion by the fretfulness and uneasiness of their natural temper, which they humor and indulge, instead of mortifying it." Soon after Henry's warning, the emerging evangelical tradition also interpreted Jeremiah's words as "a fit of passion" (John Wesley) that were at best a sign of the prophet's infirmity and at worst an occasion of sin, "the language of Jeremiah's folly and corruption." A more sympathetic approach, in John Brown's *Self-Interpreting Family Bible,* encouraged individual identification with the prophet's internal dilemma. The note suggests reading persuaded and allured rather than deceived, explaining that Jeremiah was "inwardly tormented with challenges of conscience, and frowns from God." Brown adds a sympathetic application of Jeremiah to ministers in his own fractured Scottish Presbyterian church: "To faint in the Lord's way, or to wish that we had never entered into it, because we meet with difficulties, is extremely weak and foolish. But it is an ease for burdened souls to pour out their burdens before the Lord... but absurd is sinful passion when allowed to ramble." Jeremiah's protest here becomes a flashpoint for Protestant ambivalence about the proper response to spiritual trials. Prayer in time of distress is a sign of true faith, yet raw protest like Jeremiah's might weaken faith.

For those caught up in the Enlightenment understanding of true religion not as supernatural revelation, but rather what is in accord with reason and nature, the idea that God would deceive his prophet offered a prime example of the problems with the Bible as a moral authority. In his influential Deist work *Christianity as Old as the Creation,* Matthew Tindal argues, "The common Parent of Mankind is too good and gracious, to put the Happiness of all his Children on any other Doctrines, than such as plainly shew themselves to the Will of God, even to the ignorant and illiterate, if they have but Courage and Honestly to make use of their Reason" (Tindal 1730: 231). Given this evident concord between divine will and human reason, Jeremiah's accusations of divine deception in 20:7 as well as 4:10 and 15:18 offer evidence that prophetic texts are useless for "the practice of Morality in Obedience to the Will of God." His use of Jeremiah to advance a Deistic embrace of human reason was countered by Daniel Waterland's *Scripture Vindicated* in an argument equally indebted to Enlightenment ideas. Waterland challenges Tindal, "Here again, the translation is harsh, and faulty." It should read not deceived, but "over-persuaded." He ends with the quintessential Enlightenment argument of reading in context. Jeremiah is a man of "great modesty and profound humility, in not affecting high things, or shining offices, but submitting however to the burden of them in obedience to the will of God. For what purpose, then, could the Objector [Tindal] produce this text?" (Waterland 1734: 84–85).

Scottish preacher George H. Morrison, who drew large crowds to his church in Glasgow at the beginning of the twentieth century, responded to Jeremiah's complaint in a sermon entitled "The Deceptions of God." Morrison presents divine deception as necessary to human life, as in the sweet illusions of childhood. These inevitably bring disappointment: "Think once again of how life deceives us. It is when men compare all that the years have brought with the glad and golden promise of the morning. It is then that they are tempted, not in bitterness, but in the melancholy which Jeremiah knew so well, to cry, 'O Lord, if this be life, Thou has deceived me, and I was deceived.'" Morrison sees "loving purposes" in this deception, especially enticement: "Do you think that we would ever have the heart to travel if we were not beset by stratagems of mercy? So does God lead us through the ideals of childhood, and the hopes of youth, and the letter of the promise, till at last the husk is broken in our grasp, and we find with a strange joy the hidden kernel... What in our ignorance we called deceit was nought but the ingenuity of love" (Morrison 1907: 308). This bold approach of embracing divine deception as a form of grace is reminiscent of Origen's explanation described above, but is otherwise unknown in reception history. In Morrison's austere Protestant world Jeremiah is us, and his complaint teaches that we should accept with gratitude illusions that make life sweeter for a while, even if later phases of life unmask them. His words were widely disseminated for preachers in *The Expositor's Dictionary of Texts* (Nicoll et al. 1910) and his sermon collections.

The reception of Jeremiah's words that overturned centuries of discomfort was originally hidden in the technical commentaries of two German biblical scholars. Heinrich Ewald listed the verses as part of the last of Jeremiah's six "outpourings of the heart," which Berhnard Duhm subsequently called "Confessions." Their work laid the groundwork for the mid-twentieth century interpretation, tinged with Existentialism, that persists today. Jeremiah's struggle against God is a struggle within himself, and rather than a problem represents the height of modern spiritual engagement.

The discourse of *Angst* replaces the theological and moral reservations of earlier readers. The subtitles of the biblical commentaries at Jer 20:7–14 reinforce this understanding. Wilhelm Rudolph's academic commentary (1947) refers to "Jeremiah's Inner Struggle" (*Seelenkämpfe*); the Anchor Bible's commentary calls it "The Prison Within," and the New American Bible places the heading "Jeremiah's Interior Crisis" right into the midst of the biblical text. That Jeremiah's harsh words might be a model for modern Christians is suggested in 1960 by von Rad's judgment that the confessions represent "the human spirit at its noblest" (von Rad 1965: 2:205). Michael Fishbane's idiomatic translation, "You have enticed me, YHWH, and I've been had" and his careful literary analysis of the passage culminates in a description of the prophet's prayer that makes it a model for contemporary readers: "It is in the very process of prayer that the prophet has achieved his new knowledge [verses 11–12]. What Jeremiah achieves by revealing his case to God is to see his life in a new way... God's protection is spiritualized; it is the confidence he gives His servants that their heart and service are seen and accepted" (Fishbane 1979: 102). Walter Brueggemann describes Jeremiah's Confessions as "the most direct, candid and intimate prayers," showing that Jeremiah "carried on an intense and often stormy conversation with Yahweh. These prayers are models for the depth of honesty that is appropriate in prayer" (Brueggemann 1998: 114). These receptions of Jeremiah's harsh words as commendable and true prayer mark a dramatic reversal of centuries of warnings against weak faith and blasphemous speech.

Resistance against totalitarian regimes in the mid-twentieth century gave a new reception to Jeremiah's complaint. In a sermon preached just weeks before the Third Reich began taking over the German Evangelical church, Dietrich Bonhoeffer chose Jer 20:7 as his text: "I had no idea what was coming when you seized me – and now I cannot get away from you anymore; you have carried me off as your booty. You tie us to your victory chariot and pull us along behind you, so that we have to march, chastened and enslaved, in your victory procession. How could we know that your love hurts so much, that your grace is so stern?" (Bonhoeffer 2007: 13:347). His biographer writes, "His depiction of the refractory yet obedient Jeremiah became a kind of personal confession to the congregation." Bonhoeffer identified with the torment of the prophet "whom God will not let go, who will never be rid of God... He was upbraided as a disturber of the peace, an enemy of the people, just like all those, throughout the ages until the present day, who have been possessed and seized by God, for whom God has become too strong." Bonhoeffer's actualizing of Jeremiah's conflict is apparent: "How gladly would he have shouted peace and Heil with the rest" (Bethge 1970: 346).

Whose Violence and Destruction? (20:8)

The referent of Jeremiah's "violence and destruction" is not named, making it easy for readers to see their own enemies in the prophetic cry. Septuagint seems to preserve a different textual tradition with its enigmatic, "I will be laughed at in my bitter speech; 'faithlessness' and 'wretchedness' I will be named." Origen translates the verb as a future, 'I will laugh,' reading it as eschatological proclamation informed by Luke 6:21, "Blessed are you who weep now…" (Origen 1998: 233). Jeremiah's troubles signify for Origen the future glory for which the Divine Physician is preparing him, as Origen believed was happening in the lives of his readers. In early modernity, Jeremiah's cry becomes the voice of rebellion against the religious oppression of the English monarch, as in Tyndale's illicit 1535 English translation, "because I have now preached long against malicious Tyranny." By the early twentieth century, it is read in the context of Jeremiah's "Confessions," a cry of rage and dereliction against God (Baumgartner 2015: 64).

A Reproach and a Derision (20:8)

Reception of these words highlights the disparate religious sensibilities of antiquity and modernity. Origen contrasts himself and his readers who hide their sins with the holy prophet: "Blessed Jeremiah, he who has no other reproach than the word of the Lord" (Origen 1998: 237). Also protecting Jeremiah's reputation as holy man, Theodoret explains, "What galls the prophet are not the miseries and abuse happening to him but the mockery made of the divine oracles." By the sixteenth century, Jeremiah's outburst had become a spiritual treasure. Luther identifies with Jeremiah, contemporizing his outburst as conscience: "Every magistrate and every nobleman does nothing; in fact, they despise the words… This excessive contempt for the Gospel and this blasphemy among the people causes our preachers to become altogether weary. So the prophet was mocked by excessive contempt and derision and felt like saying, 'I would just as soon keep silent altogether and let them sweat it out themselves…He could not keep silent because his conscience was driving him'" (*LW* 17:343–344). Calvin also uses Jeremiah's words to describe the disillusion of contemporary preachers and teachers, who despair that their work has only driven people away from God: "The Prophet saw no other fruit to his labor, but that men were rendered more insolent, and from being thieves became robbers, and from being disdainful became ruffians, so that they increasingly kindled God's wrath, and more fully abandoned themselves." The idea that people might be made more intransigent by God's word haunts Calvin, who is troubled by the Libertines, radical Protestants who make "the liberty of the Gospel," into "brute license, so that they sin with impunity." Others in Geneva were weary of religious controversies, even denying the existence of God. Calvin thus uses Jeremiah's despair to give voice to discouraged Christians wanting to quit their vocations.

Near the end of the nineteenth century, evangelical author F.B. Meyer softens Jeremiah's outburst in light of precedent: "Not dissimilar have been the appeals of God's servants in every age, when they have measured their weakness against the strength of the evils they have combated, and have marked their limited success: the handfuls of seed wasted upon barren soil; the word spoken in the ear of the wind" (Meyer 1894: 89). By the twentieth century, the prophet's experience resonates directly with modern sensibility: "That the effect of prophetic obedience should be the sabotaging of his right to be regarded as a serious and reasonable person and that he should be metamorphosed into a weird crank was more than could be borne" (McKane 1986: 1:471). While the "derision" of verse 8 was understood for centuries as an attack on the divine word, in modernity it became a personal attack on the prophet and a psychological burden.

A Burning Fire (20:9)

"O blameless, O blessed Jeremiah – excepting, I would say, this little sin," says Origen. Perturbed by Jeremiah's rebellion, he also identifies with it "Once someone has realized that because of the teaching and the word he has been in misery and suffered and hated, he often says: 'I will withdraw, why remain in these circumstances?... why should I not withdraw to the desert and peace?'" Yet the fire in Jeremiah's bones is also for Origen the divine fire bringing shame; therefore "he rejected the sin at the same time in the act of speaking." Origen sees Jeremiah as a model of catching oneself in the act of sin, and prays "that I also, at the same time I sin and speak a sinful word, would feel that a fire arose in my heart burning and flaming so that I could not bear it." This fire is for Origen like the divine physician, who causes pain in the present to avoid worse in the future. He concludes, "Let us each pray to God that this fire in Jeremiah comes to himself... so that he might not be kept for the other fire" (Origen 1998: 239–241). Even saints are sinners, and Origen reads Jeremiah's outburst as a warning.

Jerome defends the fire as sign of sincerity, comparing it with Paul's zeal at seeing idols in Athens (Acts 17:16) and his insistence that he does not preach voluntarily (1 Cor 9:16–17). Driven out of Rome and constantly criticized, Jerome clearly identifies with Jeremiah in his pointed comment that "even today many teachers in the church endure the same, hearing the slander of many gathered against them." Gregory the Great likewise identifies Jeremiah's outburst as a virtuous sign of justice. Commenting on Elihu's compulsion to reply to Job (Job 32:18–21) he writes, "Wise men, when they find that they are not listened to, impose silence on their lips… but when they see that the sins of the ungodly gain strength they endure a kind of violence in their spirit, and burst forth in language of open reproof… Hence Jeremiah, seeing that he was not listened to, wished to hold his peace, but when he beheld evil increasing, he no longer persisted in the same silence… For the hearts of the just burn within them when they behold the deeds of the ungodly gain strength from not being reproved, and they believe that they are themselves partakers in the guilt of those whom they allow by their own silence to go on in iniquity" (Gregory 1847: 3:17–18). Medieval Christians reading the *Glossa* understood Jeremiah's fire as divine warning to confront evil in their own time.

Fourteenth-century English mystic Walter Hilton changed the understanding of the fire in Jeremiah's bones from torment to "spiritual sweetness" when he found in it a description of mystical experience in prayer. This fire burns when

> words are used which most accord with one's feelings at the moment of prayer – things which come to mind spontaneously according to sundry considerations which have been on the person's heart… This kind of prayer pleases God greatly, for it springs exclusively from the affection of the heart… Of this kind of experience in prayer the prophet Jeremiah seems to have been speaking.… For as a physical fire burns and consumes all physical things where it burns, just so spiritual fire, the love of God, burns and consumes all carnal affections and appetites in a person's soul. And this fire is well stoked up in my bones, says the prophet of himself. By this he means to say that his love fills up the capacities of his soul, his mind, reason and will, with grace and spiritual sweetness just as marrow fills up the core of his bones. That is, the fire is within, and not produced outwardly, by means of the senses… Nevertheless this force is so mighty within that it strikes out into the body, so that all the body may quake and tremble. And because it is so far from bodily conditions which resemble it, and so unfamiliar, a person in such a state cannot control it by reason, and may not be able to bear the force of it – even falling down, as the prophet Jeremiah says, who was himself at last overcome in this way. (Jeffrey 1988: 97–99)

Hilton's guide to contemplative prayer, printed in 1494, was one of the earliest printed books in English and widely circulated, popular among an increasing population of lay Christians cultivating private devotional practices. Adapting Jeremiah's metaphor to the physical sensation of mystical prayer in late medieval England, Walter Hilton bent its reception toward a positive experience of religious intimacy. In the same century, German mystic and prior Henry Suso used Jeremiah's inner fire to describe God's presence as "Beloved when it enters the heart of the human lover, praying and longing for it" (Suso and Colledge 1994: 137).

Luther identified closely with Jeremiah's experience of fire burning in his bones. "So it was with me, Martin Luther, that I would often determine not to preach anymore." Yet just as Jeremiah "could not keep silent because his conscience was driving him," so Luther was driven to continue preaching (*LW* 17:344). His commentary on John 16:1–2 paraphrases Jeremiah's burning fire to describe his own experience: "… that is, I became so terrified and so sick at heart that I felt as though I were lying in a red-hot stove and thought that I would surely die if I kept silence." Faced with the prospect of excommunication Luther writes, "If we cease our preaching when we know that it is true and God's word – we would fare as the prophet Jeremiah did. Then God's Word would kindle in us a fire which would melt away and burn up our hearts. No man could endure this, and I would rather die ten deaths than burden my conscience in such a way; for this would soon kill me anyhow" (*LW* 24:301, 305). Jeremiah offered an image for Luther's own torment, and emboldened him to persevere.

John Milton slyly adopted Jeremiah's voice in order to disarm his political opponents. Writing *The Reason of Church Government* against the episcopacy in the English church in 1642, he poses as a loyal man of God torn by inner conflict. Insisting that he hesitated to speak against bishops, Milton clothes himself with Jeremiah's mantle: "But when God commands to take the trumpet and blow a dolorous or a jarring blast, it lies not in man's will what he shall say, or what he shall conceal. If he shall think to be silent, as Jeremiah did, because of the reproach and derision he met with daily… he would be forced to confess as he confessed, his word was in my heart…" To cloak his dangerous political attack against the established church, he takes on the guise of a prophet driven to speak against his own interests "those sharp, but saving words which would be a terror, and a torment in him to keep back" (Milton 2007).

John Wesley's intense religious experience of 1738 added new meaning to Jeremiah's words. Discouraged by a failed mission to Georgia and persistent criticism in his native England for supporting lay preachers, Wesley was trans-formed by a conversion experience which he described as "I felt my heart strangely warmed." For Wesley, the heart prepared by study and prayer was the primary locus of divine activity, manifested in strong emotion. Jeremiah's burning fire supported his own experience, and indicated for him not torment, but comforting evidence that the prophet "found in his heart a constraint to go on." Wesley assures readers in his 1765 commentary that the prophet "did not speak openly, but in his heart." British evangelical F.B. Meyer on a visit to New York contemporized Wesley's reading of Jeremiah's fire for an industrialized society by comparing it to a steam engine. Describing the steady progress of the steamer Maid of the Mist at the foot of Niagara Falls, asking how she can so calmly defy the mad rush of waters, he answers, "Because a burning fire is shut up in her heart, and her engines cannot stay, because impelled in their strong and regular motion. Similarly, within Jeremiah's heart a fire had been lit from the heart of God, and was kept aflame by the continual fuel heaped on it." Jeremiah's fire is here a model of evangelical fervor, for "after all, our main desire is to know how we have this heart on fire. We are tired of a cold heart toward God" (Meyer 1894: 90–91). Meyer's popular "spiritual biography" of Jeremiah, with its personal piety, still remains in print.

Samuel Taylor Coleridge adapted Jeremiah's image to Romantic sensibility in his 1798 poem, "The Rime of the Ancient Mariner." The haunted mariner's fate is to wander the earth alone, telling his sad tale. He is clearly a prophetic figure who learns God's justice and mercy first-hand and is compelled to warn others:

> Since then, at an uncertain hour,
> That agony returns:
> And till my ghastly tale is told,
> This heart within me burns.

Jeremiah's fire remained a mark of authenticity in nineteenth- and twentieth-century Protestantism. H.A. Ironside's widely used commentary warned, "'A burning fire' must have vent, and if the word of God be thus surging up in one's breast he simply must preach. To seek to imitate this is but folly. Any spiritual person, and many utterly godless ones, can readily detect the difference between giving forth that which has been implanted in the inmost soul by the Holy Spirit, and the mere vaporings of a wrought-up sermon." Twentieth-century reception of the burning fire reflects increasing focus on evidence that human emotion is a sign of divine activity. Duhm's historical-critical commentary shows his Romantic sensibility in claiming that the feeling of burning bestows authenticity as "an important testimony by the prophets, demonstrating better than a long theological explanation, that prophecy is not based on reflection and surmise, but that a psychic urge and force, which the prophets cannot master even in daylight's rational judgment, compels them into speech." In the late twentieth century, the theological discourse of earlier interpreters takes a psychological turn with the theory that inner conflict can be a vehicle of religious revelation. In his historical-critical commentary, William McKane writes, "It should be appreciated that the prophetic word arises out of the depths of human suffering, and that it is the product of a conflict which is both agonizing and fruitful. The prophetic word is born out of Jeremiah's human anguish, and it is because there is this great tumult of inward conflict and contradiction that he reaches that vision of the truth which stamps him as a prophet." As if in response to Origen's concern about Jeremiah's sin, McKane insists that "prophetic conflict is not to be interpreted as rebellion and guilt or reduced to human frailty" (McKane 1986: 474).

Reinhold Niebuhr also saw Jeremiah's words as marks of authenticity, though for different reasons. Disturbed by Americans unwilling to risk their security by confronting the rise of the Nazi party, he wrote: "It is instructive that the same Jeremiah who spoke so uncompromisingly against the false prophets tried to return his prophetic commission to God. He was not certain that he was worthy of it, and he doubted his courage to maintain the integrity of the word of God against the resistance of a whole generation which demanded security from religion and rejected the prophet who could offer no security on this side of repentance" (Niebuhr 1965: 110).

Jeremiah's cry resonated with Andrew Mabanji, a sculptor from Zimbabwe enduring the systemic dismantling of his country's economy and democracy by Robert Mugabe (Figure 42). He describes the work of his group of African artists, the Gota Rochisuma Affiliates, as "the explosion of negative silence, the voice of the voiceless. As members of the Shona tribe we want to release from the stone the hidden strengths of indigenous Shona culture." Here Jeremiah's words become encouragement and affirmation for a people resisting injustice by their government.

Do Saints Curse? (20:13–18)

This incongruous juxtaposition of hymn and curse has troubled readers since the fifth century. For Theodoret, Jeremiah gave the hymn in verse 13 pride of place "so as to remove any occasion of blasphemy." Evangelical preacher H.A. Ironside warned against weak faith: "Who would suppose that the same man would be in this truly blessed state of soul at one moment, and perhaps immediately afterwards be plunged into the abyss of the few remaining verses? Ah, it is an experience common to most of the children of God. While faith is in exercise, all is bright. When self is looked to, all becomes dark. In [verses 11–13] the Lord has been before the prophet's soul. In those to follow, it is with himself he is occupied. The result is a sudden depression of his spirit, akin to that of Job" (Ironside 1952: 99–100). Wilhelm Rudolph in 1968 introduced the psychiatric term "depression" to describe verses 14–18, contrasting it with the joy in verse 13 as a mood swing natural to "devout men." Most scholars now use form criticism to solve the problem, defining verses 14–18 as an independent unit and verse 13 as added by a later redactor to soften Jeremiah's harsh words.

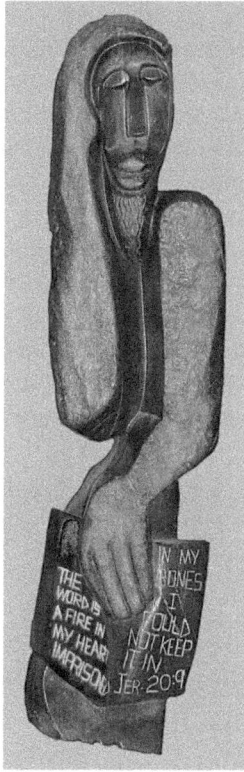

FIGURE 42 Sculpture by Andrew Mabanji. Saint John's Abbey, Collegeville, MN.

Jeremiah's curse in verses 14–18 posed consternation for some readers and opportunities for others. Origen was so troubled that he explained the curse as Jeremiah's reference to the Levitical impurities incurred by his mother during his birth (Origen 1990: 157). Rabbinic tradition before the fourth century CE told the story that Jeremiah was born in accordance with divine design on the Ninth of Ab, the same day of the year that Jerusalem would later be destroyed by the Babylonians and then the Romans. He emerged from the womb wailing, and as an adult cursed the day of his birth because it presaged the destruction of Jerusalem (Ginzberg 1982: VI:384 n.11). Rashi assumes this midrash in his comment that the "trouble and sorrow" of verse 18 are not Jeremiah's personal troubles but the destruction of Jerusalem.

Jeremiah's curse on the day of his conception was a problem in early Jewish tradition because Rabbi Yohanan had decreed that sexual relations should occur only at night (based on Esther 2:14). How could Jeremiah's righteous father, assumed to be the high priest Hilkiah, have had sexual relations in the day? Only under compulsion, the midrash explains. The marriage occurred when Jezebel was killing the prophets, so Hilkiah had to consummate the marriage immediately and flee (*Genesis Rabbah* 64.5). Rashi repeats the tradition, naming the villain as the more chronologically plausible Manasseh. For Rashi's readers in the crusades this midrash became a reflection on the complexities of living faithfully under persecution.

For Jeremiah's irrational curse of the messenger, Gregory developed an elaborate spiritual exegesis that lingered for centuries in the *Glossa*. The father is the corporeal world into which humans are born, the cursed messenger is the devil, and the newborn represents human mortality as the price of sin. Whenever someone sins, the gleeful messenger brings his good news to the father – the world – news of another mortal corrupted. *Bible moralisée* adapted Gregory's reading in a satirical condemnation of contemporary clergy (Figure 43).

FIGURE 43   Jeremiah's curse as medieval allegory condemning contemporary bishops. © M. Moliero Editor, *The Bible of St. Louis*, vol. 2, f. 141r.

The first roundel shows a messenger with Jeremiah's father. The interpretive roundel uses Gregory's spiritual sense to make literal the trope of fathering by picturing a bishop in bed with a woman, surprised by a group of condemning monks. The text quotes Gregory, "The Devil informs the father that a son is born whenever he shows one whom that corruptor has seduced from innocence by a woman." Here biblical text and figural interpretation provide cover for a trenchant indictment of corruption at the highest levels of the church.

Luther saw in Jeremiah's words the complexity of human emotion. Keenly aware from his life in the monastery that overwhelming fear of death and God's wrath could be crippling to the Christian life or, worse, lead to blasphemy, he distinguished human passion from sinful expression. Luther compares anger to the sexual desire that seizes an adolescent, which does not offend God unless it is not kept in check; likewise the "agitations of a muttering, blaspheming, and doubting heart" must be controlled so that they do not result in "disdain of God or despair." Even so, "it happens, of course, that the complaints of saints who suffer such trials also include at least an element of blasphemy... Shall we excuse Jeremiah who became bitter because God did not destroy him in the womb?" The example of Jeremiah as a good man who sinned but was "saved by grace" appealed to Luther (*LW* 13:108–109).

Calvin allowed his readers no such comfort. Although he considered the source of Jeremiah's complaint justified, his belief that feelings could lead to sin made him fence off the dangerous curse with rhetorical barbed wire. Jeremiah was "distressed inwardly in his mind, so that he was carried away contrary to reason and judgment, by turbulent emotions which even led him to give utterance to vile blasphemies. For what is here said cannot be extenuated; but the Prophet most grievously sinned when he became thus calumnious towards God." Jeremiah's state of "sacrilegious madness" warns readers against being "carried away by a violent feeling, so as to become intemperate and unruly." The Christian life always brings reproach, trouble, and the threat of despair; therefore, Calvin warns, "we ought surely to exercise the more care to restrain our feelings... to contend against such feelings... to repress and subdue them."

Calvin's caveat about policing emotions became a significant aspect of the seventeenth- and eighteenth-century Protestant reception of Jeremiah's curse. John Trapp warned his readers that Jeremiah "not without some tang and taint of human frailty, grievously complaineth," and that like Peter's denials and Thomas' unbelief, Jeremiah's outbursts should make readers "not high minded, but fear." Matthew Poole reminded his Puritan readers that Jeremiah was "encompassed with infirmities" and warned them: "These great failures of God's people stand in Scripture, as rocks in the sea appear, to mind mariners to keep off them, not to run upon them." Reflecting on what use Christians might make of this verse, Matthew Henry described it as a warning "to suppress all such intemperate heats and passions in ourselves… When the heart is hot, let the tongue be bridled."

Condemnation of Jeremiah's curse was transformed into praise when J.G. Herder's 1733 treatise *The Spirit of Hebrew Poetry* established a new discourse for biblical interpretation. Seeking the origins of Hebrew poetry, Herder invokes the categories of form and feeling:

> From without, the forms of sense flow into the soul, which puts upon them the impress of its own feeling, and seeks to express them outwardly by gestures, tones, and other significant indications. The whole universe with its movements and forms is for the outward intuition of man, a vast tablet, on which are pictured all forms of living beings. He stands in a sea of living billows, and the fountain of life, which is within his own being, flows forth and re-acts against them. Thus, what flows in upon him from without, according as he feels it and impresses his own feelings upon it, forms the genius of his poetry in its original elements. It may therefore be denominated alike human and Divine, for it is in fact both. (Herder 1833: I, 6)

Herder's concept of the poet's task as impressing his emotions onto the raw material of his sensations is at the heart of German Romanticism, which validates human emotion as a source of truth. In calling Jeremiah "a soul of the tenderest sensibilities," Herder opens the way for a new reading of Jeremiah's curse that had proved so unsettling to earlier readers (Herder 1833: I, 45).

The passions that were a doorway to sin in the sixteenth and seventeenth centuries became in the eighteenth and nineteenth centuries a sign of artistic genius and a spiritual treasure. Benjamin Blaney merged German Romanticism with emerging historical-critical scholarship in his influential commentary, defending Jeremiah's "strong poetical figures" and "imprecations" not "as so many expressions of indignation and malice, but rather of mourning and sorrow" (Blaney 1836: 165). Far from being sinful, the words are "truly and beautifully affecting" and "the pencil is guided by nature; which delights in multiplying passion, especially of the violent and tumultuous kind." Robert Lowth, biblical scholar and bishop of London, permanently changed reception of Jeremiah's words with the publication in 1787 of *Lectures on the Sacred Poetry of the Hebrews*. Lowth showed conclusively that all biblical poetry is based on couplets of parallel lines, thereby highlighting the traditional character of Jeremiah's words (Lowth 1835: 153). By the early nineteenth century, therefore, Jeremiah was understood as one whose words reflected the form and tropes of ancient Hebrew poetry, but whose soul was not very different from the reader's.

Concern over Jeremiah's near blasphemous words nevertheless lingered until the dawn of the twentieth century, when Bernhard Duhm (1901) offered a solution to Calvin's problem: "Such a poem in the mouth of a prophet is almost alarming to us. A Christian would consider it an offense to speak in this way. Here is a man who, driven by despair, exposed his emotions without concern and exhibited shocking frankness when he let the whole world know what he had experienced... As a man of natural, honest emotion Jeremiah in these Confessions wins the highest prize... We must be thankful that Jeremiah himself has allowed us to look so deeply into his inner life, as no other Old Testament writer has done" (Duhm 1901: 168). However, Duhm also uses the emerging history-of-religions approach to place Jeremiah's bitter words in their "ancient Semitic" context in which no idea of an afterlife yet existed: "Jeremiah would not have cursed his life if he had believed that his earthly life signified only a brief step in his existence" (Duhm 1901: 168). In addition, Duhm excuses Jeremiah's curse because he could not have imagined that his suffering might benefit his people. Duhm ends the section by finding Jeremiah's fulfillment in "the holy man who knew mockery and shame even to death." Duhm's Jeremiah offers a peculiar mix of modern sensibilities and ancient prefiguring of Jesus.

In some traditions, Jeremiah's curse remained dangerous. Evangelical preacher William Kelly, while acknowledging that the prophet "was bound in the greatest grief before God, and at last he vents it to the Lord," warns his readers away. "Jeremiah, however, is in wonderful contrast with the blessed Lord, Who, when most rejected, was most happy in a certain sense... If the greatest suffering would magnify God the most, He was ready to receive it" (Kelly 1938: 46). Among some contemporary Christians, Jeremiah remains a negative example: "A renewed outbreak of sufferings, however, combined with Satan's efforts, bring distress back into his heart" (George André 1988: 44).

The appreciation of Jeremiah's curse as a badge of religious integrity that flowered in German Romanticism generally became the norm in mainstream religious circles. Identification with Jeremiah lends an eerie prescience to Dietrich Bonhoeffer's 1927 meditation for young people: "Jeremiah had long ago recognized the ultimate failure of his words, but God still spoke to him and as long as that happened he had to continue to speak... Jeremiah was the unhappiest person in the whole city, because he knew both God and the people... Jeremiah's close relationship with God made him curse his life. Children, being with God does not make one happy. We learn this from Jeremiah" (Bonhoeffer 2003: 9:514).

Jesuit priest Daniel Berrigan rendered verses 14–18 into contemporary poetry, ending with these words:

> Nevertheless,
> You pillar
> cloud of unknowing,
> of undoing –
> I cling to You, fiery cling to You, burn of you
> and I sing, I raise
> a song against the night;
> my Scandal
> my Love –
> stand with me in the breach!
>
> (Berrigan 1999: 87–88)

The Burial of an Ass (22:18–19)

Jeremiah's shocking prophecy that King Jehoiakim's body would not be buried properly was a problem because of its horror and its contradiction with other accounts. 2 Kings 24:5–7 describes the king "sleeping with his fathers" but 2 Chron 5–8 reports that Nebuchadnezzar bound Jehoiakim with chains for exile to Babylon. For Josephus, writing in first-century Rome after the Jewish revolt, Jeremiah's words are a liability because they threaten disrespect for the Emperor.

Jeremiah Through the Centuries, First Edition. Mary Chilton Callaway.
© 2020 Mary Chilton Callaway. Published 2020 by John Wiley & Sons Ltd.

In *Antiquities* 10:6, Josephus transforms Jeremiah's inflammatory prophecy with a fictional narrative describing Nebuchadnezzar "not observing covenants that he had made" when he invaded Jerusalem. He slaughters young and old, including King Jehoiakim, "whom he commanded to be thrown before the walls, without any burial." In Josephus' re-telling it was not Jews, but an eastern despot who murdered and then desecrated the body of Judah's king. This tradition of attributing Jehoiakim's death to Nebuchadnezzar is expanded in *Leviticus Rabbah*. The contradiction between the three biblical texts is resolved with a set of midrashic stories that describe the king being lowered over the wall of Jerusalem to be handed over to Nebuchadnezzar in exchange for Babylonian withdrawal. In one story, Nebuchadnezzar executes Jehoiakim, puts his body into the carcass of an ass and drags him around to fulfill Jeremiah's prophecy (Rosenberg 1985: 1:242).

In Christian tradition the burial of an ass becomes a metaphor for burying sinners and a warning to the living whose misdeeds would pursue them into eternity. Eleventh-century theologian-monk Peter Damian worked to reform clerical abuses in the church, including priests living with a mistress. In a letter to the bishop of Turin, he recounts the case of a defiant priest who refused to dismiss his mistress. When the priest died suddenly, Peter Damian asked that he be buried near the church but without hymns or psalms "so that fear might be engendered in those who live impure lives, and that glory of chastity might be enhanced. Clearly, it seemed to be the proper procedure that, according to the prophet, the dead man should be buried like an ass, since during his life he refused to be bound by human law. Thus Jeremiah spoke of Jehoiakim, 'He shall be buried'" (Damian 1998: 4:275).

Jeremiah and the Lost Ark (22:29)

Jeremiah's enigmatic cry, "O earth, earth, earth, hear the word of the Lord!" echoed through the centuries. It is the fourth use of earth/land (*eretz*) in the short space of verses 26–29, where it refers twice to Babylon and once to Judah, but in verse 29 has no clear referent. In their original setting the words are part of a prophecy that the young King Jehoiachin will be taken as exile to the land of Babylon and never return to the land of Judah. The earliest use of Jeremiah's cry appears in the late first-century CE *Apocalypse of Baruch* (*2 Baruch*) in a midrashic account of the destruction of the Temple and the fate of the Ark. The story describes four angels about to drop their flaming torches onto Jerusalem when a fifth angel swoops in to stop them. Collecting up the Ark and "all the holy vessels of the tabernacle," the angel cries out Jeremiah's words to the earth, adding the command, "Receive the things which I commit to you, and guard them until the last times." The narrator reports, "The earth opened its mouth and swallowed them up" (Charlesworth 1983: 1.623). Jeremiah's mysterious words here evoke an earlier tradition explaining the mystery of the lost Ark (see p. xx in Introduction), reassuring the faithful that it, like them, remained under divine protection.

Generations of Jews and Christians contemporized Jeremiah's call to *eretz*. Targum shortens the triple *eretz* to "land of Israel" and directs the prophetic "listen to the word of the Lord" to the congregation sitting in the synagogue. In this way the translators repurposed Jeremiah's words about the fate of Jehoiachin into a warning for the present. Rashi adopted Targum's interpretation and added another: the triple "land" means that God esteems Israel above all. For Jewish readers in eleventh-century France this would be a welcome word of hope. In the twelfth century, Joseph Qimhi read Jeremiah's triple "land" as the destroyed Judah, which was God's response to the triple "temple of the LORD" spoken by smug worshippers in Jer 7:4. This scriptural echo reminded readers that divine justice, while sometimes slow, was sure.

English Bibles from the beginning translated Jeremiah's mysterious triple cry of *eretz* as earth, thereby broadening the sense from the land of Judah to the land of the contemporary reader. Jeremiah's cry echoed in John Milton's defiant words near the end of his life, when the Puritan Commonwealth had been dissolved and Charles II returned to the throne. The restoration of the monarchy in 1660 was a bitter blow for Milton, and the English king represented a new Nebuchadnezzar who would destroy England as the Babylonian king had destroyed Judah. Milton's sense of himself as a disillusioned Jeremiah who nevertheless must speak the truth blazes out in his last work, *The Readie and Easie Way* (1660). Recognizing the defeat of the Puritan cause, he invokes Jer 22:29 to warn of its consequences: "Thus much I should perhaps have said, though I was sure I should have spoken only to trees and stones: and had none to cry to, but with the prophet, 'O earth, earth, earth!' to tell the very soil itself, what her perverse inhabitants are deaf to" (Milton 2007: 138).

The Righteous Branch (23:5–6)

The playful biblical text was an invitation to readers down the centuries. In its original sixth-century context of Judean anxiety over the future of the Davidic monarchy, the words seem to affirm that God stands by the promise made to David in 2 Samuel 7, but the prophecy turns the Hebrew root *zdk* into a kaleidoscopic display of meaning. First, Jeremiah uses *tzadik* to mean "legitimate": the king will be a rightful scion of David. Then the noun *tzedakah* describes

Jeremiah Through the Centuries, First Edition. Mary Chilton Callaway.
© 2020 Mary Chilton Callaway. Published 2020 by John Wiley & Sons Ltd.

how the king will act: he will do what is right in God's eyes. Finally, the king's name, *yhwh tzidkenu,* proclaims him as link between God and people. These descriptions of the rightful/right acting future king play on the name of Zedekiah, the last king of Judah, whose righteousness is at best ambiguous in Jeremiah.

Jeremiah's hopeful prophecy is contemporized by Jews and Christians alike. In the Targum the Davidic branch is translated as God's messiah who will come. In the eleventh century, after the first crusade, Rashi interprets the messianic title "the Lord is our righteousness" to offer hope for Jews in a time of devastation that "in the time of this one [the Messiah] the Lord will vindicate us." In Christian tradition, the Davidic branch signified Christ, yet curiously Jeremiah's lyrical prophecy of divine consolation often became bitter polemic. By mid-fifth century CE it had become a staple of Christian argument, as when Theodoret chastised "stupid Jews who shamelessly endeavor to apply this to Zerubbabel." In the Reformation this oracle that the church from the beginning had interpreted as messianic became a weapon in a different theological battle, when Luther explained it at length in a 1527 sermon. It was published in an English translation as "A Fruitful and godly exposition and declaration of the kingdom of Christ and of Christian liberty, made upon the words of the Prophet Jeremiah in the 23rd chapter" (1548). The English translator notably dedicated it to Mary, sister of England's first Protestant monarch, Edward I.

Luther's title signals two of the key aspects of what is more manifesto than sermon. For him the words "the Lord is our righteousness" are key, for here he finds in Jeremiah the centerpiece of his radical theology of justification by faith, the source of Christian liberty. Luther seems to base his reading of Jeremiah on the exegesis of Nicholas of Lyra, who used Maimonides' observation that the name Lord signifies "the perfect and undifferentiated essence" while other divine names are derived from God's works. Verse 5 for Luther refers to Christ's humanity, while verse 6, with its use of the divine name, refers to Christ's divinity. Luther also divides Jeremiah's oracle, explaining that Lord refers to the divine person, "whereof he gives nothing nor participates in us," while the title "our righteousness" "concerns what his kingly office does for us." In Luther's radical theology, this kingly office extends to humanity by Christ's participation in the divine righteousness: "Now when I believe in Christ, then must Christ with his righteousness step forth before the face of God in heaven and make answer for me… Therefore when death comes to a faithful Christian he says, 'you are welcome good sir death, what seek ye here? Do you not know whom I have by my side? Christ is my righteousness'" (Luther 1548: images 31–32).

Thinly veiled in this dramatic scenario is Luther's attack on the church's practice of selling indulgences to Christians fearful of eternal torment because of sins for which they could never atone. Church teaching traditionally used Jeremiah's verse to show Christ prefigured in the prophets, but Luther read the words as freedom from spiritual captivity for ordinary Christians. He also found in Jeremiah's words the corollary to this Christian liberty – Christ's kingdom is not earthly, ruled by humans in Rome, but a spiritual one whose authority resides only in heaven. Luther ends his sermon with what will become the high rhetoric of Reformation theology concerning the role of works in the life of faith: "When I preach thus I do not mean that men should not obey the higher powers, serve them and give them their due, for Christian liberty does not touch the body, nor outward behavior and conversation but the soul. Therefore when you serve or obey higher powers it is like giving a coat to a naked man, or feeding the hungry, for it is a work of charity that flows out of faith; not that you should be made righteous through this work but that it declare your faith" (Luther 1548: images 37–38).

The lasting effect of Luther's sermon on Jeremiah 23 is evident in English Bible translations. Coverdale rendered the key words, "the Lord our righteous master," but every subsequent translation read "the Lord our righteousness." KJV added an implicit commentary with its innovation of setting all four words in small capital letters, a tradition that persists into the present in some Bibles. Across the channel, the Douay Rheims translation avoided the freighted language of justification with a literal rendering of the Vulgate (*Dominus justus noster*), "the Lord our just one." A marginal note offers a riposte to Luther: "Christ who is just of himself, who maketh others just, and without whom no man can be just."

The potent legacy of Patristic and Reformation reception exemplified the problem of religion for nineteenth-century Deists for whom naïve literalism and self-serving interpretations of biblical prophecies were detrimental to English society and to the credibility of the church. Matthew Arnold's important *Literature and Dogma* (1870) aimed to show that dogma harms religion because it presupposes a certainty proper only to science, encouraging people to adopt beliefs that can be discredited by reason and leave them bereft and cynical. The two most egregious examples of turning the poetry of the Bible into dogma are miracles and prophetic predictions, because they confuse the certainty of science with the imaginative power of literature. Interpreting Jeremiah's words in 23:5–6 as a prediction of Jesus is Arnold's chief example of misreading prophetic poetry as a narrow prediction that can only harm people's faith when they learn the truth: "And what, then, will they say as they come to know… that Jeremiah's supposed signal identification of Jesus Christ with the Lord God of Israel… runs really: 'I will raise to David a righteous branch; in his days Judah shall be saved and Israel shall dwell safely; and this is the name whereby they shall call themselves: The Eternal is our righteousness!'"

(Drury 1989: 158). Arnold uses the famous prophecy of Jeremiah to expose what he disparagingly calls "the display of supernatural prescience" as the weak foundation of belief offered by the church.

False Prophets (23:9–40)

Readers through the centuries often contemporized Jeremiah's warnings against smooth-talking prophets who offered false hope. Thomas Hobbes used them in *Leviathan* to support his political argument that Christians should submit to a sovereign ruler, whom he called "God's Prophet," lest they be bewitched by false prophets into rebellion, violence, and civil war. In Hobbes' reading, false prophets in modern guise are ambitious pretenders inciting rebellion from the legitimate sovereign. Jeremiah shows that "the prophets were generally liars," which Hobbes takes as evidence that 23:16 and 14:14 warn Christians about dissenters claiming authority against the king. Everyone "is bound to make use of his natural reason to apply to all prophecy those rules which God hath given us to discern the true from the false" (Hobbes 2011: 363–364). Hobbes enlisted Jeremiah into the Enlightenment embrace of reason in support of the monarch, whom he calls the Sovereign Prophet.

In 1937, Reinhold Niebuhr invoked Jeremiah to warn Americans about the dangers of Mussolini and Hitler. In *Beyond Tragedy,* the chapter titled "The Test of True Prophecy" opens with two full pages of quotations about false prophecy from Jer 23. Niebuhr writes, "False prophecy always means to give ultimate significance to purely individual and partial judgments. The question is: How is one to detect this false element? Jeremiah's answer is that a false prophet betrays himself by offering false security to people" (Niebuhr 1937: 17). Niebuhr applied Jer 23:17 to contemporary preachers and politicians who used a lethal combination of American optimism and triumphal Christianity to reassure people that no harm would come from Hitler.

Jeremiah's warning against false prophets who ran but were not sent (23:21) is central to the writings of early Quaker William Dewsbury. Together with George Fox, Dewsbury sent sermons across the Atlantic to fellow Quakers who had fled persecution in England as well as those arrested in England. The descriptive title page of his 1655 sermon "The Mighty Day of the Lord is Coming" uses Exile as a figure for Quakers forced to live in a world reliant on external forms rather than the "inner light." Dewsbury takes on the mantle of Jeremiah to unmask false prophets, Anglicans and Puritans who "look for the kingdom of God to come in outward observations... not regarding the motions of the Spirit of God within... who run when the Lord never sent them, as the false prophets did, when the Lord sent his true prophet Jeremiah to cry against them" (Dewsbury 1656: 158). Dewsbury notes that he writes his sermon from an English jail, and his contemporary George Fox, founder of the Society of Friends, confirms in his introduction that Dewsbury had been "beaten, stoned and imprisoned." Both men drew strength from Jeremiah's example.

Jeremiah's image of deceivers hiding in secret places foolishly thought to be invisible to God (23:23–24) takes on new meaning when these "secret places" are read in terms of human interiority. Calvin interprets the hidden places in terms of the emerging humanist trope of the many-layered self: "The heedless security of men would never be so great as it is, were they to believe that nothing is hid from God, but that he penetrates into the inmost recesses of the heart, that he discerns between the thoughts and the feelings, and leaves not unobserved the very marrow."

The image of the word as powerful hammer (23:29) became a favorite image for the Bible in the sixteenth century. A 1538 edition of Coverdale's New Testament showcases its appearance in English on the title page: "Jeremie: Is not my word like a fire saith the Lord, and like an hammer that breaketh the hard stone?" One of the more radical reformers, Thomas Müntzer (1489–1525) added "the hammer" to his signature. At the same time, English Presbyterian Thomas Bakewell described the hammer as a weapon that would smash falsehood. Describing Anabaptists like Müntzer and "all others who affect not civil government" as an unnaturally hard nut, Bakewell declares "the hammer of God's word that breaketh in pieces the rocks, Ier. 23.29, will break this nut, that all may see the devilish kernel that is in it" (Bakewell 1644: n.p.).

Jeremiah's image of stolen words (23:30) came to signify the misuse of Scripture. Jerome used it against Pelagius, who argued that humans could participate in their own salvation by doing good works; Jerome's response condemned heretics who "steal" the words of Scripture, seducing unsuspecting Christians with false hopes. Medieval Jewish exegete Rashi commented that Hananiah spied on Jeremiah prophesying doom on Elam in the upper marketplace, and then imitated his manner of speaking to falsely pronounce doom on Babylon in the lower marketplace. He may also be condemning Christians who studied Hebrew with a rabbi and then used their knowledge to turn prophetic texts against Jews. In nineteenth-century Protestant language, false prophets invaded the inner castle of the faithful Christian's heart and mind, carrying away its treasure. In a note castigating "profane clergymen," John Brown's *Self-Interpreting Bible* warns, "They 'steal my words' from the memory of their neighbor, by occupying it with other things. They 'steal my words' from the understanding, by perverting it with false doctrines. They 'steal my words' from the heart, by fostering evil affections and establishing evil habits; and thus fulfill the work of the wicked one who 'catcheth away' the seed of the word which is sown in the hearts of men, Matt 13:19."

The metaphor of wheat and chaff (23:28) captivated readers. Jerome distinguished the chaff of heretics, which cannot nourish believers, from the wheat of the church, which is heavenly bread. Repeated use of Jerome's "heretics" in the interlinear notes of the *Glossa Ordinaria* invited readers similarly to identify appropriate adversaries. In the tumultuous sixteenth-century battles about the authority of Scripture, Protestant John Lambert used Jeremiah's words to fight for his life against accusations of heresy in the English church. Extradited from Antwerp, where he was in hiding with Tyndale, Lambert had to answer, among many questions, whether he believed that "oblations and pilgrimages may be devoutly and meritoriously done to the sepulchers and relics of saints." Knowing that responding truthfully would condemn him to death, Lambert cagily responded by paraphrasing Jeremiah to distinguish human tradition from biblical command. "Christ's law… hath no chaff in it, as have men's traditions; but is pure and clean wheat, as showeth Jeremy, 'What is the chaff to the wheat? Therefore behold, I will come against the prophets that steal my word, and deceive my people in their lies and in their errors'" (Foxe 1838: 5:201). Jeremiah's words were as offensive in the sixteenth century as in his own time, and Henry VIII ordered Lambert executed in 1538.

Two Baskets of Figs (24:1–10)

The vision of the sweet and rancid figs reflected debate in Jeremiah's time over whether exiles or those who remained in Judah constituted the true people of God. Identification of the good figs as the exiles in Babylon reflects the dominant role that Judeans in Babylon took in editing the scroll of Jeremiah. In the earliest receptions there were only good figs, which were tangible signs of divine care. In the apocryphal stories of Second Temple literature these figs

Jeremiah Through the Centuries, First Edition. Mary Chilton Callaway.
© 2020 Mary Chilton Callaway. Published 2020 by John Wiley & Sons Ltd.

signify the divine care of Jeremiah's friend (see Jer 39), while in Islamic tradition they instruct the prophet about divine power (see Introduction p. xx). From the third century to the sixth, emphasis shifted to the bad figs. After a number of allegorical interpretations, Origen takes verse 1 as definitive: Jeremiah has the vision after the first exile to Babylon and defines the bad figs as those who remain in Jerusalem. For Origen these are the Jews, whom he identifies with Jerusalem, while the good figs are "strangers by nature and outside Jerusalem," that is, Christians (Origen 1998: 291–292). Origen's allegory provided fuel for centuries of anti-Jewish polemic. Caesarius of Arles (470–542) conflated it with the parable of the non-productive fig tree in his sermon on Luke 13:6–9. Interpreting this fig tree as the Law, he designated its early inedible figs as "the conceited and worthless Israelites" while the later figs, sweetened by the Gospel, were Christians. In the sixteenth century, Calvin was troubled by idea of an authoritative vision. The idea that a vision could preempt the divine word posed the challenge of Catholic tradition to the authority of the Bible. He reassured his readers that vision is ancillary, "a sort of seal to what was delivered; for in order that the Prophet might possess greater authority, they not only spoke, but as it were sealed their doctrine, as though God had graven on it, as it were by his finger, a certain mark."

Jeremiah 25

This chapter displays the complex reception of the Jeremiah tradition in antiquity. Septuagint ends it with verse 13, making chapter 25 a coda to the scroll of Jeremiah's prophecies between 627 and 605 BCE. Divine affirmation of "everything written on this scroll, which Jeremiah prophesied against all the nations" signals the early work of scribes shaping the tradition. Septuagint continues with the oracles against the nations as a proleptic fulfillment of verses 12–13. The Masoretic Text, however, situates these oracles against the nations after Jeremiah 45 as the final words of the book.

Jeremiah Through the Centuries, First Edition. Mary Chilton Callaway.
© 2020 Mary Chilton Callaway. Published 2020 by John Wiley & Sons Ltd.

The Cup of the Wine of Wrath (25:15–31)

Jeremiah's unsettling image of nations forced to drink the intoxicating cup of strong wine plays on the traditional Near Eastern trope of a cup of wine as one's portion in life. Ezekiel, who often exaggerates Jeremiah's metaphors, portrays Judah as a ruined woman forced to drunkenness (Ezekiel 23:32–33). Isaiah reverses Jeremiah's image to comfort the exiles in Babylon with hope of renewal: "I have taken from your hand the cup of staggering; you shall drink no more from the bowl of my wrath" (Isa 51:23).

Readers frequently turned Jeremiah's image against their own enemies, especially in times of persecution. The author of Revelation used it as code against Romans persecuting Christians, intensifying the image to the wine of divine wrath poured undiluted into the cup of God's anger. In this apocalyptic vision, the worshippers of false (Roman) gods drink the deadly draught to their destruction (Rev 14:10). The Geneva Bible assures Puritan readers with a note teaching that the cup of wine signifies "The extreme afflictions that God hath appointed for everyone, and this cup which the wicked drink is more bitter than that which he giveth to his children, for he measureth the one by mercy and the other by justice."

Jewish tradition read the cup as both judgment and mercy. Jews in late antiquity heard in the Targum that Gentile nations would be forced to drink the wine of God's curse against them (see commentary on 1:5). Rashi explains the command to drink as evidence that this divine judgment cannot be reversed by last-minute repentance, which in light of the First Crusade could signal that God's mercy for Israel's enemies might have limits. On the other hand, mid-rashic tradition combines the cup of 25:15 with the prophetic commission of 1:5 to highlight Jeremiah's anguish at giving the deadly cup to his own people. When he asks who should drink the deadly cup first and God replies "Jerusalem and the cities of Judah" (verse 18), the prophet cries out, "Woe is me, my mother that you bore me" (15:10). He compares himself to a priest asked to give a woman suspected of adultery "the water of bitterness" and discovers that she is his mother (Ginzberg 1941: 4:295).

The deadly effects of the cup provided useful images to leaders in the Temperance movement. The Temperance Bible Commentary makes Jeremiah's metaphor literal, suggesting that Judah's sin is drinking: "The cup of their pleasure is the sign of their punishment." The authors explicitly make the image of judgment a warning against drinking wine: "The opinion that a liquor, capable of representing calamities so dreadful, is at the same time suitable for daily use, cannot too soon pass away from among sane men" (Lees 1868: 188). Scottish clergyman Alexander Stewart writes, "Intoxicating liquor must be in itself a very bad thing, seeing the consequences of it are so frequently made use of in

Scripture to represent the most woeful and miserable conditions in which men may be placed. It deprives men of reason and judgment, thereby making them represent those who are frantic with despair – driven to 'their wit's end, staggering in all the measures they take'… it often causes men to fall never again to rise, and thus to resemble those who fall under the irresistible judgments of God" (Stewart n.d.: 331). One robust response to these uses of Jeremiah includes *The Holy Bible Repudiates "Prohibition,"* written in 1910 by George Gavin Brown, founder of Brown-Forman Distillers Corporation. In his preface, Brown, who identifies himself as "a whiskey merchant and manufacturer," distinguishes temperance from the growing movement toward prohibition. Brown explains Jeremiah's cup as metaphor: "It should be noted that the wine-cup prophesied of is not to contain ordinary wine but God's fury. There is not only no condemnation of ordinary wine here but decidedly the contrary. The people, with the approval of God, looked upon wine as a blessing, whereas they are being threatened by a deadly punishment" (Brown 1910: 49).

In 1862, Julia Ward Howe transformed Jeremiah's image of treading grapes (25:30) in "The Battle Hymn of the Republic." Combining the ominous metaphor of divine anger with the cup of the wine of wrath (see Jer 51), Howe wrote of "trampling out the vintage where the grapes of wrath are stored." Her words made the dread and urgency of Jeremiah's image a warning about divine retribution for America's sin of slavery.

Jeremiah 26–28

Jer 26 offers another tradition about the events narrated in Jer 7. Reception history of the "Temple Sermon" can be found with the comments in Chapter 7.

Jeremiah's Yoke (Jer 27:2; 28:1–17)

The dramatic confrontation between Jeremiah and Hananiah intrigued readers through the centuries, beginning with the image of the yoke. The Hebrew technical terms for "yoke" and "bars of iron" caused difficulty for ancient translators. Septuagint has bonds and collars while Jerome reads chains and a shackle.

Jeremiah Through the Centuries, First Edition. Mary Chilton Callaway.
© 2020 Mary Chilton Callaway. Published 2020 by John Wiley & Sons Ltd.

Luther's 1534 translation turned the two Hebrew words into *Joch* (yoke), and the English word yoke appears first in the Geneva Bible (1587). The scene is not illustrated until the sixteenth century, when it becomes a favorite in vernacular Bibles. It appears first in Lucas Cranach's woodcut for Luther's translation, which shows Jeremiah wearing a square wooden yoke, confronting a European king and angry mob. Cranach's contemporizing woodcut includes a Bible prominently placed in the center foreground, perhaps signaling a parallel between Jeremiah's prophetic words and Luther's translation of God's words. The engraving in the 1674 *Theatrum Biblicum* similarly presents Jeremiah as a strong individual obedient to God whatever the cost (Figure 44). The cloud of glory that he faces is the Protestant replacement for the anthropomorphic deity of medieval art. This Jeremiah, wearing the peculiar yoke, encouraged seventeenth-century Protestants in their own acts of individual conscience.

By the eighteenth century, the yoke was an embarrassment for Deists. Matthew Tindal's argument for a rational, universal Christianity devoid of "nonsense" rejected such texts in which prophets acted like "madmen or idiots" (Tindal 1730: 72–81). Cambridge scholar-cleric Daniel Waterland in turn ridiculed Tindal's literalism, describing the yoke narrative as "figurative, metaphorical language"

FIGURE 44   *Theatrum Biblicum.* 1674. Rare Books Division, The New York Public Library, Astor, Lenox and Tilden Foundations.

and an example of the "ornamental figures and affecting images" that added force to Jeremiah's message (Waterland 1732: 3:88–89).

False Prophets

The term "false prophet" does not occur in Hebrew but enters Jewish and Christian tradition through the Septuagint, where it occurs ten times, nine of which are in Jeremiah. Jer 27:9 (in the Septuagint Jer 34:9) reads, "Do not listen to your false prophets" and 28:1 (in the Septuagint Jer 35:1) reads, "Ananias the false prophet" (Jer 35:1). Early Christians adopted the term to warn readers against the threat of false prophets in their own day. Writing about Israel, the author of 2 Peter warns, "False prophets also arose among the people, just as there will be false teachers among you" (2 Peter 2:1). Josephus equates the false prophets who deceived Zedekiah with Zealots and other rebels who had incited revolt against the Romans, while Jeremiah was the one who "came forward and prophesied the truth" (*Antiquities* 10:3) His narrative is a thinly veiled defense of his own desperate act when imprisoned by the Roman government. Josephus came forward and prophesied that Vespasian would be emperor, and when Vespasian was crowned he rewarded Josephus.

Eighteenth-century educator Mrs. Trimmer warned her young readers to use common sense against false prophets in their own day: "You find, my dear, that there were also at Jerusalem false prophets, who flattered the king with hopes of deliverance from the power of Nebuchadnezzar. Zedekiah was, however, inexcusable for giving credit to them, because none of their predictions had ever been fulfilled; whereas Jeremiah was famous for the completion of his prophecies. One would have supposed that the death of Hananiah… would at least have awakened the king's attention" (Trimmer 1783: 261).

In the twentieth century, Reinhold Niebuhr repeatedly invoked Jeremiah's confrontation with false prophets in his warnings about Fascism and Nazism. He called out preachers and politicians comforting Americans with anodyne assurances in the face of grave danger, describing them as heirs of the false prophets and quoting Jeremiah repeatedly to expose their sham theology (see also commentary on Jer 23).

Jeremiah 29

The Jeremiah's letter to the Judahites taken to Babylon in 597 BCE reflects the bitter debate over the meaning of the exile, especially whether exiles in Babylon or those remaining in Judah constituted the true Israel. It offers clear evidence that the exiles settled in Babylon had the dominant voice, though not the only one, in the earliest reception of Jeremiah.

Jeremiah Through the Centuries, First Edition. Mary Chilton Callaway.
© 2020 Mary Chilton Callaway. Published 2020 by John Wiley & Sons Ltd.

Build and Plant (29:1–6)

The claim that YHWH rather than Nebuchadnezzar sent Israel into exile influenced political theology from the fifth century forward, especially when the civil society in which Christians lived was endangered. Writing after the first invasions of Rome by the Visigoths, Jerome introduces the verse as "beautiful" because it attributes exile to God's will rather than the king's power. The Geneva Bible, the work of Puritans in self-exile from England, similarly highlights the verse with a marginal note emphasizing the exile as the Lord's work, not Nebuchadnezzar's. English preacher Matthew Poole clarifies that though God was "the principal efficient cause they were ordered to be carried away, their own sins were the meritorious cause."

Jeremiah's symbolic command that parents find spouses for their sons and daughters (verse 6), intended to discourage hopes for an early return to Judah, proved useful to later readers. Jerome, who thought marriage a lesser state best avoided by Christians, used allegory to spiritualize Jeremiah's advice. Daughters signify "works" and sons are the "true faith," so Jeremiah's command urges uniting good works with a strong faith. Nicholas of Lyra also allegorized, but for a different reason. "Taking wives" refers to Jacob's wives Leah (practical wisdom) and Rachel (theological wisdom), Nicholas cagily advises. For Christians in early fifteenth-century Europe, this meant uniting the newly available writings from classical antiquity with the church's teachings to produce new forms of wisdom.

In the sixteenth century, Calvin read the words literally in order to address a new social practice he found alarming. It was increasingly common in Europe for young people to have a say in their marriage, and even to choose their own spouse. Calvin seized on the fact that Jeremiah advises parents to "take wives for your sons and give your daughters in marriage" and he warned: "It would be altogether unreasonable for young men and young women to seek partners for themselves, according to their own humor and fancy." Jeremiah's words affirm God's command "according to the usual order of nature… when he bids young men not to be otherwise joined in marriage than by the consent of parents, and that young women are not to marry but those to whom they are given."

Praying for the Enemy (29:7)

Jeremiah's command that the exiles pray for the welfare of the enemy city in which they were living nourished generations of Jews living in hostile environments. The first-century rabbinic dictum, "Pray for the peace of the government, for except for the fear of that, we should have swallowed each other alive" adapts

Jeremiah's words for Jews living in Judea under Roman rule. In that tense and oppressive context, suggesting public prayer for the Roman Emperor was not only pious but also politically astute (Herford 1987: 64–65). A prayer for the local government had become part of the Jewish prayer book in fourteenth-century Spain; after their expulsion in 1492 some Jews took the prayer to their new home in the Ottoman Empire, where they prayed for the Sultan. Expelled Jews also brought the prayer to Holland and Italy, where they prayed for the secular ruler. In 1655, Jewish scholar Manasseh ben Israel wrote his "Humble Addresses" to Cromwell arguing for overturning the thirteenth-century expulsion of the Jews from England, and one of his arguments used Jeremiah to show that Jews pray for the government of the land in which they are living. Jeremiah's prayer was also an inspiration to the eighteenth-century Jewish intellectual movement, Haskalah, whose goal was to help Jews adapt to the modern cultures in which they lived. Meir Hurwitz, living in Vilna under Russian law in 1807, warns his readers not to view Gentiles in the traditional way as idolaters and enemies, but to remember their own obligation to pray for their welfare, as Jeremiah and the sages had commanded. His argument was humanistic and utilitarian, but Jeremiah's words clothed it with Jewish authority. The prayer remained in the Jewish prayer book until the end of the nineteenth century, though by tacit agreement was often omitted from the liturgy (Lederhendler 1989: 61, 120).

Christian tradition combines Jeremiah's Realpolitik with high ideals. Origen's Gnostic interpretation describes Babylon as the "confusion" (Gen 11.9) of this mortal life to which the soul is condemned, while Jerusalem is both the origin and destination of Christian souls. Jerome identifies Jeremiah's words with Jesus' command to "love your enemies and pray for those who persecute you" (Matt 5.44), and with the advice to early Christians to pray for "kings and all who are in high positions" (1 Tim 2.1–2). The interpretations of Origen and Jerome both influenced Christian political theology. In *City of God,* Augustine combines them into an allegory of Christians living in the two cities of Babylon (the political realm) and Jerusalem (the spiritual realm). Always a shrewd politician, Augustine exhorts Christians to follow Jeremiah's advice, explaining that the peace of Babylon refers to "the peace of this world which the good and the bad share in common" (*City of God* 6:18). In a sermon Augustine also alludes to "the voice of a new Jeremiah" when he approvingly cites 1 Timothy's exhortation that Christians in the Roman Empire pray for kings so that they can live in peace (Augustine 1990: 3:29).

These early expositions permanently gave Jeremiah's words the dual motivation of spiritual generosity and political self-interest. The Geneva Bible codes the verse as comfort to Puritans in exile: "The prophet does not speak this for the affection that he bore to the tyrant, but that they should pray for the common rest and quietness that their troubles might not be increased, and that they might with more patience and less grief wait for the time of their deliverance, which God had appointed most certain: for not only the Israelites but all the world yea and the insensible creatures would rejoice when these tyrants would be destroyed, as in Isa 24.4." The plural "tyrants" implicitly includes Mary Tudor, the reason for the Puritans' exile. In seventeenth-century England, Matthew Poole similarly uses Jeremiah's words to warn his readers in 1663 living under England's Act of [Religious] Uniformity: "Do not raise tumults or seditions, nor take part with those who do… when God hath put a yoke upon our necks, we patiently wait until he takes it off." He ends with a note of self-interest: "For God having by his providence cast us under their power, our peace dependeth upon theirs."

Jeremiah's words are invoked to support a modern political argument in Spinoza's *Theologico-Political Treatise* of 1670. To eliminate religious tyranny over scientific and philosophical investigation, Spinoza argues that political power should be separate from religious authority and established solely on reasoned assent of the governed. Citing Jer 29, he writes in chapter XIX of the *Treatise* that when the sovereignty of Judah was destroyed, the religion of the Hebrews "could no longer be received as the law of a particular kingdom, but only as the universal precept of reason" (Spinoza 1951: 248). Jeremiah offers evidence for the revolutionary argument that political authority should not derive from religious beliefs, but common consent of the governed.

Dietrich Bonhoeffer address Jeremiah's words to the next generation in the darkest of times. Writing from prison in March 1944 to his infant great-nephew, Dietrich Bethge, on the eve of his baptism, Bonhoeffer offers advice on living in difficult times: "We may have to face events and changes that take no account of our wishes and our rights. But if so, we shall not give way to embittered and barren pride, but consciously submit to divine judgment, and so prove ourselves worthy to survive by identifying ourselves generously and unselfishly with the life of the community and the sufferings of our fellow-men." Bonhoeffer then quotes Jer 27:11, merging it with the words, "Seek the welfare of the city" (Bonhoeffer 2008: 160).

Seventy Years (29:10)

Seventy originally signified simply a large number, but Jeremiah's prophecy early on generated new meanings for the number. Although the period from the exile in 587 to the return under Cyrus in 539 was only forty-eight years, Jeremiah's seventy-year prediction had already begun to shape tradition by 520 BCE when it appears in the speech of an angel (Zech 1.12). It is further developed in 2 Chron 25:17–23, where Nebuchadnezzar's destruction and Cyrus' restoration are explained as "to fulfill the word of the Lord by the mouth of Jeremiah until the land made up for its Sabbaths." This reception of Jeremiah had two lasting effects. It gave Jeremiah the last word of the Bible in its original Jewish form, where Chronicles is the last book of the third scroll, and it established seventy as a number with hidden significance. During the persecutions of Antiochus (168 BCE) the anonymous author of Daniel uses Jeremiah's prediction, which he "perceived in the scrolls," as code to encourage his fellow Jews (Dan 9:2). The angel Gabriel instructs him in a vision to interpret Jeremiah's seventy years in light of 2 Chronicles, as seventy weeks of years, which will end with divine deliverance. If the land usually recovers in a sabbatical of seven years, for Daniel the sins of the people are such that it would take the land 70 times that long, or 490 years. The time between the exile and the fulfillment of Jeremiah's prophecy thus becomes the time between the exile and the time of Daniel's readers, who are living in the terrible persecutions of Antiochus IV. By actualizing Jeremiah's words, the author of Daniel helps sustain his fellow Jews during what has been called the first religious persecution. The Targum added the interpretative phrase "your memorial will come before me," sometimes used to link current trauma to the ancient promises of the covenant with Abraham. With these added words the Targum construes Jeremiah's seventy years as symbolic reminder of God's faithfulness to the covenant in every age. Finally, two foundational Jewish principles of interpreting Scripture became grounded in the authority of Scripture itself in part because of their connection to this weighty verse in Jeremiah. Interpreting one portion of Scripture (Jer 29:10) by means of another (Leviticus 25:1–7 and 26:27–3), and reading a text as code, as in Daniel 9, both become hermeneutical rules in rabbinic Judaism (Fishbane 1985: 479–489).

During the collapse of the Roman Empire, the verse offered Christians a new way to view history. After the first Visigoth invasion in 410 CE, Christian refugees who had fled to Carthage faced taunts that their god had been defeated. In response, Augustine re-worked the earlier Gnostic allegory of Jerusalem as the soul's original home and Babylon as the earthly world into which it was forced to descend. In *City of God*, Augustine writes that Christians live simultaneously in the foreign city of this life (Babylon) and the spiritual Jerusalem, the city of God. Augustine's allegorizing of Jeremiah had a long afterlife in the Christian church's liturgical calendar. It provided the basis for the early medieval church to extend the penitential season of Lent from 40 to 70 days, so Christians might metaphorically sojourn in Babylon for a time symbolic of Israel's exile. The first Sunday of this pre-Lenten penitential season was called Septuagesima, 70 days before Easter. During these 70 days in "exile," Christians did not sing or say "Alleluia," as Psalm 137 describes the exiles refusing to sing the Lord's song in a foreign land. In a popular Latin hymn from the eleventh century, Babylon, Lent, and human life merge into a single reality as Christians put away the alleluias until Easter. The hymn was translated several times and widely used from 1837 to the present.

God's Inscrutable Plans (29:11)

Fifteenth-century Jewish scholar Abarbanel interpreted the divine thoughts of shalom to refer to exile: 70 years signifies the present trials, which will humble Israel's arrogant heart and give her a future. This actualizing of Jeremiah's words served as both exhortation and encouragement to Jews expelled from Spain by Queen Isabella (Rosenberg 1989: 2, 231). Similarly, at the height of the English Civil War, Puritan preacher John Wells used Jeremiah in his pastoral essay, "The Anchor of Hope for God's tossed ones… Or, God's bowels let out, opened, proclaimed to afflicted Saints, in a little Treatise on the 29 of Jer. 11 verse." Offering encouragement to his perse-cuted readers, he writes that Jeremiah "holds forth most sweetly the tender thoughts of the merciful God towards his people in evil times" and ends with, "This is enough to keep you above water, whatever your present condition." For this preacher, God's people in Babylon enjoy divine care while the "flourishing Babylonians shall be overlooked" (Wells 1645: 2, 23, 200). Using Jeremiah's language as code, Wells encourages his suffering fellow Puritans (Israel) while slyly suggesting that God did not support the established church (Babylonians).

In modernity, the verse becomes a hallmark of personal faith and Jeremiah's plural "you" for the exilic community becomes a singular address for the individual. In her *Sacred History for Schools and Families,* Mrs. Trimmer advises, "This section affords a very instructive lesson to all persons who are in calamitous circumstances, admonishing them not to sink into despair, but to make the best of their condition, since the very dispensation which appears to them a misfortune, may be in reality a blessing in disguise" (Trimmer 1785: 98). In the twentieth century, it became a favorite among American Protestants. While English translations historically rendered the phrase "I know the thoughts I am thinking about you" twentieth-century versions uniformly read "I know the plans I have for you." This shift accords with a theology in which every aspect of an individual's life is part of a personalized divine plan. Often called a "Motivational Bible Verse," Jeremiah's words are the subject of dozens of YouTube videos of rock songs, sermons, and even an animated Jesus speaking Jeremiah's words. It is for sale on plaques, shirts, wedding bands, greeting cards, key chains, and coffee mugs.

FIGURE 45   A contemporary Jeremiah adopts Jer 29:19 to warn inhabitants of New York City.

Jeremiah as Contemporary Prophet (Jer 29:19)

Jeremiah's warning became part of Puritan preaching in the form of the Jeremiad, and was planted in the American colonies from the beginning. It has remained part of American political discourse (see Introduction p. xx), as this contemporary example (Figure 45) shows.

Hope in the Midst of Trauma (30:1–3)

The divine command that Jeremiah "write on a scroll all the words that I speak to you" is one of four references to a scroll in the book (25:13; 36:1,4,32; 51:60). The words of this scroll stand in stark contrast to the scroll of judgments mentioned in 25:13, because they offer images of comfort and restoration. Placed immediately after Jeremiah's letter to the first exiles, in which he dashed their hopes for a quick return, these optimistic words seem disconnected from reality

Jeremiah Through the Centuries, First Edition. Mary Chilton Callaway.
© 2020 Mary Chilton Callaway. Published 2020 by John Wiley & Sons Ltd.

and dissonant with the traumatic destruction of Jerusalem graphically portrayed in the chapters that follow. Some modern scholars explain the odd placement as work of scribes in Babylon, who collected oracles of salvation from the prophetic tradition to give hope to the exiles and attributed them to Jeremiah (Carroll 1986: 570). Readers through the centuries have continued to find consolation in these chapters.

The ancient allegorical interpretation reads these promises of Israel's restoration as code for the coming of Christ and the restoration of humanity. While accepting this figurative reading, Jerome also tries to make literal sense of the text's placement. He links God's command that Jeremiah write about a restoration in the distant future as evidence against the false prophets, who said in chapters 28-29 that the deported Judahites would return within two years. Glossa highlights the figurative explanation, but also presents Jerome's historical explanation to help puzzled medieval readers. In the late fourteenth century, however, Nicholas of Lyra resisted this literalism. In his addition to the Glossa, he explains that the prophets often did not observe "the sequence of time in their writing, but often wrote first what came later. Whence the Hebrew scholars [Jews] say that there is no first or last in Scripture, by which they meant Scripture does not always proceed in chronological order." Nicholas' preference for resolving the problem by appealing to Hebrew literary style instead of allegory made him a harbinger of modernity. Postmodern readers might adopt his use of rabbinic insight, and see the curious placement of these words of comfort as a window into the ancient Semitic mentalitè, a way of thinking that is not linear and logical, but imaginative and associative. In such a reception, the non-linear flow of the chapters is at least as significant as the words.

Rachel Weeps in Every Century (31:15–17)

The brief, enigmatic image of Rachel weeping for her children has never stopped haunting readers. Its complex reception begins before Jeremiah, with the difficult birth of her second son Benjamin (Gen 35:16–20), whom she names Benoni, "son of my sorrow." Benjamin is the eponymous ancestor of one of the northern tribes, as are Ephraim and Manasseh, sons of Rachel's firstborn, Joseph. When the northern tribes were taken into exile by the Assyrians in 722 BCE the tradition of Rachel weeping for her sons poignantly expressed this trauma. Rachel's weeping most likely came to Jeremiah as a traditional image which he interpreted anew for the exiles of Judah.

The image is also complicated and enriched by the double tradition about Rachel's tomb. In 1 Sam 10:2, as in Jeremiah, it is in Benjamin, north of Jerusalem, while the tradition of Gen 35:19 and 48:7 locates it "on the way to

Ephratah, which is Bethlehem." The confusion is caused by the similarity in sound between the towns Ephrat in Benjamin and Ephratah in Judah. Jewish and Christian reception of Rachel's weeping begins with this geographic ambiguity. Matthew interprets Ramah in light of the two Genesis texts that locate Ramah near Bethlehem in order to show Jeremiah's words fulfilled in the horrors of Herod's slaughter of male babies (Matt 2:17–18). In medieval Christian art, Rachel's weeping always prefigures the killings in Bethlehem; in *Biblia Pauperum* and in the stained glass of cathedrals the scene of Herod's soldiers killing Jewish babies is usually accompanied by an image of a bearded Jeremiah and his text.

Jewish tradition expands each aspect of Jeremiah's haunting image. Ramah has two meanings in Hebrew, and Targum elaborates both. In the first, its literal meaning "high" is explained as "the height of the world," which is a rabbinic title for God. The people's weeping, personified in Rachel, therefore ascends to the ears of God. The second is the place name, and Jewish tradition favors the northern location, for God hears "the house of Israel who weep and lament after Jeremiah the prophet, when Nebuzaradan sent him from Ramah… and those who weep for the bitterness of Jerusalem, as she weeps for her children… because they have gone into exile" (Hayward 1987: 131–132). Rachel's weeping teaches that God hears Israel's weeping in every exile in every era. This tradition of contemporary consolation is preserved in Rashi's commentary on Jeremiah and in Jewish teaching. *Genesis Rabbah* explains that Rachel wept as the exiles were led past her tomb on the way to Babylon. For centuries Jews in synagogue on the second day of Rosh HaShanah have linked Rachel's weeping with God's command that Abraham offer up Isaac as a sacrifice, because these verses of Jeremiah are the Haftaroth to the Torah reading of Gen 22. The story of the binding of Isaac has been linked with Jewish suffering since the early Middle Ages, and through this connection Rachel weeps for Jewish martyrs in every era.

Rachel's weeping persists in contemporary idioms. Walter Wangerin's oratorio, "Rachel Weeping for Her Children," is modeled on medieval mystery plays in which "Prophet Jeremy" addresses "people wielding power… with dominion over all the weak." Here, Rachel's voice haunts Herod, who shouts, "Shut the woman up! Remove her wailing far from me!" The author describes it as a play for "whenever the time or conflict or the state of our culture requires it… It is a cautionary play."

In the visual arts, Rachel is rendered as a lamenting mother in diverse contexts. The haunting image in German-Israeli artist Jacob Steinhardt's 1962 woodcut portrays Rachel as a contemporary woman holding her head in anguish as flames burn behind her. Linda Gisson's 11-foot tall statue outside the Sacred Heart Cathedral in Richmond, Virginia shows a contemporary Rachel bent with grief, surrounded by six flames representing the six million Jews murdered, and standing before a before a stone engraved "Remember" in English and Hebrew. The artist named it "Rachel Weeping for Her Children, in Memory of the Martyrs of the Holocaust, April 28, 1987." Nebraska artist Sondra Johnson designed a bronze life-size sculpture of Rachel in 1998 as a memorial for women who mourn the loss of a child unborn, at birth, or later. Portraying a kneeling woman holding an empty blanket, the statue has been installed in a number of cemeteries at special graves for miscarried or stillborn babies.

Rachel's voice has also echoed down the centuries in musical settings of Jer 31:15. At least six Renaissance composers wrote settings of the Vulgate "Vox in Rama audita est," most famously Heinrich Schütz. Intended for the church's observance of Herod's slaughter of the Holy Innocents on December 28, these motets gave Jeremiah's words an early modern voice. Two settings in the twenty-first century, by Willem Verkai in the Netherlands (2005) and Nobuaki Izawa in Japan (2017), suggest that Rachel still weeps for all children being killed by war and famine.

Gender-Bending (31:22)

Jeremiah's startling image of a woman surrounding a strong man as a sign of God creating something new has been a richly generative problem from the beginning. The rare Hebrew verb meaning "surround" or "envelop" occurs only in poetry, and the vowels in the Masoretic Text equate it with the verb in Deut 32:10 describing God's protection of Israel in the wilderness. Septuagint reads "The Lord has created salvation [or safety] in a new planting; men shall go about in salvation [or safety]." The church in the east knew Jeremiah through the Septuagint, so Theodoret's commentary interpreted the Lord's new planting as the church springing from Israel. The men "going about in salvation" were the apostles visiting the nations with the Gospel. Jerome's reading of the Hebrew left the most lasting influence. The Hebrew word for strong man (*geber*) some-times designates the king (2 Sam 23:1; Zech 13:7), so for Jerome it named Christ. Jeremiah's "new thing" is a woman encompassing a man "in the lap of her womb" without coitus, prefiguring Mary's virginal conception. Targum's reaction against this Christian appropriation of Jeremiah's image is apparent in its interpretation of *geber* as Torah, which is traditionally female: "The people, the house of Israel, will eagerly pursue Torah." Jerome's Christological interpretation dominated until the sixteenth century, and its significance is apparent in *Bible moralisée*. The top roundel usually portrays the plain sense, but here it shows the female as the church surrounding a medieval man with her robe while Jeremiah reprimands the Jews (Figure 46). The lower roundel

FIGURE 46   © M. Moliero Editor, *The Bible of St. Louis,* vol. 2, f. 148r.

shows a traditional Virgin and child, imaginatively attended by worshipping Jews and Gentiles. *Bible moralisée* extends Jerome's allegory to address medieval consternation over the faithfulness of Jews to their covenant with God. Around the same time rabbinic scholar David Kimḥi. responded to Christian allegories with his own: female Israel will return to and embrace her Lord (Rosenberg 1995: 2:52).

Calvin rejects traditional Catholic allegory of the woman as Mary, excusing earlier interpreters as "anxious to lay hold on whatever might seem to refer to the mystery of our salvation." Instead he interprets the woman as the Jews in exile, perhaps reflecting his own experiences of political exile, and reads the words as a promise that "the Jews shall gain the upper hand, though the strength of their enemies be great and terrible." The Geneva Bible's note transmits Patristic tradition, though without explicit reference to Mary: "Because their deliverance from Babylon was a figure of their deliverance from sin, he showeth how this should be procured, to wit, by Jesus Christ, whom a woman should conceive and bear in her womb." The note concludes with an ingenious figure using Isa 54:1 to interpret Jeremiah: "Or he meaneth that Jerusalem, which was like a barren woman in her captivity, should be fruitful as she that is joined in marriage, and whom God blesseth with children."

Interest in gender as social construction marks late twentieth-century interpretations. Australian evangelical scholar William Thompson's commentary sees a contrast between the giddy, weak Israel of the past and the new virgin Israel, who will be "something of an Amazon, and do exploits. A woman (Israel) will take the lead." William Holladay makes Jeremiah part of a different conversation about gender. He interprets the female encompassing the male as prophetic prediction of a new creation in which "the female shall be the initiator in sexual relations" and concludes: "The reassignment of sexual roles is innovative past all conventional belief, but it is not inconceivable to Yahweh" (Holladay 1989: 195). Kathleen O'Connor reads the reversals as eschatological sign: "The surprising new role of women symbolizes a changed order of relationships in a reconstituted and joyous society" (O'Connor 2012: 276).

The New Covenant (31:31–34)

Jeremiah's prophecy of a "new covenant" may have the most far-reaching effects of all his words. From antiquity to early modernity, the promise of a new covenant written on the heart resonated with communities struggling with their identity in the midst of radical change or oppression. Reception began almost immediately, with Jeremiah's exilic redactors modifying his radical image of a new covenant in 32:40 to the traditional "everlasting covenant" (Gen 9:16; 2 Sam 23:5). Ezekiel transformed Jeremiah's image of God writing Torah on Israel's heart into God giving Israel a heart transplant, replacing a stony heart with a heart of flesh (Ezek 11:19; 36:26). Both prophets speak of Israel's heart in the singular, signifying a corporate will. This Semitic idea is transformed by the Septuagint, which translates the Hebrew "on their heart" to "on their hearts," shifting the focus to the individual. Septuagint also Hellenizes Jeremiah by its translation of Hebrew *kereb* (interior) with Greek *dianoia* (mind, intellect), suggesting intellectual assent to Torah. This tension between understanding Jeremiah's new covenant as a new relation with God's people or a divinely wrought change in human nature persists from the third century BCE forward.

The Jewish sectarian group living at Qumran and responsible for the *Damascus Document* used Jeremiah to identify themselves as those "who entered the new covenant in the land of Damascus" (6.19; 8.21; 19:33–34; 20:12).

They contemporized the new covenant as their interpretation of Torah and the rule by which their community lived. Their life, deliberately cut off from the official priesthood and Temple, was legitimized by their belief that Jeremiah's prophecy was fulfilled in them. The term "new covenant" highlighted their claim to be the true heirs of Israel, and the eschatological sense of Jeremiah's new covenant particularly suited their belief that they were living in the end time.

Within a few hundred years, another Jewish group similarly found their identity in the new covenant. Like the Jews at Qumran, Christians used it to claim their identity as the new Israel. The earliest Christian use is Paul's report of the tradition of Jesus' words at the last supper, "This cup is the new covenant in my blood" (1 Cor 11:23–26). For the early church, Jeremiah's new covenant had been fulfilled in their own time, sealed with the blood of Jesus. A shift occurs in 2 Cor 3:5, in which the author describes himself as made capable by God to be minister of a new covenant, not of letter but of spirit. This polemical contrast is heightened in the Epistle to the Hebrews (10:15–17), which quotes the Septuagint of Jer 31:31–43 in full to argue that the Mosaic covenant and the Israelites were faulty and rendered obsolete by the new covenant. Such receptions of Jeremiah highlight the Christian dilemma. The early church needed to show the old covenant annulled to establish its identity and authentication as the people of the new covenant, yet the stubborn fact remained that the original covenant was crucial to the church's identity, and flourished still in the Judaism of the Roman Empire.

Jeremiah's related image of the Law written on the heart becomes an elastic metaphor stretched to fit many different circumstances. Paul uses it to signify innate moral understanding when he describes Gentiles who instinctively do what the law requires as having the law "written on their hearts, their conscience bearing witness" (Rom 2:15). Using a term from Greek philosophy (*syneideisis*) to explain the image, Paul radically shifts Jeremiah's meaning away from the particularity of Jewish Torah to a universal sense of right and wrong. John Chrysostom develops this idea in a homily on John's gospel, where he rails against ostentatious displays of wealth by ambitious Christians who show off their Scriptures written in gold on fine skins bound in ornate cases, but don't try to understand them: "The Scriptures were not given to us merely to have in such books, but to engrave in our hearts" (*Patrologia Graeca* 59, col. 187, my translation). Chrysostom adds the idea that "written on the heart" implies a change in one's character.

The most visible effect of Jeremiah's words is the legacy of the Christian Bible as Old and New Testaments. In the second century CE, the Gnostic theologian Marcion taught that the Lord in the Scriptures was a primitive and inferior deity who was unrelated to Jesus. Around 140 CE, he presented a short list of sacred books which he deemed authoritative Christian writings, excluding all of the Scriptures (Old Testament) and the Gospel texts that cited them. In response, Tertullian combined Isa 43:19 ("I am doing a new thing") with Jeremiah's new covenant to argue that the law was both given and abrogated by the creator God (*Scorpiae* 4:1). Irenaeus went further, using Jeremiah's language in parallel with Matthew's image of the master who brings out old and new treasures from his household (Matt 13:52) to affirm that God is author of both covenants. By the end of the third century CE, the church had rejected Marcion's view and affirmed the authority of Israel's Scriptures, naming them "the Old Covenant (Testament)" to make them a companion to the church's writings, the New Covenant (Testament). This designation insured a permanent place in the church for the Scriptures while also relegating them to the role of prefiguring Jesus. The division of the Christian Bible as Old and New Testament is perhaps the most visible effect of Jeremiah's new covenant.

Jewish reception from about the third through the ninth centuries was playful with Jeremiah's images. Two examples from the dozen extant references illustrate midrashic adaptation of Jeremiah to contemporary Jewish self-understanding. In the collection of rabbinic homilies from late antiquity known as *Pesikta de Rab Kahana,* a homily on the covenant made at Mt. Sinai asks why Ex 19:1 says "on this day" when "on that day" would make more sense in the narrative. It is to remind us, the homily says, that the words of Torah should not seem antiquated, but as fresh as though just given *on this day* for study. Yet in the world to come, God says, "I myself shall teach it to all Israel, and they will study it and not forget it, as it is said… in their heart will I write it" (Braude 2002: 428). Here, Jeremiah's image is a constant reminder that studying Torah links this world with the world to come, but remains necessary as long as we are in this world. Another early Jewish reception, in *Song of Songs Rabba,* uses imagery of a lover to interpret Jeremiah's new covenant. In this midrash, Torah is fixed in the hearts of the people when God says "I am the Lord your God" (Ex 20:1), but when they ask Moses to be their intermediary (Ex 20:16) they begin to see Torah as Moses' own transitory teaching and they lose their ardor for it. When they beg Moses to ask God for a second revelation, "that he would kiss us with the kisses of his lips" and fix Torah in their hearts as before, Moses replies that this will happen only in the days to come, as it says, "when I will put my Torah in their inward parts…" (Jer 31:33) (Sasson 1988: 102). Here, Jeremiah's words are imaginatively used to address the longing to return to the original moment of encounter with God, and to live up to it.

In the midst of expulsions and pogroms in medieval Europe, Jewish reception of Jeremiah's new covenant became polemical, focusing on Jewish identity and rejection of Christian claims. Two approaches in particular left their mark. The first was an insistence on the *peshat,* the plain sense, of Jeremiahs' new covenant.

Beginning with Saadia's tenth-century Arabic treatise and continuing through fourteenth century exegetical and polemical literature, Jewish exegetes reminded Christians that Torah and covenant are not synonymous (Sarason 1988: 104). David Kimhi. appealed to Jeremiah's plain sense, arguing that his words clearly do not refer to the content of a new Torah, but to a new relationship that would change the way Torah is transmitted and observed. A second approach of medieval Jewish reception was related to the first, but focused on the image of Torah written on the heart. In the thirteenth century, Nachmanides wrote that Jeremiah's new covenant signaled the end of human resistance to God's will and the restoration of humanity to its original state of harmony with God. Reading Jeremiah in light of the divine promise to circumcise Israel's heart (Deut 30:6) and Ezekiel's prophecy of a new heart (Ezek 36:26), Nachmanides found a divine promise to restore human nature to its original state before Adam's sin. In the messianic age, God will implant into people's hearts the inclination and will to observe God's laws, so the covenant will not be abrogated. Nachmanides' reading of the new covenant as an eschatological change in human nature was a popular medieval Jewish reception. In addition to resonating with medieval concerns about the state of human nature, it offered a strong riposte to Christian appropriation of the new covenant. More than one Jewish commentator noted wryly the disparity between the present world and the world of Jeremiah's new covenant, understood by Christians to be inauguration of the messianic age (Sarason 1988: 107). Merely looking around them, seeing the corruption of the world, should convince Christians that they were not living in the world of Jeremiah's new covenant!

Jeremiah's heart inscribed with Torah becomes, in seventeenth-century England, the sacred space of inner contemplation. Quaker William Dewsbury, writing from a small jail in northern England to Quakers in America, appeals to Jeremiah's words: "All people, no longer look forth; the glad tidings of the Gospel of eternal Salvation is heard within… as now witnessed with all the Children of Light, whose Minds are turned within to wait on the Lord for Teaching, to establish them in the Covenant of Life and Peace, who is performing his Promise to all that wait on him, which he declared by his Servant the Prophet Jeremiah (31–34). Therefore… turn your minds within… search and try your ways with the Light Christ Jesus hath lighted you withal…" (Dewsbury 1656: 159–160). Jeremiah's words that the Law will be written on people's hearts is here translated into the Quaker principle of the Inner Light. Most importantly, Jeremiah's prophecy offers support for the Quaker belief that individuals can know God's law by turning within, not from religious authority or liturgical ceremony.

A modern appropriation reads Jeremiah in light of Kant's categorical imperative, as knowledge of a universal moral law. The American Society of Public Administrators engaged in a debate over whether they should adopt a written code of ethics for the profession. In an argument against adopting such a code, one member cited Jeremiah: "There are many other arguments against a code of ethics. Although some of us would be uncomfortable with the comparison, a large number of American public administrators agree with the prophet Jeremiah that the laws of right behavior are written on one's heart, not on paper" (Chandler 1983: 33).

Noting that Lutherans hear this text every year on Reformation Sunday, Walter Brueggemann finds Luther's insight that "God's gracious generosity permits forgiveness and reconciliation, even for those who do not merit such grace" is indebted in part to Jeremiah's new covenant. He paraphrases, "God, says Jeremiah, is ready to forgive and forget, so that the renewed relationship is one of generosity and grace on God's part." He takes the new covenant as a challenge to American self-understanding as a people covenanted to each other: "If we carry the Jeremiah oracle toward our common civic life, the mandate that may arise from God is an invitation to a deep breath and a fresh generosity, and a move beyond petty and deep resentment toward embrace of the other" (*Huffington Post* 26 October 2011).

A Strange Real Estate Deal

Readers from the beginning wrestled with God's command to make a foolish investment. Jerome's discomfort with Jeremiah's "difficult and laughable" purchase of land just as the Babylonian army was occupying Jerusalem is apparent in his explanation. There was no actual command to buy the field; Jeremiah had only been told that Hanamel was coming with the proposition, but its outrageousness confirmed his intuition that it must be from the Lord.

Jeremiah Through the Centuries, First Edition. Mary Chilton Callaway.
© 2020 Mary Chilton Callaway. Published 2020 by John Wiley & Sons Ltd.

Jerome uses the narrative to highlight the surprises of living in faith over and against the philosopher's perfectly controlled life. For Luther, this outrageous aspect of the divine word similarly signals an important truth about the way God works: "For the prophesy which comes from God comes in such a way that it is against all reason and asserts the impossible… This was the case when Jeremiah in the very time of the siege of Jerusalem, when everything was already beyond hope, prophesied 'Houses and fields and vineyards shall again be possessed in this land, although everything had already been laid waste and the citizenry itself was already moving away'" (*LW* 25: 445).

Jeremiah's prayer of protest (verse 16) influenced later reflection on the interplay between emotion and obedience. Eleventh-century French scholar, Joseph Kara, humanized Jeremiah by suggesting that the prophet bought the land with an embittered heart because the city was surrounded by the Babylonian army, yet did not hesitate (Rosenberg 1985: 2:260). Puritan John Trapp read seventeenth-century sensibilities into Jeremiah, warning his readers that obedience with a bitter heart is empty. The prophet's prayer upon concluding his unusual real estate deal offers a valuable lesson to Christians who are doubting what God asks of them: "His heart began to boil with unbelief and carnal reasonings: he therefore setteth himself to pray down those distempers. As a man may sleep out his drunkenness, so he may pray away his perturbations" (Trapp 1660).

For Dietrich Bonhoeffer in a Nazi prison, Jeremiah's act of buying real estate when there seemed to be no hope of inhabiting it offered a sign. After a visit from his fiancée, Bonhoeffer writes to say that their love is "a sign of God's grace and kindness, which calls us to faith. We would be blind if we did not see it. Jeremiah says at the moment of his people's great need 'still one shall buy houses and acres in this land' as a sign of trust in the future. This is where faith belongs. May God give it to us daily. And I do not mean the faith which flees the world, but the one that endures the world and which loves and remains true to the world in spite of all the suffering which it contains for us" (Bonhoeffer 2009: 415).

Taking Back the Gift of Freedom (34:8–22)

When the Babylonian army began the first siege of Jerusalem, King Zedekiah decreed that all Hebrew slaves be made free. When the Babylonians suddenly withdrew, people immediately took back their slaves. For Jeremiah, this cynical breaking of their promise mirrored the people's duplicitous behavior toward YHWH.

In the Jewish lectionary, the story in verses 8–22 is read as the *haftorah* for the Torah reading of Ex 21:1–24:18. This is a unique *haftorah* because it ends by

Jeremiah Through the Centuries, First Edition. Mary Chilton Callaway.
© 2020 Mary Chilton Callaway. Published 2020 by John Wiley & Sons Ltd.

returning to Jer 33:255–226, although rabbinic rules forbid reading out of order. Yet the tradition of ending the *haftorah* with positive words overrides the rule, as Rashi notes at the end of his commentary on Lamentations. The liturgical pairing of Torah limitation on slavery with Jeremiah's indictment of Judeans who cynically violated the law is an early reception of Jer 34. The pairing eloquently highlights the double sin of cynically violating Torah after initial obedience. Seventeenth- and eighteenth-century Puritan scholars vied to name the particular sin that Jeremiah indicted. The Geneva Bible contemporizes the slave owners as sham Christians: "They would seem holy and so began some kind of reformation: but soon after they uttered their hypocrisy," while for John Trapp the sin that made them repeal their vows was covetousness. Matthew Poole adds that "these wretched hypocrites" seeing the Babylonians retreat "concluded they were now out of God's hands, and repented of their repentance."

Jeremiah 35

Jeremiah tests the resolve of the Rechabites, who for centuries had remained loyal to their ancestors' command not to drink wine or live in houses, in order to make graphic Judah's disobedience. The story is set in the reign of Jehoiakim, yet it immediately follows three chapters set some ten years later, in the reign of Zedekiah. This non-chronological sequence has perturbed readers from the ninth century to the present. Rabanus Maurus turns the problem into an opportunity, explaining that the prophet did not follow human chronology because he was guided by the Holy Spirit, who makes a different kind of connection between narratives. The confusing order is intended to remind readers that the Scriptures are

Jeremiah Through the Centuries, First Edition. Mary Chilton Callaway.
© 2020 Mary Chilton Callaway. Published 2020 by John Wiley & Sons Ltd.

not a product of human arrangement but divinely inspired. His explanation is reproduced in the *Glossa Ordinaria* into the sixteenth century. In Jewish tradition, fifteenth-century Spanish scholar Abarbanel creatively suggested that the divine command to visit the Rechabites came during Jehoiakim's reign but Jeremiah only made it public ten years later, when the Judahites' disobedience (Jer 34) reminded him of the Rechabites' obedience. In the Enlightenment, Thomas Paine scornfully wrote that the clumsy ordering was precisely evidence that the book is "a medley of detached unauthenticated anecdotes, put together by some stupid book-maker" (Paine 1796: 52). Twentieth-century scholars theorized that biblical texts are often ordered by theme or verbal association rather than chronology; in this view chapters 26–36 were designed as a unit, framed by narratives about resistance to Jeremiah. Jer 35 highlights obedience and pairs thematically, if not chronologically, with the story of Jehoiakim's disobedience that follows.

Readers through the centuries became fascinated by the Rechabites and imagined them as models of their own ideals. Kimḥi seemed to link the nomadic quality of Rechabite life with the fragility of Jewish life in medieval Europe, where pogroms and edicts made sudden relocation necessary: "Houses, fields, and vineyards keep a person from moving away from his place in the event of a catastrophe, such as famine or war, and he may die from worry" (Rosenberg 1989: 2:285). Medieval Christians read interlinear notes in the *Glossa* instructing them that, like the Rechabites, they should live in metaphorical tents with no permanent home on earth, "that you might lead a holy life." Seventeenth-century Jansenist scholar, Isaac-Louis de Sacy, made the Rechabites' story available in an illicit translation, yet his accompanying "Sens Litteral et Spirituel" instructed readers in the church's traditional interpretation. Sacy challenges his readers: "The example of the Rechabites makes almost everyone blush at their own faint-heartedness in their morality. Who among the rich regard themselves as living in tents on the earth, and even among the poor who does not wish to be settled and prosperous?" For de Sacy, the Rechabites' fidelity to tradition made them a model for French Christians, who ought to revere the teachings of their fathers (Augustine and medieval exegesis) and instruct their children to be faithful to them. For Sacy, witnessing political and cultural upheavals at the end of the seventeenth century, the Rechabites embody an elegy for lost virtue: "There are few imitators of the holy zeal of Jonadab son of Rechab for the instruction and sanctification of their people! And there is even less of the humble obedience of the Rechabites to the holy teaching of their ancestors" (de Sacy 1693: 490, 493).

English Puritans in general interpreted the Rechabite vows as recognition that earthly pleasures need strict policing. A marginal note at verse 6 in the Geneva Bible adapts the *Glossa*'s note to Puritan ideas: "Teaching them by this to flee all opportunity for intemperancy, ambition and greed and that they might know that they were strangers in the earth, and be ready to depart at all opportunity." Matthew Henry elaborates this idea: "... that they might not run into unlawful pleasures they were to deny themselves even lawful delights. The consideration that we are strangers and pilgrims should oblige us to abstain from all fleshly lusts. Let them sit loose to what they had, and then they might with less pain be stripped of it. Those are in the best frame to meet sufferings who live a life of self-denial, and who despise the vanities of the world." Anglican John Trapp, however, cautioned that the Rechabites' resolve was "not because they were persuaded as Mahomet's followers are, that in every grape there dwelt a devil" and not "to establish any new arbitrary service or any rule of greater perfection of life (as the Papists misallege it in favor of Monkery [monastic life]." At issue for Trapp was not alcohol or monasticism, but the religious identity of Anglican Christians over against the Puritans.

The Rechabites' obedience to their ancestor was also a refusal to obey Jeremiah's command to drink the wine he set before them, and this led to a defense of legitimate, even holy disobedience. Eleventh-century Benedictine, Peter Damian, invoked the Rechabites in arguments about the limits of authority. In a legal debate over schism caused by a papal election, supporting those who refused obedience to one he saw as a pretender, Damian claimed that sometimes disobedience is more holy than obedience. After reciting the story of the Rechabites, he concludes: "Because we elected the pope without the consent of the emperor, you are not at once to judge the external act, but you must rather carefully note the spirit and the intention with which it was done" (Damian 1992: 3:359). On another occasion, he counsels a brother about refusing what is not forbidden with a commendation of the Rechabites disobeying Jeremiah's command to drink: "O blessed disobedience, that was found worthy of commendation" (Damian 1998: 4:121–122).

In the seventeenth century, the Rechabites are key to an impassioned defense of natural rights and political liberty. Asking whether Jonadab's sons would have sinned if they had disobeyed their father's command, Noncomformist scholar Matthew Poole answers no, because Torah does not forbid drinking wine and living in a house: "Unquestionably parents have not a power to determine children in all things as to which God hath left them a liberty, for then they have a power to make their children slaves and to take away all their natural liberty. To marry or not, and to this or that person, is a matter of liberty... All souls are God's and conscience can be under no other dominion." Poole here endorses John Locke's developing political theory of natural rights, and uses Jer 35 to challenge the recently published work of Robert Filmer, which argued that the Bible supports absolute parental authority over children and therefore the absolute power of kings. Poole's elaborate comment on verse 19 is a thinly veiled attack on royalist theology and a robust support of individual rights.

In the nineteenth century, the temperance movement found an ideal model in the Rechabites. In his Bible commentary, Irish Methodist Adam Clarke gives Jonadab's command a modern, sensible ring – "Ye shall preserve your bodies in temperance, shall use nothing that would deprive you of the exercise of your sober reason at any time" – and concludes, "True Christians may be considered as the genuine successors of these ancient Rechabites." A long exposition in *The Temperance Bible Commentary* invokes nineteenth-century exploration to promote Jonadab as a model for contemporary Christians. It describes an early nineteenth-century British evangelist encountering a "Bedouin cavalier" in Mesopotamia who called himself a descendant of Jonadab still obeying Rechabite vows. Twelve years later he meets more Rechabites, who invite him to their tents and offer hospitality for six days, without wine, and the authors of the Commentary conclude, "What a flood of all the vices was diverted from this tribe! Happy family in which there had never been a drunkard to break his mother's heart... Would that, in the modern Church, we had more persons like-minded, willing, for the sake of the world's progress... to sacrifice even the love of a little liquor, and thereby secure for themselves... exemption from the manifold miseries and pollutions of intemperance." That the Rechabites refused a man of Jeremiah's standing offers a stern warning about the danger of "social drinking." Readers are warned to be wary of "persuasion even of men eminent for their position or personal worth... Most nobly does their conduct compare with a not infrequent desertion of the Temperance cause because the wine-cup has been associated with the hand of friendship, the smile of beauty, the seal of fashion, or the solicitation of sensuous desire" (Lees and Burns 1868: 196–197). The Temperance Education Foundation in Ohio published "The Holy Bible and Drink," a widely circulated pamphlet providing Bible passages "bearing upon the problems of intoxicating drink," where Jeremiah 35:5–6 appears under the heading "Making A Choice" and the Rechabites called "Examples of Decision" to encourage readers.

When the tradition of temperance grew into a call for prohibition in the US, some readers of Jeremiah were angered. Kentucky whiskey manufacturer George Brown wrote a pamphlet, "The Bible Repudiates Prohibition," to offer "an honest explanation" of Bible passages mentioning wine or strong drink. Of Rechabite abstinence, he argues that Jeremiah commends their faithfulness to their ancestor simply to contrast Judah's disobedience to God: "There is no more reason to conclude because of this commendation that God commands total abstinence from wine than that he does from sowing seed or building houses" (Brown 1910: 51). In *Alcohol and the Scriptures* (1968), the Temperance Committee of the Presbyterian Church of Victoria, Australia romanticizes the life of Jonadab's ancestors, "It was a life without vineyards and therefore without the curse of liquor. The vine stood for the culture of Canaan which was associated with false worship. Because it threatened the simplicity and purity of Israel's life and faith, it was a point of honor with the Rechabites to abjure the vine and its fruits in any form" (Kerr 1968: 3). In his widely read *Your Bible and You*, which went into over 40 editions, popular devotional writer Arthur S. Maxwell devotes a chapter to "Unwise Drinking." A full-page color illustration shows Jeremiah addressing an attentive group of men with their backs to wine jars and cups, men "who have refused to be deceived" by alcohol who serve as models for twentieth-century Americans.

The dramatic narrative of the king's attempts to silence the prophet and destroy his scroll engaged readers wrestling with their own religious and political threats. Its importance from the beginning is signaled by its location; scholarly consensus since the nineteenth century understands chapters 26–36 as a literary unit of narratives redacted to follow the prophetic oracles of chapters 2–25. Ancient redactors often arranged material according to theme or word association rather than narrative chronology, and here chapter 36 is situated at the end to form a frame with 26. Both chapters contrast the virulent rejection of the prophetic word, one in the Temple, the other in the palace, with divine determination to

Jeremiah Through the Centuries, First Edition. Mary Chilton Callaway.
© 2020 Mary Chilton Callaway. Published 2020 by John Wiley & Sons Ltd.

preserve the word for the future. Readers through the ages have seen encoded in chapter 36 clues about the production and transmission of the Bible as well as a meditation on the mystery of the divine word in their own time.

Free Will and Divine Omniscience (36:3, 7)

Theologians of the thirteenth century engaged with the question of whether God knew the future, which would seem to compromise human free will. Nicholas of Lyra headed off potential theological misuse of verses 3 and 7, arguing that far from suggesting God's ignorance of the future, these verses instead highlight the freedom of king and people to turn from their sinful ways. Jeremiah 36 therefore bears witness to the paradox that divine foreknowledge and human freedom co-exist. Moreover, God's desire to draw people back is manifest here in the optimistic mercy of verse 3, a verse that for Matthew Poole highlighted the crucial role of preaching: "God knew what would be, but yet he would not be wanting in means by which they might be informed in his will, and so believe the thing, for believing and reforming are here meant by hearing." Poole translates the biblical idioms of verse 7 into Protestant ones: "It teacheth us that the only means to turn away God's fierce anger ready to fall upon people is Prayer and Reformation." Like the officials in Jerusalem who could be saved only by listening to the words on Jeremiah's scroll and acting on them, Poole's readers could be saved by heeding the warnings of preachers.

Word, Scroll, Book (36:2, 5, 18)

God's command that Jeremiah "take a scroll of a book and write in it..." was actualized by Nicholas of Lyra, who updated the *Glossa Ordinaria* with his additions across the bottom of the pages. He writes, "That Jeremiah prophesied not only in speech, but also in writing, for the sake of the future and the absent, signifies that a man educated in Holy Scriptures should not teach by preaching or lecturing alone, but also by writing, so that he can benefit those who are not present and those yet to come." By this parallel between the writing prophet and the Bible scholar Nicholas cannily inscribes divine sanction into his own activity of writing commentaries.

The feat of dictating an entire scroll captured the imaginations of readers in every age, and confirmed the divine origin of Scripture. Theodoret clarifies that it was no human capability, for Jeremiah spoke while inspired by divine grace. Similarly, a comment in the *Glossa* urges readers to understand Jeremiah's tour de force as prefiguring the ready speech promised to the arrested "apostles and prophets" in Matt 10:17–20, and to Christians everywhere. Calvin took the opportunity to clarify the complex nature of Holy Scripture: "God suggested to the Prophet at the time what might have been erased from his memory; for all the things which we have some time ago said, do not always occur to us… Jeremiah then stood, as it were, between God and Baruch; for God, by his Spirit, presided over and guided the mind and tongue of the Prophet." Calvin's comments on the princes reflected his own experiences of rejection, especially in his native France. He writes that they did not believe Baruch's simple description in verse 18, but "had suspicion of some trickery, as the unbelieving imagine many such things respecting God's servants." Some 200 years later, John Wesley drew on Calvin's readings to make verse 18 witness to the truth of the Bible. Baruch's description of Jeremiah's dictation added to the princes' fear, he says, because "without a special influence of God, it had been impossible, that Jeremiah should have called to mind all that he had spoken at several times in so many years" (Wesley 1765). For the Reformers nothing less than the divine inspiration and authority of Scripture was at stake in these verses.

An interlinear note at verse 5 in the *Glossa* reminds readers that the divine word eludes human limits: "Though I am shut up the word of the Lord is not restrained." The verse offers Nicholas of Lyra an opportunity for a humanistic teaching on friendship from Aristotle. Jeremiah sending "his friend Baruch" to read the scroll shows that "what we accomplish through our friends we to some degree do ourselves."

Jehoiakim as Perennial Tyrant (36:20–26)

Jehoiakim is code for "tyrant" whenever the persecuted write about authorities too dangerous to name. Thirteenth-century Jewish scholar, David Kimḥi, describes the king listening only as far as verse 4 before demanding, "Who says so?" On hearing in the next verse that it is the Lord's doing, he cuts out every occurrence of the divine name and tosses them into the fire. For Kimḥi's readers in medieval France, the story had a chilling resonance; Jehoiakim for them represents Christian authorities who burned cartloads of Torahs and Talmuds. Kimḥi taught that just as Jehoiakim's princes should have torn their garments when they saw the scroll burning, whoever today witnesses a Torah scroll being forcibly burnt must tear his garments in mourning (Rosenberg 1995: 2:295). Jer 36 thereby instructed medieval French Jews to bear witness to the divine name in response to Christian persecution.

For students in the intellectual ferment of the University of Paris in the early twelfth century, the increasingly prominent role of philosophy, especially the newly available works of Aristotle, offered an exciting counterpoint to theological studies. *Bible moralisée* often presented visual warnings against these new teachings thought to be a threat to Christian faith. The scene of Jehoiakim cutting up Jeremiah's scroll is paired with an interpretive roundel picturing two philosophers and two Christians bent over a book. One of the philosophers, eyes narrowed in a hostile glance, wields a knife like Jehoiakim's, preparing to cut out part of page (Figure 47). The text reads, "Heretics derive confirmation for their heresies in sacred scripture. An evil man is enraged when he hears words not pleasing to him." This medieval allegory reads Jehoiakim as dangerous

FIGURE 47   © M. Moliero Editor, *The Bible of St. Louis,* vol. 2, f. 150r.

contemporary philosophers, but also as an ordinary Christian whose hardness of heart prevents him from hearing the words of Scripture.

Jehoiakim was an especially loathsome figure for English Puritans like John Trapp, who delivered a tirade expressing his outrage over the 1624 order of Pope Urban VIII to burn Luther's translation of the Bible in Catholic parts of Germany: "O madness!... Jehoiakim is the first we read of, that ever offered to burn the Bible. Antiochus indeed did the like afterwards, and Dioclesian the Tyrant, and now the Pope. But though there were not a Bible left upon earth, yet forever, O Lord, thy Word is stablished in heaven." Matthew Henry, on the other hand, finds in the complicit princes a cautionary tale for his fellow churchmen and comments:

> Shows of piety and devotion may be found even among those, who, though they keep up deep up forms of godliness, are strangers and enemies to the power of it. The princes patiently attended the reading of the whole book. They were in great fear. But even those who are convinced to the truth and importance of what they hear, and are disposed to favor those who preach it, often have difficulties and reserves about their safety, interest, or preferment, so that they do not act according to their convictions, and try to get rid of what they find troublesome... The princes showed some concern, till they saw how light the king made of it. Beware of making light of God's word!

Henry is warning his fellow Puritans to resist the lure of preferment, and not stand by silently like Jehoiakim's princes as the word of the Lord is desecrated. Non-conformist Matthew Poole barely disguises his rendering of Jehoiakim and his princes as Charles II and the enforcers of the Act of Uniformity: "It speaketh nothing but the impotency, and passion, and debauchery of human Nature to swell against any Revelations of the Divine Will; the Counsels of the Lord shall stand, and men only further entangle themselves by struggling in the Lord's net."

Calvin's personal identification with Jeremiah is reiterated in the closing words of his long commentary on chapter 36. The words "God hid them" evoke reflections on his own persecutions and a measure of comfort: "Though there may be many ways by which we may escape from our present dangers, yet our life is in God's hand, so that he hides and conceals us; for we ourselves would run headlong unto death, were we not covered by the shadow of his hand."

Twentieth-century readers saw in Jehoiakim the unsettlingly familiar figure of a totalitarian ruler. George Steiner writes, "The locus of truth is always extra-territorial; its diffusion is made clandestine by the barbed wire and watch-towers of national dogma. The quarrel is as ancient as Israel. It is that between priest and prophet, between the claims of nationhood and those of univer-sality... The mortal clash between politics and verity, between an immanent homeland and the space of the transcendent, is spelt out in Jeremiah 36–39. King Jehoiakim seizes the scroll dictated by God's clerk and bookkeeper. He cuts out the offending columns and casts the entire text into the consuming flame (governments, political censors, patriotic vigilantes burn books). God instructs the prophet: 'Take thee again another scroll...' The truth will out. Somewhere there is a pencil-stub, a mimeograph machine, a hand-press which the king's men have overlooked" (Steiner 1996: 322–323).

Words and the Word (36:27)

The distinction between scroll and words (verse 27) caught the imagination of Christian and Jewish scholars because it spoke to contemporary controversies. Theodoret usually avoided allegorical interpretation, but writing when the church was in conflict over the divine and human natures of Christ, he could not resist Jeremiah's image of the divine word persisting after destruction of the scroll: "Whereas the writing matter was consumed by fire, the divine Law remained intact; likewise also the Word, when the body that was assumed suffered, remained immune to suffering." Theodoret is writing some ten years before the Council of Chalcedon in 451 AD settled the Christological question. There he played a leading role, and his recent work on Jeremiah would have informed his thinking about the paradox of the divine word in human flesh. His allegorical reading of the scroll remained influential until the sixteenth century, reported in full in the *Glossa*. A very different parsing of the scroll and the words led Kimḥi to direct Jeremiah's words to Jewish communities experiencing violence and book-burning by Gentiles: "Lest you think that he burnt only the margins and spared the written words, Scripture relates that he burnt the written text as well. This is to teach us that anyone witnessing a Torah scroll being burnt must tear his garments twice, for the parchment and the text" (Rosenberg 1995: 2:296).

A sixteenth-century German stained-glass window, now in the Victoria and Albert Museum, demonstrates the anti-Jewish sentiment embedded in German culture of that era. Its vivid colors portray the king as a medieval Jew cutting pages from a codex, while outside the palace in the distance an imprisoned Christ-like Jeremiah dictates to Baruch.

The drama of the king burning Jeremiah's scroll took on lasting significance when Jeremiah's story resonated with early Protestants whose vernacular Bibles were confiscated and burned. In 1521, authorities in England, Venice, and Naples obeyed the papal order to burn Luther's writings; in 1529, Bishop Tunstall burned most copies of Tyndale's English New Testament; and in 1536, Tyndale himself was burned at the stake for translating the Bible into English. One of the first to illustrate the scene was Hans Sebald Beham, a Protestant so radical that

FIGURE 48 Jehoiakim watches while Jehudi burns Jeremiah's scroll. Hans Sebald Beham 1534. Pitts Theological Library Digital Image Archive.

he been expelled from Nuremburg and for whom the story of hostile officials was a reality. Ironically, his woodcut appeared in Johann Dietenberger's 1534 German translation of the Vulgate published for Catholics in Mainz as a response to Luther's translation. Publishers wanted books to sell, and Dietenberger's publisher used whatever was available to fill his volume with pictures. In Beham's contemporizing illustration, Jeremiah's scroll has become two European books, and both Jehoiakim and Jehudi are dressed as contemporary Germans. The less-detailed figures in the background have the caps and divided beards of medieval Jews, making the scene a classic sixteenth-century pastiche of biblical and contemporary worlds. The woodcut appeared three years later in Beham's own 1537 picture Bible, *Biblicae Historiae* (Figure 48).

The resonance of the narrative for Protestants is captured by Jan Luyken's engraving for his emblem book of biblical pictures. Emblem books were a popular genre of picture Bibles that offered elegant images of biblical scenes accompanied by a brief moralizing text, often in verse. Luyken, an Anabaptist Protestant, had already published an emblem book titled *Martyrs Mirror*, with images of religious persecutions from the crucifixion to seventeenth-century Switzerland. His biblical emblem book highlighted Jeremiah's persecutions with just two engravings, Jeremiah in the cistern (see commentary on Jer 38) and Jehoiakim burning the scroll. Christoph Weigel used Luyken's engravings in his popular picture Bible (Figure 49), in which the dramatic scene is accompanied by

Ian Luyken facit   IEREM.XXXVI.   *Christ. Weigel excudit*

Vix legit . allatum fibi Rex cremat igne volumen :
Hic quia Se fcelerum . fuppliciique monet .
Nempe ferox. linguisque probis , verisque . Tyrannus
Nil potius calamis , quod vereatur , habet .

Der König lieft und reißt, und läßt ins Feuer ftreuen .
Das Buch , darinnen fteht von Sünd und Straffen viel .
Warhafftig ein Tyrann hat nichts fo fehr zufcheuen ,
als eine Frome Zung , als einen wahren Kiel.

FIGURE 49   King Jehoiakim burns Jeremiah's scroll. Jan Luykens in Christoph Weigel's
Historiae celebriores Veteris Testamenti Iconibus representatae 1712. Private collection.

a quatrain in Latin and German, which reads in translation: "As soon as he reads, the king seizes the scroll and burns it with fire. Thereby he stands full of sin and judgment. Truly a Tyrant fears nothing more than a faithful tongue or a truthful pen." Weigel has updated Luykens' image of persecution to address Enlightenment embrace of reason and rejection of tyranny.

A more fanciful rendering of the scene further highlights the theme of conflict between individual conscience and political power. Weigel's engraving for his 1695 *Biblia ectypa* shows a single figure entreating the king to stop as the book is consumed in flames (Figure 50). This engraving also appeared in a 1716 edition of Luther's German Bible. The enduring popularity of emblem books and picture Bibles that presented sacred stories for contemporary tastes secured the importance of Jeremiah's burning scroll in the imagination of seventeenth- and eighteenth-century Europeans. In America, young Christians in 1836 learned in Sunday school, "Just as foolish and wicked is the conduct of those who now ridicule or hate the holy Scriptures... Many abuse it and refuse to read it, as he [Jehoiakim] did, because it reproves them of sin, and threatens the

FIGURE 50 King Jehoiakim burns Jeremiah's words. Christoph Weigel, *Biblia ectypa* 1695. Pitts Theology Library, Candler School of Theology, Emory University.

wicked with everlasting punishment. But if all the Bibles in the world were destroyed, it would do the sinner no good. God will perform what he promises or threatens, and no power can prevent it" (American Sunday-School Union 1836: 47).

The story ends with Jeremiah and Baruch re-creating the destroyed scroll according to divine command. Medieval German prior, Henry Suso, used the scene to chastise a monk wanting to give up because some converts he had brought to the faith had turned back. Jeremiah offers a model of persistence because he "did not for all this give up" and even "at the Lord's command went on writing a second volume" (Suso 1994: 181).

In the twentieth century, Jacques Derrida invokes Jeremiah at the beginning of *Writing and Difference* as an example of the dilemma of writing constraining meaning. "Writing is the anguish of the Hebraic *ruah*, experienced in solitude by human responsibility; experienced by Jeremiah subjected to God's dictation, or by Baruch transcribing Jeremiah's dictation… It is the moment at which we much decide whether we will engrave what we hear. And whether engraving preserves or betrays speech" (Derrida 1978: 9).

Jeremiah 37–38

Dungeon and Cistern

These chapters narrate two episodes in which Zedekiah's officials imprison Jeremiah in life-threatening circumstances. Early twentieth-century scholars concluded that the detail of the scenes, the use of an otherwise unknown technical term for the site of imprisonment, and the naming of the court officials indicate that the stories came from contemporary sources near the court. Yet the parallel structure of two arrests, dangerous confinements, and

Jeremiah Through the Centuries, First Edition. Mary Chilton Callaway.
© 2020 Mary Chilton Callaway. Published 2020 by John Wiley & Sons Ltd.

secret meetings with Zedekiah led the same scholars to conclude that a single event may lie behind the two chapters. Further, the account of Jeremiah being arrested as he leaves Jerusalem to buy his uncle's field contradicts the account in Jer 32, in which he arranges the purchase from his confinement in the court of the guard. In part two of *The Age of Reason* (1795), Thomas Paine judged "these two accounts are different and contradictory," part of the confused nature of the book of Jeremiah, "showing that it does not comport with reason and holds no authority for reasonable men."

The complex pre-history of the narratives is evident in 37:15–16, which uses four different terms to describe the place of confinement. The last term, *hachanuot*, occurs only here, and probably derives from the verb meaning "to bend down," in reference to a low, curved ceiling. Reception history of Jeremiah's prison begins with the ancient versions: Septuagint simply transliterates the Hebrew, while the Vulgate contemporizes the story for Roman citizens by using *ergastulum*, a prison for rebellious slaves on an estate. English versions show a similar adaptation to local culture. Coverdale contemporizes with "dungeon," evoking confinement in an English castle, and this is still used in many translations.

Ancient Allegories (38:1–13)

The dramatic account of Jeremiah violently dropped down a cistern by angry princes and creatively rescued by the king's Ethiopian official sparked the imagination of readers from the beginning. Patristic theologians found rich resources in the muddy pit and the faithful slave. Origen's homily on Jer 1 creatively claims that God foretold the ordeal in the muddy cistern when he promised support in 1:8 and his purpose is clear when he turns to encourage those who are persecuted not to be dismayed, but to continue in the model of Jeremiah and Christ. His homily on Jer 15:10 describes the task of prophets to reprove God's people and to suffer for it; as evidence, he combines the fate of prophets described in Heb 11:37 with the phrase, "they threw this one into the pit of mire" (Origen 1998: 16–17). As one who lost his father to Roman persecution, condemned by more than one bishop for his teaching, and imprisoned under the emperor Decius, Origen clearly identified with Jeremiah suffering for his obedience.

The ninth-century illustration of a sermon by the fourth-century Cappadocian bishop Gregory of Nazianzus presents a unique reception of the narrative. Gregory's sermon, preached "To the Frightened Citizens of Nazianzus and the Irate Prefect," had the double purpose of comforting the people of Nazianzus after their harvest had been destroyed by hail, and appealing to civil authorities to show mercy by not demanding the usual taxes. Gregory begins by quoting Jer 4:19 to describe his own anguish at his people's troubles. He does not mention Jer 38, but the ninth-century Greek artist illustrating a book of his homilies uses it to expand the sermon's themes of mercy and divine care. The first of three rows of images show a haloed Jeremiah being raised from the pit with rags by two men as Zedekiah looks on from a window above. A Greek inscription reads "Jeremiah in the mire." In the same frame, David bows in penance before Nathan, portrayed as a priest bestowing forgiveness. The other rows portray the Good Samaritan, two healings, and Jairus kneeling before Jesus in supplication for his daughter, pictured on a bed behind him. This last scene is diagonally opposite the raising of Jeremiah from the pit, creating a strong visual connection between Jesus' compassion in raising Jairus' daughter and Zedekiah ordering Jeremiah raised from the cistern. The unusual focus on Zedekiah as merciful is part of a ninth-century visual exegesis of Gregory's fourth-century homily that challenges contemporary political leaders to humble themselves before God (Brubaker 1999: 73–79).

Patristic allegories mark reception of Jer 38 through the middle ages. Basil the Great's fourth-century homily on Psalm 30:3, in which Hades is paralleled by a common Greek term for pit (*lakkos*), describes the prophet lowered into the pit and raised out of it as a figure of the Christian soul moving away from or toward God: "In the same way [as Jeremiah] every deed can press us down by sin to the underworld, or lift us as if on wings heavenward to God" (Basil 1963: 217). Jeremiah's cistern evokes both danger and rescue, damnation and salvation. Basil's spiritualized reading is elaborated centuries later in an anonymous comment on Ebed-Melek in the *Glossa*: "As the princes who threw the prophet into the pit are figures of devils who always want to submerge Christ's faithful into the mire of vice and the filth of sin, so this Ethiopian eunuch, who rescued the prophet because he feared God and was compassionate, figures Gentile preachers. They castrate themselves for the kingdom of heaven and look with love on the unjustly oppressed; they are zealous in word, deed and example to root out the snares of destruction." Gregory the Great's *Moralia in Job* (25.7) allegorizes the rags and ropes used to rescue Jeremiah into aids for Christian life:

> By divine warnings of helpful examples we are freed from the depths, as the prophet Jeremiah signified when he was thrown into the mud. When he was raised out of the mud, ropes and old rags were lowered to him. What do these ropes signify except teachings of the Lord, which convict and tear us when we have fallen into wickedness as they also bind and lift us out? So that these ropes might not cut when he was lifted, old rags were lowered at the same time. These signify the examples of the ancient fathers that comfort us lest the divine commands

terrify us. Their example enables us to do what in our ignorance we fear. So therefore we should hasten to be lifted from this depth: let us be tied with ropes; that is, let us be bound by the commands of the Lord, but let them be lined with old rags, with which we can be better held. They comfort us with their examples so that the commandments do not wound and terrify as they lift us.

Gregory's interpretation influenced Christians throughout the middle ages, beginning with Peter Damian's homily in preparation for Lent, "On Patience in the Battle against Our Wickedness," reproduced in the *Glossa*. Peter Abelard subsequently elaborated the rags and ropes in his description of the prophetic literature: "It was necessary that object lessons from the histories be added, in which both reward for those who obey and punishment of those who transgress are placed before [the people's] eyes. These are those old rags which were fastened into ropes to pulley Jeremiah from the well, namely, the examples of the ancient fathers, which were used with holy admonitions for pulling the sinner from the depth of vices" (Abelard 2011: 85.) In the *Glossa*, a lengthy excerpt from Gregory surrounds the text of Jer 38, ensuring that this allegory of the rags under Jeremiah's arms would persist for a thousand years, into the sixteenth century.

Jewish tradition resisted allegorizing but added a miracle. Josephus describes Jeremiah in a pit full of mud, held fast up to his neck (*Antiquities* 10.121). A homily for the Ninth of Ab in *Pesikta Rabbati* 26 describes Jeremiah thrown into a pit full of water, which God miraculously makes sink to the bottom. The mud then rises to the surface, holding Jeremiah's head above the water. To increase his torment, Jonathan the scribe taunts, "Put your head down in the mud – maybe you will have a good nap" (Braude 1968: 532). One of the few medieval illustrations of Jeremiah in the cistern is in a *Bible historiale* from 1350. His cap and black beard make him resemble a contemporary Jew, and the men wielding ropes are dressed as medieval Frenchmen. The top image, showing only Jeremiah's head above the mud and the two knaves taunting him, suggests that the artist knew the Jewish tradition about the mud in the cistern.

A Model for Political Resistance (38:1–16)

Early modern readers caught in religious wars and persecutions read Jeremiah as a model of resistance. The choice of this scene for one of the few illustrations of Jeremiah in early modern Bibles highlights the political resonance of the prophet's imprisonment described above. Many woodcuts, copper engravings, and steel engravings emphasize the rough treatment given the prophet: he is usually old and barely clothed, while his captors are strong young men with armor and weapons. The earliest modern illustration is most likely the woodcut by an anonymous artist in the workshop of Lucas Cranach, made for the first edition of his friend Martin Luther's complete German Bible printed in Wittenberg in 1534. Luther wanted illustrations as an aid to making biblical stories more familiar. Whereas medieval Latin Bibles usually portrayed Jeremiah in one historiated initial showing in miniature either the call or the apocryphal stoning, Luther's vernacular Bible included large illustrations of Jeremiah 28 and 38. The latter shows men in contemporary European dress straining at ropes as they lower the prophet into a brick-lined hole. The gloriole around Jeremiah's head evokes traditional images of saints, but the muscular figures in the picture marks a change to realism in Bible illustrations and was widely copied well into the seventeenth century.

The anachronistic translation of "dungeon" in both the Geneva and Bishops Bible encouraged Puritans and Royalists alike to identify with the prophet. In 1559, English Puritans who had fled to Geneva during the persecutions of Queen Mary completed their illegal translation of the Bible, distinguished by instructive marginal notes addressed to persecuted readers. Zedekiah's princes in Jer 38:4 evoked the Queen's bishops who were arranging the execution of Protestants: "Thus we see how the wicked when they cannot abide to hear the truth of God's word, seek to put the minister to death, as transgressors of policies." The condemnation of Zedekiah in the note accompanying verse 5 again covertly judges the English monarch as disobedient to God: "Wherein he grievously offended in that not only he would not hear the truth spoken by the Prophet but also gave him to the lusts of the wicked to be cruelly treated." Of Jeremiah's dungeon in 37:6, Calvin advises his readers, "Since then the holy Prophet was so atrociously treated, let us not think it strange, when the same thing at this day is endured by God's children, and for the same cause, even for bearing testimony to celestial truth." A century later, Anglican bishop Joseph Hall, who had been briefly imprisoned in the Tower by political enemies, invoked Jeremiah's dungeon in a sermon defending the established church against Puritan attacks, preached before King James I. Called "The Deceit of Appearance," it urged Christians to consider biblical examples of truth trumping appearance. "Should appearance be the rule, woe were God's children, happy were their enemies. Who, that had seen... Jeremiah in the dungeon, Zedekiah in the throne... would not have said... O miserable Jeremiah, John, Christ?... Yet we know... Jeremiah's dungeon had more true light of comfort, than the shining state of Zedekiah" (Hall 1863: 152–153). When Charles I was confronted with his Parliament's Grand Remonstrance censuring his actions in 1641, he jailed the leaders. One of his own clerics invoked Jeremiah to denounce him: "Pits were digged for the righteous... dungeons for Jeremy, because he would preach the truth with boldness" (Hill 1993: 88).

Jeremiah changed from martyr to rebel in Matthäus Merian's *Iconum Biblicarum* (1630). Merian used the new technology of copperplate engraving to produce a picture Bible with finely detailed full-page illustrations faced by a moralizing quatrain in Latin, German, and French. Unlike earlier images, Merian's Jeremiah is muscular and faces the viewer with a defiant look. The accompanying poem ironically explains that Jeremiah reaped the rewards of speaking the truth in faithfulness and piety – being thrown into a pit. Merian knew the power of images because his Protestant father in law had been exiled from Belgium during the Inquisition for his graphically polemical engravings of violence by Spanish explorers against inhabitants of the New World. His Jeremiah has slipped from Catholic tradition of martyrdom to Protestant ideal of prophetic confrontation.

In France, Jansenist educator Nicolas Fontaine used Merian's Jeremiah in the cistern for his own political struggle. His *L'histoire de Vieux et du Nouveau Testament* (1670) was an illustrated collection of epitomized Bible stories for his students (see Introduction). His narrative makes Jer 38 a thinly veiled commentary on the persecution of his Jansenist community and suggests to young readers that the prophet's brave resistance manifested his holiness. The accompanying engraving from Merian's *Iconum Biblicarum* supports Merian's reading of the prophet as defiant rather than defeated, and is well suited to Fontaine's Jérémie as a contemporary model for speaking against a corrupt king (Figure 51). His transformation of the prophet into bold rebel was translated and published in England, along with Merian's engraving, and subsequently in America, where it circulated widely through the nineteenth century.

Fontaine's Jansenist contemporary, Isaac-Louis le Maistre de Sacy, also used Jer 37–38 for strong political statements. Sacy's Jérémie both defies and embraces church teaching, nicely embodying Sacy's complex view of Scripture. Sacy defended his illicit translations by saying that the Bible was intended more for laypeople trying to live faithfully in the world than for mystical meditation by cloistered monks, and he compared reading the words of Scripture with eating the Word in the Eucharist. His extensive use of traditional Patristic sources in the "sens litteral et spirituel" accompanying each chapter of his commentary obeys the rules set by the Council of Trent, but he also slyly addresses contemporary politics. In the guise of exegesis, Sacy turns Jer 37–38 into an indictment of Louis XIV and his nobles. Political and ecclesial office-holders in Sacy's world were indebted to the king for their positions, so their dealings with him were carefully calibrated to maintain those positions. Their culture of posturing and dissembling was anathema to Sacy. On Jérémie's harsh response to Zedekiah's request that he intercede with God for Jerusalem, Sacy remarks, "He responded in accord with the heart of this prince who asked for prayers but dismissed the prophet's words, believing instead his cowardly sycophants (lâches flatteurs)" (Sacy 1693: 2:515–516). The biblical text nowhere suggests the flattery of sycophants, but Sacy encoded in his exegesis encouragement for readers to equate Zedekiah and his princes with the corruption of Louis XIV and his court.

JEREMIE PROPHETE. *Jeremie, chap.* XXXVIII. 307

'*Du saint Prophete Jeremie.*'

L E Prophete Jeremie eſtoit un homme d'une vertu admirable. Il ⟨Jeremie a⟩
fut ſanctifié dés le ventre de ſa mere, & il commença à preſcher ⟨commencé à prophetiſer⟩
dés l'âge de quinze ans. Il eut pluſieurs revelations ſur le ſujet des mal- ⟨l'an du M. 3375.⟩
heurs qui devoient arriver aux Juifs; & il eſt celuy de tous les pro- ⟨Avant J. C. 629 & il a⟩
phetes qui les a reſſentis, & qui les a exprimez, ſelon qu'il paroiſt ⟨prophetiſé⟩
dans ſes lamentations, en des termes plus pathetiques. Comme il en ⟨durant prés de 45 ans.⟩
eſtoit ſi vivement touché luy-meſme, il les prédiſoit auſſi aux autres
avec une force extraordinaire, & il ne ſe laſſoit point de faire reten-
tir par tout les paroles menaçantes que Dieu l'obligeoit de dire à ſon
peuple. Une liberté ſi genereuſe luy attira bien-toſt la haine des hom-
mes. Ils ne le regarderent plus que comme l'objet de leur averſion, &
ils luy ſuſciterent des perſecutions toûjours nouvelles. Ce ſaint homme ſouffrit avec un courage heroïque les outrages de ſes ennemis. Il
vit ſans s'eſtonner leurs mauvais deſſeins contre luy, leurs menaces,
& les ſupplices qu'ils luy préparoient: & bien loin d'en eſtre plus ti-
mide dans ſes prédications, il y fit au contraire paroiſtre plus de feu

Qq ij

FIGURE 51   Page from Fontaine's 1670 student story-Bible, with picture by Matthäus
Merian. Private collection.

Sacy's comment on Jer 38:4–6 heightens his political critique while also presenting Jérémie as moral exemplar. His opening sentence, "The nobles of the
king of Judah who rose up against Jérémie, according to St. John Chrysostom,
display a most unreasonable injustice…" shrewdly undermines the French

nobles with the most devastating words. The phrase "une injustice bien dérai-sonnable" explicitly evokes seventeenth-century French values of reason and justice in order to emphasize their absence from church and state. "A strange notion: this Prince of justice is so indebted to his nobles that he hands over a holy prophet simply from fear of offending them... However, this has been the pretext under which enemies of the true church have always opposed its defenders, a pretext of (false) justice and the good of the state and the church." Here, Sacy sees in Jérémie a model of moral courage imprisoned for his speech, as was Sacy himself for his Bible translations. This identification is elaborated in the comment on 38:6, which describes Jérémie in the cistern as a speech-act: "He spoke even more forcefully the divine threats than if he had been free; since the chains of his prison and the shadows of his dungeon proclaimed most loudly his suffering as proof that his prophecies were true. He would not expose himself willingly to such great hardships if he did not see himself compelled (presié) to proclaim them in his ministry" (de Sacy 1693: 2:528–529).

A century later, when church property was confiscated and priests executed preceding the French Revolution, Catholic poet Desmarais adopts the voice of the prophet, alternating between anguish and rage (see Introduction p. xx). His third "Vignette" presents "Jérémie thrown into a pit" in 107 French rhyming, metered couplets laden with baroque sensibilities: "In the dungeon he cries, 'What a dangerous abode, what a deep prison!/A stream flows nearby whose waters flood it/my feet, my hands, my body, sink down under its chains/my clothes have become rags eaten by worms/Hungry insects without number consume my black bread under cover of darkness/I hear only rocks cracking suddenly/making a terrible crash as they fall.'" In a radical departure from the biblical text, the poem describes God appearing as fire in the cold pit and Jérémie responding with Baroque emotions, "My voice, my feeble voice, has reached your ears/You deign to listen, you put an end to my tears./At last I taste the sweetness of sleep/Which my tears and sobs had destroyed." Perhaps most pertinent to Desmaris' readers is God's promise of retribution: "I tremble, you speak to me: 'Doubt not, it is your God/It is I who now come to defend you./Your vile persecutors, delivered to my vengeance/will perish before your eyes, consumed with regrets/but you can expect eternal blessedness.'" This personal reassurance to Desmaris' readers takes a political turn at the end of the poem. Having called the persecutors "blasphemers," Jérémie prays, "Hurl your weapons at this impious breed/whose destructive hand devastates my country/Destroy even the descendants of these depraved men/And let your bloody blows terrify the Universe" (Desmarais 1772: 67–68). The accompanying engraving of Jérémie being lowered into the pit includes political commentary in the identification of the official with the prominent display of the "horse's ass" (Figure 52).

Pag. 50.

P. Le Clerc Del .   *Pepin Sculp .*

FIGURE 52   A baroque Jérémie in Paris. M. Demaris, Jérémie, Poëme en quatre Chants 1771, page 56. Private collection.

The Cistern as Spiritual Prison (38:1–6).

In the eighteenth century, dungeon and cistern are the centerpiece of Samuel Wesley's representation of Jeremiah in his two-volume *History of the Old Testament in Verse* (1704). Wesley, the father of John and Charles, founders of

Methodism, began his education among the Dissenters, but changed his allegiance to the established church and the crown while at Oxford. Never fully accepted in either camp, he found in Jeremiah a spiritual model. His rendering of biblical history in heroic couplets includes Jer 37–38, which cast the prophet as a stoic Englishman. His description of the cistern as "a den profound and dark beyond the Grave" adds touches of English prisons:

> A thousand noxious Creatures had been there,
> Tho' now themselves extinct for want of Air:
> Unwholesome Damps from hollow Vaults arise
> In pestilential Fogs, and scale the Skies:
> Hither the Prophet cast, no bottom found,
> A Bog of putrid Mire deny'd the Ground.

Yet the prophet, like an English martyr, resists torment with prayer:

> Nor Chains, nor Darkness shook so firm a Mind,
> Calm as the Bless'd, and all to Heaven resign'd:
> Nor by the best of Friends forsaken there,
> Who from that dire Abyss regards his Prayer:
> By whom inspir'd good Ebed-melech goes.

Wesley ends the scene with a warning to the reader:

> With Heav'ns unchang'd Decrees we strive in vain,
> And still the more we strive, the less we gain.

By the nineteenth century, the cistern had again become a figure for the mire of sin. In *Pilgrims Progress*, John Bunyan had described the "very dark dungeon, nasty and stinking" in the castle of the Giant Despair, and elsewhere he wrote about the pit of sin. It was his nineteenth-century editor and biographer, however, who likened Jeremiah in the cistern to Bunyan in the English dungeon. In his preface to Bunyan's autobiographical *Grace Abounding*, George Offor reads Bunyan in Jeremiah's pit as a trope for spiritual and psychological torment: "If ever any victim of terror or despair might, without extravagance, compare his dark prospects to a 'horrible pit' or his dire entanglements to a 'miry clay,' it was Bunyan. This emblem is taken from the deep and damp dungeon of an ancient prison, such as that into which Jeremiah was 'let down by cords...' Unlike Jeremiah, who was imprisoned with a clear conscience, Bunyan was "a guilty man...for he had not only sinned in the face of deep convictions and signal warnings, but against solemn vows and pledges also...You cannot but feel then, that no man could escape from such a pit, or extricate himself from such clay of despair, by his own power." Bunyan's biographer uses Jeremiah's pit not only as literal parallel to Bunyan's prison cell, but more potently as metaphor for the tortures of a guilty conscience. He also contrasts Jeremiah's pit as the spiritual torment of the penitent sinner with the more dangerous pit of "mere worldly sorrows" which can harden the heart. For the unsanctified, who suffer worldly sorrow, "their 'horrible pit' becomes almost a real hell; and their 'miry clay' chains of darkness, that fix both their weakness and woe for life" (Bunyan 1850: 1:3).

In the nineteenth and twentieth centuries, Jeremiah in the cistern becomes a model of individual faith in times of trouble. Nineteenth-century Bible illustrations tend to show the prophet alone in a dungeon, relating to God rather than interacting with his human tormentors. An early nineteenth-century illustration in a family Bible from the north of England shows an almost naked prophet, with chained ankle, looking remarkably calm as he gazes upward, hands clasped in prayer (Figure 53). Here is a model of faithful patience encouraging English Christians to bear their troubles bravely. Another anonymous engraving from a family Bible shows a white-robed Jeremiah seated on ropes held by muscular men lowering him into a hole (Figure 54). His eyes and arms raised to heaven are reminiscent of nineteenth-century images of Jesus. This trope of Jeremiah's cistern as personal tribulation persists in contemporary Christian interpretation, illustrated by the 2014 drawing accompanying an online sermon from a Baptist church in Dallas (Figure 55).

Ebed-Melek Rescues Jeremiah (38:7–13)

The mysterious figure of the Ethiopian eunuch who rescues Jeremiah from the pit has consistently upended readers' cultural assumptions of the "other." In rabbinic Judaism, blacks were often considered an inferior subgroup of Gentiles; hence Ebed-Melek's positive portrayal needed commentary (Melamed 2003: 114–115). *Pesikta Rabbati* 26 highlights his exceptional nature: "He was called Cushite because just as a Cushite is recognized by his skin; so he was recognized by his good deeds among Zedekiah's men" (Braude 1968: 532). Gregory the Great claimed him as unexpected forerunner to Gentile Christians, a "eunuch for the kingdom of heaven." For Protestants who had fled their native England in the sixteenth century, Ebed-Melech symbolized the gracious foreigners in Geneva who sheltered them. The Geneva Bible marginal note (1560) at 38:9 reads, "Hereby is declared that the Prophet found more favor at this stranger's hands, than he did by all them of his country, which was to their great condemnation." John Trapp commends Ebed-Melech to English

FIGURE 53   From an eighteenth-century family Bible published in Leeds, England. Private collection.

Christians facing danger: "This stranger is a good encouragement to men to appear in a good cause, and to act vigorously for God, notwithstanding they are alone and have to encounter divers difficulties." In contrasting "the Church in the wilderness" with the established church, John Bunyan shrewdly identifies Ebed-Melech as an outsider, one of those who are "in the porch of the church." These are Old Testament figures who "prefigure the strength of the church under persecution" and are "seasonable to them that in the wilderness are faint and weary" (Bunyan 1841: 367). In *Seasonable Counsel: Or, Advice to Sufferers*, Bunyan similarly exhorts persecuted Puritans to be attentive to the way God makes up for their losses: "When Jeremiah the prophet was rejected of all, yea, the church that then was, could not help him; he was cast into the dungeon, and

FIGURE 54   Jeremiah lowered into the cistern. From an English family Bible, 1834. Private collection.

FIGURE 55   Jeremiah in the cistern for American Christians. By permission of Pastor Jeff Warren, Park Cities Baptist Church, Dallas, Texas 2014.

sunk to a great depth there in the mire. God the Creator, who ruleth the spirits of all men, stirred up the heart of Ebed-Melek the Ethiopian both to petition for his liberty, and to put him out of the dungeon by the help of thirty men" (Bunyan 1861: 730).

Ebed-Melech also provided French Jansenist theologian Isaac-Louis de Sacy with a model of the righteous outsider. In his 1693 commentary, de Sacy writes: "All means of carrying out his purposes are equal to God. However, he often chooses one who appears as a foreigner, the better to confound the pride of those who think themselves natives in this regard." Pointedly highlighting the divine spark in igniting individual conscience, he continues, "We are equally astonished at the weakness of a sovereign who hands over a prophet to the cruelty of his enemies, and the nobility of a stranger who defends an abandoned prisoner, against the opinion of the whole court and all the people, guided only by the secret voice of the One who spoke to his heart" (de Sacy 1693: 2:530). Ebed-Melech is thus a model of Jansenist piety, resisting worldly authority to obey a conscience shaped by studying the Bible.

Exploration of Africa in the nineteenth century also led to romanticizing the exotic Ethiopian. The widely influential and still used *Preacher's Commentary* (1882) observes, "The Ethiopian's skin was not changed in the land of his bondage, but his heart was. He found light shining in this deep night of Judaism, and was guided by it to the everlasting and ever-loving God. And while the children of the kingdom cast themselves out, this child of darkness and of the desert was brought in to share the inheritance of the faithful. He 'trusted' in the Lord… Jehovah singled out an Ethiopian in the court of Zedekiah, and sent to him a message of His divine and fatherly love. To God the small and the great are alike." Ebed-Melech here serves the popular Evangelical theme especially attractive to England's working class that it is not the outside (the Ethiopian's skin) but the inside (his heart) that matters (Jellie 1892: 590). Ebed-Melech also underscored the late nineteenth-century romantic vision of life in the countryside. English and American preachers using Joseph Exell's popular *Biblical Illustrator* read that he was "a slave from the Soudan. But no son of Israel is he; only a slave of the royal household, a heathen from a far-off land, with a black skin but a pure heart. The simple nature of the Ethiopian, uncorrupted by the vices of palace life, would recognize the moral and spiritual elevation of the prophet."

Ebed-Melek's exotic difference from British readers increased his usefulness as a moral exemplar in sermons: "The poor can show kindness, as well as the rich. Ebed-Melech was a poor coloured man – the slave of King Zedekiah; yet he managed to show real kindness to the prophet Jeremiah… In learning to show kindness to others, there is no telling how much good we may do." Finally, Ebed-Melek's thoughtfulness in wrapping the ropes in rags marks him as a model: "Negro though he was, Ebed-Melech was a gentleman."

Englishmen preparing sermons with the help of *The Pulpit Commentary* found homiletic gold in Ebed-Melek's sexuality as well as his race. "He was a man of an apparently inferior race. It is better to have a black skin and a humane heart than a white skin and a black heart… He was regarded as an effeminate creature. True manliness belongs to our conduct, not to our appearance and manners. God raises up friends in the most unlikely quarters." F.B. Meyer similarly describes his perplexity with Ebed-Melek's gender with phrases like, "there was great gentleness in the way this noble Ethiopian executed his purpose" and "it was an act of womanly tenderness, which makes it as fragrant as the breaking of the box over the person of the Lord." Yet "only one of God's own gentleman would have thought of the rags and clouts" (Meyer 1894: 170). Ebed-Melek's race, nationality, and sexuality posed a problem for eighteenth- and nineteenth-century preachers, which they solved by transforming him into an honorary Caucasian and, proleptically, a Christian gentleman. In the early twentieth century, by contrast, Ebed-Melek's race is highlighted. Arthur Maxwell's *The Bible Story,* published a year after the Supreme Court settled Brown vs. Board of Education, invites young readers to imagine, "How glad Jeremiah must have been to see the kind face of that dear colored man looking down from the top of the dungeon!" (Maxwell 1955: 189). In *Jeremiah and the Great Disaster,* a children's book published in England in 1987, Jeremiah's rescuer is simply called "a friend" without mention of race, but the two illustrations portray him as African.

More recently, Ebed-Melek has been presented as a universal role model for ethics in the workplace in the online "Theology of Work Project." Replacing Ethiopian with "immigrant," and calling him "a nameless Gentile slave" (because Ebed-Melek means slave of the king), the author presents him as a model of bravery instinctively responding to injustice: "Although his immigration status and racial difference made him a vulnerable worker, his faithfulness to God led him to blow the whistle on injustice in the workplace… An anonymous cog in the wheel made a life-and-death difference… Ebed-Melech could not know in advance whether going outside the chain of command would be a career-limiting move (or a life-ending move, given what happened to Jeremiah)" (www.theologyofwork.org).

Ebed-Melek was popular with seventeenth and eighteenth-century engravers, who found him both exotic and exemplary. Jan Luyken's 1712 popular emblem book of biblical pictures included a moralizing poem with each engraving. Luyken's Ebed-Melek is foregrounded from the other figures, dressed as a nobleman and directing the rescue effort (Figure 56). An abbreviated translation of the accompanying Dutch poem reads, "Whoever in his heart does not listen to his conscience, which reminds him constantly that he has forgotten God, throws Jeremiah into the muddy hole and looks like the

GESCHIEDENISSEN.   321

JEREMIAS XXXVIII: 6,7,8,9,10,11,12,13.

FIGURE 56   Ebed Melek rescues Jeremiah. Jan Luyken, 1712. Private collection.

presumptuous princes… who held onto their own will. But whoever listens to his heart, he pulls Jeremiah from the hole and will receive with Ebed-Melek the favor and friendship of God." Here, the saintly Ebed-Melek is contrasted with the willful princes, and Jer 38 has become a Protestant teaching about training one's conscience and listening to it before acting.

Ebed-Melek also became a signifier of more worldly concepts. Another illustration comes from Bernard Picart (Figure 57), whose engraving in a 1712 emblem book of biblical pictures also portrays Ebed-Melech as a foreign nobleman directing local soldiers. Ebed-Melek displays an early Enlightenment view of the nobility of foreign cultures and non-Christian religions described in the Enlightenment French work that appeared in English as *Religious Ceremonies and Customs of All the Peoples of the World* (1723–43). Jean Frederic Bernard worked with engraver Bernard Picart to produce this illustrated compendium that presented an ethnography of religious traditions presented as

FIGURE 57   Ebed Melek directs Jeremiah's rescue. Bernard Picart. Courtesy of the Pitts Theology Library, Candler School of Theology, Emory University.

equals. Picart's noble Ethiopian in a picture Bible. reflects the Enlightenment interests of Bernard's encyclopedic book.

On the eve of World War I, British artist William Kunning King found in Ebed Melech a model to inspire his fellow Brits. King had already drawn popular pictures promoting the work of the Salvation Army in rescuing abused children and later produced pictures showing selfless devotion of British soldiers to each other in battle. King saw another such model of active compassion in Ebed Melek. His dress and face make him appear more real than the Orientalized soldiers around him. King overrides the biblical text to portray Ebed Melek grasping Jeremiah's frail hand, giving the readers of *Bibby's Annual* a literal image of the common phrase "to give a hand" (Figure 58). The brief accompanying text notes that later, Ebed Melek was one of the few who escaped with his life. The purpose of the picture is then made clear: "It was well said by one of old: 'Blessed are the merciful, for they shall obtain mercy.' It is a law of Nature which is just as operative as the law of gravitation, but many people do not yet know of it." American illustrator Herbert Rudeen portrayed Ebed Melek as a handsome, friendly hero among foreign-looking old men (Figure 59). Jeremiah's white hand on Ebed Melek's black arm, and the joy in their faces, offered a message about civil rights to the wide readership of the 1959 children's picture Bible in which the illustration was featured.

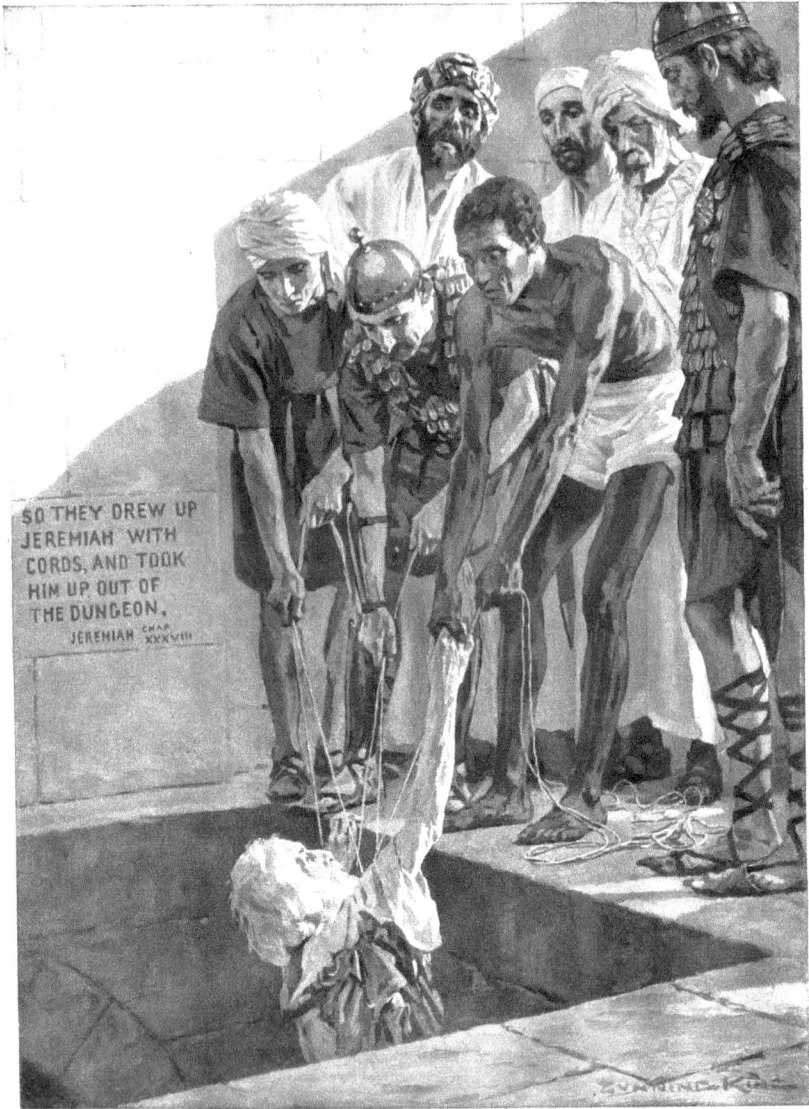

SO THEY DREW UP
JEREMIAH WITH
CORDS, AND TOOK
HIM UP OUT OF
THE DUNGEON.
JEREMIAH XXXVIII

Drawn by Gunning King]   [Copyright—Bibby's Annual

JEREMIAH BEING DRAWN UP OUT OF THE WELL INTO WHICH HE WAS CAST BY
THE ADVICE OF THE PRINCES OF KING ZEDEKIAH.

But an Ethiopian in the king's household named Ebed-Meleck, hearing of Jeremiah's misfortune, pleaded with the king that he might be allowed to take him out of the pit, and to allow him to remain in the court of the prison : this request was granted, and the Ethiopian, with his men to help him, thus saved the life of the Prophet. When the King of Babylon afterwards besieged Jerusalem and overcame Zedekiah, his servant Ebed-Meleck was one of the few who escaped with his! life : It was well said by one of old, " Blessed are the merciful, for they shall obtain mercy." It is a law of Nature which is just as operative as the law of gravitation, but many people do not yet know of it.

FIGURE 58   Jeremiah rescued by Ebed Melek rescues Jeremiah. William Gunning
King. *Bibby's Annual,* 1914. Private Collection.

FIGURE 59   An American Ebed Melek for children. Herbert Rudeen 1959. Private collection.

Jeremiah's Lie (38:24–27)

Zedekiah's command that Jeremiah lie to the princes about his conversation with Zedekiah has caused consternation from the first century CE to the present. In *Jewish Antiquities* Josephus frames the episode to contrast Jeremiah's loyalty with that of Zedekiah's officials. He begins by emphasizing the deception of Zedekiah's advisors who told him that Nebuchadnezzar would not attack, and ends with the leaders asking Jeremiah "what kind of story he had made up about them when he came to the king" (*Antiquities* 229). This sleight-of-hand to downplay Jeremiah's lie was part of Josephus' identification with Jeremiah, and part of his project to demonstrate loyalty to Roman authorities. In early modernity, the verse became a significant stumbling-block. A marginal note in the Geneva Bible warns readers that Jeremiah's lie shows "the infirmity of the prophet, who dissembled to save his life, even though it was not to the denial for his doctrine or to the hurt of any."

Calvin writes that though Jeremiah's words were in part true, "he could not by this evasion be wholly exempted from blame." He was "oppressed with extreme fear; and thus we are reminded to seek of God magnanimity of mind and resolute firmness; for he alone can strengthen and sustain us when we are terrified." Furthermore, though he obeyed the king, "he ought rather to have hearkened to God's word, in which simplicity is enjoined." On the other side, English Non-conformist Matthew Poole presents Jeremiah as a model for Christian behavior in a hostile environment: "A man is not bound in all cases to speak the whole truth, much less to those who have nothing to do to inquire of us, which these princes had not." Thomas Paine, whose *Age of Reason* argued against the authority of the Bible, highlights "the duplicity" of Jeremiah: "Thus this man of God, as he is called, could tell a lie, or very strongly prevaricate, when he supposed it would answer his purpose" (Paine 1796: 2:52).

A small book on Jeremiah published in Philadelphia for use in American Sunday schools reassures young readers that verse 26 "was, no doubt, part of what had been said, for we cannot believe that Jeremiah would have said this to the rulers (as he did) if it had not been true" (American Sunday-School Union 1836: 68). The *Self-Interpreting Bible,* widely used in families, treads a fine line between censure and endorsement: "Though no man is authorized to tell a falsehood to escape inconvenience or danger, yet no man is bound to tell an enemy what that enemy does not ask, or what that enemy has no right to demand" (Brown 1792: 621). The *Preacher's Commentary* (1892), a collection of comments compiled by Protestant preacher W. Harvey Jellie, presents justifications by the bishop of London among others. The editor rejects these modernizing interpretations with the warning that Christians might be led to find in Jeremiah a model for equivocation and subterfuge. "Truth suffers in the hands of compromising men. It brings discredit upon truth in general, if professedly holy men are discovered to tamper with it by equivocation. Souls in whom God's Light shines should never emit dim rays."

Historical-critical exegesis offered a way out of the dilemma. Bernhard Duhm's 1901 commentary includes a lengthy excursus on the difference between ancient and contemporary sensibilities. Noting that Jeremiah "willingly, calmly lies," Duhm compares the episode with Abraham's lie in Gen 20:12 and God's deception in I Kings 22:22f. He then reassures his readers that "The O.T. knows the essential differences between custom and sin. We on the contrary emphasize above all the offense against ourselves, the injury of our relationship to the good, the damage to our ethical human nature. The lie for us is a grave offense, because it poisons our inner being; we count it more than anything to be the 'worthless' thing that according to 15:19 ought not come from the prophet's mouth. We think this way because for us the human soul is the theme of religion and the focus of all ethical concerns." Duhm adopts Kant's argument that lying damages one's humanity, yet he also distinguishes the "divine Truth" for which Jeremiah staked his life from the "circumstantial truth" which Jeremiah viewed as a means to a higher end. "No prophet stands more against lies than Jeremiah, but sometimes deception can be more effective than truth against the enemy of the people's welfare." Lest readers take Jeremiah as a model, Duhm again locates the prophet in a world inaccessible to them: "One must assume that Jeremiah, if Baruch has reported accurately, did not feel any scruples with his untruth. The conscience of ancient man did not stir up injuries to the soul (Verletzungen der Seele) on its own. Jeremiah had accomplished his goal; the princes left him alone." This argument from historical difference shows Duhm's desire to rationalize the lie, which might otherwise undermine his claims that Jeremiah through his "confessions" marks a new spiritual consciousness in human history.

In the twentieth century, revelations about lapses in the personal integrity of leaders raised questions about their moral authority, and Jeremiah's lie was particularly troubling for readers taking biblical figures as models for contemporary Christians. In his widely read and still reprinted 1930 *Jeremiah: A Study in Personal Religion*, Congregational minister and scholar Raymond Caulkins writes at length to reassure American readers of Jeremiah's integrity in spite of his "partial truth": "Jeremiah obeyed the king and said what he had been told to say and no more. Did he do right, or did he do wrong? To have told the whole truth might have meant instant death for himself, and he would have betrayed the confidence of the king. Jeremiah was not keen to die… Most Bible readers will feel that if he did wrong, it was a wrong for which it is easy to forgive him. Even to-day people disagree on this point of ethics" (Caulkins 1930: 300–310). The *Apologetics Study Bible* devotes an unusually long annotation that defends Jeremiah (human life was in jeopardy) while sternly warning readers: "The Bible does not say that what Jeremiah did was commendable, or that God blessed him for it. In fact, Jeremiah remained in custody until the fall of the city." Lest readers take the prophet as a model, the note reminds them, "Jeremiah's compliance, in the face of death and suffering, contrasts with Jesus' determination in the garden of Gethsemane" (Cabal 2007: 1148). Paul Redditt's *Introduction to the Prophets* ends the chapter on Jeremiah with a full page titled, "A Problem Raised by a Study of Jeremiah," and calls the lie "a moral issue." Some would excuse it because Jeremiah was simply following orders, but invoking the international trials of Nazis who used that reasoning, Redditt warns that Jeremiah's lie cannot be justified (Redditt 2008: 128–129).

Finding grace in a dark place, Matthew Poole says of Jeremiah's imprisonment in verse 28, "Thus God hath several ways to hide his people in an evil day; he hid Josiah from it in the grave; he hid Noah in an ark, Lot in Zoar, Jeremiah in a prison, which in probability was a safer place for him than the land of Benjamin, whither he would have gone had not Irijah stopped him."

Zedekiah Captured (39:4–7)

This brief narrative about Zedekiah's capture inspired creative responses. Rashi explains that Zedekiah had built a secret underground tunnel from the palace to the wilderness in Jericho. During their escape, God sent a deer to prance before the Babylonians, and they chased it along the roof of the tunnel to the place where Zedekiah exited and captured him. Not all Jews read Zedekiah's

Jeremiah Through the Centuries, First Edition. Mary Chilton Callaway.
© 2020 Mary Chilton Callaway. Published 2020 by John Wiley & Sons Ltd.

capture with Rashi as well-deserved punishment. Nineteenth-century Lithuanian poet, Judah Lieb Gordon, read against the grain, identifying with Zedekiah as one who tried to navigate between political realities and an unyielding prophet. When Gordon lived in St. Petersburg, representing the Jewish community to the czarist government, he was arrested, imprisoned, and then deported for alleged anti-government activity. Using the outraged voice of Jeremiah's confessions in the persona of Zedekiah he rails against God for the impossible situation God dealt him.

> What then, Heavenly Power, is my crime against You?
> That you have landed such blows against me and my entire family?
> If I have acted wickedly and done what is evil in your eyes,
> Would that I alone had met my doom:
> But what have these lambs done, what have they sinned?
> Jealous and vengeful God, the God of Jeremiah!
> I, if I sinned, transgressing your word –
> Why were my children put to death – in violation of your Torah (Deut. 24:16)?

The poet breaks off his argument to bemoan "the nightmarish picture, the horrific sight" of his slaughtered "cherished babes" that he still "sees" with burning vividness in his soul. When he resumes his case against God, his argument reflects the values and reasoning of modernity, challenging the hopelessly idealistic idea of a nation ruled by both God and king:

> Why did you command that they place a king over them?
> Why did you appoint overseers to ride herd over them?
> Is that the kind of king you have in mind,
> A man whom every minor soothsayer torments?
> Thus from the day this nation came into being and onward
> There has been a quarrel between the practitioners of Torah and the government.
>
> (Nash 2003: 37, 41–42)

In the time of Haskalah, the Jewish Enlightenment, Gordon interprets Zedekiah's story to highlight contradictions in the biblical ideal of Israel and the inevitable conflicts between religious and secular powers playing out in his own time. Writing the poem in a Russian prison, he reads Zedekiah as a noble character, who like Gordon himself was caught between the harsh demands of God and a secular power intent on dominance.

Ebed-Melech Becomes Abimelech (39:15–18)

The promise of divine protection given to Ebed-Melech after the destruction of the temple generated rich embellishment after its second destruction in 70 CE. The Jewish apocryphal writing *Things Omitted from Jeremiah the Prophet* (also titled *4 Baruch*) names him Abimelech and describes his reward in an imaginative narrative. As God is about to command angels to drop burning torches onto Jerusalem, Jeremiah implores him to show what he can do for Abimelech, "for he did many good deeds for your servant Jeremiah." God instructs Jeremiah to send Abimelech to Agrippa's vineyard, where he will be sheltered "until I return the people to the city." Sent to gather figs to give to the sick, in the heat of the day Abimelech falls asleep under a tree. Awakening 66 years later, with the help of an angel Abimelech finds Baruch, with whom he writes a letter to Jeremiah in Babylon. In a Christian addition to the text, the two witness a miraculous "death and resurrection" of Jeremiah on an altar (see Introduction). In the end, Jeremiah "delivered all the mysteries that he had seen to Baruch and Abimelech" as he was being stoned, and the two bury him.

This apocryphal story of Abimelech takes on canonical status in an early fifteenth-century French bible, whose striking illustration is set between Jerome's prologue and Jer 1. Abimelech, asleep under a tree with his bag of figs spilled open nearby, wears European dress and has the divided beard that signifies the prophets in medieval art. He is being awakened by a passer-by; the difference in their dress may indicate the 66 years during which he slept. The figs develop the metaphor of Jeremiah's two baskets of figs (Jer 24), which signified divine restoration of the exiles and Jerusalem. The second century CE author of *4 Baruch* extends this traditional sense of divine restoration to the more recent idea of individual resurrection (Kaestli 1997). When Abimelech learns how long he has slept and sees the figs, he cries out in thanksgiving to God "the rest of the souls of the righteous in every place" (Charlesworth 1985: 2, 421). Then Baruch, on seeing Abimelech's fresh 66 year old figs, exclaims, "Thus it will be for you, my flesh ... he who preserved the basket of figs, the same one again will preserve you by his power" (Charlesworth 1985: 2, 421). If Abimelech's sleep is an allegory for death, as his words suggest, the figs clearly signify resurrection of the body, as Baruch's words make clear. The illustration of this apocryphal story at the beginning of Jeremiah in a fifteenth-century bible (Figure 60) replaces the traditional weeping or martyred prophet with one who gives witness to God's care for the righteous after death.

Christians in every era claimed Ebed-Melech's reward as their own. Theodoret reminds his fifth-century readers that kingship did Zedekiah no good in the end, while being a slave did not harm Ebed-Melech. His comment persists into early

FIGURE 60   Abimelech with his figs, awakened after 66 years. Beginning of Jeremiah in French bible, 1425. Pierpont Morgan Library. Ms M. 395, fol. 99r.

modernity in the *Glossa*. Ebed-Melech's reward also provided medieval Christians an allegory for the afterlife. The *Glossa* ends its comment by noting that like the Ethiopian slave, the righteous are given freedom – from future punishment – while their persecutors perish in eternal torment. Calvin's Protestant theology led him to focus instead on the last words of scene, God's promise of protection "because you trusted in me." Calvin instructs readers that Ebed-Melech models a life of faith, and is rewarded "because he trusted in God." In seventeenth-century England, Matthew Poole reflects both Patristic teaching and English society when he highlights Ebed-Melech as foreigner who becomes like us, "a type of the calling of the gentiles."

Jeremiah 40–43

These narratives describing the fate of Judeans who remained in the land were shaped by exilic redactors to highlight the chaos and disobedience in Judah. Their claim to be the true remnant of Israel is especially apparent in the few stories about Jeremiah. Beyond their original purpose, the stories shaped significant Jewish and Christian traditions that persisted into early modernity and proved to be rich sources for political and religious reflection.

Jeremiah Through the Centuries, First Edition. Mary Chilton Callaway.
© 2020 Mary Chilton Callaway. Published 2020 by John Wiley & Sons Ltd.

How Did the Prophet Escape the Burning City? (40:1–6)

The Bible presents two different narratives of Jeremiah's escape, and Jewish tradition offers a third (see commentary on 20:7). In the first (39:11–14), Nebuchadnezzar orders him released from Zedekiah's court of the guard and entrusted to Gedaliah, the Babylonian appointed governor. In the second, he is taken with other captives in chains to Babylon, but at Ramah the Babylonian captain Nebuzaradan releases him and gives him "a ration of food and a present" (40:5). The present is elaborated by Josephus to "rich gifts," highlighting the foreign invaders' appreciation of Jeremiah (*Antiquities* 10:158). Josephus continually presents Jeremiah's story as his own, here slyly signaling to the Romans the advantages of a working relation between conquered and conqueror. These gifts discomfit Calvin, who warns his readers against Jeremiah's moral failure: "Jeremiah may seem to have forgotten himself; for it was a disgrace to him to receive from an enemy of God's people, a present or gifts for his doctrine." The "doctrine" was Jeremiah's prophecies about the destruction of Jerusalem, and the suggestion that he may have profited from the enemy for his preaching discomfited the reformer. In addition, the possibility that speaking the divine word might play into the hand of one's enemies haunted Calvin in his own politically charged environment.

Rembrandt's famous painting of Jeremiah lamenting the destruction of Jerusalem (1620) foregrounds the rich gifts as golden vessels (Figure 1). Art historian Simon Schama comments that Rembrandt's juxtaposition of the mourning prophet with riches spoke to the Protestant ethic of distaining worldly treasures, even as it offered gleaming representations of their presence in art. Rembrandt's Jeremiah speaks to this ambivalent wrestling with a theology of mortality and transience in a culture newly entranced with consumer goods (Schama 1999: 281–283).

A post-colonial interpretation of Jeremiah's release deliberately reads the text from below, shifting the focus from Babylonian power to the experience of the occupied. In *Empire and Exile,* Steed Davidson highlights the prophet's agency in choosing to remain in the land, argues that his "choice of a location on the margins" makes him subject rather than object of empire, and is an act of resistance. Davidson argues, "The margins provide the space where a counter-language can be spoken that can effectively challenge the dominant power. The movement to the margins, when given the choice to accept the center, in itself rejects the values of the center; it is an act of resistance" (Davidson 2014: 124).

The Murder of Gedaliah (40:7– 41:17)

The intrigue and deception that end with the assassination of Gedaliah, whom Nebuchadnezzar had appointed to govern the remnant of Judah, resonated in times that were troubled by political murder. The story of Gedaliah's murder horrified medieval Christians in Europe, who considered him akin to a king. Guyart's *Bible historiale* typically illustrates it with a contemporizing scene, like that of a 1470 Flemish manuscript showing a knight with a long sword impaling the king asleep in his castle, amid a bloody scene of servants and the queen also being stabbed. An illuminated *Bible historiale* from early fourteenth-century France includes an elaborate full-color page showing the treacherous Ishmael kneeling as if in allegiance to Gedaliah, dressed as a French king.

How Long, O Lord? (42:7)

The ten-day delay between Jeremiah's request for guidance and God's response often perturbed readers. Fifteenth-century Jewish scholar Abarbanel notes that giving the number of days it took God to reply is unique in Scripture, warning that it cannot be used as a model (Rosenberg 1989: 2:327–328). Calvin's discomfort is clear in his piling up of explanations. He calls it shrewd on God's part, who "deferred, that the prophecy might have more weight," by showing that Jeremiah "did not instantly bring forth what had not arisen in his own head, but prayerfully waited to know what pleased God." The delay is also a model for Christians, who should "wait with calm and resigned minds" for God's answer to their prayers for guidance. A century later, Puritan John Trapp rejects the suggestion of his contemporaries that Jeremiah had prayed for ten days, but contemporizes the experience to cultivate spiritual patience in his readers: "So long God held his holy Prophet in request: and so he doth still his best servants many times."

The refusal to heed Jeremiah's plea not to flee to Egypt becomes a metaphor for stubborn disobedience leading to disaster. Jerome uses Jeremiah to address the contemporary controversy about Pelagius. In a letter to Augustine castigating his ecclesial enemies for clinging to the heretical teachings of Pelagius even after the pope has denounced him, Jerome casts himself as Jeremiah: "Captive Jerusalem is in the hands of Nebuchadnezzar, and refuses to listen to Jeremiah's advice (Kelly 1998: 325). Puritan scholars who created the Geneva Bible similarly viewed themselves as Jeremiah and his opponents as their persecutors. A marginal note focuses on "prideful" in verse 2 to condemn the persecuting English church of the most grievous sin: "This declareth that pride is the cause of rebellion, and contempt of God's ministers." Three more notes urge readers to see in the disobedient Judeans their own English persecutors who refuse to listen to God's messengers.

The Stones of Tahpanhes (43:8–13)

Jeremiah's prophetic act of burying paving stones in front of Pharaoh's residence while proclaiming that Nebuchadnezzar would set his throne above those stones and ravage Egypt caused consternation among readers from the beginning. Even the textual tradition is unstable. Septuagint describes hiding large stones "in the doorway of the entrance," the Hebrew reads "in a hidden place among the bricks which are in the doorway" and the Vulgate describes a vault under the brick wall at the entrance to the palace. In the fourteenth century, Nicholas of Lyra adds to the *Glossa* his explanation that the Hebrew describes a mud pit for making bricks, but he also adds a "*moraliter*," an allegorical warning that the stones signify sinners hardened in guilt, over whom

JEREMIAH PROPHESYING THE DEFEAT OF THE EGYPTIANS.—JER. XLIII. 9.

FIGURE 61   Jeremiah about to bury stones in Egypt. Illustration from a nineteenth-century family Bible Private collection.

FIGURE 62   Jeremiah preaches in Egypt. Woodcut from a sixteenth-century German bible. Private collection.

the devil has established his throne just as Nebuchadnezzar did. Combining Origen's allegorizing of Nebuchadnezzar as Satan with late medieval fears about death, Nicholas ominously adds that as sinners now serve the devil in guilt, they will later serve him in punishment.

A nineteenth-century illustration from an English family Bible highlights the cross-currents of influences on the reception of Jeremiah (Figure 61). The monuments and palm trees reflect interest in the *realia* of the Bible, heightened by British archeological expeditions to Palestine and contemporary imagination. The distinction between the white Jeremiah and his darker, sinister-looking fellow Judeans, however, reflects a reception of the prophet that has roots in the middle ages. Readers of this bible were encouraged to identify with Jeremiah and to hear his prophetic words directed outwardly against others.

The connection between the stones and recalcitrant sinners persists into early modernity. In this contemporizing woodcut in the 1536 Zürich Bible, a German translation by Zwingli and his colleagues, Jeremiah appears as a Protestant preacher. Here the stone is not hidden, but showcased as a warning against hardening the heart (Figure 62).

The most influential tradition about the stones is the legend that the Judahites used them to kill Jeremiah (see Chapter 44).

Stories about Jeremiah in Egypt began in early Judaism. *Lives of the Prophets* describes him performing miracles in Egypt, ridding his city of snakes and crocodiles (see Introduction). A Christian interpolation reports Jeremiah's prophecy that a child would be born of a virgin before whom Egyptian idols would fall and shatter. Peter Comestor's twelfth-century *Historia* adds a description of Egyptians making a statue of a virgin and child, and of Egyptian idols on pedestals falling over when the infant Jesus and his parents enter Egypt (Matthew 2:14). This tradition appears often in the popular late-medieval *Speculum Humanae Salvationis* with a woodcut of the flight to Egypt, idols

Jeremiah Through the Centuries, First Edition. Mary Chilton Callaway.
© 2020 Mary Chilton Callaway. Published 2020 by John Wiley & Sons Ltd.

falling into pieces, and the text, "This prophecy that the holy prophet Jeremias proclaimed [Jer 44:30] is indeed fulfilled when Christ enters Egypt with his mother, for then all the statues and idols of the Egyptian gods are dashed to the ground."

The folly of fleeing to Egypt becomes a metaphor in English history. In the closing paragraphs of *The Readie and Easie Way* (1660), John Milton, near the end of his life and bitterly disappointed by the restoration of the monarchy in England, gives a prophecy of doom explicitly modeled on Jeremiah. Responding to the argument that a return to monarchy would improve England's economy, he uses Jeremiah 44 to mock the desire "to put our necks again under kingship, as was made use of by the Jews to return back to Egypt, and to the worship of their idol queen, because they falsely imagined that they then lived in more plenty and prosperity." The Royalists' stubborn intent "to prostitute religion and liberty" by "choosing a captain back for Egypt" brings them to "a precipice of destruction." Milton's contemporary, John Trapp, also drew lessons from Jeremiah in Egypt, and the prophet as model for contemporary Christian preaching is apparent in his reading of Jeremiah 44:20. On the words "Then Jeremiah said unto all the people" he comments, "The Prophet, without any special command from God, moved with a spirit of Zeal, confuteth that blasphemy of theirs and sheweth plainly that idolatry maketh no people happy, but the contrary." With these words Trapp echoes Jeremiah's rhetoric of linking present calamity with past sins, a hallmark of Puritan theology.

Uppity Women (44:15–19)

Although the speech against Jeremiah is made by husbands and wives together, its reception has focused on the women. Calvin notes that idolatry began with the women and he reproves their husbands for tolerating "ungodly superstitions," warning that "consent was the same as the deed." The Geneva Bible's note warns, "This teaches us what a great danger it is for the husbands to permit their wives anything of which they are not assured by God's word." Trapp finds more danger in gender relations than idolatry, explaining the women's behavior by their irrational and impetuous nature: "Women, as they have less of reason than men, so more of passion, being willful in their way, and oft carrying their men along with them … as did Eve, Jezebel, etc." He playfully warns his male readers, "When man lost his freewill, saith one, women got it … in some there is a strong inclination to whoredom. Such there was in these women to idolatry; they were fully set upon it." John Bunyan invokes Jeremiah 44 when he addresses a controversy in his community over whether women should be allowed to hold prayer services without men. His short tract "A Case of

Conscience Resolved" establishes biblical warrants against the women's practice, beginning with Eve stepping out of her place and becoming "baffled, and befooled" by the serpent. Bunyan caustically notes that when the women in Jer 44 made cakes to the queen of heaven it was "as right in their own eyes, as if they had done true worship indeed," showing that women are ill equipped to design worship (Bunyan 1859: 4:409). For Bunyan this provides biblical confirmation that male permission is required for women's worship.

Early Protestant readers also seized on these verses in their polemic against Catholic use of non-biblical tradition. The people's appeal to tradition to justify their sacrificial rites (verse 17) elicits contempt from Calvin, who compares it to the way "the Papists" disregard Scripture in favor of "the fathers," and superstitious men hold sacred anything handed down from their ancestors. The Geneva Bible instructs readers that "the Papists" took Mary's title "Queen of Heaven" from this verse, and that Jeremiah here condemns them for making Christ's mother an idol. Trapp similarly comments, "Antiquity is here pleaded, and authority, and plenty and peace. These are now the Popish pleas, and the pillars of that rotten religion."

In Catholic interpretation, the Queen of Heaven in Jeremiah had long been understood in the historical sense as the moon. Rabanus Maurus in the eleventh century interprets it as "either the moon or Juno, or wife of Saturn, mother of the gods," shown to be an idol by Psalm 96:5, "God made the heavens." He offers a "mystical" interpretation of the women as "all the heretics in the Egypt of this world, which means in the darkness of error." The women's sacrifices and libations are allegories for "distorted inventions and perverse teachings for deceiving men and perverting the true faith." *Glossa* preserves this allegory, and adds interpretation of Jeremiah's phrase "walking in God's laws" as "the right path of the catholic faith." *Bible moralisée* contemporizes the women by a colorful picture of scholars turning their backs on Jesus to worship a demon, who signifies the new philosophy being taught in the Paris universities. These medieval receptions of Jer 44 repeatedly warn readers against false gods crafted by human intellect and imagination.

Enlightenment thinkers found another lesson in the women's idolatry. Mrs. Trimmer reminds her young readers that true religion is consistent with reason: "One could scarcely have supposed that any people would have acted in a manner so inconsistent with the light of reason, as to pay adoration to inanimate things; but for the Jews to do so who had been so often favored with Divine revelations, is quite astonishing ... The queen of heaven, to whom the Israelites paid adorations, is supposed to have been the moon; I need not enlarge on the folly of idolizing this planet, as I am sure, my dear, you see the absurdity of it; and must think those Jews who did so, were deserving of the punishments denounced against them" (Trimmer 1783: 286–287).

Martyrdom of Jeremiah

The tradition that Jeremiah was stoned by his own people appears in the first century CE Jewish *Lives of the Prophets*, a collection of mostly apocryphal traditions about 23 prophets. Jeremiah is introduced as born in Anathoth and died "in Taphnai of Egypt, having been thrown down by stones by his people" (Charlesworth 1985: 2:386). The Epistle to the Hebrews alludes to this tradition when it lists scriptural characters commended for their faith. Jeremiah and Isaiah are unmistakable by allusion to the traditions of their martyrdom: "They were stoned to death, they were sawn in two..." (Heb 11:37). In the late second century, Tertullian invokes the stoning in an argument against Gnostics who justified making sacrifices to Roman gods to avoid torture and death. Comparing such advice to the bite of a scorpion that kills, Tertullian offers Jeremiah as a model who endured death by stoning for telling people truths they did not want to hear (*Liber Scorpiace* 8). In the late fourth century, Jerome similarly invokes Jeremiah's death to argue against "the gospel of pleasure" taught by Jovinian, a Christian theologian who tried to make the gospel compatible with the culture of aristocratic Romans. Jerome clearly identifies with Jeremiah as one who spoke fearlessly against the dominant religious culture.

Jeremiah's martyrdom became authoritative in the seventh century, when Isidore of Seville included it in his influential catalogue of biblical figures, *De ortu et orbitu Patrum.* Peter Comestor's colorful elaboration in *Historia Scholastica,* his twelfth-century paraphrase of the Bible, educated many generations of clergy through the Middle Ages. Comestor explains that when Jeremiah spoke the words of 44:26–27 the people became so enraged that they "rose up against Jeremiah, and stoned him with stones, which he had hidden under the brick wall," as commanded in 43:9.

The most dramatic elaboration of Jeremiah's death appears in the twelfth-century Edili Bible, produced as a lectern bible for the monks of Florence cathedral. Jeremiah is introduced by Isidore of Seville's brief apocryphal biography, which contrasts the prophet's own people stoning him to death with the grateful veneration of pagan Egyptians after his prayers rid them of serpents. This unusual addition to Jerome's traditional preface encouraged the monks in the anti-Jewish readings of Jeremiah beginning to multiply in the twelfth century. The picture of the apocryphal martyrdom illustrates Isidore's parallel by showing men in contemporary dress as the angry mob hurling stones at the kneeling prophet, who raises his hands in prayer while God bestows the golden nimbus of sainthood on his head (Figure 63). The other illustration, at top left and above Jerome's prologue, is unique to this Bible. In a detailed study of the image, art historian Robert Timothy Chasson showed that the prophet lies atop the Temple, which in twelfth-century art was often

FIGURE 63   First page of Jeremiah in twelfth-century Edili Bible. Florence, The Biblioteca Medicea Laurenziana, ms. Edili 125, f.121r.

portrayed anachronistically as the blue Dome of the Rock. The scene appears to be from the apocryphal *Paraleipomena of Jeremiah,* also called *4 Baruch,* a second century CE Jewish expansion of Jeremiah with a later Christian addition. In this narrative, God commands the prophet to go into exile with his people and years later instructs him to lead the faithful back to Jerusalem. On the tenth day, as he is offering up a sacrifice, Jeremiah falls to the ground and becomes "as one of those who has given up their soul" (*4 Baruch* 9:7). While Baruch and Ebed Melek (here called Abimelech) sorrowfully prepare the body for burial, a heavenly voice warns them not to bury one who still lives. After three days Jeremiah's soul returns to his body, and he rises saying, "Glorify God and the Son of God who awakens us, Jesus Christ the light of all the aeons, the inextinguishable lamp, the life of faith." On hearing this the people become enraged and stone Jeremiah to death. The artist for the Edili Bible has apparently telescoped the events of this apocryphal narrative. Jeremiah's role in bringing the exiles home is illustrated by the figures on the left with walking sticks and travelers' bundles, while his subsequent vision of the future coming of Christ is portrayed with the artistic convention of positioning him on his side with open eyes. The prominent lock on the gates evokes the *Paraleipomena*'s story of Jeremiah's last action before leaving Jerusalem, when he throws the Temple keys to the care of the sun. The Temple, a common figure of heaven, is locked until Jeremiah's vision is fulfilled and Christ opens the gates. The unusual first page of Jeremiah in this twelfth-century Bible signaled readers to understand the prophet not only as a figure of Christ, but also as sign of the resurrection to come.

Vulgate Bibles frequently began Jeremiah with a small illustration of the prophet, often with a halo, bent under a fuselage of stones hurled by angry men. In this typical example from a fourteenth-century French Bible, the image decorates the first letter V (for *verba* = words), thereby presenting readers a hermeneutic for reading Jeremiah as a prefiguring of Christ (Figure 64).

An image from the *Bible historiale* juxtaposes Jeremiah's call and martyrdom, with the cistern in the background, signaling readers to understand Jeremiah as model of obedience and holy suffering (Figure 65).

For Christians before the sixteenth century, biblical text and Patristic tradition merge into a single narrative of Jeremiah's death by stoning. The Coptic Orthodox Church still remembers the martyrdom of St. Jeremiah the Prophet in the ninth month of its liturgical calendar. Calvin rejected the tradition as unbiblical, yet seems almost wistful at its loss: "Some think that he was on this account stoned by the Jews; but this is not probable, nay, it may be gathered from other places that he died a natural death. However this may have been, his perseverance and firmness were wonderful, for he struggled to the end, and without weariness, with those wild beasts, whose savageness he had more than

FIGURE 64 Martyrdom of Jeremiah. Incipit of Jeremiah in a Latin bible. Bibliothèque nationale de France. Latin 17198, fol. 264v.

enough experienced." The tradition of Jeremiah's stoning persisted in the notes of Douay-Rheims Catholic Bibles into the nineteenth century.

A seventeenth-century engraving by Johann Friedrich Fleischberger envelopes the prophet in Catholic imagery and apocryphal traditions (Figure 66). The inscription describes "this likeness of the prophet Jeremiah" as "found in an ancient book." The German caption distills Jeremiah into the language of Christian martyrdom: son of a priest who spoke "against godless Jews with spiritual teaching for fifty years" and was stoned to death in Egypt. With one hand he holds the Ark, veiling his hand like a priest holding a sacred object; with the other he points to the Ark with a gesture suggesting a priestly blessing. The early Jewish tradition that Jeremiah hid the Ark as the Temple was burning, to be revealed at the end of the age, had developed into a Christian tradition that Jeremiah would reveal the Ark at the time of the resurrection. (see Introduction). The scene of the stoning in the background, on the diagonal with God's hand and Jeremiah's nimbus, highlights the tradition of Jeremiah as holy martyr, prefiguring of Christ and sign of Christ's return.

FIGURE 65   Martyrdom of Jeremiah, with call and cistern in background. *Bible historiale*. Bibliothèque nationale de France. Latin 4915.

In the beleaguered Catholicism of eighteenth-century France, Jeremiah's martyrdom became newly significant. Seven years before the Revolution, a priest and poet active in the defense of the church against the *philosophes* and other critics contemporized the martyrdom in an elaborate style for his devout readers. An engraving presents the killers in contemporary dress and the text makes the prophet a blend of Christ and contemporary Catholics: "The Jews, long angry at Jerémié… throw him to the ground, and kill him, some with sticks, others with stones. The holy prophet has a most moving appearance:

FIGURE 66   Johann Friedrich Fleischberger. Private collection.

he lifts his hands to Heaven, and while dying prays for his killers. An angel appears from afar on a luminous cloud... and brings him the martyr's crown" (Desmarais 1772: 84) (Figure 67). This martyred Jerémié of baroque sensibilities is designed to heighten piety and to bring courage to French Catholics smarting under the blows of Enlightenment thinkers and *philosophes* who dismissed religion in favor of human reason (see Introduction).

FIGURE 67   Jérémie martyred in eighteenth-century France. M. Demarais. Private collection.

Long after the church officially dropped the tradition of Jeremiah's martyrdom, John Henry Newman embraced it. In his 1830 sermon "Jeremiah, A Lesson for the Disappointed," he highlights Jeremiah as "the most exact type of Christ" among the prophets because he wept over Jerusalem "and then was tortured and put to death by those He wept over" (Newman 1891: 8:126). He challenged the popular evangelical teaching that intense feelings signaled true faith, emphasizing instead obedience and disappointment as true marks of the life of faith. For him Jeremiah offered a type of Christ in his death, and a model of obedience in adversity for contemporary Christians.

The significance of God's promise to Baruch was contested during the early reception of Jeremiah's words. In the Septuagint, these five verses appear as the coda to Jeremiah's words, just before the scribal addition of chapter 52. In that position they highlight the role of Baruch as guardian of Jeremiah's words, and suggest that he is the prophet's successor. The Book of Baruch (second or first century BCE), is placed immediately after Jeremiah in the Septuagint, and presents Baruch as religious leader of the community in Babylon continuing Jeremiah's work. The placement of chapter 45 in the middle of the Hebrew text rather than at the end may reflect tensions over the legacies of the two men.

Jeremiah Through the Centuries, First Edition. Mary Chilton Callaway.
© 2020 Mary Chilton Callaway. Published 2020 by John Wiley & Sons Ltd.

Evidence of such rivalry is apparent in the way Baruch in some ways eclipsed Jeremiah in developing Jewish and Christian traditions of the Second Temple era. The popular apocalypses *2* and *4 Baruch* present colorful stories of Baruch as miracle-worker and seer who takes Jeremiah's place to address the trauma of Roman destruction of the Temple in 70 CE. This heightening of Baruch over Jeremiah is also apparent in multiple Syriac lectionary manuscripts that list an excerpt from *2 Baruch* for liturgical use (Henze and Lied 2017: 349–351). The reading prescribed is the end of Baruch's letter to the exiles in Babylon (85:1–15), which urges penance and watchfulness for the end-time: "The pitcher is near the well, and the ship to the harbor, and the journey to the city, and life to its end. Prepare yourselves so that, when you sail and ascend from the ship, you may have rest and not be condemned" (Charlesworth 1983: 1:651). The lectionaries identify the reading as "From Jeremiah," which suggests that Syriac Christians had a considerably enlarged Jeremiah tradition (see also Introduction under "Early Christianity").

Jeremiah's challenge to Baruch continued to prick the conscience of modern leaders struggling in a hostile environment. Eighteenth-century Pennsylvania Quaker John Woolman became disillusioned with commerce, not only because of the slave trade but also because of increasing consumer consumption and use of debt. Jeremiah's words prompted him to warn his colleagues and to sell his shop: "Though trading in things useful is an honest employ, yet throughout the great number of superfluities which are bought and sold through the corruption of the times, they who apply to merchandise for a living have great need to be well experienced in that precept which the prophet Jeremiah laid down for his scribe: 'Seekest thou great things for thyself? Seek them not'" (Slaughter 2008: 190). In the nineteenth century, John Henry Newman seemed to be speaking of himself when he preached Jeremiah as a model of resignation in his sermon titled "Jeremiah, A Lesson for the Disappointed." He describes the prophet "who at one time could not comfort himself, at another was sent to comfort a brother; and, in comforting Baruch, he speaks in that nobler temper of resignation which takes the place of sanguine hope and harassing fear, and betokens calm and clear-sighted faith and inward peace" (Newman 1891: 134). It is a resignation that Newman knew in his own disappointment as "that chastened spirit and weaned heart, which is the termination of all agitation and anxiety in the case of religious minds." For Newman, Jeremiah offers solace for a failed mission. A century later, Dietrich Bonhoeffer underlined in his Bible the words to Baruch. He read them sometimes as rebuke and at other times as comfort, invoking them in three letters to different people written from his prison cell in the months before his death. In one he writes hopefully that "God is about to accomplish something that… we can only receive with the greatest wonder and awe… and we shall have to repeat Jer. 45:5 to ourselves every day"

(Bonhoeffer 2009: 161). In another, his meditation on Jer 45 leads him to say, "If we can save our souls unscathed from the debris of civilization, let us be satisfied with that. If the Creator destroys his own handiwork, what right have we to lament over the destruction of ours?" (Bonhoeffer 2009: 183–184). Two months later, in a letter written to a friend on the news that the plan to assassinate Hitler had failed, Bonhoeffer reflects on his desire not to be holy, but simply to have faith. This happens, he says, "only by living completely in this world," which means abandoning attempts to make something of oneself by planning one's life. Instead, "we throw ourselves utterly in the arms of God and participate in his sufferings in the world and watch with Christ in Gethsemane. That is faith… (cf. Jer. 45)" (Bonhoeffer 2009: 226–227).

Jeremiah 46–51

> Israel is a hunted sheep driven away by lions. First the king of Assyria devoured it, and now at the end King Nebuchadrezzar of Babylon has gnawed its bones (50:17).

These words evoke the experiences that led to the rage and despair expressed in the poetry of Jer 46–51, traditionally called "oracles against the nations." The literary form and violent language of these prophecies against Israel's enemies reflect ancient Near Eastern taunt songs commonly used against adversaries; similar exaggerated threats appear as early as the third millennium in Sumerian literature. As with all prophetic poetry, exaggeration, vivid language, and

Jeremiah Through the Centuries, First Edition. Mary Chilton Callaway.
© 2020 Mary Chilton Callaway. Published 2020 by John Wiley & Sons Ltd.

shocking images are the norm. In seventh-century Israel, the prophets Nahum and Zephaniah had used such language in oracles against Assyria, and Jeremiah turned one of these against Jerusalem (see Commentary on Jer 13).

The unstable position of the oracles in the book of Jeremiah suggests a complex historical process in the earliest stage of reception. The Septuagint locates them after Jeremiah 25:13 as an anticipation of divine vindication in the future. Placement of the oracles at the end of the Hebrew scroll suggests that the final redaction of Jeremiah occurred after Babylon had fallen to Cyrus in 539 BCE. This repositioning of the oracles is further evidence that the process of re-interpretation and reception was already at work in the formation of the Jeremiah tradition. Placing the oracles at the end also opened them out to the future, encouraging readers in every century to find their own enemies encoded in the violent language of divine retribution.

For modern readers, these blood-thirsty prophecies pose problems, but earlier readers found opportunity and even comfort in the images of divine justice. What follows is a sampling of the causes for which these promises of vindication have been enlisted. God's threat that Judah would be justly punished but mercifully preserved (46:28) offered consolation in times of persecution for Jews and Christians alike. Joseph Kara, living in northern France in the early twelfth century during the First Crusade, reads hope in his paraphrase, "I will chastise you through the nations of the world, but will not destroy you completely" (Rosenberg 1989: 2:354). Jewish liturgy for the Ninth of Ab included a *piyyut* by the poet Kalil that merges the horror of Jerusalem's destruction with later Jewish experience. Zion is described as uttering the cry of Heshbon (48:3) and Mephaath (48:21), cities named in Jeremiah's oracle against Moab. She even cries out, "Woe! I have drunk the cup, have drained it!" as if enduring Babylon's own punishment (Davis 1896: 613). In this liturgical setting, Jeremiah's language of destruction gives voice to later Jewish experience.

Jewish and Christian traditions read the oracles as warnings of divine power to punish wrong-doers whoever they might be. Targum contemporizes the threat by adding the crimes of plundering and shedding innocent blood to the list in 51:35, and tyrants to the list of rulers at 51:57. Targum also teaches rabbinic theology at verses 39 and 57 by adding eschatological threats to the enemy: "They shall die 'the second death', and not live for the world to come." On Jer 48:14–47, Matthew Henry warns that it will be of more use to readers to keep in their eye "the power of God's anger and the terror of his judgments and to "get their hearts possessed with a holy awe of God and his wrath, than to search into all the figures and expressions here used."

In the twenty-first century, reception of the oracles is colored by psychological, political, and philosophical discourse. One approach reads the oracles as a form of revenge fantasies, a psychological experience and literary genre that aims to transform victim to avenger, at least in the imagination. In form and function the oracles resemble this genre, which offers "a clear and exact retributive justice" as part of psychological healing. By enabling exiles "to express their pain and rage as well as a language of resistance that enables victims to alter their narratives," the oracles offer hope and comfort and empower Israel to rewrite its history (Kalmanofsky 2015: 109–127). A different explanation comes from a postcolonial reading. This approach finds in the vengeful images a "rhetoric of collusion" encouraging the exiles to submit to Babylonian rule in the present and be sustained by hope of divine intervention in the indeterminate future. It notes that Judeans with a stake in Babylonian hegemony are closely linked with Jeremiah, notably the scribe Ahikam (Jer 26:24) and the Babylonian appointee Gedaliah (Jer 40:6). The oracles can be read as a bid for enduring present reality patiently on the part of the group with most to gain from Judean compliance with Babylon (Pyper 2015: 145–157).

Babylon, the Golden Cup in God's Hand (51:7)

Of all the oracles, those against Babylon cast the longest shadow in reception history, as readers in every age found in the lethal golden cup a compelling image for their enemies. In early Jewish and Christian writings, Babylon is code for Rome, giving cover to subversive rhetoric against the empire. Two apocalyptic Jewish writings offer hope after the destruction of Jerusalem, one expressing grief because "Babylon" is happy and Zion is destroyed (*2 Baruch* 11:1) and another shaming Nero and his flight from Rome, encoded as the terrible and shameless prince who will flee from Babylon (*Sibylline Oracles* 5:143). Targum Jonathan transforms the divine threat of making Babylon so drunk that it will "sleep a perpetual sleep and not wake" (51:39, 57) by translating "it will die the second death and not live in the world to come" into a teaching about resurrection. The apocalyptic visions of Revelation (14:8; 17:1–6; 18:1–3) make Jeremiah's image a fixture of Christian discourse, transforming the description of Babylon as the golden cup in God's hand into Babylon the whore who holds golden cup of "the wine of wrath of her fornication" (Rev 18:1–3). Like all cities in ancient Near Eastern literature, Jeremiah's Babylon is portrayed as feminine, but John's hyper-sexualized Babylon in his first-century apocalyptic visions influenced subsequent receptions of Jeremiah's image. Against third-century philosophers warning that Christianity undermined Rome's intellectual traditions, Origen responds, "Often I see the golden chalice in ornate discourse, and detect Babylon's cup in poisonous teaching." Jerome adopts Origen's metaphor to castigate him, warning Christians against the golden cup of worldly eloquence and the (Gnostic) teachings of philosophers (Wenthe 2009: 269). In his *Confessions*, Augustine, reading Babylon as sin, writes of his seduction by classical literature, "And in order that I might be more firmly mired in the very center of that city, my invisible enemy trod roughshod over me and seduced me, for I was easily seduced. For, not even she, the mother of my flesh, who had already *fled Babylon,* but delayed upon its borders, as she advised me to be modest..." (Book 2: 3.8).

In the twelfth century, the *Glossa* reports Origen's comments at length as warnings against the new philosophies taught in the university of Paris. Equally influential is Augustine's use of Babylon to signify the carnal captivity of this world contrasted with the freedom of Jerusalem as the life of grace in the church. Gregory the Great's elaboration of Babylon as earthly prizes and the golden cup as temporal attractions that inebriate foolish minds with desire appears in the *Glossa*'s comments on Jer 51. For Gregory, Babylon's golden cup had proved deadly at humanity's origins: "With this golden cup Eve was made drunk by her own will, because when she gazed at the forbidden tree with desire, seeing that it was beautiful in appearance, she ate." For centuries. medieval readers understood Jeremiah's golden cup of lethal wine as the spiritual threats in their own lives.

In early modernity, this image of Babylon as a golden cup takes on new life through Revelation's early reception. Lucas Cranach's woodcut illustrating Rev 17:1–5 for the first edition of Luther's German New Testament in 1522 is almost a political cartoon indebted to late medieval illustrations of a woman seated on a seven-headed beast, holding up an elaborate goblet (Figure 68). Cranach pointedly changes her proffered cup to a liturgical vessel and makes her headdress the triple crown of the papacy. Identification of Babylon with the Catholic church was a hallmark of early Protestantism, developed in Luther and Calvin, that persisted for centuries. Yet Augustine's reading of Babylon as the world of sin out of which Christians should flee to the freedom of Jerusalem also persisted, notably in John Bunyan's *Pilgrim's Progress.*

Jeremiah Speaks to a War-Torn Twentieth Century (51:11)

The call to battle includes a command that resonated into the twentieth century. The rare Hebrew verb means to "clean" or "polish;" the Septuagint has "prepare" and the Vulgate, "sharpen." English translations read "sharpen" until the Geneva Bible translators retrieved the Hebrew with the poetic "make bright." The King James Version, following Geneva, is the source for Edna St. Vincent Millay's famous wartime poem "Make Bright the Arrows." Written in 1940 as a wake-up call against fascism, the poem uses Jeremiah's Babylon to

FIGURE 68   Lucas Cranach, The Whore of Babylon (1522).

evoke Nazi Germany. The final lines are a warning to Americans reluctant to enter the war: "Make bright the arrows, O peaceful and wise! Gather the shields/Against surprise."

Jeremiah's image of the nation that will conqueror Babylon as God's "battle-axe and weapon of war for breaking nations in pieces" (verses 20–23) inspired Thomas Hardy at the height of the Great War. In his poem "In Time of 'The Breaking of Nation'" Hardy transforms the divine vow to "break in pieces" every aspect of Babylonian civilization, from the horse and his rider to the farmer and his oxen. Jeremiah's "horse and rider" become Hardy's evocative image of a farmer plowing with an old horse, while the young man and maid who will be broken in pieces become Hardy's "maid and her wight" on a walk whispering together in love. Hardy's subversive use of Jeremiah's violent images for peaceful, timeless occupations offered hope to English readers in 1916 by suggesting that despite the war, elemental aspects of human civilization endure.

> Only a man harrowing clods
> In a slow silent walk
> With an old horse that stumbles and nods
> Half asleep as they stalk.
>
> Only thin smoke without flame
> From the heaps of couch-grass;
> Yet this will go onward the same
> Though Dynasties pass.
>
> Yonder a maid and her wight
> Come whispering by:
> War's annals will cloud into night
> Ere their story die.

Thus Far the Words of Jeremiah (51:59–64)

Historical-critical scholars read this verse as evidence of the editorial work of scribes in Babylon. It is the fourth reference to a scroll of Jeremiah's words (see Commentary on Jer. 30), an emphasis on writing distinctive to his book. In antiquity, the verse was significant for other reasons. The rabbis agreed that prophetic books end with words of comfort, but some argued that Jeremiah instead ends with a rebuke by describing the destruction of the temple in chapter 52. The decisive argument appealed to the last words of chapter 51, which teach that Jeremiah ends with the prophecy of Babylon's fall, therefore bringing comfort to Israel.

Act of Uniformity law passed by the English Parliament in 1662 after the restoration of the monarchy under Charles II; required that the Book of Common Prayer be used in all public worship.

Alexandria city in Egypt founded in the fourth century BCE by Alexander the Great; crossroads of intellectual activity bringing together Jews, Greeks and others; became a center of allegorical exegesis of the Bible.

Allegory method of interpretation that seeks figurative meanings of spiritual or moral import.

Jeremiah Through the Centuries, First Edition. Mary Chilton Callaway.
© 2020 Mary Chilton Callaway. Published 2020 by John Wiley & Sons Ltd.

Antioch Syrian city; home of early Church Fathers who used a more historical and literal approach than the Alexandrians.

Antiphon a short sentence from Scripture sung or recited before and after a psalm or canticle.

Ark of the Covenant wooden box constructed by the Israelites in the wilderness to house the stone tablets of the Covenant (Exodus 25:1-23; 2 Samuel 6).

Balm of Gilead ancient salve made from the aromatic resin of a shrub in the region of Gilead, east of the Jordan River; used metaphorically in Christian tradition.

Bible historale a popular early medieval Bible in French that translated portions from every book of the Bible into the vernacular, along with abridged commentary from Peter Comestor's *Historia scolastica*; produced with colorful pictures for inexpensive popular editions as well as richly ornamented versions for kings and nobles; made biblical stories available to a wide range of French Christians from 1291 through the fifteenth century.

Biblicae Historiae a 1539 example of the genre of picture Bible popular in the sixteenth and seventeenth centuries; each page offers a title summarizing the biblical content, a large woodcut portraying the action, and several verses of moralizing poetry that comments on the narrative.

Bible moralisée a magnificent large-scale, often multivolume picture Bible that paired medallion illustrations of biblical scenes with matching illustrations of medieval Christians, Jews, philosophers and others who were often shown behaving badly. A fine pictorial example of allegorical exegesis as well as use of the Bible to comment on contemporary issues in medieval France.

Biblia pauperum medieval book for prayer and meditation that portrays scenes in the life of Jesus flanked by scenes and texts from the Old Testament; the Old Testament scenes are presented as prefiguring allegories of the New Testament event.

Bibliothèque Bleue inexpensive books bound in blue paper used to wrap sugar, typically sold by itinerant peddlers in the countryside from the early seventeenth century into the mid-nineteenth century, though also available in cities. Along with romances and recipes they included books of prayers and popularizing narrative Bibles. Jeremiah generally appeared in these works as wonder-worker and martyr.

Dance of Death (Danse Macabre) An illustrated literary genre popular from the late Middle Ages into early modernity; shows the inevitability of death through text and woodcuts portray death as a grinning human skeleton interacting with people of all social classes.

Deism eighteenth-century philosophical belief that God is best known through reason, human experience and natural science rather than through traditional Christian means.

Devotio Moderna late medieval religious movement started in the Netherlands by lay people seeking individual spiritual disciplines and practices outside the church in order to deepen their relation with God; way of life for the widespread religious community of people who were living out the monastic virtues of simplicity and love of God and neighbor in their own homes and families.

Douay Rheims Bible translation of the Latin Vulgate into English by English Catholics in exile during the reign of Elizabeth I, partly in response to the popularity of vernacular Bibles in England. The New Testament, translated at the Catholic college in the French city of Douay, appeared in 1582; the whole Bible was completed in the French city of Rheims in 1610. It was a Catholic Bible because it used Jerome's Latin as the original text rather than the original Greek and Hebrew, and because its copious marginal notes guidied readers to interpret the text in accord with the church's teachings.

Exile time from 587 BCE – 539 BCE when the Babylonian king Nebuchadnezzar destroyed Jerusalem and sent many inhabitants to live in Babylon. Significant portions of the Hebrew Bible were preserved and shaped during this Exile, including the book of Jeremiah. Jeremiah warned his people before it and lived through it.

Geneva Bible English translation of the Bible from Greek and Hebrew made by English Protestants who fled to Geneva during the reign of Mary Tudor. The New Testament was completed in 1557; the whole Bible in 1560. Calvin's theology and Puritan ideas are the basis of the marginal notes.

Glossa Ordinaria the most influential Christian commentary on the Bible from the twelfth into the sixteenth centuries. The *Glossa* is a compendium of Patristic and early medieval comments on every chapter of the Bible. Arranged like the Jewish Talmud, the *Glossa* set a few verses of Scripture in the center of a large page and arrayed excerpts from the church fathers around all four sides of the page. Interlinear notes guided readers to Christological interpretations of key words. Interpretations ranged from the plain sense to the allegorical and mystical, offering a diversity of readings and approaches to Scripture. Anti-Jewish readings, especially those that present the church as replacing Israel, are common throughout.

Haftarah a passage from the Hebrew Prophets selected to accompany and comment on the liturgical reading from Torah.

History of effect translation of German technical term *Wirkungsgeschichte* coined by Gadamer to describe his claim that interpretation always reflects the situated-ness and foreknowledge of the interpreter, and that interpretations over time become part of the received text.

Humanism cultural movement beginning in fifteenth-century Europe that was initiated by the retrieval of classical Greek texts, including the Greek New Testament, after the fall of Constantinople.

Interiority concept about the human person that became widespread in late medieval and early modern European and British cultures; idea of a space within the body that was considered the center of affect and privileged arena of religious experience.

Jeremiad literary form developed by English Puritans that laments the moral deficiencies of the present as a people's abandonment of their true identity and high calling; often suggests a way forward to reclaim the original promise of greatness.

Lectionary list of selected scripture readings arranged for liturgical use.

Lives of the Prophets collection of Jewish midrashic legends about twenty-three biblical prophets; extant only in editions from the first century CE with Christian additions.

Masoretic Text (MT) standard Hebrew text of the Bible produced by Jewish grammarians in the sixth to tenth centuries CE, with vowel points, accents and marginal notes for copyists.

Mentalité the assumptions and particular ways of thinking that are characteristic of people in a particular historical time and place.

Narrative Bible a book that presented biblical history from Genesis through Revelation as a single story, in the form of a continuous narrative, in the vernacular. Originated in late antiquity; was produced by multiple authors in the Middle Ages and continued into modernity in the form of children's Bibles.

Ninth of Ab Jewish holy day of mourning in remembrance of the destruction of the temple in 586 BCE and 70 CE Jeremiah's words are important in the liturgy for this day.

Pesikta de Rav Kahana sixth-century Jewish collection of midrashic homilies on the Torah and *haftarah* readings for special Sabbaths, festivals, and fast days. *Pesikta* is an Aramaic word for a portion of Scripture designated to be read in the synagogue.

Pesikta Rabbati ninth-century collection of midrashic homilies given in Palestinian synagogues for special Sabbaths and festivals and fast days. Many traditions in the earlier *Pesikta de Rav Kahana* appear in *Pesikta Rabbati*.

Philosophes French intellectuals of the eighteenth century who were influenced by Descartes and scientific thinking; rejected the authority of the monarchy and the church. Voltaire and Rousseau were among the most influential.

Plymouth Brethren a Christian Evangelical group begun in Dublin in the early nineteenth-century; rejected the English church's acceptance of biblical criticism and scientific discoveries in favor of a more literal reading of the Bible and traditional Christian practices. First met as a group in Plymouth, England in 1931; still active.

Septuagint (LXX) ancient Greek translation of the Hebrew Bible made in the third century BCE for Greek-speaking Jews in Egypt. The Hebrew text of Jeremiah underlying this Greek translation seems to represent a more ancient manuscript tradition than the Masoretic Text of Jeremiah. The Septuagint introduces Greek concepts such as the dualism of body and soul into its text of Jeremiah.

Talmud vast collection of rabbinic teachings in dialogue with each other, in the form of a commentary on the Mishnah; preserved in the Palestinian Talmud (fourth century CE) and the Babylonian Talmud (fifth century CE).

Targum Aramaic translation of the Hebrew Bible, used in Jewish worship from the fifth century BCE (cf. Ezra 4:7); the Targum to Jeremiah was written down most likely in the eighth century CE, though it preserves earlier traditions.

Vulgate fourth-century Latin translation of the Bible by Jerome; designated the only authentic Latin Bible at the Council of Trent (1545–1563).

Wycliffe Bible first complete translation of the Bible into English; named after John Wycliffe.

Brief Biographies

Abarbanel, Isaac (1437–1508) Jewish Bible scholar from Portugal; state treasurer to King Ferdinand but expelled with all Jews in 1492; brought Renaissance thinking to his biblical commentaries by considering historical aspects of ancient Israel, and beginning his commentaries with an introduction describing the time and circumstances of its composition.

Ambrose (*c*.333–397) bishop of Milan and teacher of Augustine; fought Arianism and defended Church independence against the Western Roman emperors.

Andrew of St Victor (d. 1175) biblical exegete who favored literal interpretation over the traditional allegorical approach.

Jeremiah Through the Centuries, First Edition. Mary Chilton Callaway.
© 2020 Mary Chilton Callaway. Published 2020 by John Wiley & Sons Ltd.

Aquinas, Thomas (*c*.1225–1274) a Dominican monk and the Christian church's major systematic theologian; presented Christian theological ideas in terms and methods of Aristotelian philosophy.

Augustine of Hippo (354–430) Roman citizen and intellectual who became a Christian; his imaginative merging of classical tropes and biblical language permanently influenced Christian theology.

Beard, Frank (1842–1905) American illustrator and cartoonist.

Beham, Hans Sebald (1500–1550) German artist influenced by Albrecht Dürer; used the medium of copper engraving; expelled from Nuremberg for heresy because of alliances with Protestants more radical than Luther.

Brown, John (1722–1787) Scottish weaver who became a Presbyterian minister, learned in biblical languages and history; produced the "self-interpreting Bible," which offered explanatory notes, spiritual reflections and engravings of religious scenes. Published in 1778, it remained in print for a century and present in many middle-class homes in England and America.

Bunyan, John (1628–1688) author of *Pilgrim's Progress* (1679), preacher and member of an independent congregation in Bedford, imprisoned for his beliefs.

Chagall, Marc (1887–1985) Jewish artist from Belarus who painted traditional biblical scenes with startling overlays of Eastern European motifs and modern touches.

Calvin, John (1509–1564) French Reformer; wrote major works of theology and biblical commentary, and led a theocratic regime in Geneva.

Charles I (1600–1649) English king caught up in the Puritan rejection of the church and the monarchy; executed by Parliament in 1649.

Charles II (1630–1685) English king in exile after his father was executed; brought back to the throne in the Restoration of 1660; with him the Church of England again represented the state religion.

Chrysostom, John (*c*.347–407) born in Antioch; became Archbishop of Constantinople; often considered the greatest preacher of the patristic era.

Comestor, Peter (c. 1100–1180) inventive theologian and teacher from Troyes and Paris; taught at the collegiate school of St. Victor in Paris; composed the *Historia Scholastica,* an engaging narrative paraphrase of the Bible used by medieval students.

Cranach, Lucas, the Elder (1472–1553) German painter, illustrator of Luther's Bible (1522).

Damien, Peter (1007–1072) philosopher, monk, bishop and reformer, whose creative thinking is preserved in his 180 letters.

Dewsbury, William (1621–1688) an early member of the Society of Friends (Quakers) in England, jailed for his beliefs.

Duhm, Bernhard (1847–1928) German Old Testament scholar who combined emerging historical-critical biblical scholarship with German romanticism. Introduced the term "confessions" in his commentary on Jeremiah.

Eliot, T.S. (1888–1965) American poet and critic. Awarded Nobel Prize for Literature in 1948.

Elliott-Binns, (1885–1963) English clergyman, college chaplain, parish priest and Old Testament scholar.

Erasmus, Desiderius (1466–1536) influential Dutch intellectual; one of the first to use the new methods of humanism to translate and interpret the Bible.

Fontaine, Nicholas, pseudonym Sieur de Royaumont (1625–1709) Jansenist educator who published an abbreviated and illustrated Bible in French to circumvent the prohibition on vernacular Bibles.

Forrest, Leon (1937–1997) African-American novelist whose fiction often merged ancient tropes with contemporary realism.

Foster, Charles (1822–1887) Protestant educator whose story-Bible picture books for children combined the emerging historical approaches with moral instruction.

Fox, George (1624–1691) English preacher who affirmed "inner light" over other forms of religious authority; founded the Society of Friends (the Quakers).

Gadamer, Hans-Georg (1900–2002) German philosopher who developed a philosophical hermeneutics that showed understanding to be a dialogic and situated mental activity determined by history and our contemporary situation.

Gaines, M.C. (1894–1947) creator of the comic-book format and then of Bible stories as comic-books.

Ginsberg, Allen (1926–1997) visionary American poet of the Beat Movement whose new forms, strong language and powerful critique of American society had lasting effects.

Gregory of Nazianzus (Gregory the Theologian) (330–389) one of the Cappadocian Fathers, eloquent champion of orthodoxy.

Gregory of Nyssa (333–395) one of the Cappadocian Fathers; outstanding orator, exegete and ascetical writer.

Gregory the Great (*c.*540–604) one of the four great Latin fathers of the church; on the border between the Patristic and the medieval church; used multiple approaches to interpreting Scripture.

Guyart des Moulins (1251–1222) French cleric who produced one of the first vernacular paraphrased Bibles by adapting Comestor's Latin story Bible and adding pictures of biblical characters dressed in contemporary style.

Henry, Matthew (1662–1714) non-conformist minister, author of a popular and widely influential exegetical commentary on the whole Bible.

Herbert, George (1593–1633) Welsh-born Anglican priest and poet; one of the Metaphysical poets who combined early modern sensibilities and traditional religious images.

Herder, Johann Gottfried (1744–1803) seminal German philosopher and literary critic who explored the relation between thought, feeling and language.

Robert Herrick (1591–1674) English clergyman and poet whose poems eloquently described experiences and emotions both religious and secular.

Heschel, Abraham Joshua (1907–1972) Jewish American scholar and philosopher who wrote about divine pathos and suffering.

Hippolytus of Rome (170–236) early Christian theologian and bishop of Rome; rejected authority of Pope Callistus and claimed to represent the church; wrote a liturgical handbook that gives evidence for early forms of Christian worship.

Holbein, Hans, the Younger (1498–1543) German painter and engraver whose oil portraits of Henry VIII and many in his circle remain important historical witnesses to the era.

Hopkins, Gerald Manley (1844–1889) English Jesuit poet who created a new form called sprung rhythm and used words in unexpected ways.

Howe, Julia Ward (1819–1910) writer, reformer and feminist; author of 'The Battle Hymn of the Republic'.

Ibn Ezra, Abraham (1092/3–1167) Spanish Jewish poet, grammarian, philosopher and biblical exegete, who often countered Christian allegorical interpretations notes on Hebrew grammar and on the "plain sense" of the text.

Irenaeus (*c*.120–*c*.200) Greek bishop of Lyons, fierce opponent of Gnosticism.

Ironside, H.A. (1876–1951) Canadian–American evangelist and prolific author; member of the Plymouth Brethren.

Isidore of Seville (560–636) Archbishop of Seville, declared uniformity in the Mass and tolerance of Jews; author of widely used encyclopedia of word etymologies.

Jerome (*c*.340–420) biblical scholar educated in Rome who knew multiple languages.
    Wrote commentaries on almost all books of the Bible. Best known for his translation of the Bible into Latin (Vulgate).

John of Damascus (*c*.650–750) Greek theologian who lived in Syria and Palestine.
    Author of several influential works including the *Fount of Wisdom* and by tradition *Sacra Parallela*.

Josephus, Flavius (*c*.37–*c*.100) Jewish historian, politician and soldier; author of the *Jewish War* and *Jewish Antiquities*.

Joye, George (c.1495–1553) English scholar and Bible translator who worked with Tyndale; his translation of Jeremiah was the first after Wycliffe's; used by Tyndale, Coverdale and the KJV.

Justin Martyr (*c*.100–*c*.165) philosopher and apologist in the early church who argued that human reason and the divine mind were aligned to the same truth. Used Jeremiah to argue that Jews had been replaced by Christians as God's people.
    Moved to Ephesus and Rome where he was martyred along with other Christians.

Kara, Joseph (c.1065–1135) Jewish Bible scholar; contemporary of Rashi in northern France; favored the plain sense over midrash.

Kempis, Thomas à (*c*.1380–1471) Monastic and author of *The Imitation of Christ*, which encouraged lay people to love God through practices of reading, prayer, and the way they lived. A key voice in the *Devotio Moderna*.

Kimḥi, David (also known as Radak) (*c*.1160–*c*.1235) Influential French Jewish lexicographer, grammarian and Bible translator, whose commentaries highlighted many

Klein, Abraham Moses (1909–1972) Canadian Jewish poet whose work combined contemporary Jewish experience with traditional motifs and legends.

Layton, Irving (1912–2006) Canadian Jewish poet, born in Romania, whose inventive poems about identity often incorporated Jewish motifs.

Louis IX (1214–1270) French King, canonized as St. Louis; in regency under his mother Blanche of Castile; *Bible moralisée* made for him; went on Crusade to Holy Land.

Louis XIV (1638–1715) French King known as the Sun King; suffered as a child during civil uprising and later built Versailles to make the nobles absolutely dependent on him.

Lowth, Robert (1710–1787) bishop of London and Oxford professor of poetry who changed understanding of Hebrew poetry by showing it is structured in parallel pairs.

Luther, Martin (1483–1546) German Augustinian monk and university teacher. Leader of the Reformation in Germany. Wrote extensive commentaries on the Bible.

Maimonides, Moses (Rambam) (1135–1204) influential Jewish philosopher and physician from Spain. Author *The Guide for the Perplexed*, which tried to reconcile the Torah with aspects of Aristotelian philosophy.

Marcion (c. 85–160) Gnostic Christian philosopher with a large following throughout the Roman Empire; taught that the deity of the Scriptures was inferior to a higher deity and that the Scriptures were not authoritative for the Church. Rejection of his teaching led to the early church affirming the authority of the Scriptures and naming them the Old Testament.

Maxwell, Arthur S. (1896–1970) prolific author of children's Bibles and moral story books, sometimes under the name Uncle Arthur, that reflected values of the fifties. London-born Seventh Day Adventist who moved to U.S. and influenced generations of young readers.

Merian, Matthäus, the Elder (1593–1650) Swiss engraver and etcher. His *Iconum Biblicarum* combined medieval artistic traditions with early modern ideas; his pictures remained influential for centuries.

Meyer, Frederick Brotherton (1847–1929) English Baptist clergyman, evangelical, and author of many devotional commentaries on the Bibe.

Milton, John (1609–1674) poet, nonconformist and anti-monarchist. Author of *Paradise Lost*. Often adopted Jeremiah's voice in his political writings against the English monarchy.

More, Hannah (1745–1833) English abolitionist, educator of the poor, writer of religious tracts; creator of term Jeremiad.

Moulins, Guyart des (1251–1322) enterprising French priest who produced the first French vernacular Bible by translating and shortening Comestor's Latin *Historia* and adding colorful pictures of biblical characters in medieval dress.

Nahmanides (Rabbi Moses ben Nahman, called Ramban) (1194–1270) Spanish philosopher, physician and Bible scholar who combined traditional Jewish interpretation with contemporary ideas in his commentaries.

Nicholas of Lyra (*c*.1270–1349) Influential Franciscan scholar who highlighted Bible's literal meaning while still honoring of patristic, rabbinic and medieval interpretations. His learned comments were included across the bottom of the page in editions of the *Glossa Ordinaria* beginning in the late fourteenth century.

Origen (*c*.185–235) Brilliant Bible scholar, philosopher and theologian from Alexandria who interpreted Scripture in terms of the neo-Platonic philosophy of Plotinus. Influenced Jerome and many others before his writings were destroyed as heretical because he believed in the reincarnation of souls.

Pelagius (*c*.360–418) theologian and monk from the British Isles who taught that humans should take responsibility for their salvation. He rejected Augustine's doctrine of original sin, and taught that Christ was a moral exemplar. His work was condemned as heretical in 418, yet remained influential.

Philo of Alexandria (*c*.20–*c*.50) Greek-speaking Jewish philosopher from Alexandria who interpreted biblical stories and characters as symbolic of Greek philosophical ideals.

Quarles, Francis (1592–1644) English religious poet, popular among Puritans but a Royalist politically.

Rabanus Maurus (776–856) Benedictine monk and archbishop of Mainz in the time of Charlemagne. Learned theologian and poet who compiled Patristic traditions into a commentary form for the book of Jeremiah, among others.

Rashi, Rabbi Shlomo ben Isaac (1040– 1105) French Jewish exegete, noted for emphasizing the plain (literal) sense of biblical texts in contrast to Jewish midrashic elaboration and Christian allegory. Lived during the First Crusade.

Tertullian (*c*.160–*c*.220) early Christian theologian from North Africa; one of the first to write in Latin, establishing it as the language of the church; was deeply moved by Christian martyrs and wrote in defense of martyrdom.

Theodore of Mopsuestia (*c*.350–428) Christian theologian and biblical interpreter from Antiochus, who usually favored the "plain sense" of Scripture.

Trimmer, Mrs. Sarah (1741–1810) English Christian educator, active in establishing Sunday schools for the poor, author of Ion.

Philo of Alexandria (*c*.20–*c*.50) Greek-speaking Jewish philosopher from Alexandria who interpreted biblical stories and characters as symbolic of Greek philosophical ideals.

Quarles, Francis (1592-1644) English religious poet, popular among Puritans but a Royalist politically.

Rabanus Maurus (776–856) Benedictine monk and archbishop of Mainz in the time of Charlemagne. Learned theologian and poet who compiled Patristic traditions into a commentary form for the book of Jeremiah, among others.

Rashi, Rabbi Shlomo ben Isaac (1040– 1105) French Jewish exegete, noted for emphasizing the plain (literal) sense of biblical texts in contrast to Jewish midrashic elaboration and Christian allegory. Lived during the First Crusade.

Tertullian (*c*.160–*c*.220) early Christian theologian from North Africa; one of the first to write in Latin, establishing it as the language of the church; was deeply moved by Christian martyrs and wrote in defense of martyrdom.

Theodore of Mopsuestia (*c*.350–428/9) Christian theologian and biblical interpreter from Antiochus, who usually favored the "plain sense" of Scripture.

Trimmer, Mrs. Sarah (1741–1810) Influential English educator who helped found Sunday schools; author of narrative Bibles for young people and "the unlearned."

Wesley, Charles (1707–1788) English Methodist hymn writer.

Wesley, John (1703–1791) Anglican priest and evangelist. Founder of Methodism.

Wesley, Samuel Sebastian (1663–1735) Anglican priest, father of John and Charles, and a poet.

West, Benjamin (1738–1820) American-born British painter, whose now famous paintings of Isaiah and Jeremiah were commissioned by King George III for his chapel.

Wycliffe, John (*c.*1330–1384) English Bible translator and theologian, forerunner of the Reformation. With his associates produced the first English translation of the Vulgate.

Zweig, Stefan (1881–1942) Renowned Austrian Jewish writer; left his homeland in 1934 to escape Hitler; his 1918 anti-war play about Jeremiah remains in circulation.

Bibliography

1535. The Byble which is all the holy Scripture: in whych are contayned the Olde and Newe Testament truly and purely translated into Englysh by Thomas Matthew. M,D,XXXVII, Set forth with the Kinges most gracyous lyce[n]ce. Coverdale, Miles, Tyndale, William, Rogers, John, Antwerp: Printed by Matthew Crom Tyndale for Richard Grafton and Edward Whitchurch, London.

1603. *Bibliorum sacrorum cum glossa Ordinaria*. Vol. 4. Venice. (Library of the University of Toronto). https://archive.org/details/bibliorumsacror04strauoft.

1643. *The Souldiers Pocket Bible*. London: G.B. and R.W.

Jeremiah Through the Centuries, First Edition. Mary Chilton Callaway.
© 2020 Mary Chilton Callaway. Published 2020 by John Wiley & Sons Ltd.

1648. *Jeremiah Revived: though in his Prison; or his Lamentations parall'd. Great Britain's voyce of Weeping after Great Britain's Vote of Loyalty. Being a mournfull representation of the King and his Kingdomes wretched condition.*

1652. *Bibliorum sacrorum cum glossa Ordinaria.*

1677. *Fons Lachrymarum: or a Fountain of Tears: from whence doth flow Englands Complaint; Jeremiah's Lamentations Paraphras'd with Divine Meditations; and an Elegy.* London: Obadiah Blagrave.

1685. *Histoires Abregées de l'Ancient Testament 1685* (online at the ARTFL Project of the University of Chicago, Bibliothèque Bleue de Troyes: Bbl2205).

1693. *The Doctrine of the Bible: or, Rules of Discipline. Briefelye gathered through the whole course of the Scripture, by waye of Questions and Answers.* London: Richard Bradocke.

1836. *The Life and Prophecies of Jeremiah.* The American Sunday-School Union.

1850. *The Holy Bible… in the Earliest English Versions. Made from the Latin Vulgate by John Wycliff and His Followers.* Eds. J. Forshall and F. Madden. Vol. 3. Oxford.

1878. 'Taxation of the Liquor Traffic,' *The Princeton Review*: 384–398.

1879. *The Roman Breviary, Volume 2, Summer.* Edinburgh: Blackwood & Sons.

1880. *Holy Songs, Carols, and Sacred Ballads.* Boston: Roberts Bros.

n.d. *The Holy Bible and Drink.* Westerville, Ohio: Temperance Education Foundation, Inc.

2016. Jeremiah (Book and Person), in *Encyclopedia of the Bible and Its Reception,* vol. 13, 909 – 948. Berlin: De Gruyter.

Abelard, P. 2011. *Commentary on the Epistle to the Romans, Fathers of the Church: Medieval Continuation.* Washington, D.C.: Catholic University Press.

Abboud, R. 1996. 'Jeremiah's Mad Again,' *The New England Quarterly* 68: 75–90.

Adams, T. 1614. *The Devills Banket, described in foure Sermons.* London: printed by Thomas Snodham for Ralph Mab.

Al-Tha'labi, Ahmad Ibn Muhammad ibn Ibrahim. 2002. *'Arā'is Al-Majālis Fī Qisas Al-Anbiyā' or "Lives of the Prophets".* Trans. and annotated by William M. Brinner. Studies in Arabic Literature, Vol. 23. Leiden: Brill.

André, G. 1988. *The Prophet Jeremiah.* Sunbury, PA: Believers Bookshelf Inc.

Ainsworth, W. 1652. *Medulla Bibliorum, The Marrow of the Bible.* London: George Calvert.

Akinsiku, A. 2007. *The Manga Bible.* New York: Doubleday.

Arlow, J. 1951, 1997. *Psychoanalytic Quarterly* 20: 374–397. Reprinted in *Judaism and Psychoanalysis* ed. Mortimer Ostow. New York: KTAV.

Assaf, F. 1990. 'Review of Jean Serroy, *Le Virgile travesty,' Cahiers du dix-Septième* IV (2): 277–279.

Augustine. 1960. *City of God.* Trans. W.C. Greene. Loeb Classical Library 416. Cambridge: Harvard University Press.

Augustine. 1990. Sermons. *Works of St. Augustine: A Translation for the 21st Century.* Trans. E. Hill. Ed. J. Rotelle. New City Press.

Bakewell, T. 1644. *A Confutation of Anabaptists.* London: T. Bankes.

Baldwin, L.V. 1992. *To Make the Wounded Whole: The Cultural Legacy of Martin Luther King, Jr.* Philadelphia: Fortress Press.

Barrows, C. and D. Hustad (eds.), 1968. *Crusader Hymns and Hymn Stories*. Billy Graham Evangelistic Association.

Barton, J. 1990. 'Jeremiah in the Apocrypha and Pseudepigrapha,' in A.R.P. Diamond, K. O'Connor, L. Stulman (eds.) *Troubling Jeremiah*. Sheffield: Sheffield Academic Press, pp. 306–317.

Baumgartner, W. 2015. *Jeremiah's Poems of Lament*. Trans. D.E. Orton. London: Bloomsbury Press.

Basil the Great. 1963. *St. Basil Exegetical Homilies*. Trans. Sister Agnes Clare Way. Fathers of the Church, Vol. 46. Washington, D.C.: Catholic University of America Press.

Bastiaensen, A.A.R. 1990. 'La Perdrix animal méchant figure du diable: Augustin héritier d'une tradition exégétique,' in A.A.R. Bastiaensen, B. Bruning, M. Lamberights, J. van Houtem (eds.), *Collectanea Augustiniana: mélanges T.J. van Bavel*. Leuven University Press, pp. 193–217.

Beard, F. 1899. *Fifty Great Cartoons*. Chicago: The Ram's Horn Press, unpaginated. https://ehistory.osu.edu/exhibitions/rams_horn/content/StrangerAtOurGate.

Beard, F. 1903. *Picture Puzzles or How to Read the Bible by Symbols*. Chicago: Columbia Publishing House.

Begg, C. 1995. 'The "Classical Prophets" in Josephus' Antiquities,' in R.P. Gordon (ed.) *"The Place is Too Small for Us": The Israelite Prophets in Recent Scholarship*. Winona Lake: Eisenbrauns, pp. 547–562.

Bercovitch, S. 1978. *The American Jeremiad*. University of Wisconsin Press.

Berrigan, D. 1999. *Jeremiah: The World, the Wound of God*. Augsburg: Fortress Press.

Berkowitz, M.L. 2008. *The Lovell Haggadah*. Jerusalem: Schechter Institute of Jewish Studies.

Bethge, E. 1977. *Dietrich Bonhoeffer: Theologian, Christian, Contemporary*. London: Collins.

Bialik, H.N. and J.H. Ravnitzky. 1992. *The Book of Legends: Sefer Ha-Aggadah. Legends from the Talmud and Midrash*. Schocken.

Birmingham, G.A. 1956. *God's Iron: A Life of the Prophet Jeremiah*. London: Geoffrey Bles.

Bonhoeffer, D. 2002. 'The Young Bonhoeffer,' in H. Pfeifer and C. Green (eds.) *Dietrich Bonhoeffer Works, Volume 9*. Fortress Press.

Bonhoeffer, D. 2008. 'London, 1933–1935,' in H. Pfeifer and C. Green (eds.) *Dietrich Bonhoeffer Works, Volume 13*. Fortress Press.

Bonhoeffer, D. 2009. 'Letters and Papers from Prison,' in H. Pfeifer and C. Green (eds.) *Dietrich Bonhoeffer Works, Volume 8*. Fortress Press.

Bousset, J. 1892. *Oeuvres Oratoires de Bossuet. Édition critique complete par L'Abbé J. Lebarq. Tome Quatrième. 1661–1666*. Paris: Desclée, de Brouwer et Cie.

Braude, W.G. 1968. *Pesikta Rabbati*, Yale University Press.

Braude, W.G. and I.J. Kapstein. 2002. *Pesikta de Rab Kahana*. Jewish Publication Society.

Bright, J. 1964. *Jeremiah*. The Anchor Bible, Volume 21. New York: Doubleday.

Brinner, W.M. 2002. *Ara'is Al-Majalis Fi Qisas Al-Anbiya' or "Lives of the Prophets": As Recounted by Abu Ishaq Ahmad Ibn Muhammed Ibn Ibrahim Al-Thalabi*. Leiden: Brill.

Brooke, G. and F.G. Martinez (eds.), 1994. *New Qumran Texts and Studies*. Brill.

Brooks, T. 1671. 'Seven Characters of False Teachers,' in *Precious Remedies Against Satan's Devices*. London.

Brown, G.G. 1910. *The Holy Bible repudiates "prohibition"; compilation of all verses containing the words "wine" or "strong drink", proving that the scriptures commend and command the temperate use of alcoholic beverages*. Louisville.

Brown, J., the Rev. 1792. *The Self-Interpreting Bible*. With additions by the Rev. H. Cooke. Glasgow, Edinburgh, and London: Blackie and Son.

Brubaker, L. 1999. *Vision and Meaning in Ninth-century Byzantium: Image as Exegesis in the Homilies of Gregory of Nazianzus*. Cambridge University Press.

Brueggemann, W. 1997. 'Texts That Linger, Words That Explode,' *Theology Today* 54 (2):180–199.

Brueggemann, W. 1998. *A Commentary on Jeremiah: Exile and Homecoming*. Grand Rapids: Eerdmans.

Bunyan, J. 1841. *The Practical Works of John Bunyan*. Ed. The Rev. A. Philip. London.

Bunyan, J. 1850. *The Works of John Bunyan with an Introduction to Each Treatise, Notes, and a Sketch of His Life, Times, and Contemporaries, Volume 1*. Ed. R. Philip. Glasgow: Blackie & Son.

Bunyan, J. 1859. *The Entire Works of John Bunyan, Volume* 4. Ed. H. Stebbing. Toronto: Virtue, Yorston & Co.

Bunyan, J. 1861. *The Works of John Bunyan, Volume* 2. Ed. G. Offor. Glasgow: Blackie & Son.

Cabal, T. 2007. *The Apologetics Study Bible*. Nashville: Holman Bible Publishers.

Caesarius of Arles. 1956. *Sermons of St. Caesarius of Arles*. Trans. M.M. Mueller. Fathers of the Church Series, Vol. 31. Washington, D.C.: Catholic University of America Press.

Callaway, M.C. 2004. 'The Lamenting Prophet and the Modern Self: On the Origins of Contemporary Readings of Jeremiah,' in J. Kaltner and L. Stulman (eds.) *Prophetic Speech*. Edinburgh: T. & T. Clark International, pp. 48–62.

Callaway, M.C. 2011. 'Peering Inside Jeremiah: How Early Modern English Culture Still Influences Our Reading of the Prophet,' in L. Stulman and A.R.P. Diamond (eds.) *Jeremiah (Dis)Placed: New Directions in Writing/Reading Jeremiah*. Edinburgh: T & T. Clark International, pp. 279–289.

Callaway, M.C. 2011. 'Reading Jeremiah with Some Help from Gadamer,' in L. Stulman and A.R.P. Diamond (eds.) *Jeremiah (Dis)Placed: New Directions in Writing/Reading Jeremiah*. Edinburgh: T & T. Clark International, pp. 266–278.

Calvin, J. 1559, 1989. *A Commentary on Jeremiah*. Trans. J. Owen. Carlisle: The Banner of Truth Trust.

Carruthers, M. 2008. *The Book of Memory*. Cambridge: Cambridge University Press.

Carroll, Robert P. 1986. Jeremiah: A Commentary. Philadelphia: Fortress Press.

Cassian, J. 1994. 'Conferences of John Cassian,' in P. Schaff (ed.) *A Select Library of the Christian Church: Nicene and Post-Nicene Fathers*, Second Series, Vol. XI. Peabody: Hendrickson.

Caulkins, F.M. 1841. *Children of the Bible: As Examples and as Warnings*. New York: American Tract Society.

Caulkins, R. 1930. *Jeremiah: A Study in Personal Religion*. New York: Macmillan.

Cawelti, J.G. 1997. 'Leon Forrest: The Labyrinth of Luminosity: An Introduction,' in *Leon Forrest: Introductions and Interpretations*. Bowling Green State University Popular Press, pp. 1–74.

Chandler, R.C. 1983. 'The Problem of Moral Reasoning in American Public Administration: The Case for a Code of Ethics,' *Public Administration Review* 43(1): 32–39. doi: 10.2307/975297.

Charlesworth, J.H. 1983, 1985. *The Old Testament Pseudepigrapha*. 2 vols. New York: Doubleday.

Christe, Y. and L. Brugger. 2001. '"La Bible du roi: Jérémie dans la Bible moralisée de Tolède et les vitraux de la Sainte Chapelle,' *Cahiers archeologiques* 49:101–116.

Chrysostom, J. 2003. *St. John Chrysostom: Old Testament Homilies, Volume 2*. Brookline: Holy Cross Orthodox Press.

Cohen, N.G. 1997. 'Earliest Evidence of the Haftarah Cycle for the Sabbaths between the 17th of Tammuz and Sukkot in Philo,' *Journal of Jewish Studies* 48: 225–249.

Cohen, N. 2007. *Philo's Scriptures: Citations from the Prophets and Writings: Evidence for a Haftarah Cycle in Second Temple Judaism*. Leiden: Brill.

Cohen, S. 1982. 'Josephus, Jeremiah, and Polybius,' *History and Theory* 21: 366–381.

Columbus, C. 1997. *The Book of Prophecies*. Ed. R. Rusconi. Trans. B. Sullivan, Vol. 3, *Repertorium Columbianum*. Eugene: Wipf & Stock.

Curtis, A.H.W. and T. Romer (eds.), 1997. *The Book of Jeremiah and Its Reception*. Leuven University Press.

Cyril of Jerusalem. 1838. *The Catechetical Lectures of S. Cyril*. Oxford University Press.

Damian, P. 1989–2005. *The Letters of Peter Damian*. 6 vols. Trans. O.J. Blum and I. M. Resnick. Fathers of the Church Medieval Continuation. Washington D.C.: Catholic University of America.

Davidson, S.V. 2014. *Empire and Exile: Postcolonial Readings of the Book of Jeremiah*. Edinburgh: T & T Clark.

Davis, D.B. 1986. 'American Jeremiah,' *New York Review of Books* (13 February).

Davis, K. 2014. *The Cave 4 Apocryphon of Jeremiah and the Qumran Jeremianic Traditions*. Leiden: Brill.

Davis, N. 1896. 'A Dirge for the Ninth of Ab,' *Jewish Quarterly Review* 8: 611–613.

Demacopoulos, G.E. 2007. *The Book of Pastoral Rule: St. Gregory the Great*. Yonkers: St. Vladimir's Seminary Press.

Derrida, J. 1978. *Writing and Difference*. Trans. A. Bass. Chicago: University of Chicago Press.

Desmarais, M. 1771, 1772. *Jérémie, Poëme en Quatre Chants*. Paris: A. Ipres.

Dewsbury, W. 1656. 'The Mighty Day of the Lord is Coming,' in *The Faithful Testimony of that antient [ancient] Servant of the Lord, and Minister of the everlasting Gospel*, 156. London.

Diamant, D. 2013. 'From the Book of Jeremiah to the Qumranic Apocryphon of Jeremiah in Dead Sea Discoveries,' *Dead Sea Discoveries* 20(3), 452–471.

Diamond, A.R.P. 1990. 'Jeremiah's Confessions in the LXX and MT,' *Vetus Testamentum LX* (1):50.

Diamond, A.R.P. and K.M. O'Connor. 1996. 'Unfaithful Passions: Coding Women Coding Men in Jeremiah 2-3 (4:2),' *Biblical Interpretation* 4(3): 288–310.

Dopffel, M. 2010. "Between Biblical Literalism and Scientific Inquiry: Cotton Mather's Commentary on Jeremiah 8:7,' in R. Smolinski and J. Stievermann (eds.) *Cotton Mather and Biblia Americana: America's First Bible Commentary*. Grand Rapids: Baker, pp. 203–225.

Drury, J. (ed.) 1989. *Critics of the Bible, 1724–1873*. Cambridge University Press.

Duhm, B. 1901. *Das Buch Jeremia*. Tübingen und Leipzig: J.C.B. Mohr.

Dunbar, V. 1942. 'A Word to Jeremiah,' *The Sewanee Review* 50(2): 171.

Dupont-Sommer, A. 1962. *The Essene Writings from Qumran*. Cleveland: World Publishing Co.

Duppa, B. 1660. *Private Forms of Prayer Fit for Sad Times*. London: Thomas Mabb.

Eliot, T.S. 1952. *The Complete Poems and Plays 1909-1950*. New York: Harcourt, Brace & World.

Elliott-Binns, L.E. 1941. *Jeremiah: A Prophet for a Time of War*. London: Student Christian Movement Press.

Epistle of Barnabas. 1912. Trans. and ed. K. Lake *Apostolic Fathers*, Vol 1. Loeb Classical Library. Cambridge: Harvard University Press.

Exell, J.S. 1887. *The Biblical Illustrator: Jeremiah*. London: Fleming H. Revell Co.

van den Eynde, S. 2001. 'Taking Broken Cisterns for the Fountain of Living Water: On the Background of the Metaphor of the Whore in Jeremiah,' *Biblische Notizen* 110: 86–96.

Ewald, H. 1868. *Die Propheten des Alten Bundes, in zwei Bänden*. Stuttgart: Adolph Krabbe.

Felt, E.W. 1923. *Jeremiah: Prophet and Hero*. Ed. J.G. Bennett. Madras: Christian Literature Society for India.

Fishbane, M.A. 1971. 'Jeremiah 4:23-26 and Job 3:3-13: A Recovered Use of the Creation Pattern,' *Vetus Testamentum* 21:151–167.

Fishbane, M. 1985. *Biblical Interpretation in Ancient Israel*. Oxford: Clarendon Press.

Fishbane, M. 2002. *The JPS Bible Commentary: Haftarot*. Philadelphia: Jewish Publication Society.

Fontaine, N. 1670. *L'Histoire du vieux et du nouveau testament*. Paris: Chez Pierre le Petit.

Forrest, L. 1979. 'Oh Jeremiah of the Dreamers,' *Callaloo* 6: 73–80.

Forrest, L. 1988. *There Is A Tree More Ancient Than Eden*. Chicago: Another Chicago Press.

Foster, C. 1886. *Bible Pictures and What They Teach Us*. Philadelphia: Foster Publishing Company.

Fox, G. 1683. *Concerning meeting in houses, ships, streets, mountains, by-wayes and in what places the prophet Jeremiah, Christ and the apostles taught or preached in, may be seen in this book*. London.

Frank, P. 1987. *Jeremiah and the Great Disaster*. Illustrated by Tony Morris. The Lion Story Bible 25. Tring, England: Lion Publishing.

Foxe, J. 1838. *The Acts and Monuments of John Foxe*. London: R.B. Seeley and W. Burnside.

Friedan, K. 1983. 'Stefan Zweig and the Nazis,' *Religion (Syracuse University)* 45: 39–40. http://surface.syr.edu/rel/45.

Friedman, M. 1984. 'Marc Chagall's Portrayal of the Prophet Jeremiah,' *Zeitchrift für Kunstgeschichte XLVII* (3): 374–391.

Froehlich, K. and M. Gibson. 1992. *Biblia Latina Cum Glossa Ordinaria, Introduction to the Facsimile Reprint of the Editio Princeps Adolph Rusch of Strassborg 1480/81.* Brepols-Turnhout.

Gadamer, H-G. 1998. *Truth and Method.* 2nd revised edition. Trans. revised by J. Weinsheimer and D.G. Marshall. New York: Continuum.

Gaines, M.C. 1943. 'Picture Stories from the Bible,' *Old Testament* (Issue No. 4).

Gaster, T. 1949. *Passover: Its History and Traditions.* Boston: Beacon Press.

Giblin, C.H. 1967. 'Reflections on the Sign of the Manger,' *Catholic Biblical Quarterly* 29:87–101.

Ginzberg, L. 1982. *Legends of the Jews.* 7 vols. Philadelphia: Jewish Publication Society.

Glass, W. 1853. *The Revivalist: A New Selection of Hymns and Spiritual Songs.* Columbus: Scott & Bascom.

Glaude, E.S. 2000. *Exodus! Religion, Race and Nation in early Nineteenth Century Black America.* University of Chicago Press.

Gordon, T.C. 1932. *The Rebel Prophet: Studies in the Personality of Jeremiah.* Harper & Brothers.

Gregory Nazianzus. 1890. *Nicene and Post-Nicene Fathers.* Ed. P. Schaff. Christian Classics Ethereal Library, Volume 7. Peabody: Hendrickson Publishers.

Gregory of Nyssa. 1993. *Homilies on Ecclesiastes.* Ed. G.S. Hall. Berlin: De Gruyter.

Gregory the Great. 1847. *Morals on the Book of Job, Volume 3.* Oxford: John Henry Parker.

Gregory the Great. 2007. *The Book of Pastoral Rule: St. Gregory the Great.* Yonkers: St. Vladimir's Seminary Press.

Gunner, G. and R. Smith. 2014. *Comprehending Christian Zionism: Perspectives in Comparison.* Philadelphia: Fortress Press.

Habel, N. 1965. 'The Form and Significance of the Call Narratives,' *Zeitschrift für die Alttestamentliche Wissenschaft* 77: 297–323.

Habel, N. 1967, 1970. *Are You Joking, Jeremiah?* St. Louis: Concordia Publishing House.

Hagee, J. 2006. *Jerusalem Countdown: A Warning to the World.* FrontLine.

Hall, J. 1633. *A plaine and familiar explication (by way of paraphrase) of all the hard texts of the whole divine Scripture of the Old and New Testament.* London: Miles Flesher.

Hall, J. 1863. *The Works of the Right Reverent Father in God Joseph Hall. D.D. in Ten Volumes.* Ed. Josiah Pratt. Vol. 5. London: C. Whittingham.

Hammer, R. 1987. *Sifre: A Tannaitic Comentary on the Book of Deuteronomy, Yale Judaica Series,* Vol. 24. New Haven: Yale University Press.

Harris, R. 2009. 'Twelfth-Century Biblical Exegetes and the Invention of Literature,' in Ienje van 't Spijker (ed.) *The Multiple Meaning of Scripture: The Role of Exegesis in Early-Christian and Medieval Culture,* Commentaria 2. Leiden: Brill, pp. 311–329.

Hayward, R. 1985. 'Jewish Traditions in Jerome's Commentary on Jeremiah and the Targum of Jeremiah,' *Proceedings of the Irish Biblical Association* 9(2): 100–120.

Hayward, R. 1987. *The Targum of Jeremiah*. Trans. with a Critical Introduction, Apparatus, and Notes. Wilmington: Michael Glazier.

Heiman, A. 1962. 'Jeremiah and His Girdle,' *Journal of the Warburg and Courtauld Institutes* 25: 1–8.

Heinemann, J. 1982. 'A Homily on Jeremiah and the Fall of Jerusalem,' in R. Polzin and E. Rothman (eds.) *The Biblical Mosaic: Changing Perspectives*. Fortress Press, pp. 27–41.

Hengstenberg, E.W. 1839. *Christology of the Old Testament, and A Commentary on the Predictions of the Messiah by the Prophets, Volume III*. Washington: William M. Morrison.

Henry, A. (ed.) 1987. *Biblia Pauperum: A Facsimile and Edition*. Ithaca: Cornell University Press.

Henze, M. and L. Lied. 2017. 'Jeremiah, Baruch, and Their Books: Three Phases in a Changing Relationship,' in H. Najman and K. Schmidt (eds.) *Jeremiah's Scriptures: Production, Reception, Interaction, and Transformation*. Leiden: Brill.

Herbert, G. 1842. *A Priest to the Temple, or The Country Parson, His Charter, and Rule of Holy Life*. Boston: J.B. Dow.

Herder, J.G. 1833. *The Spirit of Hebrew Poetry*. Burlington: Edward Smith.

Herford, T.R. 1987. *Pirke Avoth, The Ethics of the Talmud*. New York: Schocken.

Herrick, R. 1823. *The Works of Robert Herrick*. Ed. T. Maitland. Edinburgh: Tait.

Herrin, A.K. 2014. 'Recycling and Reforming Origins: The Double Creation in Claes Jansz Visscher's Theatrum Biblicum (1639),' in F. Dietze (ed.) *Illustrated Religious Texts in the North of Europe, 1500–1800*, 183–204. Farnham, UK: Ashgate.

Heschel, A.J. 1962. *The Prophets*. New York: Jewish Publication Society.

Hill, C. 1993. *English Bible and the Seventeenth Century Revolution*. London: Allen Lane, The Penguin Press.

Hill, J.S. 1979. *John Milton: Poet, Priest and Prophet*. London: Macmillan.

Hillyard, I. 1816. *A Wonderful and Horrible Thing is Committed in the Land*. Petersburg, VA: W. Dunnavant for William Rose.

Hippolytus of Rome. n.d. De Antichrist. http://www.earlychristianwritings.com/text/hippolytus-christ.html.

Hobbes, T. 2011. *Leviathan*. Ed. A.P. Martinich and B. Battiste. Ontario: Broadview Press.

Holladay, W.L. 1986. *Jeremiah Volume 1*. Hermeneia Series. Philadelphia: Fortress.

Holladay, W.L. 1989. *Jeremiah Volume 2*. Hermeneia Series. Philadelphia: Fortress.

Hopkins, G.M. 1986. *Gerard Manley Hopkins: The Major Works*. Ed. Catherine Phillips. New York: Oxford University Press.

Hyatt, J.P. 1958. *Jeremiah, Prophet of Courage and Hope*. New York: Abingdon.

Ironside, H.A. 1906, 1952. *Notes on the Prophecy and Lamentations of Jeremiah, "The Weeping Prophet."* New York: Loizeaux Brothers. Bible Truth Depot.

Jaeger, E. 2000. *The Book of the Heart*. University of Chicago Press.

Jassen, A. 2016. "The Rabbinic Construction of Jeremiah's Lineage," in K. Finsterbusch and A. Lange (eds.) *Texts and Contexts of Jeremiah: The Exegesis of Jeremiah 1 and 10 in Light of Text and Reception History*. Contributions to Biblical Exegesis and Theology Vol. 82. Leuven: Peeters, pp. 3–20.

Jeffrey, D.L. 1988. *English Spirituality in the Age of Wyclif*. Vancouver: Regent College Publishing.

Jellie, W.H. 1892. *The Preacher's Commentary on the Book of Jeremiah: Containing Exegesis, Homiletics, Illustrations*. The Preacher's Complete Homiletical Commentary Vol. 23. New York: Funk & Wagnalls.

Jerome, St. 1893. *Against Jovinianus*. Trans. W.H. Fremantle. Nicene and Post Nicene Fathers, Second Series, Vol. 6. Buffalo: Christian Literature Publishing Co.

Jerome 1960. S. Hieronymi Presbyteri. *In Hieremiam Prophetam*. Ed. S. Reiter. Corpus Christianorum. Series Latina. LXXIV. Pars I, 3.

Josephus, F. 1937. *Jewish Antiquities Books IX–XI*. Trans. *Ralph Marcus. Loeb Classical Library*. Cambridge: Harvard University Press.

Joye, G. 1534. *Jeremy the prophete, translated into Englisshe [sic]*. Antwerp: M. de Keyser.

Kalmanofsky, A. 2009. 'The Monstrous-Feminine in the Book of Jeremiah,' *Lectio Difficilior European Electronic Journal for Feminst Exegesis* 1: 1–21.

Kalmanofsky, A. 2015. '"As she did, do to her!" Jeremiah's OAN As Revenge Fantasies,' in E.K. Holt, H C.P. Kim, and A. Mein (eds.) *Concerning the Nations*. Edinburgh: T & T Clark. pp. 109–127.

Kannengiesser, C. 1974. 'Jérémie chez les pères de l'eglise,' in M. Viller (ed.) *Dictionnaire de spiritualité*. Paris: Beauscesne.

Kannenngieser, C. 1975. "L'Interprétation de Jérémie dans la tradition alexandrine," *Studia Patristica XII*: 317–320.

Kaestli, J-D. 1997. 'L'Influence du livre de Jérémie dans les Paralipomènes de Jérémie,' in A.H.W. Curtis and T. Römer (eds.) *The Book of Jeremiah and Its Reception*. Leuven University Press, pp. 233–253.

Kelly, J.N.D. 1998. *Jerome: His Life, Writings and Controversies*. Peabody: Hendrickson.

Kelly, W. 1938. *Jeremiah: The Tender-Hearted Prophet of the Nations*. C.A. Hammond.

Kerr, E.A. 1968. *Alcohol and the Scriptures*. Temperance Committee of the Presbyterian Church of Victoria, Australia.

Kessler, H.L. 1987. 'Prophetic Portraits in the Dura Synagogue,' *Jahrbuchfür Antike und Christentum* 30: 149–155.

King, M.L., Jr. 1992. 'The Significant Contributions of Jeremiah to Religious Thought,' in R.E. Luker and P.A. Russell (eds.), *The Papers of Martin Luther King, Jr. I. Called to Serve: January 1929–June 1951*. University of California Press.

Kitto, J. 1845. *The Pictorial Sunday Book*. London Printing and Publishing Company.

Klein, A.M. 1990. *Complete Poems*. Toronto: University of Toronto Press.

Knoppers, L.L. 1990. 'Milton's *The Readie and Easie Way* and the English Jeremiad,' in D. Lowenstein and J. Grantham Turner (eds.) *Politics, Poetics, and Hermeneutics in Milton's Prose*. Cambridge University Press, pp. 213–225.

Knox, W.H. 1931. *Talks to Young People of Any Age on the Book of Jeremiah*. Essex: S.P. Bookman.

Kutsch, E. 1956. 'Gideons Berufung und Altarbau Jdc. 6,11–24,' *Theologische Literaturzeitung* 81: 75–84.

Layton, I. 1982, 1989. *Wild Peculiar Joy: Selected Poems 1945-89*. Toronto: McClelland and Stewart.

Laytner, A. 1990. *Arguing with God: A Jewish Tradition*. Lanham MD: Rowman & Littlefield.

Ledegang, F. 1982. 'Images of the Church in Origen: the girdle (Jeremiah 13:1–11),' *Studia Patristica XVII*: 907–911.

Lederhendler, E. 1989. *The Road to Modern Jewish Politics: Political Tradition and Political Reconstruction in the Jewish Community of Tsarist Russia*. New York: Oxford University Press.

Lees, F.R. and D. Burns. 1868. *The Temperance Bible-Commentary: Giving at one view version, criticism, and exposition in regard to all passages of Holy Writ bearing on the words 'wine' and 'strong drink' or illustrating the principles of the Temperance Reformation.* London: S.W. Partridge.

Lipton, S. 1999. *Images of Intolerance: The Representation of Jews and Judaism in the Bible moralisée*. Berkeley: University of California Press.

Loewe, R. 1969. 'The Medieval History of the Latin Vulgate,' in G.W.H. Lampe (ed.) *The Cambridge History of the Bible*, Vol. 2. Cambridge: Cambridge University Press, pp. 102–154.

Longacre, L.B. 1916. 'Jeremiah as His Neighbors Knew Him,' *The Biblical World* 48 (5): 283–287.

Lord, J. 1883. *Beacon Lights of History: The Old Pagan Civilizations*. New York: Fords, Howard & Hulbert.

Lowth, R. 1835. *Lectures on the Sacred Poetry of the Hebrews*. Trans. from the Latin by G. Gregory. 3rd edition. London: Thomas Tegg & Son.

Lundbom, J. 1999. *Jeremiah 1–20*. The Anchor Bible Series. New Haven: Yale University Press.

Lurz, F. 1992. 'Jeremia in der Liturgie der Alten Kirche,' *Ecclesia Orans* 9(2): 141–171.

Luther, M. 1548. *A frutefull and godly Exposition and declaration of the kingdom of Christ, and of the Christen lybertye, made upon the words of the Prophete Jeremye in the xxiii chapter*.

Luther, M. 1955–1986. *(Cited as LW.) Luther's Works: The American Edition*. 55 vols. Concordia and Fortress Presses.

Luyken, J. 1712. *De Schriftuurlyke Geschiedenissen en Gelykenissen van het Oude en Nieuwe verbond*. Amsterdam: P. Arentz.

Maier, C.M. 'Reading Back and Forth: Gender Trouble in Jeremiah 2–3,' in J.K. Aitken, J.M.S. Clines, and C.M. Maier (eds.) *Interested Readers*. Missola: Society of Biblical Literature, pp. 137–150.

Maimonides, M. 1904. The Guide for the Perplexed. Trans. M. Friedlander. London: Routledge & Kegan Paul Ltd.

Massey, J. 2012. *Jeremiah, Lamentations, Baruch*. Dalit Bible Commentary, Vol. 17. New Delhi, Centre for Dalit/Subaltern Studies.

Mason I.L., Jr. 1969. 'Typology and the New England Way: Cotton Mather and the Exegesis of Biblical Types,' *Early American Literature* 4 (1):15–37.

Matheson, P. 2001. *The Imaginative World of the Reformation*. Minneapolis: Fortress Press.

Maxwell, A. 1955. *The Bible Story*, Vol. 5. Washington: Review and Herald Publishing Association.

McKane, W. 1986. *A Critical and Exegetical Commentary on Jeremiah, Volume 1.* Edinburgh: T & T. Clark Limited.

Melamed, A. 2003. *The Image of the Black in Jewish Culture: A History of the Other.* New York: Routledge.

Meuche, H. and N. Ingeberg. 1976. *Flugblätter der Reformation und des Bauernkrieges: 50 Blätter aus d. Sammlung d. Schlossmuseums Gotha.* Leipzig: Insel.

Meyer, F.B. 1894. *Jeremiah: Priest and Prophet.* London: Morgan and Scott.

Meyer, J.D. 1975. 'Benjamin West's Chapel of Revealed Religion: A Study in Eighteenth-Century Protestant Religious Art,' *The Art Bulletin* 57(2): 247–256.

Merian, M. 1630. *Icones Biblicæ, præcipuas Sacræ Scripturæ historias eleganter & graphicè repræsentantes: Biblische Figuren ... / durch Matthævm Merian von Basel, mit Versen und reymen in dreyen Sprachen gezieret und erkläret.* Strassburg: Lazari Zetzner.

Migne, J-P. 1844–1855. *Patrologia Latina.* Paris.

Millay, E. St. Vincent. 1940. *Make Bright the Arrows.* New York: Harper and Brothers.

Milliken, V.G. 1954. *Jeremiah: Prophet of Disaster. Heroes of God Series.* New York: Association Press.

Milton, J. 2007. *The Essential Prose of John Milton.* Ed. W. Kerrigan, J. Rumrich, and S.M. Fallon. New York: Random House.

Minter, D. "The Puritan Jeremiad as a Literary Form," in S. Bercovitch (ed.) *The American Puritan Imagination: Essays in Revaluation.* London: Cambridge University Press, pp. 45–55.

Morey, J. H. 1993. 'Peter Comestor, Biblical Paraphrase, and the Medieval Popular Bible,' *Speculum* 68: 6–35.

Morrison, H.A. 1907. *The Wings of the Morning: Addresses from a Glasgow Pulpit.* New York: A.C. Armstrong.

Morton, C. 1744. *An enquiry into the physical and literal sense of that scripture Jeremiah viii.7, by an eminent professor.* London.

Murphy, A.R. 2009. *Prodigal Nation: Moral Decline and Divine Punishment from New England to 9/11.* New York: Oxford University Press.

Najman, H. and K. Schmidt. 2017. *Jeremiah's Scriptures.* Supplements to the Journal for the Study of Judaism, Vol. 17. Leiden: Brill.

Nash, S. 2003. 'Y.L. Gordon: Zedekiah in the Prison House,' *CCAR Journal: The Reform Jewish Quarterly* Spring: 33–48.

Nasuti, H. 1986. 'A Prophet to the Nations: Diachronic and Synchronic Readings of Jeremiah 1,' *Hebrew Annual Review* 10: 249–266.

Nathan, L. 1996. 'Jeremiah Lamenting the Destruction of Jerusalem,' *Salmagundi* 109/110: 94–95.

Neusner, J. 2006. *Jeremiah in Talmud and Midrash.* Lanham: University Press of America.

Newman, J.H. 1891. *Parochial and Plain Sermons, Volume 8.* London: Longmans, Green, & Co.

Newman, J.H. 2017. 'Confessing in Exile: The Reception and Composition of Jeremiah in (Daniel and) Baruch,' in H. Najman and K. Schmid (eds.) *Jeremiah's Scriptures: Production, Reception, Interaction, and Transformation.* Leiden: Brill.

Newton, J. 1779, 2011. *John Newton's Olney Hymns*. Ed. Charles J. Doe. Minneapolis: Curiosmith.

Nicoll, W.R., J.T. Stoddart, and J. Moffatt. 1910. *Expositor's Dictionary of Texts*. New York: George H. Doran.

Niebuhr, R. 1937, 1965. *Beyond Tragedy: Essays on the Christian Interpretation of History*. New York: Scribner.

Niessen, C. 2004. 'Schuld, Strafe und Geschlecht: die Auswirkungen der Genderkonstruktionen auf Schuldzuweisungen und Gerichtsankündigungen in Jer 23,9-23 und Jer 13,20-27', *Biblische Zeitschrift* 48(1):86–96.

Norton, D. 1993. *A History of the Bible as Literature, Volume 2*. Cambridge University Press.

O'Connor, K.M. 1999. "The Tears of God and Divine Character in Jeremiah 2 – 9." In A.R.P. Diamond, K. O'Connor, and L. Stulman (eds.) *Troubling Jeremiah*. Journal for the Study of the Old Testament, Supplement Series 260. Sheffield: Sheffield Academic Press.

O'Connor, K.M. 2005. "'Jeremiah's "Prophetic Imagination": Pastoral Intervention for a Shattered World,' in C.R. Yoder, K. O'Connor, E. E. Johnson, S.P. Saunders (eds.) *Shaking Heaven and Earth*. Louisville: Westminster John Knox, pp. 59–71.

O'Connor, K.M. 2008. 'A family comes undone (Jeremiah 2:1-4:2),' *Review & Expositor* 105 (2): 201–212.

O'Connor, K.M. 2012. *Jeremiah: Pain and Promise*. Philadelphia: Fortress Press.

Origène. 1976. *Homélies sur Jérémie*. Ed. Pierre Nautin. Sources Chrétiennes, Vol. 1. Paris: Les éditions du Cerf.

Origen. 1990. *Homiles on Leviticus*. Trans. G.W. Barkley. Washington: Catholic University Press.

Origen. 1998. *Homilies on Jeremiah and 1 Kings 28*. Trans. J.C. Smith. The Fathers of the Church, Vol. 97. Washington: Catholic University Press.

Origen. 2009. *Homilies on Numbers*. Trans. T.P. Scheck. Ed. C.A. Hall. Downers Grove: IVP Academic.

Paviliers, A.S.J. 1765. *La Devotion des Predestinez*. Troyes.

Paine, T. 1795, 1796, 1811. *The Age of Reason; Being an Investigation of True and Fabulous Theology*. London: Daniel Isaac Eaton.

Philippson, L. 1839–1849. *Die Israelische Bibel*. Leipzig: Baumgartner's Buchhandlung.

Philo of Alexandra. 1929. *Philo, Volume 2*. Loeb Classical Library. Cambridge: Harvard University Press.

Philo of Alexandra. 1932. *Philo, Volume 4*. Loeb Classical Library. Cambridge: Harvard University Press.

Philo of Alexandra. 1934. *Philo, Volume 5*. Loeb Classical Library. Cambridge: Harvard University Press.

Pitman, R. 1878. 'Taxation of the Liquor Traffic,' *The Princeton Review* 2: 384–398.

Polk, T. 1984. *The Prophetic Persona*. Journal for the Study of the Old Testament, Supplement Series 32. JSOT Press.

Poole, M. 1683. *Annotations upon the Holy Bible*. London: John Richardson.

Portugés, P. 1984. 'Allen Ginsberg's Visions and the Growth of His Poetics of Prophecy,' *Poetic Prophecy in Western Literature*, ed. Raymond-Jean Frontain and Jan Wojcik. 1984. Rutherford: Fairleigh Dickinson University Press, pp. 157–173.

Pyper, H.S. 2015. 'Postcolonialism and Propaganda in Jeremiah's Oracles Against the Nations,' in A. Mein, E. Holt, H.C.P. Kim (eds.) *Concerning the Nations*. London: T & T Clark, pp. 145–157

Quarles, J. 1648, 1649. *Fons Lachrymarum: or a Fountain of Tears: from whence doth flow England's Complaint*. London.

Redditt, P. 2008. *Introduction to the Prophets*. Grand Rapids: Eerdmans.

Reventlow, H.G. 2009. *History of Biblical Interpretation, Volume 2*. Trans. J.O. Duke. Missoula: SBL Press.

Rich, J. 1648. *Jeremiah's contemplations on Jeremiah's lamentations, or, Englands miseries matcht with Sions elegies*. London: John Stevenson.

Roberts, W. 1835. *Memoirs of the Life and Correspondence of Mrs. Hannah More*. Vol 1. Third Edition. London: Seely and Burnside.

Rosenberg, A.J. 1989, 1995. *The Book of Jeremiah: A New English Translation with Rashi and A Commentary Digest. English and Hebrew Edition*. 2 vols. New York: Judaica Press.

Rudolph, W. 1947, 1968. Jeremia. Tübingen: J.C.B. Mohr.

Rupp, E.G. and P.S. Watson (eds.), 1969. *Luther and Erasmus: Free Will and Salvation*. Library of Christian Classics. Philadelphia: Westminster Press.

de Sacy, I-L. le Maistre. 1693. *Jérémie traduit en Francois, avec une explication tirée des Saints Péres & des Autheurs Ecclésiastiquesi*. Tome Second. Paris: Guillaume Desprez.

Saebø, M. (ed.), 2000–2015. *Hebrew Bible/Old Testament: The History of Its Interpretation*. 5 vols. Vandenhoeck & Ruprecht.

Sánchez, R. 2014. *Typology and Iconography in Donne, Herbert, and Milton: Fashioning the Self after Jeremiah*. Basingstoke: Palgrave Macmillan.

Sarason, R.S. 1988. 'The Interpretation of Jeremiah 31:31-34 in Judaism,' in J.J. Petuchowski (ed.) *When Jews and Christians Meet*. Albany: State University of New York Press, pp. 99–123.

Sawyer, J. 1978. 'A Note on the Brooding Partridge in Jeremiah XVII 11,' *Vetus Testamentum XXVIII*: 324–329.

Schaff, P. and H. Wace. 1894. *A Select Library of Nicene and Post-Nicene Fathers of the Church, Volume XI*. Christian Literature Company.

Schama, S. 1999. *Rembrandt's Eyes*. New York: Knopf.

Schoenfeldt, M. 1999. *Bodies and Selves in Early Modern England*. Cambridge University Press.

Schwarzbach, B.E. 2008. 'Louis-Isaac Le Maistre de Sacy,' in M. Saebø (ed.) *Hebrew Bible/ Old Testament: History of Its Interpretation*. Göttingen: Vandenhoeck & Ruprecht.

Sharp, C. 2003. *Prophecy and Ideology in Jeremiah: Struggles for Authority in the Deutero-Jeremianic Prose*. London: T & T Clark.

Sharp, C. 2011. 'Jeremiah in the Land of Aporia: Reconfiguring Redaction Criticism as Witness to Foreignness,' in A.R.P. Diamond and L. Stulman (eds.) *Jeremiah (Dis)Placed: New Directions in Writing/Reading Jeremiah*. Edinburgh: T&T Clark, pp. 35–46.

Sharp, C. 2015. 'Embodying Moab: The Figuring of Moab in Jeremiah 48 As Reinscription of the Judean Body,' in E.K. Holt, H.C.P. Kim, and A. Mein (eds.) *Concerning the Nations*. London: Bloomsbury Press, pp. 95–108.

Shaw, T. 1746. *Travels or Observations relating to several parts of Barbary and the Levant.* Oxford: Printed at the Theatre.

Sherman, K. 2010. 'Irving Layton and His Brother Jesus,' *Literature and Theology* 24(2): 150–160

Shulman, G.M. 2008. *American Prophecy: Race and Redemption in American Political Culture.* Minneapolis: University of Minnesota Press.

Signer, M.A. 1997. 'The *Glossa Ordinaria* and Medieval Anti-Judaism,' in J. Brown and W.P. Stoneman (eds.) *A Distinct Voice: Medieval Studies in Honor of Leonard E. Boyle, O.P.* Notre Dame: University of Notre Dame Press, pp. 591–605.

Signer, M.A. 2001. 'God's Love for Israel: Apologetic and Hermeneutical Strategies in Twelfth-Century Biblical Exegesis,' in M. Singer and J. van Engen (eds.) *Jews and Christians in Twelfth-Century Europe.* Indiana: University of Notre Dame, pp. 123–149.

Skinner, J. 1922. *Prophecy and Religion: Studies in the Life of Jeremiah.* Cambridge: Cambridge University Press.

Slaughter, T.P. 2008. *The Beautiful Soul of John Woolman: Apostle of Abolition.* New York: Farr, Strauss & Giroux.

Smith, J. 1660. 'On Prophecy,' *in Select Discourses.* London.

Smith, L. 2009. *Glossa Ordinaria: The Making of a Medieval Bible Commentary.* Leiden: Brill.

Smith, R.L. 1943. *Writing Scripture Under Dictators.* New York: Abingdon-Cokesbury.

Spence-Jones, H.D.M and J. Exell. 1880–97. *The Pulpit Commentary.* 23 vols. London: J. Nisbet.

de Spinoza, B. 1951. 'A Theologico-Political Treatise,' in R.H.M. Elwes (trans.) *The Chief Works of Benedict de Spinoza, Volume* 1. New York: Dover.

Steiner, G. 1996. *No Passion Spent.* New Haven: Yale University Press.

Stephen, D.J. 1923. *Jeremiah Prophet of Hope.* Cambridge: Cambridge University Press.

Stewart, A. n.d. *A Practical Bible Temperance Commentary.* Aberdeen: William Lindsay.

Stockton, I. 1999. 'Bonhoeffer's Wrestling with Jeremiah,' *Modern Believing* 40 (3):50–58.

Strindberg, A. 2006. *Master Olof: A Drama in Five Acts.* Gloucestershire: Echo Library.

Strong, J. 1676. *Balm in Gilead, or, A spur to repentance as it was lately delivered in a sermon by James Strong.* London.

Suso, H. 1994. *Wisdom's Watch Upon the Hours, Volume* 4. Ed. Edmund Colledge. Fathers of the Church: Medieval Continuation. Washington, D.C.: Catholic University of America.

Sánchez, R. 1997. *Persona and Decorum in Milton's Prose. Vancouver: Fairleigh Dickinson* University Press.

Swan, J. 1653. *Calamus mensurans the measuring reed. Or, The standard of time.* London: Printed for John Williams, at the Signe of the Crowne in Pauls Church-yard.

Swan, J. 1653. *Signa Coeli: The Signs of Heaven (bound with Calamus mensurans).* London: Printed for John Williams, at the Signe of the Crowne in Pauls Church-yard.

Tarrer, S. 2013. *Reading with the Faithful: Interpretation of True and False Prophecy in the Book of Jeremiah from Ancient to Modern Times. Journal of Theological Interpretation* Supplements 6. Winona Lake: Eisenbrauns.

Tertullian. 1951–1953. *Scorpiace in The Ante-Nicene Fathers III.* Winona Lake: Eerdmans.

Tillich, P. 1998. *Against the Third Reich: Paul Tillich's Wartime Addresses to Nazi Germany.* Eds. R.H. Stone and M.L. Weaver. Louisville: Westminster John Knox.

Tindal, M. 1730. *Christianity As Old as the Creation or, The Gospel, A Republication of the Religion of Nature.* London.

Tomes, R. 1993. 'The Reception of Jeremiah in Rabbinic Literature and in the Targum,' in A.W.H. Curtis and T. Römer (eds.) *The Book of Jeremiah and Its Reception.* Leuven: Leuven University Press, pp. 324–253.

Torjesen, K.J. 1995. 'Influence of Rhetoric on Origen's Old Testament Homilies,' in G. Dorival and A. le Boulluec (eds.) *Origeniana Sexta, Origène et la Bible.* Leuven: Leuven University Press, pp. 13–25.

Trapp, J. 1660. *A commentary or exposition upon these following books of holy Scripture Proverbs of Solomon, Ecclesiastes, the Song of Songs, Isaiah, Jeremiah, Lamentations, Ezekiel & Daniel: being a third volume of annotations upon the whole Bible.* London: Robert White.

Trimmer, S. 1783. *Sacred history selected from the Scriptures, with annotations and reflections, suited to the comprehension of young minds, Volume 4.* London: Rivington.

Trimmer, S. 1785. *A help to the unlearned in the study of the holy scriptures: being an attempt to explain the bible in a familiar way: adapted to common apprehensions and according to the opinion of approved commentators.* London: Rivington.

Veldman, I.M. 1999. 'Protestantism and the Arts: Sixteenth-and Seventeenth-Century Netherlands,' in P.C. Finney (ed.) *Seeing Beyond the Word.* Eerdmans, pp. 397–426.

Visscher, Claes Jansz. n.d. *Theatrum biblicum; hoc est historiae sacrae Veteris et Novi Testamenti tabulis aeneis expressae, editum per Nicolaum Iohannis Piscatorem.* Amsterdam.

von Rad, G. 1965. *Old Testament Theology.* New York: Harper & Row.

Voltaire. 1877. *Oeuvres complètes de Voltaire.* Nouvelle Édition. Vol. 10. Contes en vers. Satires. Épîtres. Poésies. Mêlées. Paris: Garnier Frères.

Walley, T. 1670. *Balm in Gilead to heal Sions wounds: or, A treatise wherein there is a clear discovery of the most prevailing sicknesses of New-England, both in the civil and ecclesiastical state; as also suitable remedies for the cure of them.* Cambridge: S.G. and M.J.

Waterland, D. 1734. *Scripture Vindicated, Part III.* London: John Crownfield, at the Rising-Sun in St. Paul's Church-yard.

Watts, I. 1810. *The Works of the Reverend and Learned Isaac Watts, D.D. in six volumes.* Compiled by the Rev. George Burder. London: J. Barfield.

Weitzmann, K. and K. Herbert. 1990. *The Frescoes of the Dura Synagogue and Christian Art.* Washington, D.C.: Dumbarton Oaks Research Library and Collection.

Wellhausen, J. 1885. *Prolegomena to the History of Israel.* Trans. J. Sutherland. Black and Allan Menzies: Edinburgh.

Wells, J. 1645. *The Anchor of Hope for God's tossed ones…Or, God's bowels let out, opened, proclaimed to afflicted Saints, in a little Treatise on the 29 of Jer. 11 verse.* London: Henry Overton.

Wenthe, D.O. 2009. *Jeremiah, Lamentations.* Ancient Christian Commentary on Scripture Volume XII. Downers Grove: InterVarsity Press.

Wesley, J. 1765. *John Wesley's Notes on the Whole Bible: The Old Testament*. https://www. biblestudytools.com/commentaries/wesleys-explanatory-notes/.

Wesley, J. and C. Wesley. 2012. *Poetical Works of John and Charles Wesley, Volume 10*. London: Forgotten Books.

Wesley, S. 1704. *History of the Old Testament in Verse, Volume 2*. London: C. Harper.

Wycliffe, J. 1850 [1395]. *The Holy Bible, containing the Old and New testaments, with the Apocryphal books, in the earliest English versions made from the Latin Vulgate by John Wycliffe and his followers*. Ed. the Rev. J. Forshall and Sir F. Madden. 4 vols. Oxford: University Press.

Yuval, I. J. 2006. *Two Nations in Your Womb*. Berkeley: University of California Press.

Zweig, S. 1922. *Jeremiah: A Drama in Nine Scenes*. New York: Thomas Seltzer.

Index

Jeremiah Through the Centuries, First Edition. Mary Chilton Callaway.
© 2020 Mary Chilton Callaway. Published 2020 by John Wiley & Sons Ltd.